ACT EXA]

"Study is like the light that illuminates the darkness of ignorance, and the knowledge that results is the supreme possession, for it cannot be taken away even by the most skillful of thieves. Study is the weapon that eliminates the enemy which is ignorance. It is also the best friend that guides us through all our difficult moments."

—Dalai lama

CONQUERMINDS PRESS

TABLE OF CONTENTS

Part I Introduction & Study Strategies 6

Chapter 1 Welcome To The 2025 Act Prep Guide 6

1.1 Purpose And Scope Of This Book 6

1.2 Key 2025 Updates (Online Testing, Section Retesting, Superscoring) 6

1.3 The Role Of Test-Optional Policies 7

1.4 How To Use This Guide Effectively 7

Chapter 2 Crafting Your Study Strategy 9

2.1 Study Schedules And Timelines (1 Month, 3 Months, 6 Months) 9

2.2 Time Management And Overcoming Test Anxiety 12

2.3 Setting Score Goals And Tracking Progress 14

2.4 Making The Most Of Practice Materials 15

Part II Act Sections: Theory & Practice Drills 17

Section A: English 17

Chapter 3 English Overview & Essential Grammar 17

3.1 Core Grammar And Usage (Subject-Verb Agreement, Pronouns, Verb Tenses) 17

3.2 Punctuation Rules (Commas, Semicolons, Apostrophes) 19

3.3 Sentence Structure & Rhetorical Skills (Organization, Clarity, Style) 20

3.4 Quick Editing And Proofreading Techniques 23

Chapter 4 English Practice Drills 26

4.1 Grammar Drills (Targeted Exercises By Topic) 26

4.2 Passage-Based Editing Sets 34

4.3 Mixed Mini-Tests (Timed Practice) 41

4.4 Detailed Answer Explanations 54

Section B: Math 86

Chapter 5 Math Concepts & Key Formulas 86

5.1 Pre-Algebra & Elementary Algebra (Operations, Linear Equations) 86

5.2 Intermediate Algebra & Functions (Quadratics, Inequalities, Polynomials) 89

5.3 Geometry & Trigonometry Essentials (Shapes, Volumes, Trig Ratios) 92

5.4 Calculator Usage & Quick Problem-Solving Tips 96

Chapter 6 Math Practice Drills 99

6.1 Topic-Focused Drills (Algebra, Coordinate Geometry, Plane Geometry, Trig) 99

6.2 Mixed Problem Sets (Increasing Difficulty) 109

6.3 Timed Mini-Tests & Strategies For Pacing 112

6.4 Detailed Answer Explanations 118
Section C: Reading 133
Chapter 7 Reading Strategies & Approach 133
7.1 Passage Types (Literary, Social Science, Humanities, Natural Science) 133
7.2 Active Reading Methods (Skimming, Annotation, Identifying Key Words) 135
7.3 Main Ideas, Supporting Details, Inferences 136
7.4 Timing & Passage Mapping 138
Chapter 8 Reading Practice Drills 141
8.1 Targeted Question Sets (Main Idea, Detail, Inference, Vocab In Context) 141
8.2 Mixed Passage Exercises (Varied Difficulty) 146
8.3 Timed Mini-Tests & Review 148
8.4 Detailed Answer Explanations 152
Section D: Science 160
Chapter 9 Science Reasoning & Data Analysis 160
9.1 Understanding Experiments (Variables, Controls, Hypotheses) 160
9.2 Interpreting Graphs, Tables, And Figures 162
9.3 Conflicting Viewpoints & Evaluating Claims 165
9.4 Essential Science Vocab & Quick Reasoning Tips 166
Chapter 10 Science Practice Drills 170
10.1 Data Representation & Graph Interpretation Sets 170
10.2 Research Summaries (Experimental Results) 172
10.3 Conflicting Viewpoints Mini-Tests 175
10.4 Timed Practice Drills With Solutions 177
Chapter 11 The Optional Writing Test 183
11.1 Understanding The Prompt & Perspectives 183
11.2 Structuring Your Argument (Introduction, Body, Conclusion) 184
11.3 Effective Examples & Counterarguments 186
11.4 Common Mistakes & Quick Revision Methods 189
Chapter 12 Writing Practice 192
12.1 Short Practice Prompts & Outlines 192
12.2 Sample Essays (High-, Mid-, And Low-Scoring Examples) 198
12.3 Self-Evaluation Checklist & Peer Review Suggestions 201
Part III Full-Length Practice Tests 203
Chapter 13 Full Length Practice Test 1 203
Act English Exam Section 203
Act Math Exam Section 215

Act Reading Exam Section ... 226
Act Science Exam Section ... 231
Act Writing Exam Section (Optional) ... 241
Chapter 14 Full Length Practice Test 2 ... 242
Act English Exam Section ... 242
Act Reading Exam Section ... 265
Act Science Exam Section ... 272
Act Writing Exam Section (Optional) ... 281
Chapter 15 Exam Solutions ... 282

DOWNLOAD HERE YOUR FULL LENGTH SIMULATIONS!

Dear Student,

I'm excited to accompany you on your journey toward conquering the ACT. I understand the effort, dedication, and persistence needed to succeed, and that's why I created this guide—to help you study smarter and more efficiently.

Inside this manual, you'll discover two full-length practice exams. Plus, with the included QR code, you can instantly access eight additional tests at no extra cost. I opted for this hybrid format for several key reasons:

- **Cost Savings:** Packing all ten exams into a single printed volume would have increased the weight and price. This way, you get all the content you need without a hefty cost.
- **Instant Updates:** The digital component makes it simple to roll out corrections or new materials promptly, ensuring you always have the most current information.
- **Adaptability:** Whether you prefer printing the tests at home or working on them online, this format adapts to your individual study habits.

My aim is to provide you with a comprehensive, affordable, and user-friendly resource that supports your exam preparation every step of the way. I'm here to help you reach your goals and celebrate your milestones.

Wishing you the very best of luck—happy studying and go ace that exam!

SCAN THE QR CODE!

You will get:

- 8 extra full length exam simulations
- Weekly extra exam bonus

PART I

INTRODUCTION & STUDY STRATEGIES

CHAPTER 1

WELCOME TO THE 2025 ACT PREP GUIDE

1.1 PURPOSE AND SCOPE OF THIS BOOK

The ACT is a critical step in many students' journeys toward college admissions and scholarship opportunities. With evolving requirements and increasing competition, having a clear, focused study plan is essential. The purpose of this guide is to serve as your **comprehensive companion** from the very first day of your ACT preparation until you achieve your target score.

Here is how this book fulfills its purpose:

- **Holistic Coverage**: You will find detailed explanations of key concepts for each ACT section: English, Math, Reading, Science, and the optional Writing test. Instead of overwhelming you with excessive theory, we focus on **essential knowledge** and pair it with **extensive practice**, following a 20% theory and 80% practice approach.
- **Strategic Approach**: Understanding the structure of the ACT, including question types and time constraints, is as important as mastering content. This book provides **effective study techniques**, **timing strategies**, and **test-taking tips** to help you tackle each question confidently.
- **Progressive Learning**: Whether you have a month or half a year to prepare, this guide is structured to meet you where you are. You will learn not only the "what" of the ACT but also the "how" and "why," enabling you to adapt your study plan to fit your schedule, strengths, and weaknesses.
- **Updated Insights**: ACT policies and formats evolve. The 2025 exam features **online testing**, **section retesting**, and **superscoring**—all of which can significantly influence how you approach the test. You will find detailed explanations and strategies tailored to these updates throughout the book.

Ultimately, this book aims to help you **improve your score** in the most efficient way possible. It offers structured instruction, ample practice, and relevant insights so you can walk into the test center—or log in to the online test platform—with confidence.

1.2 KEY 2025 UPDATES (ONLINE TESTING, SECTION RETESTING, SUPERSCORING)

The ACT in 2025 has introduced several changes and features that are important for every test-taker to understand. While the fundamental content and format of the ACT remain consistent—focusing on English, Math, Reading, and Science, plus an optional Writing section—**how** students take the test and **how** their scores are evaluated have evolved.

Online Testing

- **Digital Format**: Many testing centers now offer the ACT in an online format. Rather than filling out a bubble sheet, you might complete the exam on a computer.
- **System Tools**: The digital platform often includes a built-in calculator (in addition to allowing a physical calculator for math), highlighter features for reading passages, and an on-screen timer. Familiarizing yourself with these tools can save you time and minimize stress on test day.
- **Technical Readiness**: While technology can streamline some tasks, it can also introduce new challenges. Knowing how to navigate digital question screens or answer submission tools is just as important as reviewing academic content.

Section Retesting

- **Targeted Improvement**: If you are satisfied with your English and Reading scores but want to improve in Math or Science, section retesting allows you to **re-sit** for individual sections. You no longer need to retake the entire ACT if you only want to boost one or two section scores.
- **Focused Study**: This change encourages a more **targeted study approach**. Once you identify specific weaknesses, you can devote time to improving those areas without worrying about the other sections.
- **Scheduling Flexibility**: You can choose specific test dates for retaking sections. This flexibility means your overall preparation can be spread out, reducing the pressure of performing well on every section in a single test session.

Superscoring

- **Combining Best Scores**: Superscoring means that if you have multiple ACT score reports (from a standard test or from section retests), the testing service (and many colleges) will combine your highest section scores into one "super" composite score.
- **Strategic Approach**: This policy makes it even more advantageous to focus on weaker sections, as you can significantly increase your composite score by improving on one or two specific areas.
- **College Acceptance**: Most colleges accept superscored results, but it's wise to verify each institution's policy. Superscoring can influence your choice of test dates and your overall preparation strategy.

Embracing these 2025 updates will help you **plan more effectively**, **study more efficiently**, and ultimately **maximize your ACT score**. Keep these changes in mind as you navigate the rest of this guide and adapt your study plan to take advantage of them.

1.3 THE ROLE OF TEST-OPTIONAL POLICIES

In recent years, many universities and colleges have adopted **test-optional policies**, meaning they do not require standardized test scores (like the ACT) for admissions decisions. However, the ACT remains an important piece of the admissions puzzle for numerous reasons:

- **Scholarship Qualifications**: Even if a school does not require an ACT score for admission, many scholarship programs use standardized test scores to determine eligibility or award amounts. A higher ACT score can **boost your scholarship opportunities** significantly.
- **Academic Placement**: Some institutions use ACT scores for placement in first-year classes, allowing students with higher scores to bypass introductory courses.
- **Competitive Advantage**: Submitting a strong ACT score can enhance your application if your GPA or extracurricular profile needs additional support. In a test-optional environment, a high ACT score can **distinguish you** from other applicants who choose not to submit scores.
- **Demonstrated Effort**: Taking the ACT and preparing seriously for it demonstrates your **academic commitment** and willingness to take on challenges—qualities that many admissions officers appreciate.

While test-optional policies may reduce the anxiety for students who prefer not to take standardized tests, a **good ACT score** can still open doors. Understanding its relevance in the admissions and scholarship process is crucial, as it allows you to decide whether investing time in the ACT aligns with your **college and career goals**.

1.4 HOW TO USE THIS GUIDE EFFECTIVELY

This guide is structured to make your ACT prep journey both **streamlined** and **impactful**. By focusing on essential strategies, clear explanations, and abundant practice materials, you can navigate through each section of the ACT with confidence.

Below are some suggestions on how to make the most of this resource:

- **Begin with a Diagnostic**: If possible, take a short diagnostic test (or if you have prior ACT results, use those) to gauge your current performance level. This helps you decide which sections to concentrate on first.

- **Set Realistic Goals**: Know your target score or at least have a range in mind. Your goals will help shape your study schedule and influence which strategies and exercises you emphasize.
- **Use Timed Practice**: Time management is crucial on the ACT. Whenever you practice, whether it's a single passage or a full-length test, **simulate testing conditions** by timing yourself.
- **Review Mistakes Thoroughly**: One of the most effective ways to improve is by examining every incorrect answer in your practice. Understand **why** you got it wrong and how you can avoid similar mistakes in the future.
- **Rotate Subjects**: Even if one subject is your weakness, don't neglect the others. Maintaining a consistent balance ensures that you stay sharp across all sections.
- **Leverage Section Retesting**: If a particular section needs more attention, plan to retest only that portion. This approach will save you from having to revisit content you've already mastered.
- **Stay Organized**: Keep track of your practice test scores, note the question types you miss most often, and record new strategies that work for you.

Because this book takes you from initial planning to final review, you can adapt your journey as you learn more about your strengths and weaknesses. Whether you choose a one-month crash course or a more extended study plan, this guide offers the **foundational knowledge** and **practice resources** needed to excel. Each section aims to help you refine essential skills and develop the confidence to succeed on test day.

CHAPTER 2

CRAFTING YOUR STUDY STRATEGY

2.1 STUDY SCHEDULES AND TIMELINES (1 MONTH, 3 MONTHS, 6 MONTHS)

Effective ACT preparation starts with a realistic timeline. Your personal schedule should reflect the time you can dedicate each week, your current academic commitments, and the gap between your baseline scores and your target. Below are three sample timelines—**one month**, **three months**, and **six months**—each designed to help you maximize your study efforts based on the time available before test day.

One-Month Study Plan (Accelerated Approach)

A one-month timeline is challenging, but not impossible. The key is to stay focused on **high-impact** topics and practice under strict time constraints.

Recommended Weekly Structure

- **Week 1**:
  - **Diagnostic Test**: Take a full-length practice test to identify your strongest and weakest areas.
  - **Content Review Basics**: Concentrate on high-yield grammar rules, essential math formulas, and quick reading strategies.
  - **Targeted Practice**: Focus on your weakest section first. For instance, if you consistently miss algebra questions, devote extra time to practicing algebraic problem sets.
- **Week 2**:
  - **Drill & Practice**: Incorporate timed mini-tests daily for English, Math, Reading, and Science.
  - **Strategic Study**: Review only the most common question types you find challenging.
  - **Reading & Science Strategies**: Practice active reading and data interpretation under time pressure, using one passage per day for each section.
- **Week 3**:
  - **Intensive Practice Tests**: Aim for two full-length practice tests this week. Analyze every mistake carefully.
  - **Refine Timing**: Work on pacing for each section—practice finishing English and Math sections with at least 2–3 minutes to spare for reviewing flagged questions.
  - **Optional Writing**: If you plan to take the Writing test, review sample essays and write at least two timed practice essays.
- **Week 4**:
  - **Focused Review**: Spend time on final polishing. Zero in on any lingering weaknesses, such as tricky grammar rules or specific math formulas.
  - **Short Bursts of Practice**: Complete short, targeted exercises in each section to keep skills fresh.
  - **Final Full Practice Test**: Take one last test about 3–4 days before your official exam, then spend the remaining days reviewing errors and reinforcing core concepts.

Tips for Success

- **Stay Organized**: Use a daily planner or digital calendar to map out your tasks.
- **Be Efficient**: Focus on question types that appear frequently. Don't waste time on rare or highly specialized concepts.
- **Recover Quickly**: If you miss a day of study, restructure your plan rather than trying to cram an entire missed day on top of an existing schedule.

Three-Month Study Plan (Balanced & Steady)

A three-month plan offers a **more balanced** approach, allowing for both content review and plentiful practice without extreme time pressure.

Overall Strategy

1. **Initial Diagnostic (Week 1)**
   - Take a full-length, timed practice test to pinpoint starting scores and weak areas.
   - Evaluate how much time you can dedicate each week. Consider your academic workload, extracurriculars, and personal commitments.
2. **Structured Weekly Schedule**
   - **Weeks 2–4: Foundational Review**
     - **English**: Strengthen grammar fundamentals (pronouns, subject-verb agreement, punctuation).
     - **Math**: Review algebra basics, geometry formulas, and common trig identities.
     - **Reading**: Practice reading passages, focusing on identifying main ideas and critical details.
     - **Science**: Familiarize yourself with interpreting graphs and scientific data.
     - Allocate at least one practice test during these three weeks to measure progress.
   - **Weeks 5–8: Targeted Practice & Strategy**
     - **Focus on Weak Areas**: Devote extra time to problem sets or question types you frequently miss.
     - **Timed Drills**: Incorporate time constraints into daily practice to build speed.
     - **Optional Writing**: Practice organizing essays; learn to generate relevant examples quickly.
     - **Midpoint Check**: Take another full-length practice test around Week 6 or 7; adjust your schedule based on the results.
   - **Weeks 9–12: Intensive Review & Final Preparations**
     - **Full-Length Tests**: Aim for 2–3 additional full-length tests in these final weeks.
     - **Performance Analysis**: Carefully review wrong answers to identify final adjustments.
     - **Refine Pacing & Accuracy**: Work on finishing each section slightly ahead of time to allow for quick reviews.
     - **Confidence Building**: Use shorter, daily drills and flashcards to keep concepts fresh.
3. **Week-by-Week Progression**
   - As you move through this plan, gradually shift from heavy content review to more frequent practice tests.
   - Track your scores, note your most persistent mistakes, and adjust your study sessions to focus on those trouble spots.

Tips for Success

- **Stay Motivated**: Three months can feel long. Celebrate small wins, like a slight improvement in math speed or a higher reading score on a practice test.
- **Avoid Burnout**: Schedule rest days and lighter study sessions periodically to maintain enthusiasm and mental sharpness.
- **Adapt to Changes**: If you find certain topics consistently challenging, don't be afraid to adjust your schedule to allow more review time.

Six-Month Study Plan (Gradual & Comprehensive)

A six-month timeline is ideal if you want to explore **every aspect of the ACT** in-depth and truly internalize the test strategies. It's also helpful if you need substantial improvement across multiple sections or if you have a heavy academic load and can only devote a limited amount of time to ACT prep each week.

Phase Breakdown

- **Phase 1 (Weeks 1–4): Initial Assessment & Basic Review**

    - **Diagnostic Test**: Establish your baseline scores.
    - **Identify Strengths and Weaknesses**: Create a study roadmap highlighting areas that need extra attention.
    - **Light Practice**: Start with untimed practice questions to build familiarity with the ACT's structure.
- **Phase 2 (Weeks 5–12): Deep Dive into Content**
    - **English**: Thorough review of grammar rules, rhetorical skills, and style.
    - **Math**: Cover all major algebraic concepts, geometry theorems, and trigonometric identities.
    - **Reading**: Develop active reading techniques, learning how to skim passages effectively without missing key details.
    - **Science**: Practice interpreting complex charts and tables; learn strategies for Conflicting Viewpoints passages.
    - **Periodic Timed Drills**: Transition slowly to timed sets to gain speed and comfort.
- **Phase 3 (Weeks 13–16): Practice Test Galore**
    - **Frequent Full-Length Tests**: Aim for one full test every 2–3 weeks.
    - **Detailed Error Review**: Develop a habit of dissecting each incorrect answer and understanding the reasoning behind the correct one.
    - **Optional Writing**: Experiment with different essay structures and refine your approach to prompt analysis.
- **Phase 4 (Weeks 17–20): Target Weak Points & Fine-Tune Strategies**
    - **Focused Drills**: Zero in on remaining weak spots, whether it's advanced math concepts or specific reading question types.
    - **Section Retesting Strategy**: If you plan to use section retesting, determine which sections need retakes based on your practice scores.
    - **Confidence Building**: Reinforce your strongest sections to ensure you maintain high accuracy rates there.
- **Phase 5 (Weeks 21–24): Final Stretch & Consistency**
    - **Simulate Test Day**: Take your final 2–3 full-length tests in a setting as close to the actual ACT environment as possible.
    - **Last-Minute Adjustments**: Fine-tune pacing strategies and revisit any lingering question types that cause confusion.
    - **Stress Management**: Integrate light review sessions; avoid overstudying to keep your mind fresh.

Tips for Success

- **Pace Yourself**: Six months is a marathon, not a sprint. Spread out your study sessions and steadily increase the intensity.
- **Layered Learning**: Revisit key topics multiple times to ensure they stick. Early and repeated exposure is more effective than last-minute cramming.
- **Monitor Consistency**: Keep a log of your practice test scores to track gradual improvements and identify plateaus.

Putting It All Together

Choosing the right timeline depends on your personal needs, score goals, and existing commitments. Here are a few final considerations for an effective study schedule:

- **Flexibility**: Life happens—extracurriculars, family obligations, or unexpected academic challenges might interfere with your plan. Build in some buffer days to handle unforeseen events.
- **Goal-Oriented Mindset**: Regardless of your chosen timeline, keep a clear, tangible target in mind (e.g., a specific ACT score or scholarship requirement). This goal will guide your daily efforts.
- **Regular Evaluation**: Periodically check your progress. Are you improving as expected? Do you need additional support in a particular section? Adjust accordingly to make the best use of your time.

By carefully planning your timeline—whether one month, three months, or six months—you can approach your ACT prep with confidence and clarity. Use the next chapters in this guide to refine your strategy, tackle specific challenges, and optimize your results on test day.

2.2 TIME MANAGEMENT AND OVERCOMING TEST ANXIETY

Effective time management and the ability to maintain composure under pressure can dramatically impact your ACT score. Even if you know the material thoroughly, running out of time or allowing test-day nerves to take control can diminish your performance. Below are strategies to help you keep pace and stay calm throughout your preparation and on test day.

Balancing Speed and Accuracy

One of the greatest challenges of the ACT is its **tight time constraints**. Each section has a specific limit:

- **English**: 75 questions in 45 minutes
- **Math**: 60 questions in 60 minutes
- **Reading**: 40 questions in 35 minutes
- **Science**: 40 questions in 35 minutes
- **Optional Writing**: 1 essay in 40 minutes

To succeed within these time frames, **efficiency** is key.

- **Know Your Pace**
  Track how many questions you can comfortably solve in a set amount of time. If you notice you're slower in Math, for example, allocate extra practice to timed math drills until you can consistently finish within the official time limit.
- **Use Benchmarks**
  In the English section (45 minutes, 75 questions), a useful benchmark might be completing 15 questions every 9 minutes. For Math (60 minutes, 60 questions), aim for 15 questions every 15 minutes. Regular check-ins help you gauge whether you're on track or falling behind.
- **Skip Strategically**
  When stuck on a question, it's often better to **skip it temporarily** and return later, rather than risk losing precious minutes. The ACT does not penalize for guessing, so make sure to bubble in an answer for every question, even if time is almost up.

Practical Time-Management Techniques

Practicing Under Timed Conditions

- Set a timer for shorter drills (10–15 minutes) and gradually work your way up to full-length practice sections.
- If you're preparing for the online ACT, practice using digital tools like an on-screen timer or highlighting features to get accustomed to the real testing environment.

Implementing the "Two-Pass Method"

1. **First Pass**: Answer all the questions you find straightforward. Mark any tougher ones for later review.
2. **Second Pass**: Return to the flagged questions with the remaining time. You'll tackle them with a clearer mind and a sense of how much time is left.

Prioritizing Sections According to Strengths

- If section retesting is an option you plan to use, identify your strongest and weakest sections early. Devote extra practice time to sections you struggle with.
- Maintain consistency in your strong areas so that you don't lose points you could otherwise secure.

Overcoming Test Anxiety

Test anxiety can manifest as **racing thoughts**, **sweaty palms**, or **difficulty focusing**. Learning to manage these feelings will help you remain calm and concentrate on the exam.

Recognize the Symptoms

- Rapid heartbeat or breathing
- Difficulty concentrating on questions
- Negative self-talk (e.g., "I can't do this")
- Shaking or feeling jittery

Awareness is the first step in taking back control. Once you recognize you're anxious, you can apply specific strategies to counter it.

Strategies for Managing Stress

- **Preparation & Familiarity**
  The more time you spend with the format, style, and content of the ACT, the less intimidating it becomes. Practice tests and drills not only improve knowledge but also build confidence in handling the exam's structure.
- **Mindful Breathing**
  If you start feeling overwhelmed, **pause** and take a few slow, deep breaths. Breathe in through your nose for a count of four, hold for a count of four, and exhale through your mouth for a count of four. This brief technique can help steady nerves and refocus your attention.
- **Visualization**
  Before the test, picture yourself calmly and methodically working through each section. Positive mental rehearsal can reduce anticipatory anxiety.
    - Close your eyes for a moment.
    - Imagine sitting comfortably, scanning a question, and knowing exactly how to approach it.
    - Visualize feeling confident as you mark the correct answers.
- **Confidence Reminders**
  Keep a short list of reminders or mantras to boost morale. For instance, "I've prepared for this," or "One question at a time." You can mentally repeat these phrases whenever anxiety starts to creep in.
- **Routine & Sleep**
  In the final days before the test, try to maintain a **consistent sleep schedule** and a balanced routine. Exhaustion heightens anxiety and impairs concentration.
- **Healthy Outlets**
  Incorporate light exercise, hobbies, or relaxation techniques (yoga, stretching, journaling) into your study schedule. These outlets can release built-up tension, preventing burnout.

Building Confidence Through Practice

- **Analyze Weaknesses**
  If you repeatedly miss questions that involve reading data in Science, schedule daily science drills. Immediate, targeted practice can alleviate fears about that section.
- **Reward Progress**
  Celebrate small improvements, like completing an English drill a minute faster than before or increasing your accuracy in Math from 60% to 65%. Progress fosters motivation and counters self-doubt.
- **Simulate Real Conditions**
  Conduct a full-length practice test under conditions similar to the actual exam—turn off your phone, limit breaks to official durations, and sit in a quiet space. Familiarity with the test environment helps reduce anxiety on the actual test day.

Final Thoughts on Time and Anxiety

Time management and anxiety control go hand in hand. By practicing good pacing strategies and confronting stressors head-on, you can preserve energy for where it truly matters: **finding the right answers**. Cultivating calm focus might require consistent effort, but it pays off when you face the real exam and need the **mental clarity** to perform at your best.

2.3 SETTING SCORE GOALS AND TRACKING PROGRESS

Establishing clear, realistic score goals—and then consistently monitoring your progress toward them—is an essential part of any successful ACT study plan. This process helps you stay motivated, recognize areas that need extra attention, and celebrate improvements along the way. By maintaining a transparent view of how you're performing across the different sections, you can make informed decisions about where to channel your time and energy.

Defining Your Target Score

1. **Identify Your Baseline**
   - Before setting an ambitious target, take a full-length practice test under conditions that mimic the real ACT. This baseline score tells you where you stand relative to your eventual goal.
2. **Research College Requirements**
   - If you have particular colleges or scholarships in mind, find out the ACT score range of successful applicants or recipients. This information offers an idea of the scores you might need to remain competitive.
3. **Consider Personal Strengths and Weaknesses**
   - Your baseline results will often reveal distinct patterns: maybe you excel in Reading and English but struggle with Math or Science. Customizing your goals based on these insights allows you to allocate time more effectively.
4. **Set a Composite Range**
   - Instead of choosing one hard number (e.g., 30), it can be helpful to aim for a range (e.g., 28–30). This approach acknowledges that while you push for a higher score, minor variations can occur on test day.

Breaking Down Section Goals

While the ACT reports a composite score, it's equally important to think in terms of **section-level targets**. A balanced approach can increase your overall composite, especially if you focus on improving a weak area:

- **English**: If grammar and punctuation are tripping you up, set a clear goal (for instance, moving from 20 to 25).
- **Math**: Identify specific content gaps—such as algebraic manipulation or geometry theorems—and track your accuracy in these areas.
- **Reading**: Aim to improve your reading speed and comprehension. Monitor your progress by noting how many questions you miss, particularly under time pressure.
- **Science**: Track improvements in interpreting data visuals and answering more complex experimental-design questions within the allotted time.
- **Writing (Optional)**: If you're taking the writing test, define a target writing score based on the requirements of your chosen institutions or personal objectives for demonstrating writing proficiency.

Monitoring Progress Effectively

1. **Frequent Mini-Assessments**
   - Incorporate brief, targeted quizzes or timed drills into your weekly routine. These mini-checkpoints help you see if your efforts in a particular area—like punctuation rules or polynomial equations—are paying off.
2. **Full-Length Practice Tests**
   - Take periodic full exams (ideally under timed conditions) to measure how well you can sustain focus across multiple sections. Comparing these scores to your baseline helps you gauge overall progress.
3. **Score Logs and Reflection**
   - Keep a simple record of each practice test's section scores alongside notes about what felt easy or difficult.
   - Reflect on the reasons behind errors—did you misunderstand a concept, or did poor time management force you to guess?

4. **Focus on Trends**
    - Individual test performances can fluctuate for various reasons, including stress levels and daily energy. Look for **patterns** over multiple practice tests to get a more accurate picture of your growth trajectory.

Adjusting Goals and Study Plans

- **Reevaluate Periodically**
    - After a few practice sessions, you may realize your initial goals need refinement. If you're improving faster than expected, consider aiming higher. If you're struggling, break your big goals into smaller milestones to maintain motivation.
- **Target Weak Areas Aggressively**
    - If Math continues to lag behind Reading, for example, dedicate more of your study time to problem-solving drills or tutoring in that subject. Addressing lagging areas can yield significant score increases in a relatively short period.
- **Stay Flexible**
    - Life circumstances change. If you take on more extracurricular activities or face unexpected commitments, adjust your timeline and study intensity accordingly. A rigid plan that causes undue stress can be counterproductive.

Celebrating Milestones

Finally, remember to **recognize your achievements**, no matter how small. Whether it's mastering a tricky grammar rule or shaving a couple of minutes off your Math section time, each success builds momentum. By setting concrete goals and tracking your steady improvement, you ensure that your ACT preparation remains focused, motivating, and efficient—and that you see real, measurable progress leading up to test day.

2.4 MAKING THE MOST OF PRACTICE MATERIALS

The practice materials included in **this guide** are specifically designed to help you excel on the ACT. They closely mirror the exam's style, question formats, and overall difficulty. By using these materials consistently and strategically, you can develop a deep familiarity with the test, refine your problem-solving skills, and ultimately boost your confidence and performance on exam day. Below are tips on how to make the most of the resources provided in this book.

Embracing the Resources in This Guide

- **Comprehensive Practice Tests**
  Full-length practice tests in this guide replicate the structure and timing of the real ACT. Taking them under conditions similar to the actual exam—quiet environment, strict timing, minimal interruptions—helps you build endurance and manage pacing across multiple sections.
- **Focused Drills and Exercises**
  Short, targeted drills included throughout the chapters allow you to concentrate on specific skills. If you notice recurring issues in grammar, math problem-solving, or data interpretation, you can use these drills to address problem areas head-on.
- **Step-by-Step Explanations**
  Each practice question is followed by detailed explanations to help you understand **why** an answer is correct or incorrect. Make it a habit to review these clarifications thoroughly, especially when you miss a question or guess on it.

Simulating Test Day Conditions

1. **Timed Sections**
   Use a timer or stopwatch to replicate actual time limits. This approach helps you gauge your pacing and become comfortable working under pressure.

2. **Minimal Distractions**
   Turn off notifications and let those around you know you're in "test mode." Maintaining a focused environment trains you to concentrate fully when it matters most.
3. **Practice in Blocks**
   If possible, complete entire sections in one sitting. By doing this, you'll develop the stamina and concentration needed to tackle each ACT section back-to-back on exam day.

Analyzing Your Performance

- **Track Scores and Time**
  Record your scores for every practice test or drill you complete. Note your timing for each section to see where you might be moving too quickly or too slowly.
- **Identify Common Error Types**
  Look for patterns. Are you missing questions because of careless errors, lack of content knowledge, or time constraints? Zero in on these patterns during your review sessions.
- **Adjust Study Focus**
  If you spot repeated weaknesses—like difficulty with reading comprehension or confusion about certain math formulas—devote extra effort to those topics in the weeks that follow.

Using Officially Inspired Questions

While the materials in this guide are extensive, you may also choose to **briefly reference** official ACT questions for additional practice. However, the core drills, exercises, and full-length tests provided here offer an in-depth representation of the ACT's difficulty level and question types. By repeatedly working through the challenges in this guide, you'll build strong testing skills aligned with the **2025 ACT format**.

Keeping Yourself Motivated

- **Set Mini-Goals**
  For each practice session, define a small aim—such as completing all English drills with fewer than five mistakes. Celebrating these minor victories keeps you engaged and encourages steady progress.
- **Review Progress Charts**
  Create a simple table or graph in your notebook to map out your improvement over time. Seeing your scores trend upward can provide a powerful boost to your confidence.
- **Reward Yourself**
  Recognize achievements along the way, whether it's after completing a particularly challenging math section or improving your reading pace. Small rewards—like a favorite snack or a quick break doing something fun—can sustain momentum.

Final Thoughts on Utilizing Practice Materials

The exercises and tests in this guide have been carefully crafted to align with the 2025 ACT exam and equip you with the skills, strategies, and confidence needed to excel. By dedicating yourself to thoughtful practice, simulating real exam conditions, and meticulously reviewing each performance, you'll establish a solid foundation for success on test day.

PART II

ACT SECTIONS: THEORY & PRACTICE DRILLS

SECTION A: ENGLISH

CHAPTER 3

ENGLISH OVERVIEW & ESSENTIAL GRAMMAR

3.1 CORE GRAMMAR AND USAGE (SUBJECT-VERB AGREEMENT, PRONOUNS, VERB TENSES)

The ACT English section emphasizes both grammatical accuracy and clear, concise expression. Strengthening your grammar skills can immediately elevate your score because many questions target these fundamental rules. In this section, we'll focus on three core areas of English usage: **Subject-Verb Agreement**, **Pronouns**, and **Verb Tenses**. Mastering these topics will help you tackle a significant portion of the English test with confidence.

Subject-Verb Agreement

Subject-verb agreement ensures that a singular subject pairs with a singular verb, and a plural subject pairs with a plural verb. This concept may sound straightforward, but the ACT often uses phrases and structures that can obscure the subject.

Key Points:

- **Basic Rule**: Singular subjects take singular verbs; plural subjects take plural verbs.
  - Example: "The **child runs** every morning." vs. "The **children run** every morning."
- **Intervening Phrases**: Prepositional phrases or descriptive clauses between the subject and the verb can cause confusion. The core subject remains the noun outside these phrases.
  - Example: "The **group** of students **is** volunteering this weekend." (Subject = group, not students)
- **Collective Nouns**: Words like **team**, **family**, and **committee** are usually considered singular when they act as a single unit.
  - Example: "The **committee decides** on the budget."
- **Indefinite Pronouns**: Words such as **everyone**, **somebody**, and **each** are typically singular. Others, like **few** and **many**, are plural.
  - Example: "**Everyone** on the team **enjoys** the victory." (Singular subject "everyone," singular verb "enjoys")
  - Example: "**Many** of the cookies **have** disappeared." (Plural subject "many," plural verb "have")

Quick Tip: If you're unsure whether the subject is singular or plural, isolate it by temporarily removing any prepositional or descriptive phrases. Then match it directly with the verb to check for correctness.

Pronouns

Pronoun errors frequently appear in ACT English passages. You'll need to ensure proper agreement, clarity, and consistency.

Key Points:

- **Pronoun-Antecedent Agreement**: A pronoun must match its antecedent (the noun it refers to) in number and gender.
  - Example: "**The dog** wagged **its** tail." ("dog" is singular, so "its" is correct, not "their")

- **Ambiguous References**: When a pronoun could refer to more than one possible antecedent, it creates confusion.
    - Ambiguous: "When **Lily** saw **Sarah**, **she** smiled." (Who smiled? Lily or Sarah?)
    - Clear: "When Lily saw Sarah, **Lily** smiled."
- **Consistency**: If you start a sentence in the third person, do not switch to second person pronouns unintentionally.
    - Example: "A person should do **his or her** best to stay healthy." (Not "your best," unless the entire sentence is written in the second person for a specific stylistic reason.)
- **Case Errors**: Pronouns can act as subjects, objects, or show possession. Make sure you use the correct form for each scenario.
    - Example: "**He** and **I** are going to the movies." ("He" and "I" are both subjects.)
    - Example: "Our teacher spoke to **him** and **me**." ("Him" and "me" are objects of the preposition "to.")

Quick Tip: To test whether "I" or "me" is correct, remove the other subject or object from the sentence and see what sounds natural. For instance, "The principal spoke to me" makes sense, but "The principal spoke to I" does not.

Verb Tenses

Verb tense consistency is vital. The ACT checks not only whether you understand individual tenses, but also whether you can maintain logical consistency throughout a passage.

Key Points:

- **Simple Tenses**
    - **Present**: Describes current actions or states (e.g., "I walk," "They run").
    - **Past**: Describes completed actions (e.g., "I walked," "They ran").
    - **Future**: Expresses actions that have yet to occur (e.g., "I will walk," "They will run").
- **Perfect Tenses**
    - **Present Perfect** (has/have + past participle): Describes actions that began in the past and continue to the present, or actions that occurred at an unspecified time in the past (e.g., "I have lived here for five years").
    - **Past Perfect** (had + past participle): Describes an action that occurred before another past action (e.g., "I had walked the dog before it started raining").
    - **Future Perfect** (will have + past participle): Indicates an action that will be completed before another future action (e.g., "I will have finished my homework before you arrive").
- **Consistency**: Switch tenses only when the timeline changes.
    - Incorrect: "She **is** painting the fence, then she **went** inside."
    - Correct: "She **is** painting the fence, then she **goes** inside." (Maintains present tense throughout)
    - Correct (if the timeline changes logically): "She **was** painting the fence when she **heard** a loud noise." (Both actions occurred in the past simultaneously)

Quick Tip: Pay special attention to time markers like "by the time," "when," "until," and "after." They often signal a shift that requires a specific tense.

Practical Takeaways

Mastering subject-verb agreement, pronoun clarity, and verb tense consistency will strengthen your foundational grammar skills. For each sentence in the ACT English section:

- **Identify the core subject and determine if it's singular or plural.**
- **Check each pronoun and ensure it clearly matches its antecedent.**
- **Confirm that the verb tense is logical given the context.**

When you integrate these checks into your reading and editing process, you'll find that many test questions become more straightforward. In the next sections, we'll explore punctuation rules, sentence structure, and the rhetorical skills needed to refine your writing. Once you have a firm grasp on all these areas, you'll be better equipped to face the variety of questions in the English section—and catch common mistakes that can trip you up on test day.

3.2 PUNCTUATION RULES (COMMAS, SEMICOLONS, APOSTROPHES)

Punctuation marks may seem small, but they carry significant weight in the ACT English section. Properly placed commas, semicolons, and apostrophes can clarify meaning, connect ideas, and prevent ambiguity. Below is a closer look at each mark and how it commonly appears in test questions.

Commas

A comma indicates a brief pause or separation of ideas. While there are several nuanced rules for comma usage, the ACT typically tests a few key scenarios:

- **Separating Independent Clauses with a Coordinating Conjunction**
  - Commas join two independent clauses when paired with a coordinating conjunction (FANBOYS: for, and, nor, but, or, yet, so).
  - Example: "I finished my homework, **and** I went for a walk."
- **Setting Off Introductory Phrases or Clauses**
  - Use a comma after a **short introductory phrase**, **dependent clause**, or **transition word**.
  - Example: "After the sun set, we turned on the porch light."
  - Example: "However, the event was already sold out."
- **Separating Items in a Series**
  - Commas separate elements in a list of three or more.
  - Example: "We bought apples, oranges, and bananas."
  - The **Oxford comma** (the final comma before "and") is optional in standard writing but sometimes tested for consistency in usage.
- **Setting Off Nonessential Clauses or Phrases**
  - When extra information is added to a sentence that could be removed without changing its core meaning, surround it with commas.
  - Example: "The restaurant, which opened last week, already has rave reviews."
- **Avoiding Comma Splices**
  - A comma splice occurs when two independent clauses are joined by only a comma.
  - Incorrect: "I love to travel, I plan a big trip every summer."
  - Correct (adding a conjunction): "I love to travel, and I plan a big trip every summer."
  - Correct (using a semicolon): "I love to travel; I plan a big trip every summer."

Quick Check: If you can remove a phrase without affecting the main message, it usually needs commas around it. Conversely, never place a comma alone between two independent clauses.

Semicolons

Semicolons function like a **bridge** between related thoughts. They are tested less frequently than commas, but correct semicolon usage can still make a difference in your score.

- **Linking Independent Clauses**
  - Use a semicolon to connect two related independent clauses when you choose not to use a coordinating conjunction.
  - Example: "I planned to read all day; the library had just received new books."
- **Before a Transitional Phrase or Conjunctive Adverb**
  - A semicolon is often used before words such as **however**, **therefore**, **moreover**, or **nevertheless** when they connect two independent clauses.
  - Example: "She loves classical music; however, she also enjoys jazz."
- **Complex Lists**
  - When items in a list contain internal commas, semicolons separate the larger groupings.
  - Example: "The conference featured speakers from Paris, France; Rome, Italy; and Berlin, Germany."

Quick Check: If you can replace a semicolon with a period and still have two standalone sentences, the semicolon is likely correct.

Apostrophes

Apostrophes are primarily used for **contractions** and **possession**, both of which can appear in ACT English questions.

- **Contractions**
  - Apostrophes replace missing letters in contractions (e.g., **don't** for "do not," **it's** for "it is").
  - Watch for tricky words like **it's** (it is) vs. **its** (possessive).
  - Example: "It's sunny today." vs. "The dog wagged its tail."
- **Singular Possession**
  - Add an apostrophe + **s** to show that one person or object owns something.
  - Example: "The cat's tail was striped."
- **Plural Possession**
  - For most plural nouns already ending in **s**, add only an apostrophe.
  - Example: "The students' projects were impressive." (More than one student)
  - For irregular plurals not ending in **s**, add apostrophe + **s**.
  - Example: "The children's playground is closed."
- **Names Ending in S**
  - Some style guides say to add only an apostrophe (e.g., "Charles' book"), while others say apostrophe + **s** (e.g., "Charles's book"). The ACT typically accepts either as long as usage is consistent.

Quick Check: If you can rewrite the phrase using "of," then an apostrophe is often appropriate. For instance, "the cat's tail" = "the tail of the cat."

Putting It All into Practice

Punctuation rules appear throughout the ACT English test, often in subtle ways. To master them:

- **Read each question carefully** to determine the relationship between phrases.
- **Check for clause structures** (independent vs. dependent) to guide your punctuation choices.
- **Confirm apostrophe usage** by deciding if the sentence indicates possession or contraction.

When you have a firm grasp of these punctuation guidelines—along with the grammar rules covered previously—you'll be well prepared to handle a substantial portion of ACT English questions. The next section delves into **sentence structure** and **rhetorical skills**, further refining your ability to craft clear, cohesive prose.

3.3 SENTENCE STRUCTURE & RHETORICAL SKILLS (ORGANIZATION, CLARITY, STYLE)

Moving beyond basic grammar and punctuation, the ACT English section also evaluates your ability to structure sentences and paragraphs effectively, maintain clarity, and apply a consistent writing style. This broader skill set ensures that each passage reads smoothly and conveys its message with precision. Below, we delve deeper into these aspects of rhetorical skills, offering expanded insights and examples to reinforce your understanding.

Organization

Organization focuses on how information is arranged within and across paragraphs. The ACT often tests whether you can identify or create a logical flow of ideas. You may be asked to choose the best placement for a sentence, determine if a paragraph should be moved, or select a transition that links ideas coherently.

Paragraph-Level Organization

1. **Logical Sequencing**

- ACT questions may ask you to determine if the final sentence of a paragraph should actually appear earlier, or if a middle sentence should be moved to the end.
- Example:
  - Original text: "Many people travel to national parks each year. **Paragraph break** In addition, annual visitor passes are often available. These natural spaces are home to diverse wildlife."
  - Reorganized text: "Many people travel to national parks each year. These natural spaces are home to diverse wildlife. **Paragraph break** In addition, annual visitor passes are often available."
- Notice how inserting the sentence about wildlife directly after mentioning national parks clarifies the reasoning for visits, while the detail about passes serves as an add-on to close the paragraph.

2. **Focused Main Ideas**
   - Each paragraph should center on a clear topic or subtopic. Sentences that don't relate to that theme can confuse the reader.
   - Test questions sometimes highlight an off-topic sentence and ask if it should be deleted or revised to better align with the paragraph's core idea.

Effective Transitions

Transitions connect ideas between sentences and paragraphs. Common transition types include:

- **Additive**: "Furthermore," "Moreover," "Additionally"
- **Contrast**: "However," "On the other hand," "Yet"
- **Cause/Effect**: "Therefore," "Consequently," "As a result"
- **Sequence**: "First," "Next," "Finally"

Example:

- Without transition: "The weather forecast predicts heavy rain. We plan to hold the event indoors."
- With transition: "The weather forecast predicts heavy rain. **Therefore**, we plan to hold the event indoors."

Tip: Read the surrounding sentences carefully to confirm the relationship between ideas. A contrasting transition like "However" would be inappropriate if the second sentence simply continues the same idea.

Clarity

Clarity ensures your writing is comprehensible and succinct. The ACT assesses whether you can recognize and eliminate ambiguity, redundancy, and unnecessary complexity. Questions often present multiple wording choices, and your task is to identify the clearest option.

Word Choice and Specificity

1. **Avoiding Vague Language**
   - Words like "stuff," "things," or "very" can weaken a statement unless the context demands a casual tone.
   - **Weak**: "He did many things to improve the school."
   - **Stronger**: "He organized a fundraiser and established a tutoring program to improve the school."
2. **Selecting Precise Verbs and Nouns**
   - Strong, specific verbs and nouns make a sentence more direct and impactful.
   - **Weak**: "She went somewhere to do volunteer activities."
   - **Stronger**: "She traveled to the local shelter to volunteer as a mentor."

Redundancy and Wordiness

1. **Detecting Redundant Phrases**
   - Redundancies appear when an idea is repeated in multiple ways.

  - **Redundant**: "They joined together **as a group** to collaborate **together** on the project."
  - **Concise**: "They collaborated on the project."
2. **Tackling Wordiness**
  - Overly long sentences can obscure main points.
  - **Wordy**: "At this point in time, the manager is in the process of implementing a brand-new set of guidelines."
  - **Concise**: "The manager is now implementing new guidelines."

Maintaining Consistency

Clarity also involves keeping consistent subject matter, tenses, and perspectives within a passage.

- **Consistent Tenses**: If a paragraph begins in the present tense when describing a process, avoid shifting to past tense unless there's a clear time change.
- **Consistent Person (Pronouns)**: A passage written in third person should not abruptly switch to "you" or "we" unless it's stylistically intentional and logical.

Style

Style encapsulates the tone, voice, and formal or informal nature of the writing. The ACT tests whether you can keep the passage's style coherent and appropriate for its context.

Formal vs. Informal Tone

- **Formal Writing**: Often used in academic or professional texts. Avoids slang, contractions (unless necessary for clarity), and overly personal language.
- **Informal Writing**: May use contractions, idiomatic expressions, or first/second person pronouns more liberally.
- **ACT Tip**: If a passage discusses scientific research, it likely requires a formal, objective style. A personal narrative might allow for more expressive language and first-person insights.

Parallel Structure

Parallelism means using the same pattern of words for similar parts of a sentence or list. Ensuring each element matches grammatically clarifies the relationships between ideas and creates a pleasing rhythm.

- **Lists**:
  - **Not Parallel**: "She likes **dancing**, **to sing**, and **reading**."
  - **Parallel**: "She likes **dancing**, **singing**, and **reading**."
- **Comparisons**:
  - **Not Parallel**: "He is happier running than when he plays basketball."
  - **Parallel**: "He is happier running than playing basketball."

Sentence Variety

Although not always explicitly tested, sentence variety can be crucial in rhetorical improvement questions. If multiple answer choices are grammatically correct, the ACT might reward the option that improves readability and flow.

- **Example**:
  - Repetitive: "Our trip began at sunrise. We started hiking the mountain. We reached the summit at noon."
  - Varied: "We set off at sunrise and began our steep ascent. By noon, we had reached the summit."

Putting It All Together

Organization, clarity, and style are intertwined components of strong writing. In the ACT English section, you'll often need to:

- Rearrange or insert sentences for better **organization**.
- Choose precise or concise phrasing to maintain **clarity**.
- Maintain a consistent **style** that aligns with the passage's tone and intended audience.

When faced with a question testing these rhetorical skills, always consider:

1. The **main idea** of the paragraph or passage.
2. The **purpose** of each sentence within that context.
3. The **flow** between ideas—do transitions, pronouns, and conjunctions effectively link them?
4. The **economy of language**—does the chosen wording eliminate repetition and excessive detail?

By applying these principles, you'll not only succeed in the ACT English section but also improve your overall writing abilities for academic and professional contexts. Next, we'll explore **quick editing and proofreading techniques** to help refine your final drafts and catch lingering errors before submitting your best work.

3.4 QUICK EDITING AND PROOFREADING TECHNIQUES

Even well-structured writing can harbor overlooked errors if it's not carefully reviewed. The ACT English section rewards precision: **one small slip** in grammar, punctuation, or clarity can cost you points. Below is a set of practical, in-depth editing and proofreading strategies to help you catch and correct mistakes efficiently.

1. Adopt a Layered Editing Approach

One of the best ways to find errors is to **focus on one category at a time** instead of trying to correct everything in a single sweep. By breaking down your review, you can give each aspect of the text its due attention.

1. **Content and Organization**
    - Check if the main idea is clear.
    - Verify that paragraphs and sentences flow in a logical sequence.
    - Ensure that each sentence contributes to the topic at hand.
2. **Sentence Structure and Clarity**
    - Look for run-on sentences or fragments.
    - Confirm that wording is concise and free of redundancies.
    - Examine transitions between sentences and paragraphs to maintain coherence.
3. **Grammar and Usage**
    - Confirm subject-verb agreement.
    - Check pronoun usage for clarity and correctness.
    - Verify verb tense consistency throughout the passage.
4. **Punctuation**
    - Review comma usage, especially around independent clauses and introductory phrases.
    - Look for correct semicolon placement.
    - Assess apostrophes in contractions and possessives.
5. **Style and Tone**
    - Maintain the same level of formality or informality that the passage started with.
    - Watch for shifts in perspective (e.g., suddenly using "you" in an otherwise third-person passage).
    - Check for parallel structure in lists and comparisons.

2. Read Aloud or Use Silent Subvocalization

Hearing your words can highlight awkward phrasing and hidden errors:

- **Read Slowly**: Instead of skimming, articulate each sentence. Pausing after punctuation can help you catch run-ons or missing commas.
- **Listen for Natural Flow**: If you stumble over a phrase, consider that a sign of potential confusion or poor wording.

Tip: If you're short on time, move your lips slightly or "speak" the sentences in your head with clear enunciation. This silent method can still reveal issues without drawing attention to yourself in a public setting.

3. Check for Common Pitfalls

The ACT English section frequently tests particular "hot spots" of error. Quickly scanning for these can net you easy corrections:

- **Comma Splices**
  - Join independent clauses with a coordinating conjunction, semicolon, or period—not just a comma.
- **Misplaced Modifiers**
  - Place descriptive phrases next to the nouns they describe.
  - Incorrect: "Walking down the street, the flowers looked beautiful."
  - Correct: "Walking down the street, she admired the beautiful flowers."
- **Pronoun Reference**
  - Ensure every pronoun clearly refers to a specific noun.
- **Shifts in Tense**
  - Keep the timeline clear. Avoid jumping between past, present, and future without logical reasons.

4. Employ Reverse Reading for Final Checks

A **reverse reading** approach—scanning from the end of the passage to the beginning—can uncover errors your brain automatically "corrects" when reading normally:

1. **Sentence-by-Sentence**: Review the last sentence in isolation, then move upward.
2. **Word-by-Word (for Grammar/Punctuation)**: If time permits, read each sentence from right to left for a final punctuation and spelling sweep. This technique disengages the brain's tendency to assume what it expects to see.

5. Create a Personal Editing Checklist

Because each writer has unique weak spots, customizing a checklist ensures you don't overlook recurring mistakes:

- **Subject-Verb Agreement**: Check that singular/plural matches are correct.
- **Apostrophes**: Verify correct use in contractions and possessives.
- **Clear References**: Ensure all pronouns refer clearly to a specific antecedent.
- **Conciseness**: Identify and remove redundant phrases (e.g., "combine together," "end result").
- **Parallel Structures**: Confirm lists and comparisons are grammatically uniform.

Use this checklist during practice sessions to form a habit. Over time, you'll develop an eye for these errors, making your editing process faster and more accurate.

6. Manage Your Time Wisely

On the ACT English section, you can't spend unlimited time editing. A few strategies:

- **Skim for Structure**: Before addressing individual questions, briefly skim the passage to understand its overall focus. This helps you spot glaring organizational errors more quickly.
- **Prioritize Obvious Errors**: If you notice a comma splice or pronoun error right away, address it; these are often quick points.
- **Use Remaining Seconds for Proofreading**: If you finish early, do a quick pass for missed mistakes. Even 30 seconds of re-checking can catch a crucial error.

7. Leverage Practice Sessions

Within this guide, you'll find extensive practice passages and editing exercises designed to sharpen your proofreading skills. Each completed exercise is an opportunity to:

- **Refine Your Process**: Test different editing methods—layered approach, reverse reading, or a personal checklist—and see what feels most effective.
- **Identify Persistent Errors**: Notice if you repeatedly miss semicolon rules or misplace apostrophes. Focus extra practice on these areas.
- **Build Speed**: As you edit more, you'll get faster at spotting issues, a valuable skill on a timed exam.

Final Thoughts on Editing and Proofreading

Effective editing and proofreading demand **attention to detail**, **methodical review**, and **time management**. By practicing these strategies regularly with the passages and exercises in this guide, you'll develop a systematic approach to catching errors and refining your writing. Whether you're aiming for higher ACT English scores or refining your skills for academic writing, these techniques will serve you well whenever you need clarity, precision, and polish in your work.

CHAPTER 4

ENGLISH PRACTICE DRILLS

4.1 GRAMMAR DRILLS (TARGETED EXERCISES BY TOPIC)

Strengthening your command of English grammar is essential for excelling in the ACT English section. In the following exercises, you'll practice **core grammar rules** discussed in the previous chapter—covering **subject-verb agreement**, **pronouns**, **verb tenses**, **punctuation**, and more. By honing these individual skills, you'll be better prepared for more complex passage-based questions later on.

Section A: Subject-Verb Agreement

Exercise A1: Select the correct verb form.

1. The pack of wolves (roam / roams) through the forest at dusk.
2. Every one of the candidates (have / has) submitted an application.
3. Neither of the twins (were / was) ready to leave.
4. The group of musicians (perform / performs) classical pieces at local venues.
5. Many of the books on the shelf (is / are) about history.
6. The committee (debate / debates) the policy changes every month.
7. Every student and teacher (is / are) required to attend the assembly.
8. A bouquet of roses (adorn / adorns) the center of the table.
9. Neither of the solutions (work / works) for this complex problem.
10. The team of engineers (present / presents) their findings tomorrow.
11. One of the most popular books (feature / features) a detective as the main character.
12. Either the cats or the dog (make / makes) a mess in the backyard.
13. Nobody in the class (understand / understands) the puzzle yet.
14. The jury (deliberate / deliberates) carefully before announcing a verdict.
15. A cluster of bright stars (illuminate / illuminates) the night sky.
16. Several of the players (has / have) decided to skip practice today.
17. Every car in the lot (need / needs) a valid parking permit.
18. Either my siblings or my cousin (is / are) coming along on the trip.
19. Most of the water in the reservoir (evaporate / evaporates) in the summer.
20. All of the equipment (require / requires) a safety check before use.
21. The bundle of newspapers (is / are) stacked on the porch.
22. Neither the volunteers nor the coordinator (expect / expects) any reward.
23. Everyone in the program (appreciate / appreciates) the updated schedule.
24. The box of ornaments (need / needs) to be stored carefully.
25. Both of my cousins (like / likes) to play soccer after school.
26. The bouquet of tulips (brighten / brightens) the living room.
27. Either the manager or the employees (handle / handles) customer complaints.
28. A panel of experts (discuss / discusses) the new breakthrough on television.
29. The sound of the waves (calm / calms) my nerves.
30. Most of the furniture (was / were) replaced last summer.
31. My collection of photographs (span / spans) several decades.
32. Few of the recipes in that cookbook (turn / turns) out well for me.
33. Some of the cake (has / have) already been eaten.
34. Neither of the twins (enjoy / enjoys) early morning walks.
35. The flock of pigeons (scatter / scatters) when the truck drives by.
36. Everybody in the group (has / have) to submit a travel form.
37. The series of documentaries (highlight / highlights) nature's beauty.
38. Not one of my relatives (live / lives) near the coast.
39. Several of my friends (play / plays) in a band together.

40. The jury (recommend / recommends) a lenient sentence for the defendant.
41. Our family (travel / travels) abroad every summer.
42. A number of employees (seek / seeks) more flexible schedules.
43. The tray of muffins (smell / smells) delicious.
44. Everybody who attends the concert (want / wants) to hear the new songs.
45. One of the cat's toys (is / are) missing under the couch.
46. The government officials (plan / plans) to meet next week.
47. The box of crayons (contain / contains) many bright colors.
48. The board of trustees (approve / approves) the new budget plan annually.
49. Either the soup or the salads (come / comes) with fresh bread.
50. A majority of the committee members (agree / agrees) on the policy changes.
51. Several of the critics (love / loves) the movie adaptation.
52. None of the test results (indicate / indicates) a serious problem.
53. The pair of shoes (look / looks) fabulous with that outfit.
54. Neither of the solutions (solve / solves) the main issue thoroughly.
55. Our team (practice / practices) in the gym each day.
56. None of the instructions (make / makes) sense to me.
57. A handful of volunteers (assist / assists) at the donation drive each weekend.
58. The audience (wait / waits) impatiently for the star to appear.
59. Plenty of opportunities (exist / exists) in this field of work.
60. The committee (debate / debates) the proposal for hours before deciding.
61. Several in the crowd (shout / shouts) for an encore performance.
62. A fraction of the data (suggest / suggests) an error in the experiment.
63. Either your brothers or your sister (has / have) the extra key.
64. The Council on Foreign Relations (promote / promotes) international dialogue.
65. Both of my knees (hurt / hurts) after the long race.
66. The solar panel on the roof (generate / generates) enough electricity for the house.
67. Many of the city's residents (support / supports) the new park initiative.
68. Every adult and child in the auditorium (watch / watches) the performance quietly.
69. Half of the fruit in the basket (is / are) rotten.
70. Somebody in the room (forget / forgets) to mute their phone.

Exercise A2: Correct the errors in subject-verb agreement.

1. The teacher as well as her students were excited about the experiment.
2. The basketball team were practicing late into the night.
3. One of the main sources of stress are poor time management.
4. The band of merry travelers were singing songs around the fire.
5. Either the teacher or her assistants was supposed to check the homework.
6. Many of the articles in the magazine is outdated.
7. The herd of elephants make a thunderous noise as they move.
8. The mayor along with her advisors have decided to postpone the event.
9. None of the students in the class have turned in their essays on time.
10. A pack of stray dogs sometimes wander through the neighborhood at night.
11. Every one of these antiques have a fascinating history behind it.
12. The board of directors are holding separate meetings this week.
13. One of the best parts of the vacation were the guided tours.
14. Either my brothers or my mom are picking me up after practice.
15. The flock of seagulls were circling the fishing boat.
16. Everything in the instructions indicate a longer cooking time.
17. The tray of cookies smell delicious, fresh out of the oven.
18. A series of unexpected events have led us to this conclusion.
19. The team of soccer players are warming up on the field too early.
20. Neither of the solutions have fixed the problem effectively.
21. The crowd of protesters were growing louder by the minute.

22. Both the director and the producers has decided to cancel the scene.
23. Everyone on the bus were complaining about the broken air conditioner.
24. The group of hikers have reached the summit first.
25. One of my best memories were going to the carnival at night.
26. The team of surgeons were confident about the procedure.
27. Most of the water bottles was stacked improperly in the storage room.
28. Every one of the finalists were excited to compete on stage.
29. Neither the coach nor the players was ready for the final match.
30. A stack of papers were left on my desk this morning.
31. Nobody in my family are planning to visit the museum this weekend.
32. A pack of wolves roam across these hills every winter.
33. Several of the applicants is overqualified for the entry-level position.
34. The jury were divided in their decision.
35. None of the advice were particularly helpful.
36. Each of the dogs need a fresh bowl of water.
37. A swarm of bees have taken over the empty shed.
38. The pile of books were toppling over on the shelf.
39. Neither of the siblings were interested in inheriting the antique clock.
40. One of the suspects have confessed to the crime.
41. The pair of headphones are missing from the counter.
42. Either the laptop or the phone were damaged during the trip.
43. Our family were planning a surprise party for our grandmother.
44. Nobody on the committee have volunteered for the new role.
45. All of the furniture were moved to the garage for storage.
46. The herd of deer scatter when they sense danger.
47. Every painting in the gallery were carefully restored.
48. The board of trustees have announced its decision earlier.
49. Each of the students have the opportunity to speak at the seminar.
50. Both the mayor and the city council approves the new policy.
51. The swarm of locusts was ravaging the crops.
52. Many in the audience was disappointed by the short performance.
53. The staff in the office were preparing for the big presentation.
54. Not one of the recipes were easy enough for me to try.
55. A team of scientists have discovered a new species of frog.
56. None of the evidence support the defendant's claims.
57. A handful of daisies add color to the windowsill.
58. The fleet of ships were anchored at the harbor.
59. A number of graduates plans on continuing their education.
60. Neither my cousin nor my siblings is aware of the surprise party.
61. A variety of factors affects the final outcome.
62. The committee were announcing the results at noon.
63. Several of the employees takes public transportation to work.
64. One of my friends have decided to move abroad for a year.
65. The series of lectures were more interesting than I expected.
66. The pair of gloves were lying on the table all day.
67. Nobody in the building were notified about the change in security codes.
68. All of the evidence point to a single suspect.

(Write each sentence correctly in your own words.)

Section B: Pronouns

Exercise B1: Identify and Correct Unclear or Mismatched Pronouns

Instructions: Each sentence contains an ambiguous, unclear, or mismatched pronoun. Identify the problem and rewrite the sentence so that the pronoun usage is clear.

1. When Sara talked to Molly, she noticed the coffee shop was about to close.
2. A person should eat plenty of fruits and vegetables if they want to stay healthy.
3. If the dogs start barking, the neighbors will call the police if it gets too loud.
4. While Tom was tutoring Jason in algebra, he realized that geometry needed more attention.
5. Kelly informed Jackie that she would be traveling to Europe next month.
6. When the car got a flat tire, they replaced it within a few minutes.
7. Everyone who sees that movie loves it because they are so terrifying.
8. The teacher told the student that she should do more practice tests.
9. Alex told Taylor that his outfit looked great.
10. When the puppy met the kitten, it ran behind the couch.
11. Sam called Chris right after he finished taking the driving test.
12. Pat and Jordan drove to the beach, but she forgot the towels.
13. The manager emailed the employee about her new responsibilities.
14. When the firefighters arrived, they said it was too late to save the barn.
15. After Julia spoke with her mother, she decided to leave earlier than planned.
16. We called the realtor and asked if she could provide more details, but they never responded.
17. The neighbors notified the homeowners that their garden gate was left open, but they didn't lock it.
18. My brother wrote to my cousin that he was thinking about applying to college abroad.
19. Olivia texted her friend after the audition, but she didn't answer right away.
20. When the nurse checked on the patient, they noted the medication had already taken effect.

Exercise B2: Choose the Correct Pronoun Case

Instructions: Select the correct pronoun from the options given in parentheses.

1. The committee awarded the prize to (he / him) and (I / me).
2. (Who / Whom) should I speak to about the vacant position?
3. My sister and (I / me) are planning a surprise party for our parents.
4. Between you and (I / me), the plan needs serious revisions.
5. (Who / Whom) do you think wrote the anonymous note?
6. The winner of the contest was (she / her).
7. Our neighbors invited my brother and (I / me) to their backyard barbecue.
8. Do you know (who / whom) will be hosting the ceremony tonight?
9. Mr. Garcia asked Jason and (she / her) for a volunteer sign-up.
10. (Who / Whom) do you recommend for the scholarship?
11. My friend and (I / me) are going hiking this weekend.
12. The teacher recognized (we / us) as the top performers in the class.
13. They asked my coworker and (I / me) to lead the project.
14. I don't know (who / whom) the CEO chose for the role.
15. Could you tell me (who / whom) invented the printing press?
16. The producers gave (they / them) an opportunity to rewrite the script.
17. The final decision rests with (whoever / whomever) gets the most votes.
18. The judge congratulated (we / us) on our community service efforts.
19. (Who / Whom) did the principal appoint as head of the committee?
20. Everyone except (he / him) showed up early for rehearsal.

Exercise B3: Fix Any Pronoun-Antecedent Agreement Errors

Instructions: Each sentence may have a pronoun that does not agree with its antecedent. Rewrite the sentence so that the pronoun usage is correct and consistent.

1. Each of the engineers presented their unique design.
2. Everybody must take off their shoes before entering the temple.
3. Several of the employees turned in his resignation letters.
4. Every student needs to submit their homework on time.
5. Not one of the actresses remembered their lines perfectly.
6. Anyone who wants to register for the seminar must sign up before they leave today.

7. One of the technicians informed management that they would be late.
8. Neither of the mechanics believed they had the right parts.
9. If a buyer wants to return the product, they should keep the receipt.
10. Everyone in the club must renew their membership by next week.
11. Each of the applicants expressed dissatisfaction with how they were interviewed.
12. Either of the players may claim their trophy after the match.
13. One of the employees wrote a letter of complaint, claiming they were overworked.
14. If anyone misses a shift, they should notify the supervisor immediately.
15. Somebody left their backpack in the hallway after class.
16. When a driver parks illegally, they risk getting a ticket.
17. Neither of the flight attendants had their schedule confirmed.
18. Anyone traveling abroad should keep close track of their passport.
19. Everyone on the debate team presented their case convincingly.
20. If a photographer plans to sell prints, they must secure licensing first.

(Rewrite each sentence using correct pronoun usage.)

Section C: Verb Tenses

Exercise C1: Fill in the blanks with the appropriate verb tense (present, past, future, present perfect, past perfect, or future perfect).

Instructions: Use the correct verb tense (present, past, future, present perfect, past perfect, or future perfect) to complete each sentence. Begin numbering at #6.

1. By the time you arrive, I _____ **(to finish)** cooking dinner.
2. I _____ **(to study)** for three hours, and now I need a break.
3. They _____ **(to travel)** to Brazil last summer and loved the beaches there.
4. We _____ **(to plan)** a trip for next month; the tickets are already booked.
5. She _____ **(to realize)** her mistake only after submitting the assignment.
6. Last night, I _____ (to realize) that my keys were missing.
7. By the end of this year, I _____ (to save) enough money to buy a new laptop.
8. She usually _____ (to take) the bus to work, but today she's driving because she overslept.
9. I _____ (to visit) Paris twice before I moved there for a year.
10. Tomorrow at noon, we _____ (to meet) the project deadline and can finally relax.
11. They _____ (to live) in the same apartment for over a decade now.
12. By the time the rain started, I _____ (to finish) mowing the lawn.
13. He _____ (to study) history at college next semester.
14. My cousin _____ (to call) me every weekend since she moved overseas.
15. We _____ (to watch) a documentary on wildlife conservation when the power went out.
16. The students _____ (to discuss) the assignment in class tomorrow.
17. After Lisa _____ (to compare) several recipes, she chose the simplest one.
18. My parents _____ (to celebrate) their 25th wedding anniversary next month.
19. We _____ (to walk) along the beach for hours before we found the perfect spot to picnic.
20. By the time you come home, I _____ (to clean) every room in the house.

Exercise C2: Rewrite the following paragraph, correcting any tense shifts.

Paragraph 1

"Yesterday, I **visit** my grandparents in the countryside. They **are** excited to see me and **prepare** a big lunch. After we eat, my grandfather **takes** me fishing, which I always enjoy. Later that evening, I **will drive** back to the city, feeling relaxed and happy."

Paragraph 2

"I wake up this morning feeling groggy. I made coffee and sit down to check my emails. Then I realize I forgot to feed the dog, so I rushed to the kitchen. By the time I get back, my coffee was cold."

Paragraph 3

"Last Saturday, I go to the park with my friends. We brought a football and play a quick game. Halfway through, it starts raining, so we decide to head home. Later that evening, I am drying my clothes and notice my phone is still in my pocket."

Paragraph 4

"Tomorrow, I picked up my new car from the dealership. I am very excited because I saved money for years to buy it. After I sign the papers, I drive it around the neighborhood to test everything."

Paragraph 5

"The little girl sits on the swing and smiled at her father, who was pushing her gently. Suddenly, she asks him if she can go higher, and he laughed before giving her a stronger push."

Paragraph 6

"Next month, we flew to Hawaii for our vacation. We are planning to explore the volcanoes and take lots of pictures. After we arrive, we will check in at the hotel and get some rest before sightseeing."

Paragraph 7

"Yesterday, I decide to bake cookies for the charity event. I mix the ingredients together and set them in the oven. While they are baking, I realized I forgot to add sugar. In the end, they still taste fine."

Paragraph 8

"During the meeting, our manager says we should finalize the budget by the end of the day. Then she handed out spreadsheets and discusses future strategies. We will review everything again once we have finished the revisions."

Paragraph 9

"Two weeks ago, I join a gym because I wanted to get back in shape. I work out daily now, and I will see some progress already. By the time summer arrives, I hope I lost a few pounds."

Paragraph 10

"This morning, the children play in the backyard while their mother prepares breakfast. When she calls them inside, they took their time picking up toys. Later, they will watch cartoons and told stories about their favorite characters."

Paragraph 11

"On Friday, I am invited to a friend's birthday party. I buy a gift, and tomorrow I wrapped it carefully. After the party, I drove home feeling happy that I could celebrate with everyone."

(Ensure the paragraph maintains a consistent and logical timeline.)

Section D: Punctuation (Commas, Semicolons, Apostrophes)

Exercise D1: Insert commas where needed.

1. After a long day at work my mother enjoys reading a good book.
2. My favorite authors are Mark Twain Jane Austen and George Orwell.

3. Michael who lives next door mows his lawn every Saturday morning.
4. I like spicy food however my brother prefers milder dishes.
5. Because the concert was sold out we decided to watch the livestream instead.
6. I bought apples oranges mangoes and grapes at the market.
7. Despite his injury Marcus finished the race in record time.
8. Our team which has been training for months hopes to win the championship.
9. Under the old oak tree we set up our picnic blankets.
10. The restaurant served pasta salads soups and sandwiches.
11. My cousin Caroline who recently moved to Boston found a job downtown.
12. Without a doubt this is the tastiest dish on the menu.
13. As soon as the sun rose we started our hike up the mountain.
14. He whispered "Be careful" before stepping into the dark corridor.
15. Anna the youngest sibling inherited her grandmother's love of painting.
16. If you need any help feel free to call me.
17. The play was long however the acting was phenomenal.
18. On Saturday I have a soccer match and a piano recital.
19. Derek asked politely "Could you pass the salt please?"
20. When you reach the end of the trail take a moment to enjoy the view.

Exercise D2: Correct any comma splices or run-on sentences using periods, semicolons, or coordinating conjunctions.

1. I love the snow it makes everything look so peaceful.
2. She ran to catch the bus she slipped on the icy sidewalk.
3. He wants to study medicine he also wants to travel the world.
4. I finished reading the book now I need to write my report.
5. She loves to paint landscapes she also enjoys sketching portraits.
6. We wanted to leave early it started raining heavily so we stayed.
7. It's a busy time of year we have family visiting from out of town.
8. Alex played the guitar beautifully the audience gave him a standing ovation.
9. I tried to bake a cake I ran out of sugar halfway through.
10. She wanted to travel abroad she saved money for months.
11. That movie is really suspenseful I would watch it again.
12. He forgot his wallet in the car he had to go back for it.
13. I love hiking through the mountains the fresh air is invigorating.
14. The manager approved my vacation request I can't wait to go to the beach.
15. We debated the issue all night we couldn't agree on a solution.
16. She studied hard for the exam she forgot her notes at home.
17. The library is closing soon you should check out your books now.
18. Some people prefer coffee others like tea.
19. I was late to the meeting I got stuck in traffic on the highway.

Exercise D3: Fix apostrophe usage.

1. The Smiths house is on the corner.
2. Its a beautiful day for a picnic.
3. Youll find the museums entrance at the end of this street.
4. The dogs collar was loose so I tightened it.
5. Its been a while since Ive visited my grandparents farm.
6. The cats bowls need to be washed regularly.
7. Weve seen that movie three times yet its ending still surprises us.
8. Todays schedule is fully booked theres no time for a break.
9. The childrens playground is next to the teachers lounge.
10. Whos ready to begin todays lesson on punctuation?
11. The familys car broke down on the way to their vacation home.
12. Youre going to have fun at tonights concert its going to be amazing.

13. The students presentations were all impressive but Jims stood out.
14. I cant believe shes leaving for college next week.
15. The teams uniform colors changed this season.
16. The babys stroller is on the back porch dont forget it.
17. Shes looking for her mothers keys but cant find them.
18. Its important that you respect others boundaries.
19. The politicians campaign slogan was all over the citys billboards.
20. Whos responsible for cleaning the dog's bowls after dinner?

Section E: Mixed Grammar Challenges

Combine multiple skills—subject-verb agreement, pronouns, verb tenses, and punctuation—to edit these sentences.

1. My family who like to travel frequently are planning a trip to Italy next year, I hope we have saved enough money.
2. Neither Jenna nor her friends was ready for they're final exams which is tomorrow at 9:00 AM.
3. Many of the theories proposed by the scientist is controversial however they has changed how we view environmental conservation.
4. Its important to have a good nights sleep a student should get around eight hours if they want to be fully alert.
5. The group of students who is meeting every Friday are excited about their project, they are hoping to present it next week.
6. Each of the employees have turned in their resignation letter last Monday, I'm not sure why they choose to leave so suddenly.
7. We wanted to buy groceries, but the store were closed the sign said it was under renovation.
8. The teacher told the class that they should finish their assignment by tonight however some of the students asked for an extension.
9. My friend and me is planning a surprise birthday party for his brother which is happening tomorrow.
10. The dog found it's ball under the couch, after we had looked for it for hours.
11. She have been studying for weeks but she realized she forgot all her notes at home.
12. I have eat breakfast already, I usually do that before starting my day but today I completely forgot.
13. A person can lose track of time if they uses their phone too often, it distracts you from important tasks.
14. My cousins decided that he would learn guitar last week, but they changed their mind yesterday.
15. The board of directors are holding a meeting next month to discuss the companys new policy, its starting to get negative feedback from employees.
16. Who do you think you should talk to about these issues, our manager or the HR representative.
17. Talia gave her sister the keys to the car so she could run errands but she left them on the table and lost it.
18. No one want to take responsibility for the mistake, they said it wasnt theyre fault.
19. Tomorrow, I flew to California for a business trip, I wonder if I will have enough time to sightsee.
20. We has waited for two hours in line for those tickets yet none of us are complaining, is better than missing the show.

(Rewrite each sentence, addressing any issues with grammar, punctuation, and clarity.)

Tips for Working Through Grammar Drills

- **Slow Down**: Read each sentence carefully. The ACT often camouflages errors with lengthy phrases or modifying clauses.
- **Check for Multiple Errors**: Each sentence can contain more than one issue, especially when it comes to punctuation and pronouns.
- **Write It Out**: When in doubt, rewrite the sentence on a scratch sheet of paper to see if the subject matches the verb, the pronouns match their antecedents, and the punctuation is correct.
- **Reflect on Mistakes**: If you find a particular pattern (e.g., you constantly add extra commas, or you struggle with pronoun clarity), spend extra time reviewing those rules.

Looking Ahead

Once you're comfortable with these targeted grammar drills, you can move on to **Section 4.2: Passage-Based Editing Sets**, where you'll apply these rules in more context-heavy questions. With consistent practice, you'll develop sharper instincts for spotting and correcting errors—a crucial step toward earning a high score on the ACT English section.

4.2 PASSAGE-BASED EDITING SETS

Now that you've practiced **targeted grammar drills**, it's time to tackle questions in a **contextual format** more akin to the actual ACT English section. In passage-based editing sets, you'll apply your knowledge of grammar, punctuation, sentence structure, and rhetorical skills to **entire paragraphs or short passages**. This approach helps you see how individual corrections fit into the broader flow and logic of a text.

Below are two sample passages. Each passage has underlined portions followed by multiple-choice questions. The **four** answer choices reflect the ACT's structure for English questions. Some questions focus on standard grammar rules, while others test the organization, clarity, and style of the passage. Work through each underlined segment, choosing the best answer. If no change is needed, select **A. NO CHANGE**.

Passage 1

Community gardens are becoming increasingly popular in urban areas. **(1) People are discovering that growing there own vegetables can be both cost-effective and emotionally satisfying.** Some residents enjoy cultivating flowers, while others prefer herbs that will thrive in small, shared plots. In either case, people feel a sense of accomplishment when they pick fresh produce they have grown themselves. **(2) One well-known gardening program in New York City, shows how powerful these projects can be.** Through collaborative efforts, entire blocks have been transformed into green spaces where neighbors bond over shared goals.

(3) Community gardening not only improves neighborhoods appearances, but it also fosters a spirit of cooperation. Whether participants are planting tomatoes or sunflowers, they learn to respect one another's preferences and share the responsibility of maintaining a tidy, productive garden. **(4) Because of this, many local parks have begun offering educational workshops, these workshops teach new gardeners the basics of soil preparation, pest control, and sustainable gardening methods.**

1. **(1)**
   A. NO CHANGE
   B. People are discovering that growing their own vegetables can be both cost-effective, and emotional satisfying.
   C. People are discovering that growing their own vegetables can be both cost-effective and emotionally satisfying.
   D. People are discovering, that growing their own vegetables can be both cost-effective, and emotionally satisfying.

2. **(2)**
   A. NO CHANGE
   B. One well-known gardening program in New York City shows, how powerful these projects can be.
   C. One well-known gardening program in New York City shows how powerful these projects can be.
   D. One well-known gardening program in New York City: shows how powerful these projects can be.

3. **(3)**
   A. NO CHANGE
   B. Community gardening not only improves neighborhoods' appearances, it also fosters a spirit of cooperation.
   C. Community gardening, not only improves neighborhood's appearances but, it also fosters a spirit of cooperation.

D. Community gardening not only improves neighborhoods' appearances but also fosters a spirit of cooperation.

4. **(4)**
A. NO CHANGE
B. Because of this many local parks have begun offering educational workshops that teach
C. Because of this, many local parks have begun offering educational workshops; these workshops teach
D. Because of this, many local parks have begun offering educational workshops. These workshops teach

Passage 2

The invention of the printing press is widely regarded as one of the most significant events in human history. **(5) Without it, mass literacy might not have developed, and information wouldn't have been as easy to share or preserve.** Johannes Gutenberg's 15th-century innovation revolutionized how books were produced and distributed. **(6) Before his invention, scribes had to hand-copy texts a process that was time-consuming and prone to errors.** When the printed word became more accessible, scientific discoveries spread rapidly, sparking further research and cultural exchange.

(7) The printing press had many immediate benefits: it lowered the cost of books, it encouraged the translation of religious texts, and enabling the spread of different cultural perspectives. Over time, people from various regions and backgrounds gained the ability to share their ideas broadly. **(8) As a result the world witnessed a flourishing of knowledge during the Renaissance, quickly overshadowing previous eras intellectual achievements.** Modern communication technologies, from newspapers to the internet, trace their lineage back to Gutenberg's era-changing machine.

5. **(5)**
A. NO CHANGE
B. Without it mass literacy might not have developed and information wouldn't have been as easy to share or preserve.
C. Without it, mass literacy might not have developed; and information wouldn't have been as easy to share or preserve.
D. Without it, mass literacy might not have developed, and information might not have been as easy to share or preserve.

6. **(6)**
A. NO CHANGE
B. Before his invention, scribes had to hand-copy texts: a process that was time-consuming and prone to errors.
C. Before his invention, scribes had to hand-copy texts, a process, that was time-consuming and prone to errors.
D. Before his invention; scribes had to hand-copy texts, which was time-consuming and prone to errors.

7. **(7)**
A. NO CHANGE
B. The printing press had many immediate benefits: it lowered the cost of books and encouraged the translation of religious texts, enabling
C. The printing press had many immediate benefits, it lowered the cost of books, it encouraged the translation of religious texts, and enabling
D. The printing press had many immediate benefits: it lowered the cost of books, encouraged the translation of religious texts, and enabled

8. **(8)**
A. NO CHANGE
B. As a result, the world witnessed a flourishing of knowledge during the Renaissance quickly overshadowing previous eras' intellectual achievements.
C. As a result, the world witnessed a flourishing of knowledge during the Renaissance, it quickly

overshadowed previous eras' intellectual achievements.
D. As a result, the world witnessed a flourishing of knowledge during the Renaissance, quickly overshadowing previous eras' intellectual achievements.

Passage 3

Farmers' markets have grown in popularity as people seek fresh, locally sourced produce. **(9) Many shoppers appreciate the variety of goods available and that farmers can be asked questions about their cultivation practices.** These markets also serve as community hubs, bringing together neighbors who enjoy seasonal fruits, vegetables, and specialty items. **(10) Because some regions experience harsh winters when produce is scarce, many markets transitions into indoor venues.** This approach ensures that customers have access to local products year-round, **(11) improving farmer's revenues** and contributing to a stronger local economy. Still, maintaining farmers' markets requires coordination among growers, volunteers, and municipal authorities. **(12) Vendors, volunteers, and city officials often dedicates countless hours** to ensure the market's success.

Questions for Passage 3

9. **(9)**
A. NO CHANGE
B. Many shoppers appreciate the variety of goods available, they like asking farmers questions about their cultivation practices.
C. Many shoppers appreciate the variety of goods available and the opportunity to ask farmers about their cultivation practices.
D. Many shoppers appreciates the variety of goods available, and they can ask farmers questions about how they grow it.

10. **(10)**
A. NO CHANGE
B. Because some regions experience harsh winters when produce is scarce, many markets transition into indoor venues.
C. Because some regions experiences harsh winters, many markets have transitioned into indoor venues.
D. Because some regions experience harsh winters when produce is scarce, many markets transitioning into indoor venues.

11. **(11)**
A. NO CHANGE
B. improving farmers' revenues
C. improves farmer's revenue
D. improves farmers revenue

12. **(12)**
A. NO CHANGE
B. Vendors, volunteers, and city officials often dedicate countless hours
C. Vendors, volunteers, and city officials often dedicating countless hours
D. Vendors, volunteers, and city officials is often dedicating countless hours

Passage 4

Large-scale public art installations can revitalize neighborhoods. **(13) Mural projects, for example provide a visual narrative of a communitys history** and aspirations. Artists collaborate with residents to design images that reflect local culture, leading to a sense of ownership and pride among viewers. **(14) Some critics argue that murals maybe superficial solutions** to deeper social issues, but supporters counter that art can spark meaningful conversations.

(15) With enough planning, numerous communities has discovered that these installations encourage tourism and community engagement. Ultimately, **(16) if residents want bright, colorful and culturally relevant spaces** they must be actively involved in the entire process, from concept to completion.

Questions for Passage 4

13. **(13)**
    A. NO CHANGE
    B. Mural projects, for example, provide a visual narrative of a community's history
    C. Mural projects for example provides a visual narrative of a communitys history
    D. Mural projects, for example provide a visual narrative of a community's history,

14. **(14)**
    A. NO CHANGE
    B. Some critics argue that murals may be superficial solutions
    C. Some critics argue, that murals may be superficial solutions
    D. Some critics argue that murals maybe superficial solutions,

15. **(15)**
    A. NO CHANGE
    B. With enough planning, numerous communities discover
    C. With enough planning, numerous communities have discovered
    D. With enough planning numerous communities has discovered

16. **(16)**
    A. NO CHANGE
    B. if residents want bright, colorful, and culturally relevant spaces
    C. if residents want bright colorful, and culturally relevant spaces
    D. if residents want bright, colorful and culturally-relevant spaces

Passage 5

Baking bread at home has gained popularity among culinary enthusiasts. **(17) It require patience, precise measurement, and an understanding of yeast fermentation** to achieve a light, airy loaf. Some bakers experiment with sourdough starters, which offer complex flavors and unique textures. **(18) Even though mistakes can happen—like under-kneading or forgetting the salt—learning these techniques often proves rewarding.** In fact, many people argue that the aroma of fresh bread alone is worth the effort. **(19) Historically, homemade bread was often a necessity, it is now enjoying a revival** thanks to social media communities that share recipes and tips. Whether one prefers whole-grain loaves or sweet cinnamon rolls, **(20) the act of turning simple ingredients into a satisfying meal fosters a sense of pride.**

Questions for Passage 5

17. **(17)**
    A. NO CHANGE
    B. They require patience, precise measurement, and an understanding of yeast fermentation
    C. It requires patience, precise measurements, and an understanding of yeast fermentation
    D. They requires patience, precise measurement, and an understanding of yeast fermentation

18. **(18)**
    A. NO CHANGE
    B. Even though mistakes can happen—like under-kneading or forgetting the salt—learning these techniques is rewarding.
    C. Even though mistakes can happen: like under-kneading or forgetting the salt—learning these techniques often proves rewarding.
    D. Even though mistakes can happen—like under-kneading or forgetting the salt: learning these techniques often proves rewarding.

19. **(19)**
    A. NO CHANGE
    B. Historically, homemade bread was often a necessity; it is now enjoying a revival

C. Historically, homemade bread was often a necessity, and it is now enjoying a revival
D. Historically, homemade bread was often a necessity it is now enjoying a revival,

20. **(20)**
A. NO CHANGE
B. the act of turning simple ingredients into a satisfying meal fosters a sense of pride in me.
C. the act of turning simple ingredients into a satisfying meal, fosters a sense of pride.
D. turning simple ingredients into a satisfying meal fosters pride in a person.

Passage 6

(21) Designing a website requires both creativity, and technical expertise. First, a developer or designer lays out the structure and determines how users will navigate the site. They then select fonts, colors, and images to ensure a visually appealing page. **(22) Without well-planned structure though, visitors may have trouble finding what they need** and abandon the site. Moreover, **(23) frequent updates keeps content fresh** and encourage return visits. Whether it's a personal blog or a large-scale e-commerce platform, **(24) websites thrive when they is user-friendly and visually engaging.**

Questions for Passage 6

21. **(21)**
A. NO CHANGE
B. Designing a website requires both creativity and technical expertise.
C. Designing a website requires both: creativity, and technical expertise.
D. Designing a website requires, both creativity and technical expertise.

22. **(22)**
A. NO CHANGE
B. Without well-planned structure, though, visitors may have trouble finding what they need
C. Without well planned structure, though visitors may have trouble finding what they need
D. Without well-planned structure. Though visitors may have trouble finding what they need

23. **(23)**
A. NO CHANGE
B. frequent updates keep content fresh
C. frequent updates will keeps content fresh
D. frequent updates will have kept content fresh

24. **(24)**
A. NO CHANGE
B. websites thrive when it is user-friendly and visually engaging
C. websites thrive when they are user-friendly and visually engaging
D. websites thrive, when they is user-friendly and visually engaging

Passage 7

Many commuters prefer cycling to driving. **(25) Not only does it reduces carbon emissions, it also provides regular exercise.** Neighborhoods often benefit from having fewer cars on the road, which can lessen traffic congestion and improve air quality. **(26) However some people still worry about safety especially in areas lacking bike lanes** or well-lit streets. Local governments may respond by installing protected bike paths and increased signage, **(27) so that more residents feels confident** riding bicycles. Ultimately, **(28) cycling can save money on gas and parking, also benefiting the environment** along the way.

Questions for Passage 7

25. **(25)**
A. NO CHANGE
B. Not only does it reduce carbon emissions, it also provides regular exercise.

C. Not only do it reduce carbon emissions, it also provides regular exercise.
D. Not only is it reducing carbon emissions, it also providing regular exercise.

26. **(26)**
A. NO CHANGE
B. However, some people still worry about safety especially, in areas lacking bike lanes
C. However, some people still worry about safety, especially in areas lacking bike lanes
D. However some people, still worry about safety especially in areas lacking bike lanes

27. **(27)**
A. NO CHANGE
B. so that more residents feel confident
C. so more residents would feel confident
D. so, that more residents are feeling confident

28. **(28)**
A. NO CHANGE
B. cycling can save money on gas and parking, it also benefits the environment
C. cycling can save money on gas and parking; it also benefits the environment
D. cycling saves money on gas and parking which also benefiting the environment

Passage 8

(29) Researching family history is a popular hobby many people enjoy collecting old letters, photographs, and documents that reveal their ancestry. Online databases and archives have made it easier to search for birth records, marriage certificates, and census data. **(30) As a result individuals who once struggled to trace** their lineage now have access to comprehensive resources. Nevertheless, **(31) the process requires patience and a willingness to verify details thoroughly errors can lead to inaccurate family trees.** Experts recommend comparing multiple sources, such as local newspapers and oral histories, to ensure accuracy. **(32) This method often uncovers surprising connections many genealogists are thrilled** to find distant relatives they never knew existed.

Questions for Passage 8

29. **(29)**
A. NO CHANGE
B. Researching family history is a popular hobby, many people enjoy collecting old letters, photographs, and documents that reveal their ancestry.
C. Researching family history is a popular hobby, and many people enjoy collecting old letters, photographs, and documents that reveal their ancestry.
D. Researching family history, is a popular hobby many people enjoy collecting old letters, photographs, and documents that reveal their ancestry.

30. **(30)**
A. NO CHANGE
B. As a result, individuals, who once struggled to trace
C. As a result, individuals who once struggled, to trace
D. As a result, individuals who once struggled to trace

31. **(31)**
A. NO CHANGE
B. the process requires patience and a willingness to verify details thoroughly, errors can lead to inaccurate family trees.
C. the process requires patience and a willingness to verify details thoroughly. Errors can lead to inaccurate family trees.
D. the process require patience and a willingness to verify details thoroughly; errors leads to inaccurate family trees.

32. **(32)**
    A. NO CHANGE
    B. This method often uncovers surprising connections, many genealogists are thrilled
    C. This method often uncovers surprising connections; many genealogists are thrilled
    D. This method often uncovers surprising connections many genealogists are thrilled and excited

Passage 9

Volunteering at a local shelter is a rewarding way to give back to the community. **(33) Some people prefer working with animals they find satisfaction in caring** for abandoned pets. Others may choose to assist in community kitchens, senior centers, or youth programs. **(34) The key is discovering which cause resonates with you, once you find that passion** the work feels genuinely fulfilling. Research shows that volunteering can boost self-esteem, **(35) reduce stress, and helps individuals** develop new skills. Additionally, **(36) connecting with neighbors fosters a sense of belonging, that can lead** to lasting friendships and improved mental health.

Questions for Passage 9

33. **(33)**
    A. NO CHANGE
    B. Some people prefer working with animals, finding satisfaction in caring
    C. Some people prefer working with animals, and they find satisfaction caring
    D. Some people prefer working with animals by finding satisfaction in caring

34. **(34)**
    A. NO CHANGE
    B. The key is discovering which cause resonates with you. Once you find that passion,
    C. The key is discovering which cause resonates with you; once you find that passion
    D. The key, is discovering which cause resonates with you once you find that passion

35. **(35)**
    A. NO CHANGE
    B. reduce stress, and help individuals
    C. reduces stress, and help individuals
    D. reduce stress and it also helps individuals

36. **(36)**
    A. NO CHANGE
    B. connecting with neighbors fosters a sense of belonging that can lead
    C. connecting with neighbors fosters a sense of belonging, which may lead
    D. connecting with neighbors fosters a sense of belonging, that leads

Passage 10

(37) Over the past decade, social media platforms have altered how people interacts with friends, family, and even strangers worldwide. Users can share photos, exchange ideas, and form communities based on shared interests. **(38) Although critics argue that it reduces face-to-face interactions** many say these networks provide opportunities for diverse connections. **(39) For instance traveling food enthusiasts** can join groups to swap recipes, discuss local cuisine, and plan meetups. Nevertheless, it's essential to use these platforms responsibly: **(40) excessive use might impacts mental health** by leading to isolation or anxiety.

Questions for Passage 10

37. **(37)**
    A. NO CHANGE
    B. Over the past decade, social media platforms has altered how people interact
    C. Over the past decade, social media platforms have altered how people interact
    D. Over the past decade social media platforms have altered how people interacts

38. **(38)**
    A. NO CHANGE
    B. Although critics argue that it reduces face-to-face interactions,
    C. Although, critics argue that it reduces face-to-face interactions,
    D. Although critics argue, that it reduces face-to-face interactions

39. **(39)**
    A. NO CHANGE
    B. For instance, traveling-food enthusiasts
    C. For instance, traveling food enthusiasts
    D. For instance; traveling food-enthusiasts

40. **(40)**
    A. NO CHANGE
    B. excessive use might impact mental health
    C. excessive use might impacted mental health
    D. excessive use might impacting mental health

How to Use These Passages

1. **Read Each Passage** carefully before deciding on the best answer for each underlined portion.
2. **Check for Grammar & Style**: Look for errors in subject-verb agreement, pronoun reference, verb tense, punctuation, parallel structure, and clarity.
3. **Apply ACT Strategies**: If "NO CHANGE" seems correct, verify that no improvement is needed. If a choice fixes one error but creates another, rule it out.
4. **Review Thoroughly**: Practice explaining why the correct choice is better than the others, reinforcing your understanding of each concept.

These passages and questions mirror **ACT English**-style items, giving you more contextual practice beyond isolated drills. Good luck!

How to Approach Passage-Based Editing Sets

1. **Read the Entire Paragraph**: Glancing only at the underlined portion might lead you to miss context clues that affect your choice.
2. **Anticipate Common Errors**: Think about punctuation usage, agreement, clarity, and style—just like in the grammar drills.
3. **Check for Rhetorical Flow**: Some questions ask which sentence best fits the passage's purpose or organizes ideas effectively.
4. **Use the Process of Elimination**: If two answer choices introduce new grammatical errors, discard them. If another choice alters the meaning drastically, it's likely incorrect.

Moving Forward

After finishing these passage-based edits, compare your answers to the **detailed explanations** in a later section (Chapter 4.4) to see how each revision improves or maintains the text's correctness and coherence. This step is crucial for cementing the lessons you're learning—when you understand **why** a specific change is correct or incorrect, you'll be better equipped to handle similar challenges on the ACT English test.

4.3 MIXED MINI-TESTS (TIMED PRACTICE)

Now that you've sharpened your skills through targeted grammar drills and passage-based editing, it's time to **simulate real test conditions** with shorter, timed practice sets. These **Mixed Mini-Tests** combine questions on grammar, punctuation, sentence structure, and rhetorical skills—mirroring the variety you'll encounter on the ACT English section.

Below are two short passages. Each passage is followed by 5 multiple-choice questions (A–D). Treat each set as a mini-exam: set a **strict time limit**—for instance, **7–8 minutes per passage**—and work through the questions without interruption. When you finish, you can check your answers in the **Detailed Answer Explanations** (Chapter 4.4) to evaluate your performance and learn from any mistakes.

Mini-Test 1

Passage A

[1] Growing vegetables at home can be both rewarding and cost-effective. [2] **Although** many individuals choose to grow herbs like basil and mint, **they** are easy to maintain in small pots. [3] If you're short on space, try vertical gardening techniques that maximize your area. [4] **For example** using hanging planters or tiered shelves allows even apartment dwellers to cultivate a variety of plants. [5] Fresh produce that you harvest on your own not only tastes better but is also free from harmful chemicals, making it a healthier choice for many families.

1. **(2)**
   A. NO CHANGE
   B. Although many individuals choose to grow herbs like basil and mint, which are easy to maintain, they are often overlooked by beginners.
   C. Many individuals choose to grow herbs like basil and mint because they are easy to maintain in small pots.
   D. Although many individuals choose to grow herbs like basil and mint, it is easy to maintain them in small pots.
2. **(4)**
   A. NO CHANGE
   B. For example, using hanging planters or tiered shelves
   C. For example: using hanging planters or tiered shelves
   D. For example; using hanging planters or tiered shelves
3. The best placement for the sentence **"Some people even repurpose old wooden pallets to create stacked gardens."** would be:
   A. Before sentence [1].
   B. After sentence [1].
   C. After sentence [3].
   D. After sentence [5].
4. Which choice best combines sentences [4] and [5] for clarity and flow, without introducing errors?
   A. "For example, using hanging planters or tiered shelves allows apartment dwellers to cultivate a variety of plants, and fresh produce that you harvest on your own tastes better while also being free from harmful chemicals."
   B. "For example, using hanging planters or tiered shelves allows even apartment dwellers to cultivate a variety of plants; and fresh produce not only tastes better but is healthier because it lacks harmful chemicals."
   C. "For example, using hanging planters or tiered shelves allows even apartment dwellers to cultivate a variety of plants, and such fresh produce is not only tastier but also free from harmful chemicals."
   D. "For example, using hanging planters or tiered shelves allows cultivation; fresh produce that you harvest on your own is free from harmful chemicals."
5. The writer wants to emphasize that homegrown vegetables can be cheaper than store-bought produce. Which sentence could most effectively be added at the end of the paragraph to achieve this?
   A. "Growing vegetables and herbs can be a relaxing hobby for many people who work long hours."
   B. "In addition, these simple gardening techniques can save families money that they would otherwise spend at grocery stores."
   C. "Herbs such as thyme and rosemary also add flavor to many dishes."
   D. "Other gardeners prefer flowers to vegetables, focusing on brightening their homes."

Mini-Test 2

Passage B

[1] Situated in the heart of the city, the **Hargrove Museum** houses a collection of rare manuscripts and historical artifacts. [2] Founded in 1920, **it's** mission has always been to preserve and share cultural treasures with the public. [3] The museum offers daily tours that allow visitors to delve deeper into each exhibit and learn about the broader social context. [4] **However**, new exhibits are frequently announced, so returning guests often discover something new to explore.

1. **(2)**
   A. NO CHANGE
   B. its' mission
   C. its mission
   D. it has mission
2. Which of the following best revises sentence [4] to maintain the paragraph's consistent tone and style?
   A. "Dude, new exhibits get announced all the time, so there's always rad stuff to check out."
   B. "Moreover, the museum frequently announces new exhibits, ensuring returning guests consistently find something fresh to explore."
   C. "Consequently, they show off different exhibits all the time, meaning frequent visitors never get bored."
   D. "On the other hand, new exhibits are regularly announced, leading to more changes than some visitors like."
3. The writer wants to add a sentence about how the museum focuses on historical significance in its collection. The best placement would be:
   A. After sentence [1].
   B. Before sentence [1].
   C. After sentence [3].
   D. After sentence [4].
4. Which choice most improves the clarity of sentence [3]?
   A. The museum offers daily tours, giving visitors a chance to learn a lot.
   B. Offering daily tours, the museum presents in-depth insights into each exhibit, placing them within their social context.
   C. Tours that are offered daily allow visitors to delve deeper into each exhibit to learn broad social context.
   D. The museum, which offers daily tours, helps visitors delve deeper, gleaning information about each exhibit's societal role.
5. If the writer wants to clarify that the museum's artifacts date from ancient civilizations to the modern era, which additional sentence would be most relevant at the end of the paragraph?
   A. "Many of the museum's pieces were donated by a local historian who traveled extensively."
   B. "Throughout its rich history, the museum has seen changes in leadership and curatorial focus."
   C. "Ranging from ancient scrolls to contemporary art pieces, the artifacts cover numerous historical periods."
   D. "The gift shop is well-stocked with souvenirs for all types of visitors."

Mini-Test 3

Passage A

[1] Ocean currents play a pivotal role in regulating Earth's climate. [2] **However** some people **believes** that these massive movements of water only affect coastlines. [3] In reality, they transport heat, nutrients, and even marine organisms across vast distances. [4] This process influences weather patterns, impacts fishing industries, and helps shape biodiversity in different regions.

1. **(2)**
   A. NO CHANGE
   B. However, some people believe

C. However; some people believes
D. However, some people believes

2. Which revision of sentence [2] best clarifies its meaning while maintaining a formal tone?
A. "However, some people aren't really sure currents do anything except affect coastal areas."
B. "However, some people mistakenly think that these vast water movements only impact coastlines."
C. "And, some people guess that ocean currents mostly matter along beaches."
D. "So, some still consider ocean currents to be less important inland than they are on the shore."

3. The writer wants to insert the sentence **"Oceanographers study how these currents originate as well as the temperature and salinity differences that drive them."** Where would it best fit?
A. After sentence [1]
B. After sentence [2]
C. After sentence [3]
D. After sentence [4]

4. Which choice most effectively combines sentences [3] and [4]?
A. "In reality, they transport heat, nutrients, and even marine organisms across vast distances, which influences weather patterns and helps shape biodiversity in different regions, also impacting fishing industries."
B. "In reality, they transport heat, nutrients, and even marine organisms across vast distances and, by doing so, influence weather patterns, impact fishing industries, and help shape biodiversity in different regions."
C. "In reality, these currents carry nutrients, heat, and organisms, impacting fishing industries, shaping biodiversity, and influences weather patterns in different regions."
D. "In reality, they carry many resources; it influences fishing industries and weather patterns, shaping biodiversity in different regions."

5. To underscore the significance of ocean currents on inland weather patterns, the writer wants to add a concluding sentence. Which of the following would best achieve that purpose?
A. "Scientists agree that inland climates can vary, depending on factors like altitude and vegetation."
B. "Therefore, communities far from the sea may still feel the effects of shifting currents in their yearly rainfall and temperature ranges."
C. "However, some researchers doubt the connection between currents and any weather changes at all."
D. "Still, many people living along coastlines are more aware of ocean-related phenomena than those farther inland."

Passage B

[1] The **Hamilton Public Library** has unveiled its new digital media lab. [2] In this cutting-edge space, patrons can record podcasts, edit videos, and experiment with graphic design software. [3] **Additionally** they can convert old VHS tapes or film reels into digital formats, preserving family memories for future generations. [4] Staff members are available to provide tutorials, ensuring that even novices feel comfortable using the equipment.

1. **(3)**
A. NO CHANGE
B. Additionally, you can convert old VHS tapes or film reels
C. Additionally, patrons can convert old VHS tapes or film reels
D. Additionally, one can convert old VHS tapes or film reels

2. Which choice most clearly maintains a **consistent point of view** throughout the passage?
A. NO CHANGE (they/they)
B. (you/can) in sentence [3], shifting the rest to second-person as well
C. (patrons/patrons) in sentence [3], matching the third-person usage in the rest of the paragraph
D. (one/one) in sentence [3], shifting the entire passage to a more formal indefinite perspective

3. The writer wants to combine sentences [2] and [3] to emphasize the diverse media activities. Which answer best accomplishes this without introducing errors?

A. “In this cutting-edge space, patrons can record podcasts, edit videos, and experiment with graphic design software, additionally they can convert old VHS tapes or film reels.”
B. “In this cutting-edge space, patrons can record podcasts, edit videos, experiment with graphic design software, and even convert old VHS tapes or film reels into digital formats.”
C. “Since you can record podcasts or edit videos, the lab also let’s you convert old tapes or reels.”
D. “Experimentation with graphic design software can be performed, and old tapes or reels are easily converted here.”

4. Which sentence, if added after sentence [4], would best conclude the passage by **highlighting the library’s commitment to broader community engagement**?
A. “The staff is also in charge of maintaining hardware and assisting the digital media lab’s budget.”
B. “As a result, local schools have begun scheduling class trips so students can discover the possibilities of digital creation.”
C. “It’s clear that libraries have changed over the years, shifting from books to digital media labs.”
D. “Any damage to the equipment may result in repair fees, so patrons must exercise caution.”

5. The writer is considering adding the following sentence:

“In fact, it’s rumored that the lab may expand soon to include 3D printing stations.”
Where would this sentence most logically fit?
A. Before sentence [1]
B. After sentence [2]
C. After sentence [3]
D. After sentence [4]

Mini-Test 4

Passage A

[1] **Air purifiers** are becoming a common household appliance for health-conscious individuals. [2] They claim to remove dust, pollen, and even bacteria from indoor air. [3] Studies show that people with allergies or respiratory issues benefit the most. [4] **However, it’s important to clean the filters regularly, otherwise the device might lose it’s effectiveness.**

1. **(4)**
A. NO CHANGE
B. However, it’s important to clean the filters regularly; otherwise, the device might lose its effectiveness.
C. However; it’s important to clean the filters regularly, otherwise, the device might lose it’s effectiveness.
D. However: it’s important to clean the filters regularly. Otherwise the device might lose its effectiveness?

2. Which phrase would most effectively replace “They claim to remove dust, pollen, and even bacteria from indoor air” (sentence [2]) to be more precise and concise?
A. “These purifiers claim that they can rid a home’s atmosphere of many contaminants.”
B. “These purifiers are said to remove dust, pollen, and even bacteria from the air indoors.”
C. “Supporters of these devices suggest they can cut down dust, pollen, and all sorts of bacterial matter inside.”
D. “They supposedly clean up indoor air by extracting dust, pollen, and bacteria that people dislike.”

3. The writer wants to add a sentence about the importance of choosing the right purifier size for a room’s square footage. The best placement would be:
A. Immediately after sentence [1].
B. Immediately after sentence [2].
C. Immediately after sentence [3].
D. Immediately after sentence [4].

4. Which revision of sentence [3] maintains parallel structure and clarity?
   A. "Studies show that people with allergies, or respiratory issues, get the most benefits from these devices."
   B. "Studies show that these devices benefit mostly those with allergies and who have respiratory issues."
   C. "Studies show that individuals with allergies or respiratory issues tend to benefit most from these devices."
   D. "Studies show, that allergies and respiratory issues can be addressed by these devices for maximum benefits."

5. To emphasize scientific evidence for the purifiers' effectiveness, which sentence could be added at the end of the paragraph?
   A. "It's generally agreed that a dust-free room can make people feel more comfortable."
   B. "A recent university experiment found that certain models removed up to 99 percent of airborne particles."
   C. "Manufacturers continue to add new features, such as silent modes and smartphone compatibility."
   D. "People who live in rural areas may not need a purifier at all."

Passage B

[1] **Digital note-taking apps** have surged in popularity among students and professionals. [2] They allow users to organize notebooks, embed images, and share collaborative documents. [3] Although some argue that handwriting strengthens memory, using digital tools can be more efficient in fast-paced environments. [4] **Ultimately, personal preference plays a key role** in deciding whether analog or digital methods will be more beneficial.

1. Which choice best improves the transition at the beginning of sentence [3]?
   A. NO CHANGE
   B. However, some argue that handwriting strengthens memory
   C. Still, it is argued by some that handwriting is better
   D. On the contrary, some people who take notes by hand see results

2. The writer wants to clarify that embedding images can help illustrate complex ideas. Where in the passage should this detail be added for greatest effect?
   A. After sentence [1]
   B. After sentence [2]
   C. After sentence [3]
   D. At the end of sentence [4]

3. Which revision of sentence [2] best maintains parallel structure?
   A. "They allow users to organize notebooks, they can also embed images, and collaborative documents are shared."
   B. "They allow users not only to organize notebooks but also to embed images and share collaborative documents."
   C. "They allow users to organize notebooks, embed images, and you can share collaborative documents."
   D. "They allow users to organize notebooks but images can also be embedded, plus shared documents."

4. The passage would most benefit from a concluding sentence that:
   A. Reiterates why handwriting is impractical.
   B. Includes additional examples of digital note-taking apps.
   C. Links the choice between handwritten and digital notes to personal circumstances.
   D. Discusses the potential disadvantages of digital note-taking, such as battery issues.

5. To offer concrete data supporting digital note-taking, which of the following statements, if added, would best accomplish this?
   A. "Some universities now provide tablets to incoming freshmen, shifting classroom culture."
   B. "In a recent survey, 70% of professionals reported improved productivity after switching to digital

notes."
C. "Although many prefer classic pen and paper, the tactile feel can't be replicated digitally."
D. "Most note-taking apps are free to download, making them accessible."

Mini-Test 5

Passage A

[1] The **Artisan Food Fair** is an event held annually in Belmont Park. [2] Visitors can sample artisanal cheeses, homemade jams, and freshly baked bread, **it** also offers cooking demonstrations led by local chefs. [3] The fair aims to celebrate regional produce while encouraging food enthusiasts to discover new flavors and techniques. [4] **In addition**, several workshops teach everything from canning to sourdough bread-making, ensuring a hands-on experience.

1. Which choice most effectively corrects the problem in sentence [2]?
   A. Visitors can sample artisanal cheeses, homemade jams, and freshly baked bread while it also offers cooking demonstrations led by local chefs.
   B. Visitors can sample artisanal cheeses, homemade jams, and freshly baked bread; it also offers cooking demonstrations led by local chefs.
   C. Visitors sample cheeses, jams, and bread, also offering cooking demonstrations by local chefs.
   D. Visitors can sample artisanal cheeses, homemade jams, and freshly baked bread, with cooking demonstrations led by local chefs as well.
2. If the writer wants to emphasize the unique benefit of learning food preservation, which sentence could best be added at the end of the passage?
   A. "Hence, some families choose to buy all their ingredients from organic suppliers."
   B. "This skill lets home cooks enjoy their favorite seasonal foods long after harvest."
   C. "Many prefer to watch cooking shows on television rather than preserve food themselves."
   D. "Overall, it's wise to check local regulations before attempting any home canning."
3. Which version of sentence [4] is most concise yet clear?
   A. NO CHANGE
   B. Several workshops instruct participants in a variety of techniques, such as canning and sourdough bread-making, for a hands-on experience.
   C. In addition, there are multiple workshops that teach everything from canning to sourdough bread-making, giving people a hands-on experience.
   D. Furthermore, a number of workshops is teaching things like canning or sourdough bread-making for a hands-on experience.
4. The writer is considering adding a sentence about how local farmers supply produce for the event. The best placement would be:
   A. Before sentence [1]
   B. After sentence [1]
   C. After sentence [3]
   D. After the new concluding sentence
5. Which transition word could replace "In addition" in sentence [4] to create a smoother flow with the preceding sentence?
   A. Similarly,
   B. However,
   C. Consequently,
   D. Otherwise,

Passage B

[1] **Job-shadowing programs** allow students to gain firsthand exposure to various careers. [2] By observing professionals in their work environment, participants learn daily responsibilities and skills essential for success. [3] **Unfortunately** many students find these programs enlightening enough to help them choose the right career

path. [4] Because they can witness both the challenges and rewards of a given field, job-shadowing experiences often become pivotal moments in a student's academic journey.

1. **(3)**
   A. NO CHANGE
   B. Consequently many students find these programs enlightening enough
   C. In fact, many students find these programs so enlightening
   D. Moreover many students find these programs too enlightening
2. If the writer wants to clarify that students often realize a job isn't what they expected, where should this detail be added?
   A. Immediately after sentence [1]
   B. At the end of sentence [2]
   C. After sentence [3]
   D. After sentence [4]
3. Which sentence could best introduce a **contrasting** viewpoint before sentence [4]?
   A. "Some participants enter these programs hoping to expand their skills in a specific area."
   B. "However, a few critics argue that short-term observation may not be enough to reveal the full scope of a career."
   C. "Statistics show that job-shadowing programs are increasing in popularity among schools."
   D. "On average, students find these programs more helpful than lectures or textbooks."
4. Which choice best revises sentence [4] to maintain consistent tone and clarity?
   A. "They get to see the ups and downs, so it totally helps them figure out how they feel about that field."
   B. "Upon witnessing both the rewards and difficulties of a field, students often make more informed academic choices."
   C. "And so job-shadowing is cool since it shows if the job is tough or if it's basically super easy."
   D. "Challenges and rewards are obviously present in many professions, so people should weigh them carefully."
5. The writer wants a concluding sentence that highlights the **practical advantages** of job-shadowing. Which sentence best fits this purpose?
   A. "Students often miss class to participate in these programs, which can set them behind academically."
   B. "Ultimately, job-shadowing saves participants time and money by helping them pinpoint the right career before investing in specialized training."
   C. "Many industries are hesitant to allow minors into professional spaces due to liability concerns."
   D. "Because so many students enjoy the experience, job-shadowing is destined to become even more popular."

Mini-Test 6

Passage A

[1] **Urban rooftop gardens** are sprouting up in cities worldwide. [2] They provide green space, produce fresh vegetables, and can even help insulate buildings. [3] Some high-rise apartment owners use hydroponic systems to maximize yield in limited space. [4] **Ultimately** a simple wooden planter box filled with herbs can enhance apartment living and provide a relaxing hobby.

1. Which revision of sentence [4] best clarifies the idea?
   A. NO CHANGE
   B. Ultimately, even a humble wooden planter box filled with herbs can improve apartment living while offering a relaxing hobby.
   C. Ultimately, a simple wooden planter box is something that is good because it's relaxing and enhances living for an apartment.
   D. Ultimately, a wooden planter box that is full of herbs, can enhance living spaces at times.

2. If the writer wants to highlight environmental benefits further, which sentence could be added at the end of the passage?
   A. "Many people also enjoy different types of houseplants in their living rooms."
   B. "These rooftop gardens can reduce stormwater runoff and decrease carbon footprints."
   C. "Apartment living sometimes makes people feel trapped in concrete surroundings."
   D. "Some buildings require permits before installing large planter boxes."
3. Which transitional phrase could be added to the beginning of sentence [3] to emphasize the **innovation** of hydroponics?
   A. In other words,
   B. For instance,
   C. Conversely,
   D. Even so,
4. The writer is considering adding a sentence that explains how much sunlight rooftop gardens need. The most logical placement would be:
   A. Immediately after sentence [1]
   B. Immediately after sentence [2]
   C. Immediately after sentence [3]
   D. At the very end of the paragraph
5. The writer wants to mention that rooftop gardens can be aesthetically pleasing. Which revision of sentence [2] would best include this detail while maintaining parallel structure?
   A. They provide green space, produce fresh vegetables, can add visual appeal, and even help insulate buildings.
   B. They provide green space, fresh vegetables, plus a visually appealing environment, and can insulate buildings.
   C. They provide green space, produce fresh vegetables, add visual appeal, and can even help insulate buildings.
   D. They provide green space, produce fresh vegetables, so it is visually appealing, and can even help insulate buildings.

Passage B

[1] **Mountain biking** is an exhilarating sport, but it requires skill, preparation, and the right gear. [2] Riders need to wear helmets, sturdy shoes, and make sure their bikes are well-maintained. [3] **Otherwise** they could face mechanical failures on steep trails, which can lead to dangerous falls. [4] Enthusiasts often recommend beginners take lessons, learn basic maintenance, and build endurance before tackling more advanced paths.

1. **(2)**
   A. NO CHANGE
   B. Riders need to wear helmets and sturdy shoes, also making sure their bikes are well-maintained.
   C. Riders need to wear helmets, sturdy shoes, and ensure their bikes are well-maintained.
   D. Riders need to wear helmets, and sturdy shoes, and also to make sure the bike is well-maintained.
2. Which sentence below would best serve as a new concluding statement for the paragraph, reinforcing the advice given?
   A. "Research indicates that mountain biking is more popular than road biking in some regions."
   B. "That is why specialized biking gear can be so expensive and hard to locate."
   C. "With the proper precautions and ongoing practice, riders can safely enjoy this thrilling outdoor pursuit."
   D. "Mountain bikes typically feature thicker tires and sturdier frames than road bikes."
3. The writer is thinking about adding a sentence on the **importance of hydration**. Where should it be placed for the best effect?
   A. Immediately after sentence [1]
   B. Immediately after sentence [2]

C. Immediately after sentence [3]
D. Replacing sentence [4]

4. Which choice provides the most consistent style when revising sentence [3]?
A. "Failing that, mechanical mishaps can happen on steep trails; it's definitely risky."
B. "If they don't, they risk mechanical failures on steep trails, leading to hazardous falls."
C. "Should they fail to meet these guidelines, it may result in mechanical breakdowns on precarious inclines."
D. "Otherwise, a lack of bike maintenance and gear is leading to potential accidents."

5. If the writer wants to highlight the **camaraderie** among mountain bikers, which sentence could be inserted after sentence [4]?
A. "Riders often exchange tips on trail conditions and gear, forming supportive communities."
B. "Long-distance rides can sometimes extend over 50 miles, proving quite grueling."
C. "Spending a lot of money on a mountain bike doesn't guarantee better skills."
D. "Many experts claim that road biking requires more stamina than mountain biking."

Mini-Test 7

Passage A

[1] The **Orion Strings Ensemble** is known for its innovative performances that blend classical and contemporary music. [2] Audiences praise the group's ability to reinterpret traditional compositions, adding fresh elements that attract younger listeners. [3] **Moreover** many established critics appreciate their willingness to experiment, thereby expanding the boundaries of the classical genre. [4] This success has led to invitations from international festivals, ensuring that Orion Strings will continue reaching broader audiences.

1. **(3)**
A. NO CHANGE
B. Moreover, many established critics appreciate
C. Moreover: many established critics appreciates
D. Moreover, many established critics appreciates

2. Which sentence, if added after sentence [2], would best clarify how the group adds modern touches to classical pieces?
A. "They often incorporate instruments like electric guitars or electronic sound effects to create a unique blend."
B. "Their repertoire includes works by Beethoven, Brahms, and Mozart."
C. "Some fans say these concerts often run longer than expected."
D. "Tickets to these concerts can be purchased through the ensemble's website."

3. The writer wants to mention the group's origin story. The most logical placement for a brief sentence about how the quartet formed in college is:
A. Immediately after sentence [1]
B. Immediately before sentence [2]
C. Immediately before sentence [3]
D. At the end of sentence [4]

4. Which revision of sentence [4] ensures parallel structure and clarity?
A. "This success has led to invitations from international festivals, ensuring that Orion Strings will continue to reach broader audiences."
B. "This success leads to more invitations from festivals abroad, so Orion Strings keeps on reaching an ever-broader audience."
C. "This success has lead them to invite from festivals abroad, and reach bigger audiences."
D. "Due to success, they will be able to continue traveling to festivals, by which means they get a chance to reach broad audiences."

5. Which new concluding sentence would best emphasize the Ensemble's future plans and appeal?
A. "Ultimately, Orion Strings is just one of many musical groups trying to innovate."

B. "Such popularity indicates that the ensemble might soon add international pop songs to its playlist."
C. "Soon, the group will record a full-length album blending orchestral arrangements with modern soundscapes, aiming to captivate audiences worldwide."
D. "Nevertheless, it's difficult to predict exactly how far their success will go in this highly competitive market."

Passage B

[1] **Solar-powered charging stations** are appearing in parks, campuses, and urban squares. [2] They allow users to plug in laptops and phones, relying on renewable energy instead of power from the grid. [3] This convenience is especially valuable during outdoor events, where people often need quick recharges. [4] **Despite that** setting them up can be costly, the long-term benefits include reduced carbon footprints and community engagement.

1. **(4)**
   A. NO CHANGE
   B. Although
   C. Meanwhile,
   D. In fact,
2. Where would a sentence about how these stations benefit tourists be most effectively placed?
   A. After sentence [1]
   B. After sentence [2]
   C. After sentence [3]
   D. Before sentence [4]
3. To clarify the **specific costs** involved, which addition would be most relevant as a follow-up to sentence [4]?
   A. "Costs can range from $2,000 to $10,000 per unit, depending on capacity and design."
   B. "Citizens frequently voice concerns about budget allocations for roads, schools, and infrastructure."
   C. "However, cities like Phoenix and Dallas have different weather patterns affecting solar use."
   D. "In addition, many people are unfamiliar with how solar technology works."
4. Which transition in sentence [3] would best connect the ideas in sentences [2] and [3]?
   A. NO CHANGE (This convenience…)
   B. For instance,
   C. Conversely,
   D. Moreover,
5. The writer wants to highlight how some stations include interactive screens showing energy usage data. Which sentence would best introduce that detail after sentence [1]?
   A. "Energy usage data might not matter to everyone, though."
   B. "Many people, especially those who love technology, find them fascinating."
   C. "Some stations even have interactive displays to show how much solar power is currently being harnessed."
   D. "These stations often feature a bold design, making them a conversation piece."

Mini-Test 8

Passage A

[1] **Local theater productions** are a great way for aspiring actors and directors to hone their skills. [2] These small-scale shows, often staged in community centers or school auditoriums, allow participants to experiment with unique scripts and innovative staging. [3] **Although some fear** limited budgets reduce the quality of local productions, **they** frequently produce impressive performances that rival professional troupes. [4] In many cases, dedicated volunteers manage everything from set design to marketing.

1. **(3)**
   A. NO CHANGE

B. Although some fear that limited budgets can reduce the quality of local productions, they
C. Although some fear that limited budgets reduce the quality of local productions, these
D. Although some fear limited budgets reduce the quality of local productions, it

2. Which choice most effectively clarifies the subject of "they" in sentence [3]?
A. NO CHANGE (they)
B. the local productions themselves
C. these groups
D. community centers

3. The writer wants to emphasize the **impact** on volunteers. Which sentence, if added at the end, best accomplishes this?
A. "Because of their efforts, many volunteers find new career paths or life-long friendships."
B. "Without them, most local theater groups would never succeed in selling enough tickets."
C. "After all, marketing costs can be quite high, and set design is very time-consuming."
D. "In fact, some volunteers dislike the lack of critical feedback provided by small audiences."

4. To include a phrase about **improvisational workshops**, where would it best fit?
A. Before sentence [1]
B. After sentence [1]
C. After sentence [2]
D. At the end of sentence [4]

5. Which revision of sentence [4] best maintains parallel structure and clarity?
A. "In many cases, dedicated volunteers manage everything, such as set design and marketing, from start to finish."
B. "In many cases, dedicated volunteers manage everything from set design to marketing, ensuring a cohesive production."
C. "Often dedicated volunteers manage everything from the set design, marketing, and coordinating with sponsors."
D. "In many cases, volunteers were dedicated to everything from set design to marketing, so that the production is cohesive."

Passage B

[1] **Organic cotton clothing** has grown in popularity, mainly due to consumers' environmental concerns. [2] Proponents claim that fewer pesticides and chemicals are used, reducing harm to farmers and local ecosystems. [3] **Nevertheless** organic cotton can sometimes be more expensive, making it less accessible to budget-conscious shoppers. [4] Despite this, many companies strive to lower production costs so more people can afford these sustainable options.

1. **(3)**
A. NO CHANGE
B. Consequently organic cotton can be more expensive
C. However, organic cotton can sometimes be more expensive
D. Indeed organic cotton can sometimes be more expensive

2. Which sentence could be added between sentences [2] and [3] to further explain **why** organic cotton uses fewer pesticides?
A. "Cotton farmers, in general, rely heavily on irrigation and fertilizer."
B. "In many regions, it's the government that decides what chemicals are permissible."
C. "Farmers who grow organic cotton often use natural pest control methods like introducing beneficial insects."
D. "Most consumers have little idea how cotton is cultivated or what chemicals are necessary."

3. The writer wants to highlight that farmers receive a fair price for organic cotton due to certification programs. Where is the best placement for this detail?
A. After sentence [1]

B. After sentence [2]
C. After sentence [3]
D. After sentence [4]

4. Which choice best revises sentence [4] to **expand** on how companies try to make organic cotton more affordable?
A. "Despite this, many companies look for ways to reduce production costs, such as improving logistics and sourcing local materials, so more people can afford these sustainable options."
B. "Despite this, many companies apparently attempt to lower costs for the sake of more customers' budgets, yet some do not."
C. "Despite this, many companies do not make enough changes, meaning it is still inaccessible."
D. "Despite this, many companies are working on it, so the clothes should be cheaper in the future."

5. Which concluding sentence would best underscore the **positive global impact** of shifting to organic cotton?
A. "In some countries, synthetic fabrics remain more popular than cotton."
B. "Many designers now use organic cotton for high-end fashion."
C. "By choosing organic cotton, consumers contribute to a healthier environment and support fair labor practices worldwide."
D. "Those who cannot afford organic cotton tend to prefer other natural fibers like wool or linen."

How To Use These Mini-Tests

1. **Time Yourself**: Spend **7–8 minutes per mini-tests** (8 tests total across 10 questions each).
2. **Apply ACT Strategies**: Read each short passage thoroughly, consider the context, and check the grammar, punctuation, and rhetorical flow.
3. **Review Answers**: Compare your responses with the official explanations (to be provided in your Answer Key section). Focus on **why** the correct choice is best and **why** the others are weaker or incorrect.

By simulating timed conditions and diverse question types, you'll build the stamina and agility needed for the actual ACT English section.

Timed Practice Tips

- **Work Quickly, But Accurately**: The ACT English section allows an average of **36 seconds per question** (75 questions in 45 minutes). For these mini-tests, practice striking a balance between reading carefully and maintaining a steady pace.
- **Skip, Then Return**: If you find yourself stuck on a question, mark your best guess and move on. Return to it if time allows.
- **Keep Track of Mistakes**: After checking your answers, note which topics (punctuation, subject-verb agreement, rhetorical skills, etc.) you missed. This will help you target specific weaknesses in future study sessions.

Looking Ahead

Upon completion, proceed to **Chapter 4.4: Detailed Answer Explanations** to verify your responses. Understanding why a particular choice is correct—or why others are incorrect—is vital for **reinforcing concepts** and **adapting your strategies** before test day. By consistently simulating timed conditions with mixed-question sets like these, you'll develop the confidence and speed necessary for a high score on the ACT English test.

4.4 DETAILED ANSWER EXPLANATIONS

ANSWER KEY: Grammar Drills

Section A: Subject-Verb Agreement

Exercise A1

Select the correct verb form in parentheses.

1. **roams**
2. **has**
3. **was**
4. **performs**
5. **are**
6. **debates**
7. **is**
8. **adorns**
9. **works**
10. **presents**
11. **features**
12. **makes**
13. **understands**
14. **deliberates**
15. **illuminates**
16. **have**
17. **needs**
18. **is**
19. **evaporates**
20. **requires**
21. **is**
22. **expects**
23. **appreciates**
24. **needs**
25. **like**
26. **brightens**
27. **handle**
28. **discusses**
29. **calms**
30. **was**
31. **spans**
32. **turn**
33. **has**
34. **enjoys**
35. **scatters**
36. **has**
37. **highlights**
38. **lives**
39. **play**
40. **recommends**
41. **travels**
42. **seek**
43. **smells**
44. **wants**
45. **is**
46. **plan**
47. **contains**
48. **approves**
49. **come**
50. **agree**
51. **love**
52. **indicates**
53. **looks**
54. **solves**
55. **practices**
56. **makes**
57. **assist**
58. **waits**
59. **exist**
60. **debates**
61. **shout**
62. **suggests**
63. **has**
64. **promotes**
65. **hurt**
66. **generates**
67. **support**
68. **watches**
69. **is**
70. **forgets**

Exercise A2

Correct each sentence so the subject and verb agree properly. Below, each original sentence is followed by a suggested correction in italics. Where applicable, the crucial subject-verb correction is underlined.

1. **Original**: The teacher as well as her students **were** excited about the experiment.
   Corrected: *The teacher, as well as her students,* ***was*** *excited about the experiment.*
2. **Original**: The basketball team **were** practicing late into the night.
   Corrected: *The basketball team* ***was*** *practicing late into the night.*
3. **Original**: One of the main sources of stress **are** poor time management.
   Corrected: *One of the main sources of stress* ***is*** *poor time management.*
4. **Original**: The band of merry travelers **were** singing songs around the fire.
   Corrected: *The band of merry travelers* ***was*** *singing songs around the fire.*
5. **Original**: Either the teacher or her assistants **was** supposed to check the homework.
   Corrected: *Either the teacher or her assistants* ***were*** *supposed to check the homework.*
6. **Original**: Many of the articles in the magazine **is** outdated.
   Corrected: *Many of the articles in the magazine* ***are*** *outdated.*
7. **Original**: The herd of elephants **make** a thunderous noise as they move.
   Corrected: *The herd of elephants* ***makes*** *a thunderous noise as they move.*
8. **Original**: The mayor along with her advisors **have** decided to postpone the event.
   Corrected: *The mayor, along with her advisors,* ***has*** *decided to postpone the event.*

9. **Original**: None of the students in the class **have** turned in their essays on time.
   Corrected: *None of the students in the class* ***has*** *turned in their essays on time.*
   (Strict formal usage treats "none" as singular. In modern usage, "have" is also widely accepted, but standardized tests often prefer the singular form.)
10. **Original**: A pack of stray dogs sometimes **wander** through the neighborhood at night.
    Corrected: *A pack of stray dogs sometimes* ***wanders*** *through the neighborhood at night.*
11. **Original**: Every one of these antiques **have** a fascinating history behind it.
    Corrected: *Every one of these antiques* ***has*** *a fascinating history behind it.*
12. **Original**: The board of directors **are** holding separate meetings this week.
    Corrected: *The board of directors* ***is*** *holding separate meetings this week.*
13. **Original**: One of the best parts of the vacation **were** the guided tours.
    Corrected: *One of the best parts of the vacation* ***was*** *the guided tours.*
14. **Original**: Either my brothers or my mom **are** picking me up after practice.
    Corrected: *Either my brothers or my mom* ***is*** *picking me up after practice.*
15. **Original**: The flock of seagulls **were** circling the fishing boat.
    Corrected: *The flock of seagulls* ***was*** *circling the fishing boat.*
16. **Original**: Everything in the instructions **indicate** a longer cooking time.
    Corrected: *Everything in the instructions* ***indicates*** *a longer cooking time.*
17. **Original**: The tray of cookies **smell** delicious, fresh out of the oven.
    Corrected: *The tray of cookies* ***smells*** *delicious, fresh out of the oven.*
18. **Original**: A series of unexpected events **have** led us to this conclusion.
    Corrected: *A series of unexpected events* ***has*** *led us to this conclusion.*
19. **Original**: The team of soccer players **are** warming up on the field too early.
    Corrected: *The team of soccer players* ***is*** *warming up on the field too early.*
20. **Original**: Neither of the solutions **have** fixed the problem effectively.
    Corrected: *Neither of the solutions* ***has*** *fixed the problem effectively.*
21. **Original**: The crowd of protesters **were** growing louder by the minute.
    Corrected: *The crowd of protesters* ***was*** *growing louder by the minute.*
22. **Original**: Both the director and the producers **has** decided to cancel the scene.
    Corrected: *Both the director and the producers* ***have*** *decided to cancel the scene.*
23. **Original**: Everyone on the bus **were** complaining about the broken air conditioner.
    Corrected: *Everyone on the bus* ***was*** *complaining about the broken air conditioner.*
24. **Original**: The group of hikers **have** reached the summit first.
    Corrected: *The group of hikers* ***has*** *reached the summit first.*
25. **Original**: One of my best memories **were** going to the carnival at night.
    Corrected: *One of my best memories* ***was*** *going to the carnival at night.*
26. **Original**: The team of surgeons **were** confident about the procedure.
    Corrected: *The team of surgeons* ***was*** *confident about the procedure.*
27. **Original**: Most of the water bottles **was** stacked improperly in the storage room.
    Corrected: *Most of the water bottles* ***were*** *stacked improperly in the storage room.*
28. **Original**: Every one of the finalists **were** excited to compete on stage.
    Corrected: *Every one of the finalists* ***was*** *excited to compete on stage.*
29. **Original**: Neither the coach nor the players **was** ready for the final match.
    Corrected: *Neither the coach nor the players* ***were*** *ready for the final match.*
30. **Original**: A stack of papers **were** left on my desk this morning.
    Corrected: *A stack of papers* ***was*** *left on my desk this morning.*
31. **Original**: Nobody in my family **are** planning to visit the museum this weekend.
    Corrected: *Nobody in my family* ***is*** *planning to visit the museum this weekend.*
32. **Original**: A pack of wolves **roam** across these hills every winter.
    Corrected: *A pack of wolves* ***roams*** *across these hills every winter.*
33. **Original**: Several of the applicants **is** overqualified for the entry-level position.
    Corrected: *Several of the applicants* ***are*** *overqualified for the entry-level position.*

34. **Original**: The jury **were** divided in their decision.
    Corrected: *The jury **was** divided in its decision.*
    *(Alternatively, "The jury members **were** divided..." is also correct if you make "members" the subject.)*
35. **Original**: None of the advice **were** particularly helpful.
    Corrected: *None of the advice **was** particularly helpful.*
36. **Original**: Each of the dogs **need** a fresh bowl of water.
    Corrected: *Each of the dogs **needs** a fresh bowl of water.*
37. **Original**: A swarm of bees **have** taken over the empty shed.
    Corrected: *A swarm of bees **has** taken over the empty shed.*
38. **Original**: The pile of books **were** toppling over on the shelf.
    Corrected: *The pile of books **was** toppling over on the shelf.*
39. **Original**: Neither of the siblings **were** interested in inheriting the antique clock.
    Corrected: *Neither of the siblings **was** interested in inheriting the antique clock.*
40. **Original**: One of the suspects **have** confessed to the crime.
    Corrected: *One of the suspects **has** confessed to the crime.*
41. **Original**: The pair of headphones **are** missing from the counter.
    Corrected: *The pair of headphones **is** missing from the counter.*
42. **Original**: Either the laptop or the phone **were** damaged during the trip.
    Corrected: *Either the laptop or the phone **was** damaged during the trip.*
43. **Original**: Our family **were** planning a surprise party for our grandmother.
    Corrected: *Our family **was** planning a surprise party for our grandmother.*
44. **Original**: Nobody on the committee **have** volunteered for the new role.
    Corrected: *Nobody on the committee **has** volunteered for the new role.*
45. **Original**: All of the furniture **were** moved to the garage for storage.
    Corrected: *All of the furniture **was** moved to the garage for storage.*
46. **Original**: The herd of deer **scatter** when they sense danger.
    Corrected: *The herd of deer **scatters** when they sense danger.*
47. **Original**: Every painting in the gallery **were** carefully restored.
    Corrected: *Every painting in the gallery **was** carefully restored.*
48. **Original**: The board of trustees **have** announced its decision earlier.
    Corrected: *The board of trustees **has** announced its decision earlier.*
49. **Original**: Each of the students **have** the opportunity to speak at the seminar.
    Corrected: *Each of the students **has** the opportunity to speak at the seminar.*
50. **Original**: Both the mayor and the city council **approves** the new policy.
    Corrected: *Both the mayor and the city council **approve** the new policy.*
    (Compound subject => plural verb)
51. **Original**: The swarm of locusts **was** ravaging the crops.
    Corrected:
    - *No change needed if treating "swarm" as singular.*
    - *The swarm of locusts **was** ravaging the crops.*
52. **Original**: Many in the audience **was** disappointed by the short performance.
    Corrected: *Many in the audience **were** disappointed by the short performance.*
53. **Original**: The staff in the office **were** preparing for the big presentation.
    Corrected: *The staff in the office **was** preparing for the big presentation.*
54. **Original**: Not one of the recipes **were** easy enough for me to try.
    Corrected: *Not one of the recipes **was** easy enough for me to try.*
55. **Original**: A team of scientists **have** discovered a new species of frog.
    Corrected: *A team of scientists **has** discovered a new species of frog.*
56. **Original**: None of the evidence **support** the defendant's claims.
    Corrected: *None of the evidence **supports** the defendant's claims.*
    ("Evidence" is noncount; "none" here is taken as singular.)
57. **Original**: A handful of daisies **add** color to the windowsill.
    Corrected:
    - *This can be correct as is* if you treat "a handful of daisies" as a plural idea (the daisies).

- Some style guides might prefer "adds color" (treating "a handful" as singular), but **"add color"** is also acceptable.

58. **Original**: The fleet of ships **were** anchored at the harbor.
    Corrected: *The fleet of ships **was** anchored at the harbor.*
59. **Original**: A number of graduates **plans** on continuing their education.
    Corrected: *A number of graduates **plan** on continuing their education.*
    ("A number of" is usually treated as plural.)
60. **Original**: Neither my cousin nor my siblings **is** aware of the surprise party.
    Corrected: *Neither my cousin nor my siblings **are** aware of the surprise party.*
    (Second subject is "siblings," which is plural.)
61. **Original**: A variety of factors **affects** the final outcome.
    Corrected: *A variety of factors **affect** the final outcome.*
    ("factors" is plural; "A variety of" implies a plural subject.)
62. **Original**: The committee **were** announcing the results at noon.
    Corrected: *The committee **was** announcing the results at noon.*
63. **Original**: Several of the employees **takes** public transportation to work.
    Corrected: *Several of the employees **take** public transportation to work.*
    ("Several" is plural.)
64. **Original**: One of my friends **have** decided to move abroad for a year.
    Corrected: *One of my friends **has** decided to move abroad for a year.*
65. **Original**: The series of lectures **were** more interesting than I expected.
    Corrected: *The series of lectures **was** more interesting than I expected.*
66. **Original**: The pair of gloves **were** lying on the table all day.
    Corrected: *The pair of gloves **was** lying on the table all day.*
67. **Original**: Nobody in the building **were** notified about the change in security codes.
    Corrected: *Nobody in the building **was** notified about the change in security codes.*
68. **Original**: All of the evidence **point** to a single suspect.
    Corrected: *All of the evidence **points** to a single suspect.*
    ("Evidence" is treated as a singular noncount noun.)

Final Notes

- In modern usage, certain words (e.g., *none, any, all, majority, none of the students, none of the instructions*) can take either singular or plural verbs depending on context. However, the **ACT** (and many standardized tests) often prefers the traditional singular usage unless the phrase clearly points to a plural subject.
- Collective nouns (e.g., *team, committee, family, board*) are typically treated as singular unless the sentence emphasizes the individual members acting separately.
- For compound subjects joined by "or/nor," the verb usually agrees with the nearest subject. For compound subjects joined by "and," the verb is usually plural (except when the entire phrase is meant to function as a single unit).

Use these corrections and explanations to guide your study and clarify any tricky points of subject-verb agreement.

Section B: Pronouns

Exercise B1: Identify and Correct Unclear or Mismatched Pronouns

Task: Each original sentence has an ambiguous or unclear pronoun. The **Corrected Version** shows one way to remove ambiguity or mismatch.

1. **Original**: When Sara talked to Molly, she noticed the coffee shop was about to close.
   Problem: "she" is unclear (Sara or Molly?).
   Corrected: *When Sara talked to Molly, **Sara** noticed the coffee shop was about to close.*
   (Alternatively, clarify that Molly noticed it if that is the intended meaning.)
2. **Original**: A person should eat plenty of fruits and vegetables if they want to stay healthy.
   Problem: "A person" is singular, but "they" is plural/ambiguous.

Corrected: *A person should eat plenty of fruits and vegetables if **he or she** wants to stay healthy.*
(Or use a plural subject: "People should eat plenty of fruits and vegetables if they want to stay healthy.")

3. **Original**: If the dogs start barking, the neighbors will call the police if it gets too loud.
Problem: "it" is unclear (the barking or something else?).
Corrected: *If the dogs start barking, the neighbors will call the police if **the noise** gets too loud.*
4. **Original**: While Tom was tutoring Jason in algebra, he realized that geometry needed more attention.
Problem: "he" could mean Tom or Jason.
Corrected: *While Tom was tutoring Jason in algebra, **Tom** realized that geometry needed more attention.*
5. **Original**: Kelly informed Jackie that she would be traveling to Europe next month.
Problem: "she" could mean Kelly or Jackie.
Corrected: *Kelly informed Jackie that **Kelly** would be traveling to Europe next month.*
(Or "...that **Jackie** would be traveling..." if Jackie is the traveler.)
6. **Original**: When the car got a flat tire, they replaced it within a few minutes.
Problem: "they" is unclear—who replaced the tire?
Corrected: *When the car got a flat tire, **the driver** replaced it within a few minutes.*
(Or "the repair crew," "my friends," etc., depending on context.)
7. **Original**: Everyone who sees that movie loves it because they are so terrifying.
Problem: "they" is unclear—refers to "movie," "scenes," or "everyone"?
Corrected: *Everyone who sees that movie loves it because **its scenes** are so terrifying.*
8. **Original**: The teacher told the student that she should do more practice tests.
Problem: "she" could be the teacher or the student.
Corrected: *The teacher told the student, "**You** should do more practice tests."*
(Or "The teacher told the student that **the student** should do more practice tests.")
9. **Original**: Alex told Taylor that his outfit looked great.
Problem: "his" could belong to Alex or Taylor.
Corrected: *Alex told Taylor, "**Your** outfit looks great."*
(Or "Alex told Taylor that **Alex's** outfit looked great," if that's the intended meaning.)
10. **Original**: When the puppy met the kitten, it ran behind the couch.
Problem: "it" is ambiguous (the puppy or the kitten?).
Corrected: *When the puppy met the kitten, **the puppy** ran behind the couch.*
(Or "...the kitten ran behind the couch.")
11. **Original**: Sam called Chris right after he finished taking the driving test.
Problem: "he" could be Sam or Chris.
Corrected: *Sam called Chris right after **Sam** finished taking the driving test.*
(Or "Chris" if that's intended.)
12. **Original**: Pat and Jordan drove to the beach, but she forgot the towels.
Problem: "she" is unclear if Pat or Jordan.
Corrected: *Pat and Jordan drove to the beach, but **Pat** forgot the towels.*
13. **Original**: The manager emailed the employee about her new responsibilities.
Problem: "her" could be the manager's or the employee's responsibilities.
Corrected: *The manager emailed the employee about **the employee's** new responsibilities.*
14. **Original**: When the firefighters arrived, they said it was too late to save the barn.
Problem: Typically not very ambiguous, but to clarify:
Corrected: *When the firefighters arrived, **the firefighters** said it was too late to save the barn.*
(Or simply "they," if context is clear.)
15. **Original**: After Julia spoke with her mother, she decided to leave earlier than planned.
Problem: "she" could be Julia or her mother.
Corrected: *After Julia spoke with her mother, **Julia** decided to leave earlier than planned.*
16. **Original**: We called the realtor and asked if she could provide more details, but they never responded.
Problem: Mixed pronouns ("she" then "they") for the same realtor.
Corrected: *We called the realtor and asked if **she** could provide more details, but **she** never responded.*
17. **Original**: The neighbors notified the homeowners that their garden gate was left open, but they didn't lock it.

Problem: "they" could mean the neighbors or the homeowners.
Corrected: *The neighbors notified the homeowners that their garden gate was left open, but **the homeowners** didn't lock it.*
(Or "the neighbors didn't lock it," depending on context.)

18. **Original**: My brother wrote to my cousin that he was thinking about applying to college abroad.
Problem: "he" could mean the brother or the cousin.
Corrected: *My brother wrote to my cousin that **my brother** was thinking about applying to college abroad.*
(Or "...that **my cousin** was thinking about applying...")
19. **Original**: Olivia texted her friend after the audition, but she didn't answer right away.
Problem: "she" could be Olivia or her friend.
Corrected: *Olivia texted her friend after the audition, but **her friend** didn't answer right away.*
(Or "Olivia didn't answer right away," if that's the meaning.)
20. **Original**: When the nurse checked on the patient, they noted the medication had already taken effect.
Problem: "they" could refer to the nurse or the patient.
Corrected: *When the nurse checked on the patient, **the nurse** noted that the medication had already taken effect.*

Exercise B2: Choose the Correct Pronoun Case

Task: The correct pronoun choice is in **bold**.

1. The committee awarded the prize to **him** and **me**.
2. **Whom** should I speak to about the vacant position?
3. My sister and **I** are planning a surprise party for our parents.
4. Between you and **me**, the plan needs serious revisions.
5. **Who** do you think wrote the anonymous note?
6. The winner of the contest was **she**.
7. Our neighbors invited my brother and **me** to their backyard barbecue.
8. Do you know **who** will be hosting the ceremony tonight?
9. Mr. Garcia asked Jason and **her** for a volunteer sign-up.
10. **Whom** do you recommend for the scholarship?
11. My friend and **I** are going hiking this weekend.
12. The teacher recognized **us** as the top performers in the class.
13. They asked my coworker and **me** to lead the project.
14. I don't know **whom** the CEO chose for the role.
15. Could you tell me **who** invented the printing press?
16. The producers gave **them** an opportunity to rewrite the script.
17. The final decision rests with **whoever** gets the most votes.
18. The judge congratulated **us** on our community service efforts.
19. **Whom** did the principal appoint as head of the committee?
20. Everyone except **him** showed up early for rehearsal.

Exercise B3: Fix Any Pronoun-Antecedent Agreement Errors

Task: Each original sentence contains a pronoun that disagrees (in number or gender) with its antecedent. The **Corrected Version** provides proper agreement. (In formal grammar, indefinite pronouns like "everyone," "each," "anyone" are singular, so "he or she" is often recommended. Alternatively, you can rewrite to use plural forms for more natural-sounding sentences.)

1. **Original**: Each of the engineers presented their unique design.
Corrected: *Each of the engineers presented **his or her** unique design.*
(Or "All of the engineers presented their unique designs.")
2. **Original**: Everybody must take off their shoes before entering the temple.
Corrected: *Everybody must take off **his or her** shoes before entering the temple.*
(Or "All visitors must take off their shoes before entering the temple.")

3. **Original**: Several of the employees turned in his resignation letters.
   Corrected: *Several of the employees turned in **their** resignation letters.*
4. **Original**: Every student needs to submit their homework on time.
   Corrected: *Every student needs to submit **his or her** homework on time.*
   (Or "All students need to submit their homework on time.")
5. **Original**: Not one of the actresses remembered their lines perfectly.
   Corrected: *Not one of the actresses remembered **her** lines perfectly.*
6. **Original**: Anyone who wants to register for the seminar must sign up before they leave today.
   Corrected: *Anyone who wants to register for the seminar must sign up before **he or she** leaves today.*
7. **Original**: One of the technicians informed management that they would be late.
   Corrected: *One of the technicians informed management that **he or she** would be late.*
8. **Original**: Neither of the mechanics believed they had the right parts.
   Corrected: *Neither of the mechanics believed **he** had the right parts.*
9. **Original**: If a buyer wants to return the product, they should keep the receipt.
   Corrected: *If a buyer wants to return the product, **he or she** should keep the receipt.*
10. **Original**: Everyone in the club must renew their membership by next week.
    Corrected: *Everyone in the club must renew **his or her** membership by next week.*
11. **Original**: Each of the applicants expressed dissatisfaction with how they were interviewed.
    Corrected: *Each of the applicants expressed dissatisfaction with how **he or she** was interviewed.*
12. **Original**: Either of the players may claim their trophy after the match.
    Corrected: *Either of the players may claim **his** trophy after the match.*
13. **Original**: One of the employees wrote a letter of complaint, claiming they were overworked.
    Corrected: *One of the employees wrote a letter of complaint, claiming **he or she** was overworked.*
14. **Original**: If anyone misses a shift, they should notify the supervisor immediately.
    Corrected: *If anyone misses a shift, **he or she** should notify the supervisor immediately.*
15. **Original**: Somebody left their backpack in the hallway after class.
    Corrected: *Somebody left **his or her** backpack in the hallway after class.*
16. **Original**: When a driver parks illegally, they risk getting a ticket.
    Corrected: *When a driver parks illegally, **he or she** risks getting a ticket.*
17. **Original**: Neither of the flight attendants had their schedule confirmed.
    Corrected: *Neither of the flight attendants had **his or her** schedule confirmed.*
18. **Original**: Anyone traveling abroad should keep close track of their passport.
    Corrected: *Anyone traveling abroad should keep close track of **his or her** passport.*
19. **Original**: Everyone on the debate team presented their case convincingly.
    Corrected: *Everyone on the debate team presented **his or her** case convincingly.*
    (Or "All members of the debate team presented their cases convincingly.")
20. **Original**: If a photographer plans to sell prints, they must secure licensing first.
    Corrected: *If a photographer plans to sell prints, **he or she** must secure licensing first.*

Final Notes

- **B1** focuses on clarity: make sure each pronoun clearly refers to its intended noun.
- **B2** focuses on **subjective** (I, he, she, who) vs. **objective** (me, him, her, whom) pronoun usage.
- **B3** addresses singular vs. plural forms (and sometimes gender) to ensure that pronouns match their antecedents correctly.

Section C: Verb Tenses

Answer Key: Exercise C1

Task: Fill in the blanks with the appropriate verb tense (present, past, future, present perfect, past perfect, or future perfect).

1. **By the time you arrive, I will have finished (to finish) cooking dinner.**
   - Future Perfect: *will have finished*
2. **I have been studying (to study) for three hours, and now I need a break.**

- Present Perfect Continuous: *have been studying*
  ("I have studied" is also acceptable, but "have been studying" emphasizes ongoing activity.)

3. **They traveled (to travel) to Brazil last summer and loved the beaches there.**
   - Simple Past: *traveled*
4. **We are planning (to plan) a trip for next month; the tickets are already booked.**
   - Present Continuous: *are planning*
5. **She realized (to realize) her mistake only after submitting the assignment.**
   - Simple Past: *realized*
6. **Last night, I realized (to realize) that my keys were missing.**
   - Simple Past
7. **By the end of this year, I will have saved (to save) enough money to buy a new laptop.**
   - Future Perfect
8. **She usually takes (to take) the bus to work, but today she's driving because she overslept.**
   - Simple Present
9. **I had visited (to visit) Paris twice before I moved there for a year.**
   - Past Perfect
10. **Tomorrow at noon, we will have met (to meet) the project deadline and can finally relax.**

- Future Perfect

11. **They have lived (to live) in the same apartment for over a decade now.**

- Present Perfect

12. **By the time the rain started, I had finished (to finish) mowing the lawn.**

- Past Perfect

13. **He will study (to study) history at college next semester.**

- Simple Future
  ("He is going to study" is also acceptable.)

14. **My cousin has called (to call) me every weekend since she moved overseas.**

- Present Perfect

15. **We were watching (to watch) a documentary on wildlife conservation when the power went out.**

- Past Continuous

16. **The students will discuss (to discuss) the assignment in class tomorrow.**

- Simple Future

17. **After Lisa had compared (to compare) several recipes, she chose the simplest one.**

- Past Perfect (followed by Simple Past: *chose*)

18. **My parents will celebrate (to celebrate) their 25th wedding anniversary next month.**

- Simple Future

19. **We had been walking (to walk) along the beach for hours before we found the perfect spot to picnic.**

- Past Perfect Continuous (emphasizing duration)

20. **By the time you come home, I will have cleaned (to clean) every room in the house.**

- Future Perfect

Answer Key: Exercise C2

Task: Each paragraph below contains inconsistent verb tenses. **Rewrite** them with a logical, consistent timeline. The suggested revisions keep each paragraph either entirely in **past** tense, **present** tense, or **future** tense, depending on context.

Paragraph 1

"Yesterday, I visit my grandparents in the countryside. They are excited to see me and prepare a big lunch. After we eat, my grandfather takes me fishing, which I always enjoy. Later that evening, I will drive back to the city, feeling relaxed and happy."

Corrected Version

"**Yesterday, I visited** my grandparents in the countryside. They **were** excited to see me and **prepared** a big lunch. After we **ate**, my grandfather **took** me fishing, which I always **enjoyed**. Later that evening, I **drove** back to the city, feeling relaxed and happy."

Paragraph 2

Original:
"I wake up this morning feeling groggy. I made coffee and sit down to check my emails. Then I realize I forgot to feed the dog, so I rushed to the kitchen. By the time I get back, my coffee was cold."

Corrected (Past Tense):

"This morning, I **woke** up feeling groggy. I **made** coffee and **sat** down to check my emails. Then I **realized** I had forgotten to feed the dog, so I **rushed** to the kitchen. By the time I **got** back, my coffee **was** cold."

Paragraph 3

Original:
"Last Saturday, I go to the park with my friends. We brought a football and play a quick game. Halfway through, it starts raining, so we decide to head home. Later that evening, I am drying my clothes and notice my phone is still in my pocket."

Corrected (Past Tense):

"Last Saturday, I **went** to the park with my friends. We **brought** a football and **played** a quick game. Halfway through, it **started** raining, so we **decided** to head home. Later that evening, I **was** drying my clothes and **noticed** my phone **was** still in my pocket."

Paragraph 4

Original:
"Tomorrow, I picked up my new car from the dealership. I am very excited because I saved money for years to buy it. After I sign the papers, I drive it around the neighborhood to test everything."

Corrected (Future Tense):

"**Tomorrow, I will pick up** my new car from the dealership. I **am** very excited because I **have saved** money for years to buy it. After I **sign** the papers, I **will drive** it around the neighborhood to test everything."

Paragraph 5

Original:
"The little girl sits on the swing and smiled at her father, who was pushing her gently. Suddenly, she asks him if she can go higher, and he laughed before giving her a stronger push."

Corrected (Past Tense):

"The little girl **sat** on the swing and **smiled** at her father, who **was** pushing her gently. Suddenly, she **asked** him if she **could** go higher, and he **laughed** before giving her a stronger push."

Paragraph 6

Original:
"Next month, we flew to Hawaii for our vacation. We are planning to explore the volcanoes and take lots of pictures. After we arrive, we will check in at the hotel and get some rest before sightseeing."

Corrected (Future Tense):

"Next month, we **will fly** to Hawaii for our vacation. We **are** planning to explore the volcanoes and take lots of pictures. After we **arrive**, we **will** check in at the hotel and get some rest before sightseeing."

Paragraph 7

Original:
"Yesterday, I decide to bake cookies for the charity event. I mix the ingredients together and set them in the oven. While they are baking, I realized I forgot to add sugar. In the end, they still taste fine."

Corrected (Past Tense):

"Yesterday, I **decided** to bake cookies for the charity event. I **mixed** the ingredients together and **put** them in the oven. While they **were** baking, I **realized** I had forgotten to add sugar. In the end, they still **tasted** fine."

Paragraph 8

Original:
"During the meeting, our manager says we should finalize the budget by the end of the day. Then she handed out spreadsheets and discusses future strategies. We will review everything again once we have finished the revisions."

Corrected (Past Tense):

"During the meeting, our manager **said** we should finalize the budget by the end of the day. Then she **handed** out spreadsheets and **discussed** future strategies. We **reviewed** everything again once we **had finished** the revisions."

Paragraph 9

Original:
"Two weeks ago, I join a gym because I wanted to get back in shape. I work out daily now, and I will see some progress already. By the time summer arrives, I hope I lost a few pounds."

Corrected (Mixed Tenses Appropriately):

"Two weeks ago, I **joined** a gym because I **wanted** to get back in shape. I **work out** daily now, and I am already **seeing** some progress. By the time summer arrives, I hope I **will have lost** a few pounds."

Paragraph 10

Original:
"This morning, the children play in the backyard while their mother prepares breakfast. When she calls them inside, they took their time picking up toys. Later, they will watch cartoons and told stories about their favorite characters."

Corrected (Past Tense):

"This morning, the children **played** in the backyard while their mother **prepared** breakfast. When she **called** them inside, they **took** their time picking up toys. Later, they **watched** cartoons and **told** stories about their favorite characters."

Paragraph 11

Original:
"On Friday, I am invited to a friend's birthday party. I buy a gift, and tomorrow I wrapped it carefully. After the party, I drove home feeling happy that I could celebrate with everyone."

Corrected (Future Focus):

"On Friday, I **am going** to a friend's birthday party. I **will buy** a gift, and tomorrow I **will wrap** it carefully. After the party, I **will drive** home feeling happy that I could celebrate with everyone."

(Alternatively, keep the entire paragraph in past tense if the event already happened.)

Final Notes

- Use **simple past** for completed actions (yesterday, last Saturday, etc.).
- Use **present tense** when describing general truths or ongoing habits (e.g., "I usually take the bus.").
- Use **future tense** for upcoming events (tomorrow, next week, next month, etc.).
- If an action happened **before another past action**, consider **past perfect** ("had done") to show sequence.
- For an action ongoing from the past to present, use **present perfect** ("have done" / "have been doing").

Section D: Punctuation (Commas, Semicolons, Apostrophes)

Exercise D1: Insert Commas Where Needed

Goal: Add commas to correct places—after introductory words/phrases, around nonrestrictive clauses, in lists, and to separate independent clauses joined by conjunctions.

1. After a long day at work, my mother enjoys reading a good book.
2. My favorite authors are Mark Twain, Jane Austen, and George Orwell.
3. Michael, who lives next door, mows his lawn every Saturday morning.
4. I like spicy food; however, my brother prefers milder dishes.
   (Using a semicolon before "however" is most precise when it connects two independent clauses.)
5. Because the concert was sold out, we decided to watch the livestream instead.
6. I bought apples, oranges, mangoes, and grapes at the market.
7. Despite his injury, Marcus finished the race in record time.
8. Our team, which has been training for months, hopes to win the championship.
9. Under the old oak tree, we set up our picnic blankets.
10. The restaurant served pasta, salads, soups, and sandwiches.
11. My cousin Caroline, who recently moved to Boston, found a job downtown.
12. Without a doubt, this is the tastiest dish on the menu.
13. As soon as the sun rose, we started our hike up the mountain.
14. He whispered, "Be careful," before stepping into the dark corridor.
15. Anna, the youngest sibling, inherited her grandmother's love of painting.
16. If you need any help, feel free to call me.
17. The play was long; however, the acting was phenomenal.
18. On Saturday, I have a soccer match and a piano recital.
19. Derek asked politely, "Could you pass the salt, please?"
20. When you reach the end of the trail, take a moment to enjoy the view.

Exercise D2: Correct Comma Splices or Run-On Sentences

Goal: Use periods, semicolons, or coordinating conjunctions (and, but, or, so, etc.) to fix run-ons or comma splices.

1. I love the snow; it makes everything look so peaceful.
   (Alternatively: "I love the snow because it makes everything look so peaceful.")
2. She ran to catch the bus, but she slipped on the icy sidewalk.
3. He wants to study medicine, and he also wants to travel the world.
4. I finished reading the book, and now I need to write my report.
   (Or: "I finished reading the book. Now I need to write my report.")
5. She loves to paint landscapes; she also enjoys sketching portraits.
   (Or: "…landscapes, and she also enjoys…")
6. We wanted to leave early, but it started raining heavily, so we stayed.
7. It's a busy time of year; we have family visiting from out of town.

8. Alex played the guitar beautifully, and the audience gave him a standing ovation.
9. I tried to bake a cake, but I ran out of sugar halfway through.
10. She wanted to travel abroad, so she saved money for months.
11. That movie is really suspenseful; I would watch it again.
12. He forgot his wallet in the car, so he had to go back for it.
13. I love hiking through the mountains because the fresh air is invigorating.
    (Or: "I love hiking through the mountains; the fresh air is invigorating.")
14. The manager approved my vacation request; I can't wait to go to the beach.
15. We debated the issue all night, but we couldn't agree on a solution.
16. She studied hard for the exam, but she forgot her notes at home.
17. The library is closing soon, so you should check out your books now.
18. Some people prefer coffee; others like tea.
19. I was late to the meeting because I got stuck in traffic on the highway.
    (Or: "I was late to the meeting; I got stuck in traffic on the highway.")

Exercise D3: Fix Apostrophe Usage

Goal: Ensure contractions (e.g., it's, can't, you're) are correct and show possession accurately (e.g., dog's collar, children's toys).

1. The Smiths' house is on the corner. (Assuming the home belongs to the entire Smith family.)
2. It's a beautiful day for a picnic. ("It's" means "it is.")
3. You'll find the museum's entrance at the end of this street.
4. The dog's collar was loose, so I tightened it. (One dog.)
5. It's been a while since I've visited my grandparents' farm.
   (It's = it has; I've = I have; grandparents' = plural possessive.)
6. The cats' bowls need to be washed regularly.
   (Multiple cats.)
7. We've seen that movie three times, yet its ending still surprises us.
   (We've = we have; "its" is possessive without apostrophe.)
8. Today's schedule is fully booked; there's no time for a break.
   (Today's = belonging to today; there's = there is.)
9. The children's playground is next to the teachers' lounge.
   (Children's = belonging to the children; teachers' = belonging to multiple teachers.)
10. Who's ready to begin today's lesson on punctuation?
    (Who's = who is.)
11. The family's car broke down on the way to their vacation home.
12. You're going to have fun at tonight's concert; it's going to be amazing.
    (You're = you are; it's = it is.)
13. The students' presentations were all impressive, but Jim's stood out.
    (Students' = multiple students; Jim's = belonging to Jim.)
14. I can't believe she's leaving for college next week.
    (Can't = cannot; she's = she is.)
15. The team's uniform colors changed this season.
    (One team. If multiple teams, then "teams'.")
16. The baby's stroller is on the back porch; don't forget it.
    (Baby's = belongs to the baby; don't = do not.)
17. She's looking for her mother's keys, but can't find them.
    (She's = she is; can't = cannot.)
18. It's important that you respect others' boundaries.
    (It's = it is; others' = belonging to multiple people.)
19. The politician's campaign slogan was all over the city's billboards.
    (One politician; one city.)
20. Who's responsible for cleaning the dog's bowls after dinner?
    (Who's = who is; dog's = belonging to one dog. If multiple dogs, dogs'.)

Final Notes

- **Exercise D1 (commas)**: Watch for places to insert commas after introductory phrases, around nonessential clauses, and in compound sentences (comma + coordinating conjunction).
- **Exercise D2 (run-ons/comma splices)**: You can correct them in various ways—such as adding a period, a semicolon, or a comma with a coordinating conjunction.
- **Exercise D3 (apostrophes)**: Remember that "it's" is a contraction for "it is" or "it has," while "its" is possessive. Also, watch for singular vs. plural possession (family's vs. families', cat's vs. cats', etc.).

Section E: Mixed Grammar Challenges

1

Original
"My family who like to travel frequently are planning a trip to Italy next year, I hope we have saved enough money."

Corrected
"My family, who **likes** to travel frequently, **is** planning a trip to Italy next year. I hope we **have** saved enough money."

- **Explanation**:
  - "family" is singular ("likes," "is").
  - Split the run-on sentence at "…next year. I hope…".

2

Original
"Neither Jenna nor her friends was ready for they're final exams which is tomorrow at 9:00 AM."

Corrected
"Neither Jenna nor her friends **were** ready for **their** final exams, which **are** tomorrow at 9:00 AM."

- **Explanation**:
  - "friends" is plural, so the verb is "were."
  - Use "their" (possessive) instead of "they're" (contraction).
  - "exams" is plural, so "which are tomorrow."

3

Original
"Many of the theories proposed by the scientist is controversial however they has changed how we view environmental conservation."

Corrected
"Many of the theories proposed by the scientist **are** controversial; however, they **have** changed how we view environmental conservation."

- **Explanation**:
  - "Many … are controversial" (plural).
  - Use semicolon before "however" to avoid a run-on.
  - "they have changed," not "they has."

4

Original
"Its important to have a good nights sleep a student should get around eight hours if they want to be fully alert."

Corrected
"It's important to have a good **night's** sleep. A student should get around eight hours if **he or she** wants to be fully alert."

- **Explanation**:
  - "It's" = "it is."
  - "night's" = possessive form of "night."
  - Split the run-on sentence.
  - Use "he or she" for singular "student," or rewrite in plural form if preferred.

5

Original
"The group of students who is meeting every Friday are excited about their project, they are hoping to present it next week."

Corrected
"The group of students who **meet** every Friday **is** excited about their project. They are hoping to present it next week."

- **Explanation**:
  - "group … is" (collective noun in singular form).
  - "who meet every Friday" (agreeing with "students" in that clause).
  - Split the comma splice into two sentences.

6

Original
"Each of the employees have turned in their resignation letter last Monday, I'm not sure why they choose to leave so suddenly."

Corrected
"Each of the employees **turned** in **his or her** resignation letter last Monday. I'm not sure why they **chose** to leave so suddenly."

- **Explanation**:
  - "Each" is singular ("turned," "his or her").
  - Past tense "chose" matches "last Monday."
  - Separate the run-on sentence.

7

Original
"We wanted to buy groceries, but the store were closed the sign said it was under renovation."

Corrected
"We wanted to buy groceries, but the store **was** closed. The sign said it was under renovation."

- **Explanation**:
  - "store … was" (singular).
  - Split into two sentences to fix the run-on.

8

Original
"The teacher told the class that they should finish their assignment by tonight however some of the students asked for an extension."

Corrected
"The teacher told the class that they should finish their assignment by tonight; however, some of the students asked for an extension."

- **Explanation**:
  - Semicolon before "however" to avoid a run-on sentence.
  - "they" refers to "the class," which is acceptable in modern usage (the entire group).

9

Original
"My friend and me is planning a surprise birthday party for his brother which is happening tomorrow."

Corrected
"My friend and **I are** planning a surprise birthday party for his brother, which is happening tomorrow."

- **Explanation**:
  - "friend and I" (subject form).
  - Plural subject => "are."
  - Added comma before nonessential clause "which is happening tomorrow."

10

Original
"The dog found it's ball under the couch, after we had looked for it for hours."

Corrected
"The dog found **its** ball under the couch after we had looked for it for hours."

- **Explanation**:
  - "its" = possessive pronoun.
  - Removed the comma to avoid a comma splice (or use a period if you want two sentences).

11

Original
"She have been studying for weeks but she realized she forgot all her notes at home."

Corrected
"She **has** been studying for weeks, but she realized she forgot all her notes at home."

- **Explanation**:
  - Use "has" (third-person singular).
  - Comma before "but" to join two independent clauses.

12

Original
"I have eat breakfast already, I usually do that before starting my day but today I completely forgot."

Corrected
"I have already **eaten** breakfast. I usually do that before starting my day, but today I almost forgot."

- **Explanation**:
  - "have eaten" is correct present perfect.
  - Split the run-on.
  - Note: The original sentence had conflicting ideas (claimed the speaker ate breakfast yet forgot). The above correction assumes they *did* manage to eat but almost forgot.

13

Original
"A person can lose track of time if they uses their phone too often, it distracts you from important tasks."

Corrected
"A person can lose track of time if **he or she uses** a phone too often. It distracts **him or her** from important tasks."

- **Explanation**:
  - "A person" is singular.
  - "he or she uses" for subject-verb agreement.
  - Remove the run-on by using a period.

(Alternatively, use a plural subject: "People can lose track of time if they use their phones too often. They distract themselves from important tasks.")

14

Original
"My cousins decided that he would learn guitar last week, but they changed their mind yesterday."

Corrected
"My **cousins** decided that **they** would learn guitar last week, but **they** changed **their** minds yesterday."

- **Explanation**:
  - "cousins" = plural.
  - Use "they" and "their minds" for consistency.

15

Original
"The board of directors are holding a meeting next month to discuss the companys new policy, its starting to get negative feedback from employees."

Corrected
"The board of directors **is** holding a meeting next month to discuss the **company's** new policy. **It's** starting to get negative feedback from employees."

- **Explanation**:
  - "board of directors" treated as a single entity => "is holding."
  - Possessive "company's."
  - "It's" = "It is."
  - Break the run-on sentence.

16

Original
"Who do you think you should talk to about these issues, our manager or the HR representative."

Corrected
"**Whom** do you think you should talk to about these issues—our manager or the HR representative?"

- **Explanation**:
  - Strictly, "whom" is correct as the object of "talk to."
  - Change punctuation to a question mark.
  - The em dash (—) separates the second clause, but a question mark is crucial.

("Who do you think…" is also common in everyday usage.)

17

Original
"Talia gave her sister the keys to the car so she could run errands but she left them on the table and lost it."

Corrected
"Talia gave her sister the keys to the car so she could run errands, but her sister left them on the table and lost **them**."

- **Explanation**:
  - Clarify pronoun references: "lost them" (referring to the keys).
  - Comma before "but."

18

Original
"No one want to take responsibility for the mistake, they said it wasnt theyre fault."

Corrected
"No one **wants** to take responsibility for the mistake; they said it **wasn't their** fault."

- **Explanation**:
  - "No one wants" (singular or standard usage).
  - Use semicolon or period to avoid run-on.
  - "wasn't" = was not, "their" = possessive.

19

Original
"Tomorrow, I flew to California for a business trip, I wonder if I will have enough time to sightsee."

Corrected
"Tomorrow, I **will fly** to California for a business trip. I wonder if I will have enough time to sightsee."

- **Explanation**:
  - Change "flew" (past) to "will fly" (future) for consistency with "Tomorrow."
  - Split the run-on with a period.

20

Original
"We has waited for two hours in line for those tickets yet none of us are complaining, is better than missing the show."

Corrected
"We **have** waited for two hours in line for those tickets, yet none of us are complaining. **It's** better than missing the show."

- **Explanation**:
  - "We have waited."
  - Break the sentence to avoid a run-on.
  - "It's better than missing the show."

General Tips for Mixed Grammar Challenges

- **Subject-Verb Agreement**: Identify the true subject (singular vs. plural). Collective nouns (family, board of directors) are often singular.
- **Pronoun Usage**: Match pronouns (singular or plural) to their antecedents; watch for who/whom.
- **Verb Tenses**: Keep the timeline consistent (past with past, future with future, etc.).

- **Punctuation**: Fix comma splices and run-ons by using periods, semicolons, or coordinating conjunctions.
- **Apostrophes**: Distinguish between contractions (it's = it is) and possessive forms (its, company's).

By applying these corrections, each sentence maintains **grammatical consistency** and **clarity**.

ANSWER KEY: Passage-Based Editing Sets

Passage 1

(Questions #1–4)

Original Passage Text

[1] Community gardens are becoming increasingly popular in urban areas. **(1) People are discovering that growing there own vegetables can be both cost-effective and emotionally satisfying.** Some residents enjoy cultivating flowers… [etc.]

1. (1)

- **Correct Answer: C.**
  - **Explanation**:
    - "There" should be "their" to show possession.
    - Parallel structure with "cost-effective and emotionally satisfying."
    - The phrase "emotional satisfying" is incorrect; it should be "emotionally satisfying."

2. (2)

- **Correct Answer: C.**
  - **Explanation**:
    - Eliminate unnecessary comma after "New York City."
    - "shows how powerful these projects can be" is the most natural flow.
    - (A) has a comma that creates a comma splice. (B) incorrectly places a comma. (D) uses an awkward colon.

3. (3)

- **Correct Answer: D.**
  - **Explanation**:
    - "not only improves neighborhoods' appearances but also fosters" is the proper parallel conjunction structure.
    - (A) leaves out the possessive apostrophe in "neighborhoods appearances."
    - (B) is a run-on or missing a conjunction.
    - (C) uses misplaced commas.

4. (4)

- **Correct Answer: D.**
  - **Explanation**:
    - A semicolon or a period is needed between two independent clauses ("…workshops" and "These workshops…").
    - Splitting into two sentences is acceptable: "Because of this, many local parks have begun offering educational workshops. These workshops teach…"
    - (C) has a semicolon plus "these workshops teach," which is also okay but doesn't split into two separate sentences—(D) does so more cleanly.

Passage 2

(Questions #5–8)

Original Passage Text

[2] The invention of the printing press is widely regarded as one of the most significant events in human history. **(5) Without it, mass literacy might not have developed, and information wouldn't have been as easy to share or preserve.** [etc.]

5. (5)

- **Correct Answer: D.**
  - **Explanation**:
    - Adds "might not have been" for parallelism: "mass literacy might not have developed, and information might not have been as easy…"
    - (A) is okay but not as precise; (B) lacks crucial punctuation; (C) incorrectly uses a semicolon before "and."

6. (6)

- **Correct Answer: B.**
  - **Explanation**:
    - A colon after "texts" works well to introduce an explanation.
    - "a process that was time-consuming" is a descriptive phrase clarifying how scribes worked.
    - (A) has no punctuation separating "texts" and "a process…," leading to a run-on.
    - (C) adds unnecessary commas. (D) misuses a semicolon.

7. (7)

- **Correct Answer: D.**
  - **Explanation**:
    - "had many immediate benefits: it lowered… encouraged…, and enabled…" uses parallel structure.
    - (A) ends with an "and enabling" that breaks the parallelism.
    - (B) has "and enabling" without a conjunction that parallels the first verbs.
    - (C) is a run-on or comma splice.

8. (8)

- **Correct Answer: D.**
  - **Explanation**:
    - Comma before "quickly overshadowing…" clarifies that it's a participial phrase describing how the Renaissance overshadowed previous eras.
    - (A) has no comma. (B) incorrectly punctuates the possessive "eras." (C) is a run-on.

Passage 3

(Questions #9–12)

Original Passage Text

Farmers' markets… **(9) Many shoppers appreciate the variety of goods available and that farmers can be asked questions about their cultivation practices.** [etc.]

9. (9)

- **Correct Answer: C.**
  - **Explanation**:
    - This choice uses parallel structure: "appreciate the variety of goods available and the opportunity to ask farmers…"
    - (A) is repetitive and somewhat confusing. (B) is a comma splice. (D) has subject-verb mismatch ("Many shoppers appreciates").

10. (10)

- **Correct Answer: B.**
  - **Explanation**:
    - "many markets transition into indoor venues" matches subject-verb agreement in present tense.
    - (A) "transitions" is incorrect for the plural "markets." (C) mixes "experiences" (wrong number) with "have transitioned" (switching tenses). (D) is a fragment or incomplete structure.

11. (11)

- **Correct Answer: B.**
  - **Explanation**:
    - "improving farmers' revenues" corrects the possessive (farmers') and keeps a participial phrase that modifies "ensures that customers have…"
    - (A) "farmer's revenues" is singular. (C) changes the sentence's structure incorrectly. (D) lacks an apostrophe.

12. (12)

- **Correct Answer: B.**
  - **Explanation**:
    - "Vendors, volunteers, and city officials often dedicate countless hours…" uses plural subject "Vendors, volunteers, and city officials" => "dedicate."
    - (A) "dedicates" is singular. (C) "often dedicating" is incomplete. (D) "is often dedicating" is incorrect in number and tense.

Passage 4

(Questions #13–16)

Original Passage Text

Large-scale public art installations… **(13) Mural projects, for example provide a visual narrative of a communitys history** and aspirations. [etc.]

13. (13)

- **Correct Answer: B.**
  - **Explanation**:
    - Need a comma after "for example," and "community's" with an apostrophe.
    - "Mural projects, for example, provide a visual narrative of a community's history…"
    - (A) is missing the possessive apostrophe. (C) changes "provide" to "provides" which fails subject-verb agreement. (D) adds an extra comma at the end.

14. (14)

- **Correct Answer: B.**
  - **Explanation**:
    - "may be" should be two words, not "maybe."
    - (A) has the incorrect "maybe." (C) and (D) add commas incorrectly or keep "maybe."

15. (15)

- **Correct Answer: C.**
  - **Explanation**:
    - "With enough planning, numerous communities **have discovered** that these installations encourage tourism…"
    - Present perfect "have discovered" is consistent and agrees with plural "communities."

        - (A) "has discovered" is singular. (B) "discover" in the simple present is possible, but "have discovered" typically fits the context of something ongoing. (D) misses a comma after "planning."

16. (16)

- **Correct Answer: B.**
    - **Explanation**:
        - Insert commas between items in a list: "bright, colorful, and culturally relevant spaces."
        - (A) lacks the serial comma. (C) has partial but inconsistent comma use. (D) hyphenates "culturally-relevant" unnecessarily.

Passage 5

(Questions #17–20)

Original Passage Text

Baking bread at home has gained popularity… **(17) It require patience, precise measurement, and an understanding of yeast fermentation** [etc.]

17. (17)

- **Correct Answer: C.**
    - **Explanation**:
        - "It requires patience, precise measurements, and an understanding of yeast fermentation."
        - "require" is wrong for "it." Also add "measurements" for parallelism with "patience" and "understanding."

18. (18)

- **Correct Answer: A. (NO CHANGE)**
    - **Explanation**:
        - "Even though mistakes can happen—like under-kneading or forgetting the salt—learning these techniques often proves rewarding." is smooth, coherent, and properly punctuated.
        - (B) might be acceptable but changes the sentence structure unnecessarily.
        - (C) incorrectly uses a colon. (D) misplaces a colon.

19. (19)

- **Correct Answer: B.**
    - **Explanation**:
        - Use a semicolon or a period to separate two independent clauses: "Historically, homemade bread was often a necessity; it is now enjoying a revival…"
        - (A) is a comma splice. (C) is also possible, but the semicolon is a bit more concise. (D) is incomplete or incorrectly punctuated at the end.

20. (20)

- **Correct Answer: A. (NO CHANGE)**
    - **Explanation**:
        - "the act of turning simple ingredients into a satisfying meal fosters a sense of pride" is correct, clear, and concise.
        - (B) and (D) alter the meaning or style unnecessarily. (C) adds an unnecessary comma.

Passage 6

(Questions #21–24)

Original Passage Text

(21) Designing a website requires both creativity, and technical expertise. [etc.]

21. (21)

- **Correct Answer: B.**
  - **Explanation**:
    - Remove unnecessary comma before "and technical expertise."
    - "Designing a website requires both creativity and technical expertise."

22. (22)

- **Correct Answer: B.**
  - **Explanation**:
    - Insert commas around "though" properly: "Without well-planned structure, though, visitors may have trouble…"
    - (A) lumps "though" awkwardly. (C) lacks one of the needed commas. (D) inserts a period that causes a fragment.

23. (23)

- **Correct Answer: B.**
  - **Explanation**:
    - "frequent updates keep content fresh" matches subject-verb agreement with "updates" => "keep."
    - (A) "keeps" is incorrect for plural "updates." (C) and (D) change tense inappropriately.

24. (24)

- **Correct Answer: C.**
  - **Explanation**:
    - "websites thrive when they are user-friendly and visually engaging" matches the plural "websites" => "they are."
    - (A) "when they is user-friendly" is wrong. (B) changes the pronoun incorrectly to singular. (D) repeats the error "they is."

Passage 7

(Questions #25–28)

Original Passage Text

Many commuters prefer cycling to driving. **(25) Not only does it reduces carbon emissions, it also provides regular exercise.** [etc.]

25. (25)

- **Correct Answer: B.**
  - **Explanation**:
    - Correct subject-verb usage: "Not only does it reduce carbon emissions, it also provides…"
    - (A) "reduces" conflicts with "does." (C) "do it reduce" is incorrect. (D) changes the meaning and tense awkwardly.

26. (26)

- **Correct Answer: C.**
  - **Explanation**:
    - Insert commas around "especially in areas lacking bike lanes."
    - "However, some people still worry about safety, especially in areas lacking bike lanes."

            - (A) lacks needed punctuation. (B) misplaces commas. (D) is missing a key comma after "However."

27. (27)

- **Correct Answer: B.**
    - **Explanation**:
        - "so that more residents feel confident" matches plural "residents" => "feel."
        - (A) "feels confident" is singular. (C) "would feel" changes the tense unnecessarily. (D) is more wordy and less standard.

28. (28)

- **Correct Answer: C.**
    - **Explanation**:
        - Use semicolon to separate two independent clauses: "cycling can save money on gas and parking; it also benefits the environment…"
        - (A) is ambiguous with the phrase "also benefiting." (B) merges them in a comma splice. (D) incorrectly uses "which" in a fragment form.

Passage 8

(Questions #29–32)

Original Passage Text

(29) Researching family history is a popular hobby many people enjoy collecting old letters… [etc.]

29. (29)

- **Correct Answer: C.**
    - **Explanation**:
        - A comma or conjunction needed between two independent clauses: "Researching family history is a popular hobby, and many people enjoy…"
        - (A) is a run-on. (B) is a comma splice. (D) incorrectly inserts a comma after "history" and results in confusion.

30. (30)

- **Correct Answer: D.**
    - **Explanation**:
        - "As a result, individuals who once struggled to trace their lineage…" is correct punctuation.
        - (A) has no comma after "result." (B) adds commas that break up the sentence oddly. (C) also misplaces commas.

31. (31)

- **Correct Answer: C.**
    - **Explanation**:
        - Splitting into two sentences avoids a run-on: "The process requires patience and a willingness to verify details thoroughly. Errors can lead to inaccurate family trees."
        - (A) is a run-on. (B) is also a run-on with only a comma. (D) changes subject-verb forms incorrectly.

32. (32)

- **Correct Answer: C.**
    - **Explanation**:
        - A semicolon separates two independent clauses: "This method often uncovers surprising connections; many genealogists are thrilled…"

        - (A) is another run-on. (B) repeats the comma splice problem. (D) adds extraneous words.

Passage 9

(Questions #33–36)

Original Passage Text

Volunteering at a local shelter… **(33) Some people prefer working with animals they find satisfaction in caring** for abandoned pets. [etc.]

33. (33)

- **Correct Answer: B.**
    - **Explanation**:
        - A comma is needed to clarify: "Some people prefer working with animals, finding satisfaction in caring for abandoned pets."
        - (A) is a run-on. (C) is missing words for clarity. (D) is awkwardly phrased.

34. (34)

- **Correct Answer: B.**
    - **Explanation**:
        - "The key is discovering which cause resonates with you. Once you find that passion, the work feels genuinely fulfilling."
        - Splitting it into two sentences avoids a run-on. (A) is a run-on as written. (C) is also workable with a semicolon, but the second half is missing a natural break. (D) inserts a comma incorrectly.

35. (35)

- **Correct Answer: B.**
    - **Explanation**:
        - Maintain parallelism: "reduce stress, and help individuals develop new skills."
        - "help" must match "reduce." (A) "helps" is singular, clashing with "reduce." (C) "reduces stress, and help" is inconsistent. (D) is wordier.

36. (36)

- **Correct Answer: B.**
    - **Explanation**:
        - "connecting with neighbors fosters a sense of belonging that can lead…"
        - Eliminates the comma before "that." (A) is a comma splice. (C) changes meaning slightly, but also acceptable in some contexts. (D) is incomplete.

Passage 10

(Questions #37–40)

Original Passage Text

(37) Over the past decade, social media platforms have altered how people interacts with friends, family, and even strangers worldwide. [etc.]

37. (37)

- **Correct Answer: C.**
    - **Explanation**:
        - "Over the past decade, social media platforms have altered how people interact…"
        - Plural "platforms have," plus "people interact," is correct. (A) uses singular "interacts."

38. (38)

- **Correct Answer: B.**
  - **Explanation**:
    - "Although critics argue that it reduces face-to-face interactions," plus a comma, clarifies the subordinate clause.
    - (A) lacks a comma. (C) and (D) add commas incorrectly.

39. (39)

- **Correct Answer: A. (NO CHANGE)**
  - **Explanation**:
    - "For instance traveling food enthusiasts can join groups to swap recipes…" is slightly awkward, but typically we'd place a comma after "For instance."
    - However, (A) is acceptable if the test's style is flexible. If you prefer more clarity, "For instance, traveling food enthusiasts…" could be best.
    - Check the official ACT style: "For instance, traveling food enthusiasts…" is likely better. If forced to pick among these, (C) is typically correct with a comma after "For instance."

(If strictly following standard punctuation, we might argue for (C). On the sample, though, if the original is considered correct by the provided solutions, it may be an instance of "No Change.")

40. (40)

- **Correct Answer: B.**
  - **Explanation**:
    - "excessive use might impact mental health" is consistent in tense and subject-verb usage.
    - (A) "impacts" can work in the present tense, but "might impacts" is ungrammatical. (C) and (D) shift tense awkwardly.

***Note**: For #39, if the original test considered "For instance traveling food enthusiasts" correct, it might be a less strict approach to punctuation. However, many style guides would suggest a comma after "For instance." Since the question is multiple-choice, the best fit among the provided might be "NO CHANGE" if all other choices create bigger errors.*

Final Notes

1. **Run-on Sentences**: Often fixed with a period, semicolon, or coordinating conjunction.
2. **Parallel Structure**: Make sure verbs or nouns in a series match in form.
3. **Subject-Verb Agreement**: Check whether your subject is singular or plural.
4. **Pronoun Usage**: Correct "their/its" vs. "they're," or subject vs. object forms.
5. **Possessive Apostrophes**: Distinguish "it's" (it is) from "its" (possessive), "their" from "they're," and so on.
6. **Commas**: Use them after introductory phrases, around extra (nonrestrictive) clauses, and in lists.
7. **Semicolons**: Use to separate two related independent clauses when you want a closer connection than a period or if there's a transitional phrase like "however."
8. **Clarity & Style**: Some questions test whether a revision improves flow, reduces wordiness, or maintains clarity.

ANSWER KEY: Passage-Based Editing Sets

Mini-Test 1

Passage A

(Sentences are labeled [1]–[5]. Questions #1–5 refer to specific underlined segments or revision tasks.)

1. **(2)**
   - **Correct Answer: C**
   - **Explanation**: "Many individuals choose to grow herbs like basil and mint **because they are easy to maintain in small pots.**" This removes the awkward use of "Although" and clarifies **why** people choose these herbs.
2. **(4)**
   - **Correct Answer: B**
   - **Explanation**: A comma after "For example" is needed. "**For example, using hanging planters or tiered shelves...**" introduces an illustrative example smoothly.
3. **Best placement for** "Some people even repurpose old wooden pallets to create stacked gardens."
   - **Correct Answer: C (After sentence [3])**
   - **Explanation**: Sentence [3] discusses space-saving vertical techniques, so adding the pallet idea right after it makes sense and maintains logical flow.
4. **Combining sentences [4] and [5]**
   - **Correct Answer: C**
   - **Explanation**: "For example, using hanging planters or tiered shelves allows even apartment dwellers to cultivate a variety of plants, **and such fresh produce is not only tastier but also free from harmful chemicals.**" This unifies the ideas clearly while maintaining parallel structure and avoiding run-ons.
5. **Adding a sentence emphasizing that homegrown vegetables can be cheaper**
   - **Correct Answer: B**
   - **Explanation**: "**In addition, these simple gardening techniques can save families money that they would otherwise spend at grocery stores.**" directly addresses cost-effectiveness.

Mini-Test 2

Passage B

1. **(2)**
   - **Correct Answer: C**
   - **Explanation**: The museum's "mission" is possessive: "**its mission**." "it's" = "it is," which is incorrect here.
2. **Best revision of sentence [4]** to maintain style and tone
   - **Correct Answer: B**
   - **Explanation**: "**Moreover, the museum frequently announces new exhibits, ensuring returning guests consistently find something fresh to explore.**" This maintains a formal, cohesive tone.
3. **Adding a sentence about historical significance in the collection**
   - **Correct Answer: A (After sentence [1])**
   - **Explanation**: Sentence [1] introduces the museum's general purpose and holdings; adding a note about historical significance right after that provides clarity and context.
4. **Improving clarity of sentence [3]**
   - **Correct Answer: B**
   - **Explanation**: "**Offering daily tours, the museum presents in-depth insights into each exhibit, placing them within their social context.**" Streamlines the sentence and keeps focus on how tours deepen visitors' understanding.
5. **Clarifying the artifacts' range from ancient to modern**
   - **Correct Answer: C**
   - **Explanation**: "**Ranging from ancient scrolls to contemporary art pieces, the artifacts cover numerous historical periods.**" directly addresses the timeline span.

Mini-Test 3

Passage A

(Ocean currents)

1. **(2)**
   - **Correct Answer: B**
   - **Explanation**: Insert a comma and correct the verb: "**However, some people believe** that these massive movements of water only affect coastlines."
2. **Revising sentence [2]** for clarity and formality
   - **Correct Answer: B**
   - **Explanation**: "**However, some people mistakenly think that these vast water movements only impact coastlines.**" is concise and maintains a formal tone.
3. **Best place to add**: "Oceanographers study how these currents originate as well as the temperature and salinity differences that drive them."
   - **Correct Answer: B (After sentence [2])**
   - **Explanation**: After correcting the misconception about coastlines, it's logical to introduce oceanographers' research on the *actual* complexity of currents.
4. **Combining sentences [3] and [4]**
   - **Correct Answer: B**
   - **Explanation**: "**In reality, they transport heat, nutrients, and even marine organisms across vast distances and, by doing so, influence weather patterns, impact fishing industries, and help shape biodiversity.**"
5. **Concluding sentence underscoring inland effects**
   - **Correct Answer: B**
   - **Explanation**: "**Therefore, communities far from the sea may still feel the effects of shifting currents in their yearly rainfall and temperature ranges.**" emphasizes inland impact.

Passage B

(Digital media lab)

1. **(3)**
   - **Correct Answer: C**
   - **Explanation**: "**Additionally, patrons can convert old VHS tapes or film reels…**" keeps the third-person "patrons" consistent.
2. **Maintaining consistent point of view**
   - **Correct Answer: C**
   - **Explanation**: The entire passage uses "patrons" and third-person references, so "patrons/patrons" is the best for consistency.
3. **Combining sentences [2] and [3]**
   - **Correct Answer: B**
   - **Explanation**: "**In this cutting-edge space, patrons can record podcasts, edit videos, experiment with graphic design software, and even convert old VHS tapes…**" captures all activities smoothly.
4. **Concluding sentence highlighting community engagement**
   - **Correct Answer: B**
   - **Explanation**: "**As a result, local schools have begun scheduling class trips so students can discover the possibilities of digital creation.**" shows broader community benefit.
5. **Placement of** "In fact, it's rumored that the lab may expand soon to include 3D printing stations."
   - **Correct Answer: B (After sentence [2])**
   - **Explanation**: After describing the existing resources (recording, editing, design), it's natural to hint at future expansion.

Mini-Test 4

Passage A

(Air purifiers)

1. **(4)**
   - **Correct Answer: B**

- **Explanation**: **"However, it's important to clean the filters regularly; otherwise, the device might lose its effectiveness."** fixes punctuation and "its" is the correct possessive form.

2. **Most concise revision of** "They claim to remove dust, pollen, and even bacteria…"
   - **Correct Answer: B**
   - **Explanation**: **"These purifiers are said to remove dust, pollen, and even bacteria from indoor air."** is direct and clear.
3. **Best placement for** choosing the right purifier size
   - **Correct Answer: B (After sentence [2])**
   - **Explanation**: Right after discussing what purifiers do, logically add a note about matching purifier size to your room.
4. **Parallel structure for sentence [3]**
   - **Correct Answer: C**
   - **Explanation**: **"Studies show that individuals with allergies or respiratory issues tend to benefit most from these devices."**
5. **Ending sentence emphasizing scientific evidence**
   - **Correct Answer: B**
   - **Explanation**: **"A recent university experiment found that certain models removed up to 99 percent of airborne particles."** underscores evidence-based effectiveness.

Passage B

(Digital vs. handwritten notes)

1. **Best transition for sentence [3]**
   - **Correct Answer: B**
   - **Explanation**: **"However, some argue that handwriting strengthens memory…"** introduces a contrast effectively.
2. **Where to add detail about embedding images**
   - **Correct Answer: B (After sentence [2])**
   - **Explanation**: Sentence [2] discusses organizing notebooks and embedding images. Immediately after is perfect for clarifying *why* images can help illustrate complex ideas.
3. **Parallel structure in sentence [2]**
   - **Correct Answer: B**
   - **Explanation**: **"They allow users not only to organize notebooks but also to embed images and share collaborative documents."**
4. **Best concluding sentence type**
   - **Correct Answer: C**
   - **Explanation**: The passage contrasts digital vs. handwritten. A conclusion linking personal circumstances (like learning style or environment) is most fitting.
5. **Concrete data supporting digital note-taking**
   - **Correct Answer: B**
   - **Explanation**: **"In a recent survey, 70% of professionals reported improved productivity after switching to digital notes."** directly offers relevant statistics.

Mini-Test 5

Passage A

(Artisan Food Fair)

1. **Fixing the problem in sentence [2]**
   - **Correct Answer: B**
   - **Explanation**: "Visitors can sample artisanal cheeses, homemade jams, and freshly baked bread; **it** also offers cooking demonstrations…" A semicolon correctly separates two independent clauses.
2. **Emphasizing the unique benefit of learning food preservation**
   - **Correct Answer: B**

- **Explanation**: **"This skill lets home cooks enjoy their favorite seasonal foods long after harvest."** highlights the practical payoff.

3. **Most concise version of sentence [4]**
   - **Correct Answer: B**
   - **Explanation**: **"Several workshops instruct participants in a variety of techniques, such as canning and sourdough bread-making, for a hands-on experience."** is clear and parallel.
4. **Placement for mention of local farmers supplying produce**
   - **Correct Answer: B (After sentence [1])**
   - **Explanation**: Right after introducing the fair, it's logical to note that local farmers provide fresh ingredients for the event.
5. **Replacing "In addition" in sentence [4]**
   - **Correct Answer: A ("Similarly,")**
   - **Explanation**: This maintains a smooth, additive transition from the preceding sentence about celebrating local produce and techniques.

Passage B

(Job-shadowing programs)

1. **(3)**
   - **Correct Answer: C**
   - **Explanation**: **"In fact, many students find these programs so enlightening**…" is a positive extension, not negative. "Unfortunately" is inappropriate.
2. **Where to clarify that students often realize a job isn't what they expected**
   - **Correct Answer: C (After sentence [3])**
   - **Explanation**: Right after stating that students find job-shadowing enlightening, it's logical to mention that *some discover* the reality isn't as they'd imagined.
3. **Contrasting viewpoint before sentence [4]**
   - **Correct Answer: B**
   - **Explanation**: **"However, a few critics argue that short-term observation may not be enough…"** provides a contrast to the otherwise positive statements.
4. **Revising sentence [4]**
   - **Correct Answer: B**
   - **Explanation**: **"Upon witnessing both the rewards and difficulties of a field, students often make more informed academic choices."** is clear, formal, and consistent.
5. **Concluding sentence highlighting practical advantages**
   - **Correct Answer: B**
   - **Explanation**: **"Ultimately, job-shadowing saves participants time and money by helping them pinpoint the right career before investing in specialized training."**

Mini-Test 6

Passage A

(Rooftop gardens)

1. **(4)**
   - **Correct Answer: B**
   - **Explanation**: **"Ultimately, even a humble wooden planter box filled with herbs can improve apartment living while offering a relaxing hobby."** clarifies the statement.
2. **Adding more about environmental benefits**
   - **Correct Answer: B**
   - **Explanation**: **"These rooftop gardens can reduce stormwater runoff and decrease carbon footprints."** emphasizes ecological value.
3. **Transitional phrase for sentence [3]**
   - **Correct Answer: B ("For instance,")**
   - **Explanation**: Introduces the hydroponic systems example as an illustrative detail.

4. **Placement for how much sunlight rooftop gardens need**
    - **Correct Answer: B (Immediately after sentence [2])**
    - **Explanation**: After describing benefits in [2], it's logical to add that **sufficient sunlight** is a key requirement before examples like hydroponics in [3].
5. **Including aesthetic appeal in sentence [2]**
    - **Correct Answer: C**
    - **Explanation**: "**They provide green space, produce fresh vegetables, add visual appeal, and can even help insulate buildings.**" maintains parallel structure.

Passage B

(Mountain biking)

1. **(2)**
    - **Correct Answer: C**
    - **Explanation**: "Riders need to wear helmets, sturdy shoes, **and ensure** their bikes are well-maintained." is parallel and concise.
2. **Best concluding statement**
    - **Correct Answer: C**
    - **Explanation**: "**With the proper precautions and ongoing practice, riders can safely enjoy this thrilling outdoor pursuit.**" unifies the advice and emphasizes a positive outcome.
3. **Placement for detail on hydration**
    - **Correct Answer: B (Immediately after sentence [2])**
    - **Explanation**: After listing gear (helmets, shoes, well-maintained bike), highlighting hydration is a logical next step in readiness.
4. **Consistent style when revising sentence [3]**
    - **Correct Answer: B**
    - **Explanation**: "**If they don't, they risk mechanical failures on steep trails, leading to hazardous falls.**" is concise, direct, and matches the passage's tone.
5. **Adding a sentence about camaraderie after sentence [4]**
    - **Correct Answer: A**
    - **Explanation**: "**Riders often exchange tips on trail conditions and gear, forming supportive communities.**" highlights teamwork and shared learning.

Mini-Test 7

Passage A

(Orion Strings Ensemble)

1. **(3)**
    - **Correct Answer: B**
    - **Explanation**: Insert a comma after "Moreover": "**Moreover, many established critics appreciate** their willingness…" clarifies the transitional phrase.
2. **Adding how they modernize classical pieces**
    - **Correct Answer: A**
    - **Explanation**: "**They often incorporate instruments like electric guitars or electronic sound effects…**" clarifies the ensemble's modern touches after discussing "fresh elements" in [2].
3. **Origin story (quartet formed in college)**
    - **Correct Answer: A (Immediately after sentence [1])**
    - **Explanation**: Right after naming the ensemble and describing its innovative style, a brief origin story naturally fits.
4. **Revising sentence [4]**
    - **Correct Answer: A**
    - **Explanation**: "**This success has led to invitations from international festivals, ensuring that Orion Strings will continue to reach broader audiences.**"
5. **Concluding sentence emphasizing future plans and appeal**

- **Correct Answer: C**
- **Explanation**: "**Soon, the group will record a full-length album blending orchestral arrangements with modern soundscapes, aiming to captivate audiences worldwide.**" looks ahead positively.

Passage B

(Solar-powered charging stations)

1. **(4)**
    - **Correct Answer: B ("Although")**
    - **Explanation**: "**Although setting them up can be costly, the long-term benefits…**" is a clear contrast. "Despite that" is awkward.
2. **Where to note benefits for tourists**
    - **Correct Answer: C (After sentence [3])**
    - **Explanation**: Sentence [3] discusses convenience for outdoor events; adding a mention of tourists who also need quick recharges is logical next.
3. **Specifying costs** after sentence [4]**
    - **Correct Answer: A**
    - **Explanation**: "**Costs can range from $2,000 to $10,000 per unit…**" clarifies what "costly" means.
4. **Best transition in sentence [3]**
    - **Correct Answer: B ("For instance,")**
    - **Explanation**: "**For instance, this convenience is especially valuable…**" smoothly exemplifies how these stations are used.
5. **Adding detail about interactive screens** after sentence [1]**
    - **Correct Answer: C**
    - **Explanation**: "**Some stations even have interactive displays to show how much solar power is currently being harnessed.**" logically follows the introduction of solar-powered stations.

Mini-Test 8

Passage A

(Local theater productions)

1. **(3)**
    - **Correct Answer: B**
    - **Explanation**: "**Although some fear that limited budgets can reduce the quality of local productions, they frequently produce impressive performances…**" adds clarity with "that" and uses "can reduce."
2. **Clarifying the subject of "they"**
    - **Correct Answer: B ("the local productions themselves")**
    - **Explanation**: Replacing "they" with "the local productions themselves" removes ambiguity.
3. **Emphasizing volunteer impact** as final sentence
    - **Correct Answer: A**
    - **Explanation**: "**Because of their efforts, many volunteers find new career paths or life-long friendships.**" highlights the personal payoff for volunteers.
4. **Placement of improvisational workshops**
    - **Correct Answer: C (After sentence [2])**
    - **Explanation**: Sentence [2] mentions "experimenting with unique scripts and innovative staging," so referencing "improv workshops" fits perfectly next.
5. **Revising sentence [4]** for parallel structure
    - **Correct Answer: B**
    - **Explanation**: "**In many cases, dedicated volunteers manage everything from set design to marketing, ensuring a cohesive production.**" is concise and parallel.

Passage B

(Organic cotton clothing)

1. **(3)**
    - **Correct Answer: C**
    - **Explanation**: **"However, organic cotton can sometimes be more expensive…"** fits the contrast from sentence [2].
2. **Adding why organic cotton uses fewer pesticides**
    - **Correct Answer: C**
    - **Explanation**: **"Farmers who grow organic cotton often use natural pest control methods like introducing beneficial insects."** explains the "why" directly.
3. **Mentioning farmers receive fair price via certification**
    - **Correct Answer: B (After sentence [2])**
    - **Explanation**: Right after explaining fewer chemicals benefit farmers, it makes sense to note certification programs help them get fair pricing.
4. **Revising sentence [4]** to show cost-lowering efforts
    - **Correct Answer: A**
    - **Explanation**: **"Despite this, many companies look for ways to reduce production costs, such as improving logistics and sourcing local materials, so more people can afford these sustainable options."**
5. **Concluding sentence underscoring global impact**
    - **Correct Answer: C**
    - **Explanation**: **"By choosing organic cotton, consumers contribute to a healthier environment and support fair labor practices worldwide."** highlights broad positive consequences.

Final Note on Scoring and Review

After you've **timed yourself** on each Mini-Test and selected your answers, compare them with the solutions here. For any discrepancies, focus on **why** the correct choice is superior—whether due to grammar, punctuation, logic, or style. Over time, these insights will help you approach ACT English questions with confidence and efficiency.

SECTION B: MATH

CHAPTER 5

MATH CONCEPTS & KEY FORMULAS

5.1 PRE-ALGEBRA & ELEMENTARY ALGEBRA (OPERATIONS, LINEAR EQUATIONS)

A solid understanding of **pre-algebra** and **elementary algebra** is essential for success on the ACT Math section. These foundational skills underpin more advanced topics, ensuring you can tackle everything from basic arithmetic to early algebraic expressions with confidence. Below is a thorough overview of the concepts you need to master, along with key formulas and problem-solving tips.

1. Arithmetic Operations & Number Properties

1.1 Order of Operations (PEMDAS)

The correct sequence in which to perform operations is:

1. **P**arentheses (or any grouping symbols, like brackets)
2. **E**xponents (including roots)
3. **M**ultiplication and **D**ivision (from left to right)
4. **A**ddition and **S**ubtraction (from left to right)

Example:
Evaluate $6 - 2 \times (3 + 1)^2$.

1. Inside parentheses: $3 + 1 = 4$
2. Exponents: $4^2 = 16$
3. Multiplication: $2 \times 16 = 32$
4. Subtraction: $6 - 32 = -26$

1.2 Integers, Fractions, and Decimals

- **Adding & Subtracting Integers**:
  - Keep track of signs. If they are the same, add absolute values; if different, subtract absolute values and keep the sign of the larger absolute value.
- **Multiplying & Dividing Integers**:
  - A negative times a negative is positive; a negative times a positive is negative.
- **Fractions**:
  - To add or subtract fractions, find a **common denominator**.
  - To multiply, multiply numerators together and denominators together.
  - To divide, multiply by the reciprocal of the divisor.
- **Decimals**:
  - When adding or subtracting, line up the decimal points.
  - When multiplying, the total number of decimal places in the product equals the sum of the decimal places in the factors.

1.3 Absolute Values and Number Lines

- The **absolute value** of a number x is its distance from zero on the number line, denoted $| x |$.
- **Key Property**: $| x | \geq 0$ for all x.
- **Equations** involving absolute values may split into two scenarios: x inside the absolute value could be positive or negative, leading to different algebraic expressions.

2. Basic Algebraic Expressions

2.1 Variables & Constants

- A **variable** (e.g., x, y) represents an unknown or changeable quantity.
- A **constant** (e.g., 5, -3) has a fixed value.

2.2 Combining Like Terms

- **Like terms** have the same variable part raised to the same power.
  - Example: $3x$ and $-7x$ are like terms, but $3x$ and $3x^2$ are not.
- **Combine** like terms by adding or subtracting their coefficients.
  - Example: $5x + 2x = 7x$.

2.3 Distributive Property

The **distributive property** states that for real numbers a, b, and c:

$$a(b + c) = ab + ac$$

Example:

$$4(x + 5) = 4x + 20$$

Also apply this property in reverse for **factoring out** common terms:

$$6x + 12 = 6(x + 2)$$

2.4 Exponents & Roots (Basic)

- **Exponent Notation**: a^n means a multiplied by itself n times.
- **Multiplying with Same Base**: $a^m \times a^n = a^{m+n}$.
- **Dividing with Same Base**: $a^m \div a^n = a^{m-n}$.
- **Zero Exponent**: $a^0 = 1$ (provided $a \neq 0$).
- **Negative Exponents**: $a^{-n} = \frac{1}{a^n}$.
- **Square Roots**: $\sqrt{a^2} = |a|$. For the ACT, typically $\sqrt{}$ indicates the **principal (positive) root**.

3. Linear Equations

Linear equations represent **straight lines** on the coordinate plane and take forms such as $y = mx + b$ or $ax + by = c$. The ACT frequently tests your ability to **solve** these equations for x and interpret the slope-intercept form.

3.1 Solving One-Variable Linear Equations

1. **Isolate the Variable**:
   - Use inverse operations (adding vs. subtracting, multiplying vs. dividing) to get x alone on one side.
2. **Check for No/Infinite Solutions**:
   - If the equation simplifies to a contradiction (e.g., $0 = 5$), there is **no solution**.
   - If it simplifies to a true identity (e.g., $0 = 0$), there are **infinitely many solutions** (the solution set is all real numbers).

Example:

$$2x - 3 = 7$$

$$2x = 7 + 3 = 10$$

$$x = 5$$

3.2 Slope-Intercept Form

- The **slope-intercept form** of a line is $y = mx + b$, where:
  - m = slope (rise over run)
  - b = y-intercept (the y-value where the line crosses the y-axis)
- **Slope** m can be calculated if you have two points, (x_1, y_1) and (x_2, y_2):

$$m = \frac{y_2 - y_1}{x_2 - x_1}$$

3.3 Standard Form

- The **standard form** of a linear equation is $Ax + By = C$, where A, B, and C are integers (and $A \geq 0$).
- You can convert between **slope-intercept** and **standard** form as needed for different problem types.

3.4 Parallel & Perpendicular Lines

- **Parallel** lines have **equal slopes** (e.g., slopes m and m).
- **Perpendicular** lines have slopes that are **negative reciprocals** of each other (e.g., slopes m and $-\frac{1}{m}$, assuming $m \neq 0$).

4. Systems of Linear Equations (Basics)

While more complex systems might appear in **Intermediate Algebra**, the fundamentals can appear here:

- **System of Two Linear Equations**:
  - **Substitution Method**: Solve one equation for one variable, then substitute into the other equation.
  - **Elimination Method**: Add or subtract equations to eliminate one variable.
- **Possible Outcomes**:
  - **One unique solution** (the lines intersect at a single point).
  - **No solution** (the lines are parallel).
  - **Infinitely many solutions** (the lines coincide).

Example:

$$\begin{cases} x + y = 5 \\ 2x - y = 1 \end{cases}$$

Using elimination:

1. Add the equations: $(x + y) + (2x - y) = 5 + 1$
2. $3x = 6 \Rightarrow x = 2$
3. Substitute $x = 2$ into $x + y = 5 \Rightarrow 2 + y = 5 \Rightarrow y = 3$

Solution: $(2,3)$

5. Common Formulas & Tips

5.1 Formulas at a Glance

- **Slope**: $m = \frac{y_2 - y_1}{x_2 - x_1}$
- **Distance on a Number Line**: If a and b are points on a line, the distance is $|\ a - b\ |$.
- **Arithmetic Mean (Average)**: Mean $= \frac{\text{Sum of terms}}{\text{Number of terms}}$
- **Sum of Interior Angles in a Polygon** (though more relevant in geometry, can appear in earlier algebra contexts as well): $(n - 2) \times 180°$ for an n-sided polygon (especially triangles and quadrilaterals).

5.2 Quick Strategies for Pre-Algebra & Elementary Algebra

1. **Check for Extraneous Solutions**: If you perform operations like squaring both sides, verify solutions by plugging them back into the original equation. (More common in Intermediate Algebra but good to keep in mind.)
2. **Estimate & Eliminate**: If faced with multiple-choice answers, sometimes you can do a quick check or approximation to rule out unlikely options.
3. **Number Sense**: Simplify fractions and factor out common terms before you dive into complex calculations—this saves time and reduces mistakes.
4. **Watch Out for Negative Signs**: Keep track of minus signs, especially when distributing or factoring expressions.

Summary & Next Steps

Pre-algebra and elementary algebra topics lay the **cornerstone** for all subsequent math on the ACT. By mastering arithmetic operations, basic algebraic manipulation, and linear equations, you'll streamline your problem-solving and free up mental resources for more advanced questions in geometry, trigonometry, and beyond.

Next, in **Section 5.2: Intermediate Algebra & Functions**, we'll delve into quadratics, polynomials, inequalities, and function basics—vital areas for boosting your ACT Math score further.

5.2 INTERMEDIATE ALGEBRA & FUNCTIONS (QUADRATICS, INEQUALITIES, POLYNOMIALS)

Intermediate Algebra often appears in the **middle to later** questions of the ACT Math section, testing your fluency with more advanced equations, inequalities, and functions. Below is a thorough overview of the key concepts—**quadratic equations**, **inequalities**, **polynomials**, and **basic function principles**—along with problem-solving strategies and common pitfalls.

1. Quadratic Equations

A **quadratic equation** is typically written in the form $ax^2 + bx + c = 0$, where $a \neq 0$. The ACT frequently tests your ability to:

- Solve for x using factoring or the quadratic formula.
- Interpret quadratic graphs, particularly the vertex and roots (x-intercepts).

1.1 Factoring Quadratics

Factoring transforms a quadratic into a product of binomials:

$$ax^2 + bx + c = (px + q)(rx + s)$$

where $p \times r = a$ and $q \times s = c$, and $prx^2 + (ps + qr)x + qs = ax^2 + bx + c$.

Example:

$$x^2 + 5x + 6 = 0 \quad \rightarrow \quad (x + 2)(x + 3) = 0$$

Thus, $x = -2$ or $x = -3$.

1.2 Completing the Square

Completing the square rewrites a quadratic in **vertex form**:

$$ax^2 + bx + c \quad \rightarrow \quad a\left(x + \frac{b}{2a}\right)^2 + \text{constant}$$

Example:

$$x^2 + 6x + 5 = 0$$

1. Move constant aside: $x^2 + 6x = -5$
2. Half of 6 is 3; square it (9) and add to both sides:

$$x^2 + 6x + 9 = -5 + 9$$

3. Factor left side:

$$(x + 3)^2 = 4$$

4. Take square root:

$$x + 3 = \pm 2$$

$$x = -3 \pm 2 \quad \rightarrow \quad x = -1 \text{ or } x = -5$$

1.3 Quadratic Formula

When factoring is difficult or not feasible, use the **quadratic formula**:

$$x = \frac{-b \pm \sqrt{b^2 - 4ac}}{2a}$$

where the discriminant $\Delta = b^2 - 4ac$ indicates:

- $\Delta > 0$: 2 real solutions
- $\Delta = 0$: 1 real solution (double root)
- $\Delta < 0$: No real solutions (2 complex solutions)

1.4 Graphing Quadratics

A quadratic function $y = ax^2 + bx + c$:

- Opens **upward** if $a > 0$ and **downward** if $a < 0$.
- Has a **vertex** at $\left(-\frac{b}{2a}, f\left(-\frac{b}{2a}\right)\right)$.
- The x-intercepts (if they exist) are the solutions to $ax^2 + bx + c = 0$.
- The y-intercept occurs at $(0, c)$.

2. Inequalities

Inequalities show a range of possible solutions instead of a single value. You'll encounter linear, polynomial, and absolute value inequalities on the ACT.

2.1 Linear Inequalities

A **linear inequality** looks like $ax + b > 0$ or $ax + b \leq 5$. Solve similarly to linear equations:

1. **Isolate** x: Perform arithmetic operations on both sides.
2. **Reverse Inequality When Multiplying/Dividing by a Negative**:
   - Example: $-2x < 4 \quad \rightarrow \quad x > -2$.

The solution can be written in **inequality form** (e.g., $x > -2$) or **interval notation** (e.g., $(-2, \infty)$).

2.2 Compound Inequalities

A **compound inequality** combines two inequalities, often using "and" or "or."

- **"And"** (intersection): $2 < x < 7$ means x is between 2 and 7.
- **"Or"** (union): $x < -1$ or $x \geq 4$ represents all values less than -1 or greater than or equal to 4.

2.3 Polynomial Inequalities

For **higher-degree** inequalities like $x^2 - 5x + 6 > 0$:

1. Solve the related equation $x^2 - 5x + 6 = 0$ to find critical points (roots).
2. Plot these on a number line to divide it into intervals.
3. Test a point in each interval to see if the inequality holds there.
4. Combine intervals where the inequality is true.

2.4 Absolute Value Inequalities

An inequality such as $|x - 3| \leq 4$ expands to:

$$-4 \leq x - 3 \leq 4$$

$$-4 + 3 \leq x \leq 4 + 3$$

$$-1 \leq x \leq 7$$

For strict inequalities, e.g., $|x - 3| < 4$, the principle is similar, but the endpoint values are not included in the solution set.

3. Polynomials

A **polynomial** is an expression involving non-negative integer exponents of variables. The ACT may test polynomial arithmetic, factoring techniques, or the properties of polynomial functions.

3.1 Polynomial Operations

1. **Addition/Subtraction**: Combine like terms (same variable and exponent).
2. **Multiplication**: Distribute each term in the first polynomial over each term in the second polynomial.
3. **Division**: May involve **long division** or **synthetic division** if the polynomial is divided by a binomial of the form $x - a$.

3.2 Factoring Polynomials

Beyond quadratics, factoring can involve:

- **Greatest Common Factor (GCF)**: Factor out the highest coefficient and any common variables.
- **Grouping**: Group terms in pairs and factor out common terms from each pair.
- **Special Products**:
  - **Difference of Squares**: $a^2 - b^2 = (a - b)(a + b)$
  - **Sum/Difference of Cubes**:

$$a^3 - b^3 = (a - b)(a^2 + ab + b^2)$$

$$a^3 + b^3 = (a + b)(a^2 - ab + b^2)$$

3.3 Zeros & Roots of Polynomials

If $x - r$ is a factor of a polynomial $P(x)$, then r is a **root** (or zero) of $P(x)$. Solving for roots often involves:

- Factoring if possible.
- Using the **Remainder Theorem**: If $P(r) = 0$, then $x - r$ is a factor.

4. Introduction to Functions

A **function** is a rule that assigns each input exactly one output. The ACT might present function notation $f(x)$, transformations, or basic domain/range questions.

4.1 Function Notation

- $f(x)$ denotes the output when the input is x.

- Example: If $f(x) = x^2 + 1$, then $f(3) = 10$.

4.2 Domain & Range

- The **domain** is the set of all permissible x-values for $f(x)$.
- The **range** is the set of all possible output values $f(x)$ can take.

4.3 Basic Transformations

While more advanced transformations may go beyond ACT basics, you should recognize:

- **Vertical Shifts**: $f(x) + k$ moves the graph up or down.
- **Horizontal Shifts**: $f(x - h)$ moves the graph h units right (if $h > 0$) or left (if $h < 0$).
- **Reflections**: $-f(x)$ reflects vertically across the x-axis; $f(-x)$ reflects horizontally across the y-axis.

Key Formulas & Concepts

1. **Quadratic Formula**: $x = \frac{-b \pm \sqrt{b^2 - 4ac}}{2a}$
2. **Vertex of a Parabola**: $\left(-\frac{b}{2a}, f\left(-\frac{b}{2a}\right)\right)$
3. **Absolute Value Inequality**: $|x - a| < b \Leftrightarrow a - b < x < a + b$
4. **Difference of Squares**: $a^2 - b^2 = (a - b)(a + b)$
5. **Polynomial Remainder Theorem**: If a polynomial $P(x)$ is divided by $x - r$, the remainder is $P(r)$.

Tips for Success

1. **Practice Factoring**: Quick, accurate factoring can save time on the ACT—especially for quadratic and polynomial questions.
2. **Watch Signs**: Inequalities flip when multiplying/dividing by negative values. Also keep track of negatives in polynomial operations.
3. **Know When to Use the Quadratic Formula**: If factoring isn't straightforward (e.g., large coefficients, prime numbers), the formula is a surefire solution.
4. **Check Special Cases**: For absolute value and polynomial roots, test potential solutions to avoid extraneous answers.
5. **Use Graphical Insights**: A rough sketch of a parabola or polynomial can help you anticipate the number of real solutions or shape of the function.

Wrapping Up

Intermediate Algebra and basic function knowledge form a significant portion of the ACT Math test, bridging simpler pre-algebra concepts with more advanced topics like logarithms or advanced trigonometry. Mastering **quadratics, inequalities, polynomials**, and **functions** ensures you're well-equipped to handle a broad array of questions. Next, in **Section 5.3: Geometry & Trigonometry Essentials**, we'll dive into the shapes, volumes, and trigonometric ratios that round out the ACT Math syllabus.

5.3 GEOMETRY & TRIGONOMETRY ESSENTIALS (SHAPES, VOLUMES, TRIG RATIOS)

Geometry and trigonometry questions on the ACT range from basic principles (angles, perimeter, area) to more advanced concepts (3D volumes, trigonometric ratios). Mastery of these topics allows you to handle a variety of questions, from quick formula-based tasks to multi-step geometric reasoning problems. Below is a detailed overview of the essentials you need.

1. Basic Shapes & Properties

1.1 Lines, Angles, and Triangles

- **Lines and Angles**
  - **Straight Line**: Measures 180°.
  - **Complementary Angles**: Sum to 90°.
  - **Supplementary Angles**: Sum to 180°.
  - **Vertical Angles**: Formed by intersecting lines; they are **equal** in measure.
- **Triangles**
  - The sum of interior angles in any triangle is 180°.
  - **Types**:
    - **Right Triangle**: One angle is 90°.
    - **Isosceles**: Two sides (and two angles) are equal.
    - **Equilateral**: All sides and angles are equal (60° each angle).
  - **Pythagorean Theorem** (for right triangles):

$$a^2 + b^2 = c^2$$

where c is the hypotenuse.

1.2 Quadrilaterals & Polygons

- **Quadrilaterals**
  - Sum of interior angles = 360°.
  - Common types: Square, Rectangle, Parallelogram, Trapezoid.
    - **Square**: All sides equal, all angles 90°.
    - **Rectangle**: Opposite sides equal, all angles 90°.
    - **Parallelogram**: Opposite sides parallel and equal. Opposite angles equal.
    - **Trapezoid**: One pair of opposite sides parallel.
- **Polygons**
  - Sum of interior angles of an n-sided polygon:

$$(n - 2) \times 180°$$

1.3 Circles

- **Diameter (d)**: A line passing through the center from one point on the circle to another.
- **Radius (r)**: Half of the diameter.
- **Circumference**:

$$C = 2\pi r = \pi d$$

- **Area**:

$$A = \pi r^2$$

- **Arc Length**: For a circle of circumference C, an arc subtending θ degrees (out of 360°) has length

$$\text{Arc Length} = \frac{\theta}{360} \times C$$

- **Sector Area**:

$$\text{Sector Area} = \frac{\theta}{360} \times \pi r^2$$

2. Area & Perimeter of Common 2D Shapes

- **Rectangle**:
  - Perimeter: $P = 2(L + W)$
  - Area: $A = L \times W$
- **Square**:

- Perimeter: $P = 4s$
- Area: $A = s^2$

- **Triangle**:
  - Perimeter: $P = a + b + c$ (sum of all sides)
  - Area: $A = \frac{1}{2}(\text{base})(\text{height})$
- **Parallelogram**:
  - Area: $A = (\text{base})(\text{height})$
- **Trapezoid**:
  - Area:

$$A = \frac{(b_1 + b_2)}{2} \times h$$

where b_1 and b_2 are the lengths of the parallel sides, and h is the height.

(Remember, the height is the perpendicular distance from one base to the other.)

3. Volume & Surface Area of 3D Shapes

3.1 Prisms & Cylinders

- **Rectangular Prism**:
  - Volume: $V = \text{length} \times \text{width} \times \text{height}$
  - Surface Area: Sum of the areas of all 6 faces

$$S = 2(lw + lh + wh)$$

- **Cylinder**:
  - Volume: $V = \pi r^2 h$
  - Lateral Surface Area: $2\pi r \times h$
  - Total Surface Area: $2\pi r^2 + 2\pi rh$ (Top and bottom circles + curved surface)

3.2 Pyramids & Cones

- **Right Pyramid** (square base as an example):
  - Volume: $V = \frac{1}{3}(\text{Area of Base}) \times h$
- **Cone**:
  - Volume: $V = \frac{1}{3}\pi r^2 h$
  - Lateral Surface Area: $\pi r \times \ell$ (where ℓ is the slant height)
  - Total Surface Area: $\pi r^2 + \pi r\ell$

3.3 Spheres

- **Volume**:

$$V = \frac{4}{3}\pi r^3$$

- **Surface Area**:

$$S = 4\pi r^2$$

(Spheres are less common on the ACT, but still possible.)

4. Trigonometry Basics

Trigonometry on the ACT generally covers right-triangle ratios, the unit circle for specific angles, and basic trigonometric identities. You'll often see these concepts tied in with geometry.

4.1 Right Triangle Trig Ratios

For a right triangle with an acute angle θ, **opposite** side opp, **adjacent** side adj, and **hypotenuse** hyp:

- **Sine**: $\sin(\theta) = \frac{\text{opp}}{\text{hyp}}$
- **Cosine**: $\cos(\theta) = \frac{\text{adj}}{\text{hyp}}$
- **Tangent**: $\tan(\theta) = \frac{\text{opp}}{\text{adj}}$

4.2 Special Right Triangles

- **45-45-90 Triangle**:
    - Side ratios are $1:1:\sqrt{2}$.
    - The legs are equal; the hypotenuse is $\sqrt{2}$ times a leg.
- **30-60-90 Triangle**:
    - Side ratios are $1:\sqrt{3}:2$.
    - The shortest side (opposite 30°) is x, the longer leg (opposite 60°) is $x\sqrt{3}$, and the hypotenuse is $2x$.

4.3 Basic Trig Identities & Equations

- **Pythagorean Identity**:

$$\sin^2(\theta) + \cos^2(\theta) = 1$$

- **Tangent in Terms of Sine and Cosine**:

$$\tan(\theta) = \frac{\sin(\theta)}{\cos(\theta)}$$

- **Inverse Trigonometric Functions**: The ACT may ask for angles given the ratio. For instance, if $\sin(\theta) = 0.5$, then $\theta = \sin^{-1}(0.5)$. Familiarity with common angles (e.g., $30°, 45°, 60°$) helps here.

5. Additional Geometric & Trig Tips

1. **Draw Accurate Diagrams**: A well-labeled sketch can reveal relationships like parallel sides, special angles, or similar triangles.
2. **Look for Similar Triangles**: Proportional sides can simplify ratio-based questions.
3. **Use Known Formulas Efficiently**: Remember key area and volume formulas. The ACT often provides some formulas, but knowing them by heart saves time.
4. **Angle Chasing**: For polygons or circle geometry, angle properties (e.g., inscribed angles, central angles) can unlock quick solutions.
5. **Apply Trig to Non-Right Triangles (if needed)**: Occasionally, you might see the **Law of Sines** or **Law of Cosines** in advanced questions, but the standard ACT tends to focus on right-triangle trigonometry. If encountered, recall:
    - Law of Sines:

$$\frac{\sin(A)}{a} = \frac{\sin(B)}{b} = \frac{\sin(C)}{c}$$

    - Law of Cosines:

$$c^2 = a^2 + b^2 - 2ab\cos(C)$$

Final Thoughts

Geometry and trigonometry form a substantial part of the ACT Math section, requiring both **memory of formulas** and **analytical reasoning**. By mastering properties of shapes, calculating volumes, and applying trigonometric ratios, you'll be well-prepared for a wide range of questions—from straightforward computations to more intricate geometric proofs. In **Section 5.4: Calculator Usage & Quick Problem-Solving Tips**, we'll explore how to leverage calculators effectively and streamline your approach for faster, more accurate problem-solving.

5.4 CALCULATOR USAGE & QUICK PROBLEM-SOLVING TIPS

A **strategic calculator approach** can help you work more efficiently and avoid mistakes on the ACT Math section. While strong mental math skills are advantageous, the ACT allows you to use an approved calculator for certain steps. Below you'll find essential guidelines on **calculator usage**, alongside **problem-solving tips** to boost accuracy and speed.

1. Knowing Your Calculator

1.1 Approved Calculators

ACT Regulations generally permit:

- **Most graphing calculators** (e.g., TI-84 series),
- **Scientific calculators**,
- **Four-function calculators** (though these might be too limited for some tasks).

Not Allowed:

- Calculators with built-in computer algebra systems (CAS) that can perform symbolic manipulations or have QWERTY keyboards (e.g., TI-89, TI-Nspire CAS unless in a specific "non-CAS" mode).
- Internet-capable devices, laptops, cell phones, or tablets.

(Always check the latest guidelines on the official ACT website to confirm allowed models.)

1.2 Familiarity & Speed

- **Practice with the Calculator You'll Use**: Learning new calculator functions on test day wastes time and risks errors. Stick to a model you know well.
- **Explore Common Functions**: Make sure you're comfortable with basic operations, exponent keys, fraction input, and clearing the memory or mode settings.

1.3 Potential Pitfalls

- **Mode Errors**: Ensure the calculator is in **degree mode** for trigonometric problems (the ACT typically uses degrees, not radians).
- **Accidental Rounding**: If you store intermediate values, be cautious about rounding too early. Keep enough decimal places to maintain accuracy.
- **Time Loss**: Over-reliance on the calculator can slow you down. Some questions are faster to solve with mental math or by hand.

2. Quick Problem-Solving Techniques

2.1 Estimation & Elimination

- **Estimation**:
    - If you see an expression like $\sqrt{50}$, estimate it as $\sqrt{49} = 7$. For multiple-choice questions, approximate to see which answers are plausible.
    - For geometry problems with unusual decimals, a rough calculation of area or perimeter might help you eliminate extreme choices.

- **Elimination**:
  - If certain answer choices are obviously too large or too small, you can narrow your options quickly.
  - For algebraic equations, sometimes plugging in the answer choices to test them is more efficient than solving from scratch.

2.2 Plugging In Values

- **Strategic Substitution**:
  - When an algebraic expression feels cumbersome, try plugging in simple numbers (like 0, 1, or 2) for the variables—assuming the problem allows it (i.e., no constraints like $x \neq 0$).
  - If the expression matches a certain outcome, see which answer choice aligns with that outcome.
- **Plugging In for Variables in Word Problems**:
  - Word problems often describe real-life scenarios but can be boiled down to an equation. If you're stuck, guess a realistic value for the variable (e.g., "number of apples = 10") and see what the expression yields.

2.3 Back-Solving from Answer Choices

- **Efficient for Algebra/Geometry**:
  - If a question asks for a certain x and provides discrete answer choices, start with the **middle** choice. If it's too big or too small, you can decide which direction to go.
- **Check for Extraneous Solutions**:
  - Some equations (especially those involving absolute values or radicals) may produce "solutions" that don't satisfy the original equation. Always verify by plugging back in.

3. Timing & Pacing

3.1 Time Allocation

- The ACT Math section has **60 questions** with **60 minutes** total—**1 minute per question** on average. However, certain questions (especially later ones) may require more time. Plan to move quickly through easier questions so you can devote more time to tougher problems near the end.

3.2 Skipping & Returning

- **Mark and Move**: If you're stuck on a question, make a quick guess (since there's no penalty for guessing) and circle the question in your booklet. Return to it if you have time at the end.
- **Prioritize**: Easy or moderate questions first. Harder questions often involve multiple steps or advanced concepts like trigonometry or systems of equations. Aim to preserve a few minutes at the end to revisit these.

3.3 Practice Under Real Conditions

- **Simulate Test Day**: Find a quiet area, set a 60-minute timer, and do a full set of 60 math questions.
- **Use One Calculator**: Resist switching between calculators or fiddling with advanced modes. Mimic exam constraints closely.

4. Specific Calculator Strategies

1. **Smart Use of Parentheses**:
   - For expressions like $(4 + 5)/(3 \times 2)$, explicitly use parentheses to ensure your calculator interprets the input correctly.
2. **Trig Ratios & Inverse Trig**:
   - Double-check **degree mode** for angles. If your answer appears nonsensical (like a huge angle for a small ratio), see if your calculator is in radians.
3. **Memory Functions**:
   - Some calculators let you store specific values or expressions, reducing repeated typing. Just remember to label or recall correctly.

4. **Check Results for Reasonableness**:
   - If you compute a triangle's side length and get 300 for a side that's supposed to be smaller than the others, you may have made a mistake in data input.

5. Final Tips to Streamline Problem-Solving

1. **Draw Diagrams**: A quick sketch can clarify geometry problems or systems of equations that can be graphed.
2. **Identify Question Type**: Recognize if a problem is testing algebra, geometry, trigonometry, or a combination. This helps you recall the relevant formulas quickly.
3. **Simplify First**: Before reaching for the calculator, see if you can reduce fractions, factor out common terms, or combine like terms.
4. **Mark Key Words**: In word problems, highlight details like "maximum," "minimum," "exact," "approximately," or specific constraints (e.g., integer solutions only).
5. **Check Oddities**: Be mindful of domain restrictions (e.g., $x \neq 0$, angles must be between 0° and 180°, etc.). The ACT often includes subtle conditions that might change your solution approach.

Wrapping Up

Mastering **calculator usage** and refining **problem-solving tactics** can give you a significant edge on the ACT Math section. By combining careful planning, efficient pacing, and a clear-eyed approach to each problem, you'll be able to handle the exam's challenges with confidence. Up next, in **Chapter 6: Math Practice Drills**, you'll apply these strategies in **topic-focused exercises**, **mixed problem sets**, and **timed mini-tests** to solidify your understanding and further improve your speed and accuracy.

CHAPTER 6

MATH PRACTICE DRILLS

6.1 TOPIC-FOCUSED DRILLS (ALGEBRA, COORDINATE GEOMETRY, PLANE GEOMETRY, TRIG)

These **topic-focused drills** provide targeted practice in each major area of the ACT Math section. Work through the problems in **Algebra**, **Coordinate Geometry**, **Plane Geometry**, and **Trigonometry** to reinforce key concepts and sharpen your problem-solving skills. Each set includes **multiple-choice questions** (five answer choices, A–E) to mirror the ACT Math format. Refer to **Section 6.4: Thorough Answer Explanations** for detailed solutions and strategies.

A. Algebra Drills (25 Problems)

1. **If $2x - 3 = 13$, what is the value of x?**
   A. 5
   B. 6
   C. 7
   D. 8
   E. 10

2. **Which of the following is the solution to the inequality $3x + 1 > 7$?**
   A. $x > 2$
   B. $x > -2$
   C. $x < 2$
   D. $x < -2$
   E. $x \geq 3$

3. **For the system of equations:**

$$\begin{cases} 2x + y = 11 \\ x - y = 1 \end{cases}$$

   What is the ordered pair (x, y) that satisfies both?
   A. $(3,5)$
   B. $(4,3)$
   C. $(5,1)$
   D. $(6,-1)$
   E. $(7,4)$

4. **What are the solutions to the quadratic equation $x^2 - 5x + 6 = 0$?**
   A. $x = -6, x = 1$
   B. $x = -2, x = -3$
   C. $x = 2, x = 3$
   D. $x = -1, x = -6$
   E. $x = 5, x = 1$

5. **Which expression factors to $(2x - 1)(x + 4)$?**
   A. $2x^2 + 8x - x - 4$
   B. $2x^2 - x + 8x + 4$
   C. $2x^2 + 7x + 4$
   D. $2x^2 + 8x - x - 4$ but simplifies to $2x^2 + 7x - 4$
   E. $2x^2 + 7x - 4$

6. **If $P(x) = x^3 - 4x^2 + x - 1$, what is $P(2)$?**
   A. -3

B. -1
C. -7
D. 1
E. 3

7. **Simplify $\sqrt{50}$.**
A. $5\sqrt{2}$
B. $25\sqrt{2}$
C. $5\sqrt{5}$
D. $10\sqrt{2}$
E. 25

8. **Which of the following is equivalent to $(3x^2)(2x^5)$?**
A. $6x^7$
B. $5x^5$
C. $5x^8$
D. $6x^3$
E. $6x^{10}$

9. **If $\frac{x+3}{2} = 5$, what is the value of x?**
A. 7
B. 8
C. 9
D. 10
E. 13

10. **Solve the system $\begin{cases} 3x + 2y = 8 \\ 2x - y = 7 \end{cases}$. Which ordered pair (x, y) is correct?**
A. $(3,1)$
B. $(2,-1)$
C. $\left(\frac{22}{7}, -\frac{5}{7}\right)$
D. $(5,-4)$
E. $(1,-11)$

11. **Which of the following is the complete factorization of $3x^2 - 11x + 6$?**
A. $(3x + 2)(x - 3)$
B. $(3x - 2)(x + 3)$
C. $(3x - 2)(x - 3)$
D. $(3x + 1)(x - 6)$
E. Not factorable over the integers

12. **Solve the equation $x^2 - 2x = 8$.**
A. $x = 2, x = 4$
B. $x = -4, x = 2$
C. $x = 4, x = -2$
D. $x = 0, x = 8$
E. No real solutions

13. **Solve the inequality $2(x + 1) < 5$.**
A. $x < 3$
B. $x < \frac{5}{2}$
C. $x > \frac{3}{2}$
D. $x < \frac{3}{2}$
E. $x > 2$

14. **If $f(x) = x^2 - 3x + 2$, then $f(4) =$**
A. 2
B. 4
C. 6
D. 8
E. 10

15. **Which integer is a root of the polynomial $x^3 - 6x^2 + 5 = 0$?**
A. 1
B. 2
C. 3
D. 5
E. No integer solutions

16. **What is $(3x^2 + 2x - 1) + (2x^2 - 5x + 4)$?**
A. $5x^2 - 3x + 3$
B. $5x^2 + 7x - 3$
C. $1x^2 - 3x + 3$
D. $1x^2 - 3x + 4$
E. $5x^2 - 7x + 3$

17. **If $\frac{a}{b} = \frac{3}{4}$, which of the following must be true for $4a$?**
A. $4a = 3b$
B. $4a = 12$
C. $4a = \frac{3}{b}$
D. $4a = 4b$
E. $4a = 12b$

18. **A car travels at 60 mph for 2.5 hours. How far does it go?**
A. 90 miles
B. 100 miles
C. 120 milcs
D. 150 miles
E. 180 miles

19. **Solve the equation $| 2x - 1 |= 5$.**
A. $x = 2$ or $x = 3$
B. $x = 3$ or $x = -2$
C. $x = 2$ or $x = -3$
D. $x = 1$ or $x = 6$
E. $x = 4$ or $x = -4$

20. **In an arithmetic sequence, the 4th term is 11 and the 7th term is 20. What is the 10th term?**

- Let the first term be a and common difference d.

A. 26
B. 29
C. 32
D. 35
E. 38

21. **In a geometric sequence, the 2nd term is 6 and the 4th term is 54. What is the 5th term?**
A. 81
B. 108
C. 162
D. 216
E. 324

22. $\log_2(8) = ?$
   A. 1
   B. 2
   C. 3
   D. 4
   E. 8

23. **If $\log_{10}(x) = 2$, which of the following must be true?**
   A. $x = 2$
   B. $x = 20$
   C. $x = 100$
   D. $x = 1000$
   E. $x = 10$

24. **What is the sum of the first 4 terms of the arithmetic sequence where $a_1 = 5$ and $d = 3$?**
   A. 14
   B. 38
   C. 26
   D. 32
   E. 40

25. **Which of the following is the solution set of the inequality $\frac{x-2}{3} \geq 4$?**
   A. $x \leq 14$
   B. $x \geq 14$
   C. $x \leq \frac{10}{3}$
   D. $x < 2$
   E. $x \geq 6$

B. Coordinate Geometry Drills (15 Problems)

1. **The slope of the line passing through $(2,4)$ and $(6,12)$ is:**
   A. $\frac{4}{6}$
   B. $\frac{8}{4}$
   C. $\frac{12}{6}$
   D. 2
   E. $\frac{1}{2}$

2. **Which equation represents a line parallel to $y = 3x - 5$?**
   A. $y = 3x + 2$
   B. $y = x - 5$
   C. $y = -3x - 5$
   D. $y = -3x + 2$
   E. $x + y = 3$

3. **What is the x-intercept of the line $2x + 3y = 12$?**
   A. $(0,4)$
   B. $(2,0)$
   C. $(4,0)$
   D. $(6,0)$
   E. $(12,0)$

4. **If a line is perpendicular to $y = \frac{2}{3}x - 1$, which of the following could be its slope?**
   A. $\frac{2}{3}$
   B. $\frac{3}{2}$

C. $-\frac{3}{2}$
D. $-\frac{2}{3}$
E. 0

5. **In the coordinate plane, the midpoint of the segment joining $(-2,4)$ and $(6,-2)$ is:**
A. $(4,-6)$
B. $(2,1)$
C. $(3,2)$
D. $(2,0)$
E. $(4,1)$

6. **Which ordered pair lies on the line $y = 2x - 3$?**
A. $(0,-2)$
B. $(2,2)$
C. $(3,3)$
D. $(1,-1)$
E. $(2,1)$

7. **What is the distance between the points $(1,2)$ and $(5,2)$?**
A. 2
B. 3
C. 4
D. $\sqrt{16}$
E. 6

8. **A circle in the coordinate plane has equation $(x-2)^2 + (y+1)^2 = 16$. What is its center?**
A. $(2,-1)$
B. $(-2,1)$
C. $(2,1)$
D. $(0,-1)$
E. $(2,0)$

9. **If the slope of a line is -3 and it passes through $(1,4)$, which of the following points also lies on this line?**
A. $(2,7)$
B. $(2,1)$
C. $(0,4)$
D. $(1,1)$
E. $(4,-5)$

10. **Which of the following could be the equation of a vertical line?**
A. $y = 5$
B. $y = 0$
C. $x = -2$
D. $y = -2x + 6$
E. $2x + y = 4$

11. **The line $y = \frac{1}{2}x + 4$ is translated 3 units down. Which is the new equation?**
A. $y = \frac{1}{2}x + 7$
B. $y = \frac{1}{2}x + 1$
C. $y = \frac{1}{2}(x-3) + 4$
D. $y = \frac{1}{2}x - 3$
E. $y = -\frac{1}{2}x + 4$

12. **What is the slope of the line $3x + 2y = 10$?**
   A. $-\frac{3}{2}$
   B. $\frac{3}{2}$
   C. $\frac{2}{3}$
   D. $-\frac{2}{3}$
   E. 0

13. **Which point is on the line segment connecting $(-1, -1)$ and $(4,9)$ and divides it into two equal lengths?**
   A. $\left(\frac{3}{2}, 4\right)$
   B. $(2,4)$
   C. $(1,4)$
   D. $\left(\frac{5}{2}, 8\right)$
   E. $(0,0)$

14. **In the equation $y = -2x + 6$, what is the y-intercept?**
   A. -2
   B. 3
   C. 6
   D. -6
   E. $\frac{6}{-2}$

15. **Which equation represents a line passing through $(0,2)$ and $(2,0)$?**
   A. $y = x + 2$
   B. $y = -x + 2$
   C. $y = 2x + 2$
   D. $y = -\frac{1}{2}x + 2$
   E. $y = \frac{1}{2}x + 2$

C. Plane Geometry Drills (15 Problems)

1. **In triangle ABC, angle $A = 50°$, angle $B = 70°$. What is angle C?**
   A. 60°
   B. 70°
   C. 80°
   D. 90°
   E. 100°

2. **A rectangle has a perimeter of 26 units. If its length is 8, what is its width?**
   A. 5
   B. 8
   C. 10
   D. 13
   E. 26

3. **A circle has a radius of 5. What is its area?**
   A. 5π
   B. 10π
   C. 25π
   D. 50π
   E. 100π

4. **The volume of a rectangular box is 480 in^3. If length = 10 in and width = 8 in, what is its height in inches?**
   A. 4
   B. 5
   C. 6
   D. 8
   E. 12

5. **A trapezoid has bases 6 and 10, and a height of 4. What is its area?**
   A. 16
   B. 32
   C. 40
   D. 64
   E. 80

6. **A square has side length 7. What is its area?**
   A. 7
   B. 14
   C. 28
   D. 49
   E. 56

7. **In $\triangle DEF$, if $DE = 5$, $EF = 5$, and $DF = 6$, which statement best describes $\triangle DEF$?**
   A. It is an isosceles triangle.
   B. It is an equilateral triangle.
   C. It is a right triangle.
   D. It cannot exist by the triangle inequality.
   E. It is a scalene triangle.

8. **If two parallel lines are cut by a transversal, which pair of angles must be equal?**
   A. Alternate interior angles
   B. Adjacent angles
   C. Exterior angles on the same side of the transversal
   D. Complementary angles
   E. Supplementary angles

9. **A right triangle has legs of length 6 and 8. What is the length of its hypotenuse?**
   A. $\sqrt{14}$
   B. $\sqrt{100}$
   C. 8
   D. 10
   E. 12

10. **The measure of an interior angle of a regular hexagon is:**
   A. 90°
   B. 108°
   C. 120°
   D. 135°
   E. 150°

11. **What is the circumference of a circle with diameter 12?**
   A. 12π
   B. 24π
   C. 36π
   D. 6π
   E. 48π

12. **In a parallelogram, opposite sides are**
    A. Not equal in length and never parallel
    B. Equal in length and parallel
    C. Equal in length but never parallel
    D. Parallel, but the diagonals are perpendicular
    E. Congruent only if it's a rectangle

13. **A triangle has sides of lengths 4, 7, and 9. Which best describes it?**
    A. Equilateral
    B. Isosceles
    C. Right triangle
    D. Obtuse triangle
    E. Cannot be determined

14. **A rectangular prism has dimensions 4 by 5 by 10. What is its surface area?**

- Surface Area $= 2(lw + lh + wh)$.
    A. 100
    B. 120
    C. 220
    D. 140
    E. 160

15. **In $\triangle ABC$, the side lengths are $AB = 8$, $BC = 8$, and $AC = 8$. What is the measure of each interior angle?**
    A. 45°
    B. 60°
    C. 90°
    D. 120°
    E. Cannot be determined from the given information

D. Trigonometry Drills (15 Problems)

1. **In a right triangle, if $\sin(\theta) = \frac{3}{5}$ and θ is acute, then $\cos(\theta) =$**
    A. $\frac{4}{5}$
    B. $\frac{3}{5}$
    C. $\frac{5}{4}$
    D. $\frac{3}{4}$
    E. $\frac{4}{3}$

2. **Which angle θ satisfies $\tan(\theta) = 1$?**
    A. 30°
    B. 45°
    C. 60°
    D. 90°
    E. 120°

3. **A 30-60-90 triangle has a hypotenuse of 14. What is the length of the shorter leg?**
    A. 7
    B. $7\sqrt{3}$
    C. $\frac{14}{\sqrt{3}}$
    D. $\frac{14\sqrt{3}}{2}$
    E. $7\sqrt{2}$

4. **For a right triangle with acute angles α and β, if $\sin(\alpha) = \frac{4}{5}$ and $\alpha + \beta = 90°$, what is $\tan(\beta)$?**

A. $\frac{4}{5}$
B. $\frac{3}{4}$
C. $\frac{4}{3}$
D. $\frac{5}{4}$
E. $\frac{3}{5}$

5. **In $\triangle ABC$, $AB = 10$, $BC = 14$, and $\angle B = 90°$. If $\sin(A) = \frac{10}{\text{hypotenuse}}$, which of the following is true?**

A. The hypotenuse is 14, so $\sin(A) = \frac{10}{14}$.
B. $AC = 4$, so $\sin(A) = \frac{4}{10}$.
C. $\triangle ABC$ cannot be right-angled with the given sides.
D. $AC = \sqrt{196 - 100} = \sqrt{96}$.
E. $\sin(A) = \frac{10}{\sqrt{196}}$.

6. **If $\cos(\theta) = \frac{12}{13}$ for an acute angle θ, then $\sin(\theta) =$**

A. $\frac{5}{13}$
B. $\frac{12}{5}$
C. $\frac{13}{5}$
D. $\frac{13}{12}$
E. $\frac{\sqrt{5}}{13}$

7. **Which of the following angles satisfies $\sin(\theta) = \frac{\sqrt{2}}{2}$?**

A. 30°
B. 45°
C. 60°
D. 90°
E. 120°

8. **A right triangle has legs 9 and 12. If θ is the angle opposite the leg of length 9, then $\tan(\theta) =$**

A. $\frac{9}{12}$
B. $\frac{12}{9}$
C. $\frac{9}{\sqrt{81+144}}$
D. $\frac{12}{\sqrt{81+144}}$
E. 1

9. **In a 45-45-90 triangle, each leg measures 6. What is the hypotenuse?**

A. 6
B. $6\sqrt{2}$
C. 12
D. $\frac{12}{\sqrt{2}}$
E. $\frac{6}{2}$

10. **If $\csc(\theta) = \frac{5}{3}$, then $\sin(\theta) =$**

A. $\frac{5}{3}$

B. $\frac{3}{5}$
C. $\frac{4}{5}$
D. $\frac{5}{4}$
E. 1

11. **Which identity is always true for an acute angle θ?**
    A. $\sin^2(\theta) + \cos^2(\theta) = 1$
    B. $\sin(\theta) \cdot \cos(\theta) = 1$
    C. $\tan(\theta) = \frac{\cos(\theta)}{\sin(\theta)}$
    D. $\sin(\theta) = \tan(\theta) \cdot \cos(\theta)$
    E. $\sec^2(\theta) = \cot^2(\theta) + 1$

12. **If $\tan(\theta) = 2$, which expression equals $\sin(\theta)$ assuming θ is acute?**
    A. $\frac{2}{\sqrt{1+2^2}} = \frac{2}{\sqrt{5}}$
    B. $\frac{2}{2^2+1} = \frac{2}{5}$
    C. $\frac{\sqrt{5}}{2}$
    D. $\sqrt{1+2^2}$
    E. $\frac{1}{\sqrt{5}}$

13. **In a right triangle, if one acute angle is $30°$, which is the sine of the other acute angle?**
    A. $\frac{1}{2}$
    B. $\frac{\sqrt{3}}{2}$
    C. $\frac{\sqrt{2}}{2}$
    D. $\frac{3}{2}$
    E. 1

14. **Which of the following angles has $\cos(\theta) = 0$?**
    A. 30°
    B. 60°
    C. 90°
    D. 120°
    E. 180°

15. **A right triangle has hypotenuse 20 and one angle θ with $\cos(\theta) = \frac{4}{5}$. What is the length of the leg adjacent to θ?**
    A. 16
    B. 12
    C. 10
    D. 8
    E. 4

Using These Drills

1. Work through each set under **timed conditions** to build speed and accuracy.
2. Check answers in **Section 6.4: Thorough Answer Explanations** to see how each solution is reached.
3. Focus on **why** an answer is correct and **why** others are incorrect—this deeper insight helps you master the concepts rather than just memorize solutions.

These **Algebra, Coordinate Geometry, Plane Geometry, and Trigonometry** exercises offer a broad sampling of the math skills tested on the ACT. Good luck!

6.2 MIXED PROBLEM SETS (INCREASING DIFFICULTY)

In these **mixed problem sets**, you'll encounter questions that blend concepts from **algebra, geometry, trigonometry, and more**—mimicking the diverse range of topics on the ACT Math section. Each set is designed to **escalate in difficulty**, starting with simpler problems and moving toward more complex, multi-step questions. Practice pacing yourself, applying problem-solving strategies, and recognizing when a quick substitution or estimation approach might be your best route.

Set 1 (Medium Difficulty)

1. **Algebra / Exponents**
   If $2^{x+1} = 32$, what is the value of x?
   A. 3
   B. 4
   C. 5
   D. 6
   E. 7

2. **Geometry / Circles**
   A circle has a circumference of 24π. What is the circle's radius?
   A. 4
   B. 6
   C. 8
   D. 12
   E. 24

3. **Systems of Equations**

$$\begin{cases} x + 2y = 7 \\ 3x - 2y = 1 \end{cases}$$

   What is the ordered pair (x, y) that satisfies both equations?
   A. $(1,3)$
   B. $\left(2,\frac{5}{2}\right)$
   C. $(3,2)$
   D. $\left(4,\frac{3}{2}\right)$
   E. $(5,1)$

4. **Inequalities**
   Which inequality is equivalent to $-3(x - 2) > -6$?
   A. $x - 2 < 2$
   B. $x - 2 > 2$
   C. $x + 2 > 2$
   D. $x < 0$
   E. $x > 0$

5. **Right Triangles**
   A right triangle has legs of length 6 and 8. What is the length of its hypotenuse?
   A. 7
   B. 9
   C. 10
   D. $\sqrt{100}$
   E. 14

6. **Factoring Polynomials**
   Which of the following expressions is a factorization of $4x^2 + 4x - 3$?
   A. $(4x - 3)(x + 1)$

B. $(2x-1)(2x+3)$
C. $(4x+3)(x-1)$
D. $(2x+3)(2x-1)$
E. $(2x-3)(2x-1)$

7. **Coordinate Geometry**
   The line $y = 2x + 1$ intersects the line $y = -x + 10$ at point P. What are the coordinates of P?
   A. (3,7)
   B. (2,5)
   C. (1,3)
   D. (1,9)
   E. (4,3)

Set 2 (More Challenging)

1. **Polynomials / Synthetic Division**
   If $x = -2$ is a root of the polynomial $x^3 + 3x^2 - 4x - 12$, what is the other factor after dividing by $(x+2)$?
   A. $x^2 + x - 6$
   B. $x^2 - 3x - 6$
   C. $x^2 + 5x + 6$
   D. $x^2 + x + 6$
   E. $x^2 + x - 6$

2. **Word Problem / System of Equations**
   A landscaping company charges a fixed fee for initial consultation and then a per-hour rate. If a 2-hour job costs \$120 and a 5-hour job costs \$210, which system of equations represents the situation (where f is the fixed fee, and r is the hourly rate)?
   A.
   $$\begin{cases} 2f + 1r = 120 \\ 5f + 1r = 210 \end{cases}$$
   B.
   $$\begin{cases} f + 2r = 120 \\ f + 5r = 210 \end{cases}$$
   C.
   $$\begin{cases} 2 + 120r = f \\ 5 + 210r = f \end{cases}$$
   D.
   $$\begin{cases} f + 2r = 120 \\ f + 5r = 210 \end{cases}$$
   E.
   $$\begin{cases} 2f + 2r = 120 \\ 5f + 5r = 210 \end{cases}$$

3. **Circles / Angles**
   In a circle, an arc subtends a central angle of 60°. If the circle's radius is 9, what is the length of the arc?
   A. 3π
   B. 6π
   C. 9π
   D. 12π
   E. 18π

4. **Plane Geometry / Coordinate Plane**
   A rectangle is placed in the coordinate plane with one vertex at the origin $(0,0)$ and the opposite vertex at $(6,4)$. Which of the following points does **not** lie on the perimeter of this rectangle?
   A. $(0,4)$
   B. $(6,0)$
   C. $(3,4)$
   D. $(6,2)$
   E. $(4,3)$

5. **Logarithms & Exponents**
   If $\log_2(16) = x$ and $\log_3(81) = y$, what is $\frac{x}{y}$?
   A. 1
   B. 2
   C. $\frac{3}{2}$
   D. $\frac{4}{3}$
   E. 4

6. **Trigonometry / Law of Sines**
   In $\triangle ABC$, $\angle A = 30°$, $\angle B = 50°$, and side $BC = 10$. Using the Law of Sines, what is the length of side AC? (Note: $\angle C = 100°$.)
   A. $\frac{10\sin(30°)}{\sin(50°)}$
   B. $\frac{10\sin(50°)}{\sin(30°)}$
   C. $\frac{10\sin(100°)}{\sin(30°)}$
   D. $\frac{10\sin(50°)}{\sin(100°)}$
   E. $\frac{10\sin(30°)}{\sin(100°)}$

7. **Applied Geometry / Volume & Surface Area**
   A right circular cylinder has a volume of 216π cubic inches. If its height is 6 inches, what is the total surface area of this cylinder?

   - **Recall**: Volume of a cylinder $V = \pi r^2 h$; Surface area $S = 2\pi r^2 + 2\pi r h$.
     A. 36π
     B. 72π
     C. 108π
     D. 144π
     E. 180π

Best Practices for Mixed Sets

1. **Identify the Concept**: Before diving into calculations, pinpoint the main idea (e.g., system of equations, geometry theorem).
2. **Check for Shortcuts**: Sometimes plugging in answer choices or using a known geometry ratio is faster than traditional algebraic methods.
3. **Manage Your Time**: As difficulty increases, some questions may take longer. Don't get bogged down—move on if stuck, then return if time allows.
4. **Always Verify the Result**: Especially if you use back-solving or an approximation. A quick mental check can save you from careless errors.

Next Steps

After working through these sets, move on to **Section 6.3: Timed Mini-Tests & Strategies for Pacing**, where you'll face **shorter, high-pressure quizzes** designed to simulate real ACT conditions. Finally, consult **Section 6.4** for **Thorough Answer Explanations**, ensuring you understand the reasoning behind each correct solution.

6.3 TIMED MINI-TESTS & STRATEGIES FOR PACING

The **ACT Math section** allots **60 minutes** for **60 questions**, which translates to an average of **1 minute per question**. However, questions range from relatively simple to quite complex, so **pacing** is crucial. In this section, you'll find **two mini-tests** designed to simulate the time pressure and variety of the ACT. Each mini-test includes a mix of algebra, geometry, and trigonometry questions—like you'd see in the actual exam.

Recommended approach:

- Set a **time limit** for each mini-test (e.g., 10 questions in 10 minutes).
- Work through the problems in order.
- If a question stumps you, make your best educated guess, mark it, and return if time allows.

Mini-Test 1 (10 Questions, ~10 Minutes)

1. **Coordinate Geometry**
   A line passes through the points $(-1,2)$ and $(3,6)$. What is the slope of this line?
   A. $\frac{4}{2}$
   B. $\frac{6}{3}$
   C. 2
   D. $\frac{2}{4}$
   E. 1

2. **Algebraic Expressions**
   Which of the following simplifies to $3x^2 - 4x + 1$?
   A. $(x^2 - 4x + 1) + (2x^2)$
   B. $(3x^2 + x) - (4x - 1)$
   C. $(2x^2 - 4x) + (x^2 + 1)$
   D. $(2x^2 + x) + (x^2 - 4x + 1)$
   E. $(4x^2 - 1) - (x^2 + 4x)$

3. **Systems of Equations**

$$\begin{cases} 2x + y = 10 \\ x - y = 1 \end{cases}$$

   Solve for x.
   A. $\frac{11}{3}$.
   B. 4
   C. 5
   D. 6
   E. 7

4. **Quadratic Equations**
   The roots of $x^2 - 4x - 5 = 0$ are:
   A. 5 and -1
   B. 1 and -5
   C. 4 and -1
   D. 3 and 1
   E. 2 and -5

5. **Inequalities**
   Solve $-x + 3 > 7$.
   A. $x > -4$
   B. $x < -4$
   C. $x > 10$

D. $x < 10$
E. $x < 4$

6. **Trigonometry**
   In a right triangle, if $\cos(\theta) = \frac{4}{5}$, then $\sin(\theta)$ is:
   A. $\frac{3}{5}$
   B. $\frac{1}{5}$
   C. $\frac{4}{5}$
   D. $\frac{5}{4}$
   E. $\frac{9}{16}$
7. **Geometry / Circles**
   If a circle has a radius of 6, what is its circumference?
   A. 6π
   B. 12π
   C. 18π
   D. 24π
   E. 36π
8. **Plane Geometry**
   A trapezoid has bases of lengths 8 and 12, and a height of 5. What is its area?
   A. 20
   B. 40
   C. 50
   D. 80
   E. 100
9. **Exponents**
   Simplify $(x^3)^2$.
   A. x^5
   B. x^6
   C. x^9
   D. x^2
   E. $x^{1/6}$
10. **Problem-Solving**
    A car travels 150 miles in 3 hours. At this rate, how long does it take to travel 350 miles?
    A. 5 hours
    B. 6 hours
    C. 7 hours
    D. 8 hours
    E. 10 hours

(Stop here if 10 minutes have elapsed.)

Mini-Test 2 (10 Questions, ~10 Minutes)

1. **Factoring Polynomials**
   Factor $6x^2 + x - 2$.
   A. $(3x - 2)(2x + 1)$
   B. $(3x + 1)(2x - 2)$
   C. $(2x - 1)(3x + 2)$
   D. $(6x - 2)(x + 1)$
   E. $(3x - 1)(2x + 2)$

2. **Coordinate Geometry**
Which point lies on the line $y = -x + 4$?
A. $(0,0)$
B. $(2,2)$
C. $(4,0)$
D. $(1,3)$
E. $(3,3)$

3. **Systems / Word Problem**
A phone plan charges $15 per month plus $0.10 per minute. If your monthly bill was $31.50, how many minutes did you use?
A. 16.5
B. 100
C. 165
D. 200
E. 315

4. **Geometry / Triangles**
In a right triangle, the hypotenuse is 13 and one leg is 5. Find the other leg.
A. 8
B. 10
C. 12
D. $\sqrt{169}$
E. 18

5. **Inequalities**
Which inequality describes all x such that $2x - 5 \leq 3$?
A. $x \leq -4$
B. $x \geq 4$
C. $x \leq 4$
D. $x \leq 1$
E. $x \geq 1$

6. **Logarithms**
If $\log_{10}(x) = 2$, which of the following is true?
A. $x = 2$
B. $x = 10^2$
C. $x = 100$
D. Both B and C are correct.
E. $(10^2)^2 = x$

7. **Trigonometry**
For a right triangle with angles 30°, 60°, and 90°, the side opposite 30° measures 6. What is the hypotenuse?
A. 6
B. $6\sqrt{3}$
C. 12
D. $3\sqrt{6}$
E. $6\sqrt{2}$

8. **Advanced Geometry**
The volume of a cylinder is 225π cubic inches. If its radius is 5, what is its height?
A. 4.5
B. 5
C. 9
D. 15
E. 25

9. **Expressions & Radicals**
   Simplify $\sqrt{8} \cdot \sqrt{2}$.
   A. $\sqrt{10}$
   B. $\sqrt{16}$
   C. 4
   D. $2\sqrt{2}$
   E. $2\sqrt{8}$

10. **Coordinate Geometry**
   A line is perpendicular to $y = 3x + 1$ and passes through the point $(0,4)$. Which is its equation?
   A. $y = -\frac{1}{3}x + 4$
   B. $y = -3x + 4$
   C. $y = 3x + 4$
   D. $y = \frac{1}{3}x + 4$
   E. $y = -\frac{1}{3}x - 4$

(Stop here if 10 minutes have elapsed.)

Mini-Test 3 (10 Questions, ~10 Minutes)

1. **Exponents & Simplification**
   If $(x^4)^3 = x^n$, what is n?
   A. 12
   B. 7
   C. 1
   D. 4
   E. 9

2. **Solving Linear Equations**
   Solve for y in the equation $2y + 3 = 15$.
   A. $y = -9$
   B. $y = 6$
   C. $y = 9$
   D. $y = 12$
   E. $y = 18$

3. **Trigonometry (Right Triangles)**
   In a right triangle, $\sin(\theta) = \frac{1}{2}$. Which angle measure could θ be (assuming θ is acute)?
   A. 30°
   B. 45°
   C. 60°
   D. 90°
   E. 15°

4. **Systems of Equations**

$$\begin{cases} x + y = 9 \\ x - y = 3 \end{cases}$$

   Find x.
   A. 1
   B. 2
   C. 3
   D. 4
   E. 6

5. **Coordinate Geometry (Slope)**
   The slope of the line passing through points (4,3) and (6,7) is:
   A. 2
   B. 1
   C. $\frac{4}{2}$
   D. 3
   E. $\frac{1}{2}$

6. **Polynomials (Factoring)**
   Which factorization is correct for $x^2 + x - 6$?
   A. $(x - 2)(x - 3)$
   B. $(x + 2)(x - 3)$
   C. $(x + 3)(x + 2)$
   D. $(x - 6)(x + 1)$
   E. $(x - 2)(x + 3)$

7. **Plane Geometry (Perimeter & Area)**
   A rectangle has width $w = 5$ and length $l = 9$. What is its perimeter?
   A. 14
   B. 28
   C. 45
   D. 20
   E. 32

8. **Word Problem (Ratio / Proportions)**
   If 3 pounds of apples cost $4.50, how much will 5 pounds cost at the same rate?
   A. $6.00
   B. $7.50
   C. $5.00
   D. $9.00
   E. $7.00

9. **Inequalities**
   Solve $4x - 2 \leq 10$.
   A. $x \leq 3$
   B. $x \geq 3$
   C. $x \leq 4$
   D. $x \leq 2$
   E. $x \geq 2$

10. **Circles**
    A circle has diameter $d = 10$. What is its area?
    A. 25π
    B. 50π
    C. 100π
    D. 10π
    E. 5π

(Time's up after ~10 minutes.)

Mini-Test 4 (10 Questions, ~10 Minutes)

1. **Quadratic Equation**
   What are the solutions to $x^2 - 2x - 8 = 0$?
   A. $x = 4, x = -2$
   B. $x = 2, x = -4$
   C. $x = -2, x = -4$

D. $x = 2, x = 4$
E. $x = -2, x = 4$

2. **Coordinate Geometry (Midpoint)**
If M is the midpoint of the segment joining $(2,-2)$ and $(6,2)$, what are the coordinates of M?
A. $(8,4)$
B. $(3,0)$
C. $(4,0)$
D. $(2,2)$
E. $(4,-1)$

3. **Logarithms**
Which equation is equivalent to $\log_5(125) = k$?
A. $k^5 = 125$
B. $5^k = 125$
C. $5^{125} = k$
D. $\log_{125}(5) = k$
E. $\log_5(5) = 125$

4. **Trigonometry (Tangent)**
In a right triangle, if $\tan(\alpha) = \frac{5}{12}$, which ratio represents $\sin(\alpha)$?
   - Hint: Recall $\tan(\alpha) = \frac{\text{opp}}{\text{adj}}$ and $\sin(\alpha) = \frac{\text{opp}}{\text{hyp}}$.

   A. $\frac{5}{13}$
   B. $\frac{12}{13}$
   C. $\frac{5}{12}$
   D. $\frac{5}{\sqrt{119}}$
   E. $\frac{12}{\sqrt{119}}$

5. **Systems of Equations / Elimination**

$$\begin{cases} 4x + 2y = 14 \\ 2x + 3y = 13 \end{cases}$$

Which ordered pair (x, y) solves the system?
A. $(2,3)$
B. $\left(2, \frac{3}{2}\right)$
C. $\left(3, \frac{2}{3}\right)$
D. $(3,1)$
E. $(4,1)$

6. **Geometry (Volume)**
A right rectangular prism has length 8, width 3, and height 5. What is its volume?
A. 16
B. 24
C. 40
D. 120
E. 240

7. **Factoring Polynomials**
Factor completely: $2x^2 + 7x + 3$.
A. $(2x + 1)(x + 3)$
B. $(2x + 3)(x + 1)$
C. $(2x + 1)(x + 3)$ but results in $2x^2 + 6x + x + 3 = 2x^2 + 7x + 3$ so check carefully.

D. $(2x - 1)(x + 3)$
E. $(x + 1)(x + 3)$

8. **Plane Geometry (Angles)**
A pentagon has internal angles summing to:
A. $360°$
B. $540°$
C. $720°$
D. $900°$
E. $1080°$

9. **Word Problem (Distance / Rate)**
A train travels at 40 mph for 3 hours and then 50 mph for 2 hours. How far does it travel in total?
A. 130 miles
B. 150 miles
C. 160 miles
D. 170 miles
E. 220 miles

10. **Inequalities**
Which solution set satisfies $2x + 1 < 0$?
A. $x > -\frac{1}{2}$
B. $x < -\frac{1}{2}$
C. $x > 0$
D. $x = -\frac{1}{2}$
E. $x < 0$

(Stop here if ~10 minutes have elapsed.)

Test-Taking Tips

1. **Remember the 1-Minute Rule**: On the official ACT, you have 60 questions in 60 minutes. Practice quickly reading each question and identifying the main concept.
2. **Flag Hard Questions**: Skip and return if you're stuck—no point is worth sacrificing multiple others.
3. **Use Estimation**: If the numbers are awkward, approximate to see which answer is reasonable.
4. **Never Leave Blanks**: There's **no penalty for guessing**, so fill in every bubble.
5. **Review**: If you finish early, double-check for arithmetic or sign errors.

By cycling through these mini-tests with discipline and carefully reviewing your mistakes, you'll continue **building both speed and precision**—key ingredients for excelling on the ACT Math section.

6.4 DETAILED ANSWER EXPLANATIONS

Topic-Focused Drills (Algebra, Coordinate Geometry, Plane Geometry, Trig)

A. Algebra Drills (25 Questions)

1. $2x - 3 = 13$
   - **Answer: D. 8** (since $x = 8$).
2. $3x + 1 > 7$
   - **Answer: A.** $x > 2$
3. **System** $\begin{cases} 2x + y = 11 \\ x - y = 1 \end{cases}$
   - **Answer: B.** $(4,3)$

4. $x^2 - 5x + 6 = 0$
    - **Answer: C.** $x = 2, x = 3$
5. **Factors to** $(2x - 1)(x + 4)$
    - **Answer: E.** $2x^2 + 7x - 4$
6. **If** $P(x) = x^3 - 4x^2 + x - 1$**, what is** $P(2)$ **?**
    - **Answer:** *C. -7*
7. $\sqrt{50}$
    - **Answer: A.** $5\sqrt{2}$
8. $(3x^2)(2x^5)$
    - **Answer: A.** $6x^7$
9. $\frac{x+3}{2} = 5$
    - **If** $\frac{x+3}{2} = 5$**, what is the value of** x**?**
    - **Answer: A. 7**
10. **System** $\begin{cases} 3x + 2y = 8 \\ 2x - y = 7 \end{cases}$
    - Solve quickly: from $2x - y = 7 \quad \Rightarrow \quad y = 2x - 7$. Substitute into $3x + 2(2x - 7) = 8 \quad \Rightarrow \quad 3x + 4x - 14 = 8 \quad \Rightarrow \quad 7x = 22 \quad \Rightarrow \quad x = \frac{22}{7}$. Then $y = 2\left(\frac{22}{7}\right) - 7 = \frac{44}{7} - \frac{49}{7} = -\frac{5}{7}$.
    - **Answer: C.** $\left(\frac{22}{7}, -\frac{5}{7}\right)$
11. **Factor** $3x^2 - 11x + 6$
    - Correct factorization is $(3x - 2)(x - 3)$.
    - **Answer: C.** $(3x - 2)(x - 3)$
12. **Solve** $x^2 - 2x = 8$
    - Rewrite: $x^2 - 2x - 8 = 0$. Solutions are $x = 4$ or $x = -2$.
    - **Answer: C.** $x = 4, x = -2$
13. **Solve** $2(x + 1) < 5$
    - $2x + 2 < 5 \quad \Rightarrow \quad 2x < 3 \quad \Rightarrow \quad x < \frac{3}{2}$.
    - **Answer: D.** $x < \frac{3}{2}$
14. **If** $f(x) = x^2 - 3x + 2$**, find** $f(4)$
    - $f(4) = 16 - 12 + 2 = 6$.
    - **Answer: C. 6**

16. $x^3 - 6x^2 + 5 = 0$**. Which integer is a root?**
    - Test small integers; $x = 1$ works $(1 - 6 + 5 = 0)$.
    - **Answer: A. 1**

16. $(3x^2 + 2x - 1) + (2x^2 - 5x + 4)$
    - Combine like terms: $5x^2 - 3x + 3$.

- **Answer: A.** $5x^2 - 3x + 3$

17. **If** $\frac{a}{b} = \frac{3}{4}$**, then** $4a = ?$
    - $\frac{a}{b} = \frac{3}{4} \quad \Rightarrow \quad a = \frac{3b}{4} \quad \Rightarrow \quad 4a = 3b.$
    - **Answer: A.** $4a = 3b$

18. **Car travels 60 mph for 2.5 hours. Distance?**
    - Distance $= 60 \times 2.5 = 150.$
    - **Answer: D. 150 miles**

19. **Solve** $| \ 2x - 1 \ | = 5$
    - Two cases: $2x - 1 = 5$ or $2x - 1 = -5$. The solutions: $x = 3$ or $x = -2$.
    - **Answer: B.** $x = 3$ **or** $x = -2$

20. **Arithmetic sequence: 4th term=11, 7th term=20. Find 10th term.**
    - Let first term a, difference d. Then 4th term $a + 3d = 11$ and 7th term $a + 6d = 20$. Subtracting gives $(a + 6d) - (a + 3d) = 20 - 11 \quad \Rightarrow \quad 3d = 9 \quad \Rightarrow \quad d = 3$. Then $a + 3(3) = 11 \quad \Rightarrow \quad a = 2$. The 10th term $= a + 9d = 2 + 9 \cdot 3 = 2 + 27 = 29$.
    - **Answer: B. 29**

21. **Geometric sequence: 2nd term=6, 4th term=54. Find 5th term.**
    - Let first term a, ratio r. Then $ar = 6$ and $ar^3 = 54$. Dividing yields $r^2 = 9 \Longrightarrow r = 3$ (positive ratio). Then $a \cdot 3 = 6 \Longrightarrow a{=}2$. The 5th term $= ar^4 = 2 \times 3^4 = 2 \times 81 = 162$.
    - **Answer: C. 162**

22. $\log_2(8) = ?$
    - $8 = 2^3 \quad \Rightarrow \quad \log_2(8) = 3.$
    - **Answer: C. 3**

23. **If** $\log_{10}(x) = 2$**, then** $x =?$
    - $x = 10^2 = 100.$
    - **Answer: C. 100**

24. **Sum of first 4 terms if** $a_1 = 5$ **and** $d = 3$.
    - Terms: 5,8,11,14. Sum $= 5 + 8 + 11 + 14 = 38$.
    - **Answer: B. 38**

25. **Solve** $\frac{x-2}{3} \geq 4$
    - $x - 2 \geq 12 \quad \Rightarrow \quad x \geq 14.$
    - **Answer: B.** $x \geq 14$

B. Coordinate Geometry Drills (15 Questions)

1. **Slope through** $(2,4)$ **&** $(6,12)$
    - Slope $= \frac{12-4}{6-2} = \frac{8}{4} = 2.$
    - **Answer: D. 2**
2. **Line parallel to** $y = 3x - 5$

- Must have slope 3 => $y = 3x +$ (constant).
- **Answer: A.** $y = 3x + 2$

3. **x-intercept of** $2x + 3y = 12$
   - Set $y = 0 \quad \Rightarrow \quad 2x = 12 \quad \Rightarrow \quad x = 6.$
   - **Answer: D.** $(6,0)$
4. **Perpendicular slope to** $\frac{2}{3}$
   - Negative reciprocal = $-\frac{3}{2}$.
   - **Answer: C.** $-\frac{3}{2}$
5. **Midpoint of** $(-2,4)$ **and** $(6,-2)$
   - $\left(\frac{-2+6}{2}, \frac{4+(-2)}{2}\right) = (2,1).$
   - **Answer: B.** $(2,1)$
6. **Which ordered pair is on** $y = 2x - 3$**?**
   - Check each. $(3,3)$ satisfies $3 = 2 \cdot 3 - 3 = 6 - 3 = 3$.
   - **Answer: C.** $(3,3)$
7. **Distance between** $(1,2)$ **and** $(5,2)$
   - $\sqrt{(5-1)^2 + (2-2)^2} = \sqrt{4^2 + 0} = 4.$
   - **Answer: C. 4**
8. **Circle** $(x-2)^2 + (y+1)^2 = 16$**, center=?**
   - Center is $(2,-1)$.
   - **Answer: A.** $(2,-1)$
9. **Line with slope** -3 **through** $(1,4)$**. Which point also on this line?**
   - Equation: y = $-4 = -3\,(x-1) \quad \Rightarrow \quad y = -3x + 3 + 4 = -3x + 7$. Plug in x=2 => y=1 => (2,1).
   - **Answer: B.** $(2,1)$
10. **Equation of a vertical line**
    - A vertical line is $x =$ constant.
    - **Answer: C.** $x = -2$
11. $y = \frac{1}{2}x + 4$ **translated 3 units down**
    - Becomes $y = \frac{1}{2}x + 4 - 3 = \frac{1}{2}x + 1.$
    - **Answer: B.** $y = \frac{1}{2}x + 1$
12. **Slope of** $3x + 2y = 10$
    - Rewrite: $2y = -3x + 10 \quad \Rightarrow \quad y = -\frac{3}{2}x + 5.$
    - **Answer: A.** $-\frac{3}{2}$
13. **Midpoint dividing segment** $(-1,-1)$ **&** $(4,9)$

- $\left(\frac{-1+4}{2}, \frac{-1+9}{2}\right) = \left(\frac{3}{2}, 4\right)$.
- **Answer: A.** $\left(\frac{3}{2}, 4\right)$

14. **y-intercept of** $y = -2x + 6$
    - Setting $x = 0 \quad \Rightarrow \quad y = 6$.
    - **Answer: C. 6**
15. **Line through** $(0,2)$ **&** $(2,0)$
    - Slope $= \frac{0-2}{2-0} = -1$. Using y-int at $(0,2)$ => $y = -x + 2$.
    - **Answer: B.** $y = -x + 2$

C. Plane Geometry Drills (15 Questions)

1. $\triangle ABC$**, A=50°, B=70°.**
    - Sum of angles=180 => C=60°.
    - **Answer: A.** 60°
2. **Rectangle perimeter=26, length=8 ⇒ width=?**
    - Perimeter=2(L+W)=26 => 8+W=13 => W=5.
    - **Answer: A. 5**
3. **Circle radius=5 ⇒ area=?**
    - Area=$\pi r^2 = 25\pi$.
    - **Answer: C.** 25π
4. **Box volume=480 in³, L=10, W=8 ⇒ height=?**
    - Volume=10×8×h=80h=480 => h=6.
    - **Answer: C. 6**
5. **Trapezoid, bases=6 & 10, height=4 ⇒ area=?**
    - Area=$\frac{(6+10)}{2} \times 4 = 8 \times 4 = 32$.
    - **Answer: B. 32**
6. **Square side=7 ⇒ area=?**
    - Area=49.
    - **Answer: D. 49**
7. $\triangle DEF$**, DE=5, EF=5, DF=6**
    - Two sides=5 => isosceles.
    - **Answer: A. It is an isosceles triangle.**
8. **Two parallel lines + transversal ⇒ which angles are equal?**
    - Alternate interior angles are congruent.
    - **Answer: A. Alternate interior angles**
9. **Right triangle legs=6,8 ⇒ hypotenuse=?**
    - By Pythagorean theorem: $\sqrt{6^2 + 8^2} = \sqrt{36 + 64} = 10$.

- **Answer: D. 10**

10. **Interior angle of a regular hexagon**
    - Each interior angle=120°.
    - **Answer: C.** 120°
11. **Circumference of circle with diameter=12**
    - Circumference=π×diameter=12π.
    - **Answer: A.** 12π
12. **Parallelogram opposite sides**
    - Are equal in length and parallel.
    - **Answer: B. Equal in length and parallel**
13. **Triangle sides=4,7,9.**
    - Check if right, acute, or obtuse. Since $9^2 = 81$ and $4^2 + 7^2 = 16 + 49 = 65$, 81>65 => obtuse.
    - **Answer: D. It is an obtuse triangle.**
14. **Rectangular prism 4×5×10 ⇒ surface area?**
    - SA=2(lw+lh+wh)=2(4×5 +4×10 +5×10)=2(20+40+50)=2(110)=220.
    - **Answer: C. 220**
15. $\triangle ABC$, **AB=BC=AC=8**
    - All sides equal => equilateral => each angle=60°.
    - **Answer: B.** 60°

D. Trigonometry Drills (15 Questions)

1. **Right triangle,** $\sin(\theta) = \frac{3}{5}$ **(acute** θ**)** ⇒ $\cos(\theta) =?$
    - $\cos(\theta) = \frac{4}{5}$.
    - **Answer: A.** $\frac{4}{5}$
2. $\tan(\theta) = 1 \Rightarrow \theta =?$
    - $\theta = 45°$ in the principal range.
    - **Answer: B.** 45°
3. **30-60-90 triangle, hyp=14 ⇒ shorter leg=?**
    - In 30-60-90, shorter leg= hyp/2 => 14/2=7.
    - **Answer: A. 7**
4. **Right triangle angles** α, β **with** $\sin(\alpha) = \frac{4}{5}$, $\alpha + \beta = 90°$. $\tan(\beta) =?$
    - $\beta = 90° - \alpha$ => $\sin(\beta) = \cos(\alpha) = \frac{3}{5}$ and $\cos(\beta) = \sin(\alpha) = \frac{4}{5}$.
    - $\tan(\beta) = \frac{\sin(\beta)}{\cos(\beta)} = \frac{3/5}{4/5} = \frac{3}{4}$.
    - **Answer: B.** $\frac{3}{4}$
5. $\triangle ABC$, **AB=10, BC=14,** $\angle B = 90°$. **If** $\sin(A) = \frac{10}{\text{hypotenuse}}$, **which is true?**

- BC=14 is the hypotenuse => $\sin(A) = \frac{AB}{BC} = \frac{10}{14} = \frac{5}{7}$.
- **Answer: A. "The hypotenuse is 14, so** $\sin(A) = \frac{10}{14}$**."**

6. $\cos(\theta) = \frac{12}{13}$ **(acute** θ**)** $\Rightarrow \sin(\theta) = ?$
   - By Pythagorean identity, $\sin(\theta) = \frac{5}{13}$.
   - **Answer: A.** $\frac{5}{13}$
7. $\sin(\theta) = \frac{\sqrt{2}}{2} \Rightarrow \theta = ?$
   - $\sin(45°) = \frac{\sqrt{2}}{2}$.
   - **Answer: B.** 45°
8. **Right triangle, legs=9 and 12.** θ **opposite leg 9** $\Rightarrow \tan(\theta) = ?$
   - $\tan(\theta) = \frac{9}{12} = \frac{3}{4}$.
   - **Answer: A.** $\frac{9}{12}$ **(which simplifies to** $\frac{3}{4}$**)**
9. **45-45-90 triangle with legs=6 ⇒ hyp=?**
   - Hyp= $6\sqrt{2}$.
   - **Answer: B.** $6\sqrt{2}$
10. $\csc(\theta) = \frac{5}{3} \Rightarrow \sin(\theta) = ?$
    - $\sin(\theta) = \frac{3}{5}$.
    - **Answer: B.** $\frac{3}{5}$
11. **Which identity is always true for acute** θ**?**
    - $\sin^2(\theta) + \cos^2(\theta) = 1$.
    - **Answer: A.** $\sin^2(\theta) + \cos^2(\theta) = 1$
12. **If** $\tan(\theta) = 2$**, find** $\sin(\theta)$ **(acute** θ**).**
    - $\sin(\theta) = \frac{\tan(\theta)}{\sqrt{1+\tan^2(\theta)}} = \frac{2}{\sqrt{1+4}} = \frac{2}{\sqrt{5}}$.
    - **Answer: A.** $\frac{2}{\sqrt{5}}$
13. **In a right triangle, one acute angle=30°. Sine of the other acute angle=?**
    - The other angle=60°, $\sin(60°) = \frac{\sqrt{3}}{2}$.
    - **Answer: B.** $\frac{\sqrt{3}}{2}$
14. **Which angle has** $\cos(\theta) = 0$**?**
    - $\cos(90°) = 0$.
    - **Answer: C.** 90°

15. **Right triangle hypotenuse=20,** $\cos(\theta) = \frac{4}{5}$**. Adjacent=?**

- Adj side= $\frac{4}{5} \times 20 = 16$.
- **Answer: A. 16**

Mixed Problem Sets (Increasing Difficulty)

Set 1 (Medium Difficulty)

1. **Algebra / Exponents**
Problem: If $2^{x+1} = 32$, what is the value of x?
   - **Step-by-Step**: Recognize $32 = 2^5$.
   $$2^{x+1} = 2^5 \quad \Rightarrow \quad x + 1 = 5 \quad \Rightarrow \quad x = 4.$$
   - **Answer**: **B. 4**

2. **Geometry / Circles**
Problem: A circle has a circumference of 24π. What is the circle's radius?
   - **Step-by-Step**: Circumference $C = 2\pi r$. Given $C = 24\pi$, so
   $$2\pi r = 24\pi \quad \Rightarrow \quad r = \frac{24\pi}{2\pi} = 12.$$
   - **Answer**: **D. 12**

3. **Systems of Equations**
$$\begin{cases} x + 2y = 7 \\ 3x - 2y = 1 \end{cases}$$
Problem: Find (x, y).
   - **Step-by-Step**: Add the two equations to eliminate y:
   $$(x + 2y) + (3x - 2y) = 7 + 1 \quad \Rightarrow \quad 4x = 8 \quad \Rightarrow \quad x = 2.$$
   Substitute $x = 2$ into the first equation $x + 2y = 7$:
   $$2 + 2y = 7 \quad \Rightarrow \quad 2y = 5 \quad \Rightarrow \quad y = \frac{5}{2}.$$
   - **Answer**: **B.** $\left(2, \frac{5}{2}\right)$

4. **Inequalities**
Problem: Which inequality is equivalent to $-3(x - 2) > -6$?
   - **Step-by-Step**: Distribute and simplify carefully:
   $$-3(x - 2) > -6 \quad \Rightarrow \quad -3x + 6 > -6 \quad \Rightarrow \quad -3x > -12 \quad \Rightarrow \quad x < 4$$
   because dividing by -3 **reverses** the inequality sign.
   Compare $x < 4$ to the given multiple-choice forms. The choice $x - 2 < 2$ is equivalent to $x < 4$.
   - **Answer**: **A.** $x - 2 < 2$

5. **Right Triangles**
Problem: A right triangle has legs of length 6 and 8. What is the length of its hypotenuse?
   - **Step-by-Step**: By the Pythagorean theorem,

$$\text{hypotenuse} = \sqrt{6^2 + 8^2} = \sqrt{36 + 64} = \sqrt{100} = 10.$$

- **Answer**: **C. 10**

6. **Factoring Polynomials**
   Problem: Which factorization is correct for $4x^2 + 4x - 3$?

   - **Step-by-Step**: We look for two binomials $(ax + b)(cx + d)$ such that $ac = 4, bd = -3, ad + bc = 4$.
     One systematic approach is to rewrite $4x^2 + 4x - 3$ as

     $$4x^2 + 6x - 2x - 3 \quad \Rightarrow \quad 2x(2x + 3) - 1(2x + 3) \quad = \quad (2x - 1)(2x + 3).$$

   - **Answer**: **D.** $(2x + 3)(2x - 1)$ (same as $(2x - 1)(2x + 3)$ in reverse order)

7. **Coordinate Geometry**
   Problem: The lines $y = 2x + 1$ and $y = -x + 10$ intersect at point P. Find P.

   - **Step-by-Step**: At intersection, set $2x + 1 = -x + 10$.

     $$2x + 1 = -x + 10 \quad \Rightarrow \quad 3x = 9 \quad \Rightarrow \quad x = 3.$$

     Then $y = 2(3) + 1 = 7$.

   - **Answer**: **A.** $(3,7)$

Set 2 (More Challenging)

1. **Polynomials / Synthetic Division**
   Problem: If $x = -2$ is a root of $x^3 + 3x^2 - 4x - 12$, what is the other factor when dividing by $(x + 2)$?

   - **Step-by-Step**: Perform synthetic division with root -2:

     $$\begin{array}{rrrrr} -2 & 1 & 3 & -4 & -12 \\ & & -2 & -2 & 12 \\ & 1 & 1 & -6 & 0 \end{array}$$

     This leaves a quotient of $x^2 + x - 6$.

   - **Answer**: **A.** $x^2 + x - 6$

2. **Word Problem / System of Equations**
   Problem: A landscaping company charges a fixed fee f plus a per-hour rate r. A 2-hour job costs \$120; a 5-hour job costs \$210. Which system is correct?

   - **Step-by-Step**: The total cost for t hours is $f + r \cdot t$. For 2 hours, $f + 2r = 120$. For 5 hours, $f + 5r = 210$.

   - **Answer**: **B** (which shows $\begin{cases} f + 2r = 120 \\ f + 5r = 210 \end{cases}$)

3. **Circles / Angles**
   Problem: A central angle of 60° in a circle of radius 9. Find the arc length.

   - **Step-by-Step**: If $\theta = 60°$, that is $\frac{60}{360} = \frac{1}{6}$ of the full circle's circumference. The full circumference is $2\pi \cdot 9 = 18\pi$. Thus the arc length is $\frac{1}{6} \times 18\pi = 3\pi$.

   - **Answer**: **A.** 3π

4. **Plane Geometry / Coordinate Plane**
   Problem: A rectangle's corners are $(0,0)$ and $(6,4)$. Which point is **not** on its perimeter?

   - **Rectangle's Perimeter**: All points where $x = 0$ or $x = 6$ (vertical edges) or $y = 0$ or $y = 4$ (horizontal edges).

- (0,4), (6,0), (3,4), (6,2) are on edges.
- (4,3) is strictly inside (since $0 < x < 6$ and $0 < y < 4$ without hitting the boundary).

  - **Answer**: **E.** (4,3)

5. **Logarithms & Exponents**
   Problem: If $\log_2(16) = x$ and $\log_3(81) = y$, find $\frac{x}{y}$.
   - **Step-by-Step**:
     $\log_2(16) = \log_2(2^4) = 4, \quad \log_3(81) = \log_3(3^4) = 4$. Hence $x = 4, y = 4$, so $x/y = 4/4 = 1$.
   - **Answer**: **A. 1**
6. **Trigonometry / Law of Sines**
   - **Step-by-Step**: By the Law of Sines,
     $$\frac{AC}{\sin B} = \frac{BC}{\sin A} \quad \Rightarrow \quad AC = \frac{\sin B}{\sin A} \times BC.$$
     Substitute $\sin(50°)$ for $\sin B$, $\sin(30°) = \frac{1}{2}$, and $BC = 10$. Thus
     $$AC = \frac{\sin(50°)}{\frac{1}{2}} \times 10 = 10 \times 2 \times \sin(50°) = 20\sin(50°).$$
     Among the expressions given, that corresponds to $\frac{10\sin(50°)}{\sin(30°)}$
   - **Answer**: **B.** $\frac{10\sin(50°)}{\sin(30°)}$
7. **Applied Geometry / Cylinder**
   Problem: A right circular cylinder has volume 216π. Its height $h = 6$. Find total surface area.
   - **Step-by-Step**:
     i. Volume $V = \pi r^2 h = 216\pi$. Then
     $$\pi r^2 \cdot 6 = 216\pi \quad \Rightarrow \quad r^2 = \frac{216}{6} = 36 \quad \Rightarrow \quad r = 6.$$
     ii. Total surface area $S = 2\pi r^2 + 2\pi rh$. Plug in $r = 6, h = 6:
     $S = 2\pi(6^2) + 2\pi(6)(6) = 2\pi \cdot 36 + 2\pi \cdot 36 = 72\pi + 72\pi = 144\pi.$
   - **Answer**: **D.** 144π

Answer Recap

Set 1
1. B
2. D
3. B
4. A
5. C
6. D

7. A
Set 2
1. A
2. B
3. A
4. E
5. A

6. B

7. D

Timed Mini-Tests & Strategies For Pacing

Mini-Test 1 (10 Questions, ~10 Minutes)

1. **Coordinate Geometry**
   A line passes through $(-1,2)$ and $(3,6)$. Find its slope.
   - **Calculation**: Slope $m = \frac{6-2}{3-(-1)} = \frac{4}{4} = 1$.
   - **Answer**: **E. 1**
2. **Algebraic Expressions**
   Which choice simplifies to $3x^2 - 4x + 1$?
   - **Check (A)**: $(x^2 - 4x + 1) + (2x^2) = x^2 - 4x + 1 + 2x^2 = 3x^2 - 4x + 1$.
   - **Answer**: **A**
3. **Systems of Equations**
   $\begin{cases} 2x + y = 10 \\ x - y = 1 \end{cases}$. Solve for x.
   - **Combine**: Adding the two equations gives $3x = 11 \Rightarrow x = \frac{11}{3} \approx 3.666$.
   - **Answer**: **A.** $\frac{11}{3}$
4. **Quadratic Equations**
   The roots of $x^2 - 4x - 5 = 0$ are:
   - **Solve**: $x = \frac{4\pm\sqrt{16+20}}{2} = \frac{4\pm\sqrt{36}}{2} = \frac{4\pm6}{2}$.
     - Roots: 5 and -1.
   - **Answer**: **A. 5 and -1**
5. **Inequalities**
   Solve $-x + 3 > 7$.
   - **Steps**: $-x > 4 \Rightarrow x < -4$.
   - **Answer**: **B.** $x < -4$
6. **Trigonometry**
   In a right triangle, if $\cos(\theta) = \frac{4}{5}$, then $\sin(\theta) =$?
   - By Pythagorean identity, $\sin(\theta) = \frac{3}{5}$.
   - **Answer**: **A.** $\frac{3}{5}$
7. **Geometry / Circles**
   A circle has radius 6. Its circumference is $2\pi r = 12\pi$.
   - **Answer**: **B.** 12π
8. **Plane Geometry**
   A trapezoid has bases 8 and 12, height 5. Area = $\frac{(8+12)}{2} \times 5 = 10 \times 5 = 50$.
   - **Answer**: **C. 50**

9. **Exponents**

$$(x^3)^2 = x^{3\cdot 2} = x^6.$$

  - **Answer**: **B.** x^6

10. **Problem-Solving**
A car travels 150 miles in 3 hours ⇒ 50 mph. At the same speed, time for 350 miles is $\frac{350}{50} = 7$ hours.

- **Answer**: **C. 7 hours**

Mini-Test 2 (10 Questions, ~10 Minutes)

1. **Factoring Polynomials**
Factor $6x^2 + x - 2$.
   - **Steps**: Look for pairs that multiply to $(6)(-2) = -12$ and sum to $+1$. That pair is $+4$ and -3. The factorization is $(2x - 1)(3x + 2)$.
   - **Answer**: **C.** $(2x - 1)(3x + 2)$
2. **Coordinate Geometry**
Which point lies on $y = -x + 4$?
   - Check each quickly: For (2,2), LHS=2; RHS= -2+4=2 ✓.
   - **Answer**: **B.** (2,2)
3. **Systems / Word Problem**
Phone plan: $15 plus $0.10/minute. Bill was $31.50. Find minutes.
   - **Steps**: 31.50 -15=16.50; 16.50 / 0.10=165 minutes.
   - **Answer**: **C. 165**
4. **Geometry / Triangles**
Right triangle with hypotenuse=13, one leg=5. The other leg = $\sqrt{13^2 - 5^2} = \sqrt{169 - 25} = \sqrt{144} = 12$.
   - **Answer**: **C. 12**
5. **Inequalities**
Solve $2x - 5 \leq 3$.
   - **Steps**: $2x \leq 8 \Rightarrow x \leq 4$.
   - **Answer**: **C.** $x \leq 4$
6. **Logarithms**
If $\log_{10}(x) = 2$, then $x = 10^2 = 100$. That matches both B and C, so the best answer is "Both B and C."
   - **Answer**: **D**
7. **Trigonometry**
Right triangle angles 30°, 60°, 90°. If side opposite 30°=6, the hypotenuse= double that=12.
   - **Answer**: **C. 12**
8. **Advanced Geometry**
Cylinder volume= 225π. Radius = 5. Then $\pi \cdot 52 \cdot h = 225\pi \Rightarrow 25h = 225 \Rightarrow h = 9$.
   - **Answer**: **C. 9**
9. **Expressions & Radicals**

$$\sqrt{8} \cdot \sqrt{2} = \sqrt{16} = 4.$$

   - **Answer**: **C. 4**

10. **Coordinate Geometry**
    A line perpendicular to $y = 3x + 1$ has slope $-\frac{1}{3}$. Through $(0,4)$ means $y = -\frac{1}{3}x + 4$.

- **Answer**: **A.** $y = -\frac{1}{3}x + 4$

Mini-Test 3 (10 Questions, ~10 Minutes)

1. **Exponents & Simplification**

$$(x^4)^3 = x^{4\cdot 3} = x^{12}.$$

    - **Answer**: **A. 12**

2. **Solving Linear Equations**
    2y+3=15⟹2y=12⟹y=6

    - **Answer**: **B. 6**

3. **Trigonometry (Right Triangles)**
    $\sin(\theta) = \frac{1}{2}$ and θ is acute $\Longrightarrow \theta = 30°$

    - **Answer**: **A. 30°**

4. **Systems of Equations**
    $\begin{cases} x + y = 9 \\ x - y = 3 \end{cases}$. Find x.

    - Adding: 2x = 12 ⟹ x = 6.
    - **Answer**: **E. 6**

5. **Coordinate Geometry (Slope)**
    Slope through (4,3) and (6,7) $= \frac{7-3}{6-4} = \frac{4}{2} = 2.$

    - **Answer**: **A. 2**

6. **Polynomials (Factoring)**
    Factor $x^2 + x - 6$. Product= -6, sum= +1 => $(x + 3)(x - 2)$.

    - **Answer**: **E.** $(x - 2)(x + 3)$

7. **Plane Geometry (Perimeter)**
    Rectangle with = $w = 5,\ l = 9.$ Perimeter $= 2(l + w) = 2(9 + 5) = 2(14) = 28$

    - **Answer**: **B. 28**

8. **Word Problem (Ratio / Proportion)**
    3 lb apples cost $4.50 => $1.50/lb. For 5 lb => $1.50×5=$7.50.

    - **Answer**: **B. $7.50**

9. **Inequalities**
    4x – 2 ≤ 10 ⟹ 4x ≤ 12 ⟹ x ≤ 3.

    - **Answer**: **A.** $x \leq 3$

10. **Circles**
    Circle diameter=10 => radius=5 => area= $\pi r^2 = 25\pi$.

- **Answer**: **A.** 25π

Mini-Test 4 (10 Questions, ~10 Minutes)

1. **Quadratic Equation**
    Solve $x^2 - 2x - 8 = 0$.

- **Steps**: $x = \frac{2 \pm \sqrt{4+32}}{2} = \frac{2 \pm \sqrt{36}}{2} = \frac{2 \pm 6}{2}$.
    - Roots: 4 or -2.
- **Answer**: **A.** $x = 4, x = -2$

2. **Coordinate Geometry (Midpoint)**
   Midpoint of $(2, -2)$ & $(6,2)$:
   - $\left(\frac{2+6}{2}, \frac{-2+2}{2}\right) = (4,0)$.
   - **Answer**: **C.** $(4,0)$
3. **Logarithms**
   $\log_5(125) = k$. Since $125 = 5^3$, $k = 3$. That means $5^k = 125$.
   - **Answer**: **B.** $5^k = 125$
4. **Trigonometry (Tangent)**
   $\tan(\alpha) = \frac{5}{12}$ → opposite=5, adjacent⟹12, hypotenuse=13. Then $\sin(\alpha) = \frac{opp}{hypp} = \frac{5}{13}$
   - **Answer**: **A.** $\frac{5}{13}$
5. **Systems of Equations / Elimination**
   $\begin{cases} 4x + 2y = 14 \\ 2x + 3y = 13 \end{cases}$. Solve for (x, y).
   - Multiply second eqn by 2 => $4x + 6y = 26$. Compare with $4x + 2y = 14$.
   - Subtract => 4y = 12⟹ y = 3. Then 4x+2(3) = 14 ⟹ 4x + 6 = 14 ⟹ 4x = 8 ⟹ x = 2
   - **Answer: A. (2,3)**
6. **Geometry (Volume)**
   A rectangular prism L=8, W=3, H=5 => volume= $8 \times 3 \times 5 = 120$.
   - **Answer**: **D. 120**
7. **Factoring Polynomials**
   Factor $2x^2 + 7x + 3$.
   - Checking $(2x + 1)(x + 3) = 2x^2 + 6x + x + 3 = 2x^2 + 7x + 3$.
   - **Answer**: **A.** $(2x + 1)(x + 3)$
8. **Plane Geometry (Angles)**
   A pentagon's internal angles sum to $(5 - 2) \times 180° = 3 \times 180° = 540°$.
   - **Answer**: **B.** 540°
9. **Word Problem (Distance / Rate)**
   A train goes 40 mph for 3 hrs=120 miles, then 50 mph for 2 hrs=100 miles, total=220 miles.
   - **Answer**: **E. 220**
10. **Inequalities**
    Solve 2x + 1 < 0 ⟹ 2x < −1 ⟹ x < $-\frac{1}{2}$

- **Answer**: **B.** $x < -\frac{1}{2}$

Answer Recap

Mini-Test 1
1. E
2. A
3. A
4. A
5. B
6. A
7. B
8. C
9. B
10. C
Mini-Test 2
1. C
2. B
3. C
4. C
5. C
6. D
7. C
8. C
9. C
10. A
Mini-Test 3
1. A
2. B
3. A
4. E
5. A
6. E
7. B
8. B
9. A
10. A
Mini-Test 4
1. A
2. C
3. B
4. A
5. A
6. D
7. A
8. B
9. E
10. B

SECTION C: READING

CHAPTER 7

READING STRATEGIES & APPROACH

7.1 PASSAGE TYPES (LITERARY, SOCIAL SCIENCE, HUMANITIES, NATURAL SCIENCE)

The ACT Reading section typically presents **four passages**—each from a **distinct genre**—to evaluate your reading comprehension, analytical thinking, and ability to draw inferences from text. Familiarizing yourself with these passage types helps you adapt your reading strategy to different writing styles, structures, and content. Below is an overview of each passage type, along with tips to maximize your performance.

1. Literary Narrative (Prose Fiction)

What to Expect

- Excerpts from novels, short stories, or sometimes memoirs.
- Often focus on character development, plot progression, and descriptive language.
- May include dialogue, internal monologues, and detailed settings.

Key Strategies

1. **Focus on Characters and Relationships**: Note how characters interact, their motives, and any conflicts or resolutions.
2. **Track the Plot**: Identify key events (conflicts, turning points) and how they affect characters' emotions or decisions.
3. **Tone and Mood**: Pay attention to descriptive words that convey emotion, setting the atmosphere of the story.

Typical Questions

- **Theme or Main Idea**: What does the passage suggest about human nature or relationships?
- **Character Analysis**: How does a character change or respond to a challenge?
- **Contextual Vocabulary**: Unfamiliar words often appear, so interpret them based on surrounding text.

2. Social Science

What to Expect

- Factual, research-based passages relating to sociology, psychology, history, or current events.
- May include references to studies, surveys, or historical documentation.
- Often features a neutral or explanatory tone, focusing on data or historical context.

Key Strategies

1. **Identify the Argument or Thesis**: Determine the central claim the author is making about a societal phenomenon or historical event.
2. **Look for Evidence**: Facts, statistics, and studies usually back up the thesis. Note how evidence is presented and whether it supports or contrasts the main point.
3. **Assess Cause-and-Effect Relationships**: Social science passages often explain how one factor influences another. Look for words like "because," "therefore," or "consequently."

Typical Questions

- **Author's Purpose**: Why did the author reference a certain statistic or historical event?
- **Evidence-Based Analysis**: Which piece of evidence best supports the author's conclusion?
- **Cause and Effect**: What caused a specific outcome in society or history?

3. Humanities

What to Expect

- Topics may include art, music, literature, cultural studies, philosophy, or ethics.
- Passages can blend factual information with personal perspective or critique.
- Style can range from formal academic analysis to a more reflective essay style.

Key Strategies

1. **Grasp the Central Theme**: Whether discussing a piece of art or a cultural movement, identify the main argument or viewpoint.
2. **Note the Author's Perspective**: Is the passage objective, critical, or appreciative? Look for language cues like "significantly," "surprisingly," "controversial," etc.
3. **Interpret References and Allusions**: Humanities passages may allude to historical periods, famous works of art or literature, or philosophical concepts. A brief mental recap of what you know can clarify context.

Typical Questions

- **Author's Attitude**: How does the author feel about the cultural practice or work of art?
- **Comparisons**: Passages might compare two artistic or cultural trends—understand the similarities and differences.
- **Supporting Evidence**: Quotes, references to other works, or historical context might serve as evidence for the author's viewpoint.

4. Natural Science

What to Expect

- Passages focus on scientific topics: biology, chemistry, physics, geology, or technology.
- Generally expository, detailing experiments, observations, or theories.
- May include technical terminology, though usually explained within the passage.

Key Strategies

1. **Identify the Main Concept**: The text might describe a study, scientific phenomenon, or technological innovation. Pinpoint the core idea quickly.
2. **Separate Details from Core Findings**: Scientific passages can contain detailed data, but you only need enough to understand the main points and the evidence supporting them.
3. **Note Hypotheses and Conclusions**: Identify the question being investigated and the conclusion drawn. Check how experimental results support or contradict the initial hypothesis.

Typical Questions

- **Cause-Effect or Process Explanation**: How does a certain mechanism or biological process work?
- **Data Interpretation**: You may need to interpret a summarized experiment or theoretical model.
- **Inferences and Predictions**: What can be concluded about future research or applications?

Why Knowing Passage Types Matters

1. **Targeted Reading Approach**: When you recognize the passage type, you can anticipate the style, vocabulary, and question types.
2. **Efficient Skimming**: For instance, in a **Literary Narrative**, you might skim for character interactions, while in **Natural Science**, you look for experimental results or data.
3. **Better Comprehension**: By aligning your reading strategy with the passage's genre, you allocate mental energy more effectively, reducing the chance of missing critical details.

7.2 ACTIVE READING METHODS (SKIMMING, ANNOTATION, IDENTIFYING KEY WORDS)

Effective reading is more than just moving your eyes across the page. The ACT Reading section demands **engaged, strategic reading** that enables you to capture central ideas, spot key evidence, and answer questions accurately—even under time pressure. Below are three crucial methods—**skimming**, **annotation**, and **key word identification**—that will help you read actively and **maximize comprehension**.

1. Skimming

Why Skim?

ACT Reading passages are lengthy. Skimming allows you to gather **main ideas** and **structural clues** without getting lost in details. You can return to specific paragraphs or lines as needed.

How to Skim Effectively

1. **Read the First & Last Lines of Paragraphs**
   - These lines often contain topic sentences or summary statements.
   - Look for transitional words like "however," "thus," or "on the other hand" to spot shifts in argument or perspective.
2. **Check for Headings or Breaks**
   - Not all ACT Reading passages have subheadings, but if they do, quickly note them.
   - Boldfaced or italicized words can signal critical concepts.
3. **Avoid Getting Stuck**
   - If you encounter a complex sentence or unfamiliar term, don't dwell on it during this first pass.
   - Focus on identifying the **core idea** of each paragraph (e.g., "This paragraph explores the protagonist's inner conflict" or "This section outlines the study's methodology").

Tip: Skimming should only take **30–45 seconds** per passage. The goal is a rough **mental map** of where certain ideas or data appear.

2. Annotation

Why Annotate?

Annotation makes your reading **interactive**. By underlining, circling, or jotting brief notes (if allowed) on scratch paper, you remain engaged and can **quickly locate** important details later.

Practical Annotation Techniques

1. **Brief Notes or Symbols**
   - Use short comments like "conflict," "example," or "definition" in the margins (or on scratch paper).
   - For longer passages, number each paragraph or section if it helps you navigate.
2. **Highlight Key Phrases**
   - Mark major shifts in argument: "In contrast," "On the contrary," "Therefore."
   - Underline or circle **names**, **dates**, or **statistics**, as they often show up in detail-oriented questions.
3. **Identify the Author's Tone**
   - If the passage is argumentative or evaluative, note words or phrases that convey the author's attitude (e.g., "regrettably," "surprisingly," "critical," "enthusiastic").

Tip: Keep annotations concise. You should **not** rewrite entire sentences—just enough to jog your memory. Over-annotation can waste time and crowd your notes.

3. Identifying Key Words

Why Key Words Matter

Key words anchor the passage's **main idea**, **supporting details**, and **transitions**. Spotting them helps you quickly answer questions about purpose, structure, and specific evidence.

Categories of Key Words

1. **Directional Words**
   - Indicate the flow of ideas: "however," "moreover," "nevertheless," "thus," "finally."
   - Signal changes in viewpoint or emphasis that are often tested in questions.
2. **Names, Dates, Places**
   - Commonly appear in detail-focused questions or to contextualize an event.
   - Especially important in **Social Science** (historical dates) or **Literary** passages (character names, setting).
3. **Technical Terms or Jargon**
   - In **Natural Science** passages, specialized words can hint at an experiment or theory's core concept.
   - In **Humanities** passages, certain philosophical or artistic terms may be crucial to the argument.
4. **Comparatives and Superlatives**
   - Words like "most," "least," "best," "highest," "lower," "faster" can set up contrasts or define extremities, often critical to understanding the passage's stance.

Putting It All Together

1. **Skim First**
   - Spend a short time scanning the passage, looking for paragraph topics and overall structure.
2. **Annotate Purposefully**
   - As you read in more detail, mark key transitions, main ideas, or specialized terms.
   - Maintain a system (symbols or short notes) to quickly reference significant points.
3. **Zero In on Key Words**
   - Pay close attention to directional words and terms that define the passage's direction or argument.
   - Highlight or note them succinctly, so you can jump back to those sections when questions demand it.

Benefits of Active Reading

- **Greater Focus**: Active methods counter "mind wandering," helping you stay alert and engaged.
- **Faster Lookup**: Marked passages let you quickly find relevant lines or data for question references.
- **Improved Accuracy**: When you've captured the main idea and critical details, you minimize guesswork.

7.3 MAIN IDEAS, SUPPORTING DETAILS, INFERENCES

After you've skimmed the passage and annotated critical points, the next step is to identify the **main ideas**, examine **supporting details**, and draw **inferences**. These three elements are interconnected—understanding the main idea requires spotting supporting evidence, and making valid inferences depends on accurately interpreting both. The ACT Reading section frequently tests your ability to move seamlessly among these levels of understanding.

1. Main Ideas

What is the Main Idea?

- The main idea (or central thesis) of a passage is the **overarching point** the author wants to convey.
- This can be explicitly stated—often at the beginning or end of the passage—but sometimes you'll need to infer it from context.

Tips for Identifying the Main Idea

1. **Look for Thesis Statements**
   - In **Social Science** or **Natural Science** passages, the author might lay out the main argument or hypothesis near the opening.
   - In **Literary** passages, the main idea might be more subtle, tied to a theme or character's journey.
2. **Check Introductions and Conclusions**
   - The first paragraph frequently frames the topic, while the last paragraph may summarize or reinforce the main argument.
   - Watch for transitions like "In conclusion," "Overall," or "Ultimately," which suggest a wrap-up.
3. **Pay Attention to Repetition**
   - If an idea or term appears repeatedly throughout the text, it's likely significant to the main idea.

Example: A passage about environmental conservation might introduce the concept of "sustainable farming" in the first paragraph, refer to it multiple times as a solution to ecological challenges, and conclude with a statement reinforcing its importance. Here, **sustainable farming** is clearly the main focus.

2. Supporting Details

What Are Supporting Details?

- These are **facts, examples, anecdotes, statistics**, or **quotes** that back up the main idea or subpoints.
- Supporting details can appear in **multiple paragraphs**, each introducing a different facet or piece of evidence related to the central theme.

Identifying Supporting Details

1. **Look for Specific Evidence**
   - Stats or dates in a **Social Science** passage, quotes or personal experiences in a **Literary** piece, or data summaries in a **Natural Science** passage.
2. **Check Transitional Phrases**
   - Words like "for example," "to illustrate," "as shown by," or "one instance of" usually introduce supporting details.
3. **Match Details to Claims**
   - Mentally link each piece of evidence to the specific claim or sub-topic it's meant to strengthen.
   - If a paragraph states that "noise pollution affects human health," look for the supporting detail—perhaps a study or anecdote—demonstrating that effect.

Example: A Humanities passage praising a particular composer might feature references to the composer's well-received works, quotes from critics, or historical anecdotes about performances that highlight public admiration—these are all supporting details reinforcing the composer's significance.

3. Drawing Inferences

What is an Inference?

- An inference is a **logical deduction** based on the information provided. The author doesn't state it outright, but the text contains **enough clues** to lead to a reasonable conclusion.

Approaches to Making Inferences

1. **Bridge the Gap**
   - Use provided details to arrive at a conclusion that is consistent with the passage, even if not explicitly spelled out.
   - Example: If a literary passage shows a character avoiding social gatherings and frequently referencing loneliness, you might infer that they struggle with social anxiety.
2. **Avoid Overgeneralizing**

- ACT questions often set traps by offering "inferences" that go beyond or contradict the provided information.
    - Stick to conclusions that the text genuinely supports.
3. **Ask "Why?"**
    - For each significant detail, consider why the author included it. If a detail doesn't fit neatly into the text's explicit statements, it might point toward a subtle or underlying idea.

Types of Inference Questions

- **Author's Intent**: Why did the author choose a particular example or phrase?
- **Character Motivations** (in Literary passages): What drives a character's decisions?
- **Implications of Data** (in Science passages): What do the findings imply for future research or understanding of a phenomenon?

Putting It All Together

1. **Find the Main Idea**
    - Start by locating the central concept. Questions about "overall purpose" or "primary message" hinge on this understanding.
2. **Identify Relevant Details**
    - When a question asks, "Which of the following best supports the author's claim?" know which lines or facts back up that claim.
3. **Make Logical Inferences**
    - For more challenging questions, determine what follows logically from the text but isn't explicitly stated.

Practical Example

Consider a **Natural Science** passage discussing the decline of bee populations. The **main idea** might be that "certain pesticides and habitat loss are leading to a rapid decrease in bees, which could have severe ecological consequences." **Supporting details** could include statistics showing the drop in bee numbers over the past decade and references to studies highlighting the role of pesticides. An **inference** question might ask you to conclude how the author believes a change in farming practices might help reverse bee decline, even if they don't say so directly.

Final Notes on Main Ideas, Supporting Details, and Inferences

- **Integrate**: Effective reading means continuously linking details back to the main idea and checking if they suggest any unspoken conclusions.
- **Stay Within the Text**: Base all inferences on the passage content; the ACT doesn't reward speculation beyond what's logically implied.
- **Apply to All Passage Types**: Literary, Social Science, Humanities, and Natural Science passages all rely on these same reading principles.

7.4 TIMING & PASSAGE MAPPING

The ACT Reading section gives you **35 minutes** for **4 passages**, each with its own set of questions. Balancing speed and comprehension is crucial. **Timing** strategy and **passage mapping** can help you tackle each passage efficiently—reducing the risk of running out of time or missing details.

1. Timing Guidelines

Although you have 35 minutes for 40 questions, you can't simply spend 8–9 minutes on each passage without being flexible. Some passages may be more challenging, requiring slightly more time, while others can be completed faster. Here are some **general timing benchmarks**:

1. **Skimming & Annotation**
    - Aim to spend **1–2 minutes** reading the passage, focusing on the main idea and structure.

- Keep notes or brief annotations to guide your return to the text.

2. **Answering Questions**
    - Allocate **5–6 minutes** to respond to the 10 questions tied to each passage (on average).
    - If a question stumps you, eliminate obvious wrong choices, pick the best remaining option, and move on. Revisit if time permits.
3. **Pacing Checkpoints**
    - Every passage: Glance at the clock after finishing.
    - By the time you complete 2 passages, ideally you've used **about half your total time** (17–18 minutes).
    - If you're behind, adjust your speed on the remaining passages.

2. Passage Mapping Techniques

Passage mapping means creating a **mental or physical 'map'** of the text so you can quickly locate details. Combined with active reading methods (skimming, annotation), this approach helps you return to specific lines or sections when questions require deeper analysis.

2.1 Dividing the Passage into Sections

1. **Paragraph Tags**
    - Label each paragraph with a letter or short descriptor on scratch paper (if allowed).
    - Example: In a 5-paragraph passage, note the main focus of each paragraph in 1–2 words (e.g., "Intro," "Study results," "Counterargument," etc.).
2. **Key Transitions**
    - Mark or note major transition points, such as when the author shifts from background info to new research, or from a character's exposition to a conflict in a literary text.
3. **Quote & Example Markers**
    - If the passage includes quotes, statistics, or specific case studies, mark their approximate location with a quick note: "Stats para 2," "Case study para 3."

2.2 Locating Answers Quickly

- **Reference the Map**: When a question says "According to lines 25–30…," you'll know which paragraph or note to revisit.
- **Shortcut for Detail Questions**: If you annotated or mapped out "Example about migratory birds in paragraph 4," jump straight there instead of re-reading from the beginning.
- **Reuse the Structure**: Some questions (e.g., "Which of the following was mentioned first?") become simpler if you recall the order in which topics appeared.

3. Balancing Depth & Speed

Don't Over-Map

- Spending too long on hyper-detailed notes can eat into your time for answering questions. **Strive for brevity**: a single word or symbol might suffice to remind you what each paragraph does.

Preview Questions (If Helpful)

- Some students prefer briefly scanning the questions before reading the passage, to know what to focus on. However, if this approach confuses you or disrupts your reading flow, skip it. **Find the method that feels most natural**.

Practice Under Timed Conditions

- Timing and passage mapping strategies are best honed in practice sessions. Test different annotation styles, see how quickly you can map a passage, and aim to refine your technique before exam day.

4. What to Do If You're Behind Schedule

1. **Skim Faster, Answer Strategically**

    - If you have only a few minutes left for a passage, do a very quick skim focusing on the first and last sentences of paragraphs.
    - Then jump to the questions, looking for evidence clues (e.g., line references) to help pinpoint where to read more carefully.
2. **Guessing Wisely**
    - If time is almost up, fill in any remaining answers—**no penalty for guessing**. A quick guess can earn points you'd lose by leaving blanks.
3. **Stay Calm**
    - Rushing can lead to mistakes in reading or frantic scanning that misses key words. Keep a steady pace, and use your mapping to jump to relevant text quickly.

Final Thoughts on Timing & Passage Mapping

Efficient reading on the ACT involves more than just comprehension. You need to handle **strict time constraints** while keeping track of crucial details. With thoughtful **passage mapping** and clear **time management**, you'll avoid last-minute panics and maximize your accuracy. Up next, we'll reinforce these strategies in **Chapter 8: Reading Practice Drills**, featuring **targeted question sets** and **mixed passage exercises** to help you solidify your approach under realistic conditions.

CHAPTER 8

READING PRACTICE DRILLS

8.1 TARGETED QUESTION SETS (MAIN IDEA, DETAIL, INFERENCE, VOCAB IN CONTEXT)

Strengthening specific reading skills can significantly boost your performance on the ACT Reading section. Below are **four targeted question sets**—each focusing on a key category: **main idea**, **detail**, **inference**, and **vocabulary in context**. Work through each set to sharpen your ability to identify the central point of a passage, locate supporting evidence, draw logical conclusions, and interpret unfamiliar words based on surrounding text.

Tip: You can time yourself for each set—or for multiple sets combined—to simulate exam pressure. Then, check your answers and review the provided rationale to clarify any misunderstandings.

A. Main Idea Questions

For each short passage or excerpt, determine the **best statement** of the passage's main idea. These passages are brief, but the skills translate directly to longer texts on the actual test.

Passage A

Most city planners believe that public parks should offer multiple recreational activities. However, some local citizens argue that parks must also serve as conservation zones for native plants and wildlife. Striking a balance between recreation and preservation remains a challenge, as space and resources are limited. Experts recommend careful landscaping and designated wildlife areas, ensuring both goals can be met.

1. **Which of the following best states the passage's main idea?**

   A. Public parks are better for wildlife than for human recreation.
   B. Striking a balance between recreation and conservation in city parks is essential but challenging.
   C. All parks should be focused solely on offering recreational activities.
   D. Planners and citizens often disagree on the definition of public recreation.

Passage B

In the early days of aviation, pilots navigated primarily by sight, using landmarks like rivers and mountain ranges to find their way. As aircraft technology advanced, navigation instruments became crucial. Compass readings and early radio aids drastically improved safety, enabling flights in poor weather and over long distances. Modern aviation now relies on satellite-based systems, which have almost eliminated the risk of pilots getting lost.

2. **Which choice best captures the main idea of this passage?**

   A. Modern aviation no longer relies on compasses or visual landmarks.
   B. Pilots in the early days of aviation often flew only short distances.
   C. Navigational technology has evolved from simple visual methods to sophisticated satellite systems.
   D. Radio navigation was the greatest achievement of early aviation pioneers.

Passage C

Farmers across the country are experimenting with more sustainable practices, such as rotating crops and reducing chemical fertilizers. While these methods may initially lower crop yields, many experts argue that long-term benefits—improved soil health and reduced pollution—are well worth the trade-off. Consumers, too, are increasingly interested in supporting eco-friendly farming, which adds market incentives for such practices.

3. What is the main idea of this passage?

   A. Sustainable farming practices always reduce yields permanently.
   B. Farmers are forced to rotate crops due to government regulations.
   C. Adopting sustainable agriculture methods can have long-term ecological and economic benefits.
   D. Consumers remain largely indifferent to how farms operate.

Passage D

In recent years, electric bicycles (e-bikes) have grown in popularity among commuters looking for a greener, more convenient way to travel. Unlike traditional bicycles, e-bikes use battery-powered motors to assist pedaling, allowing riders to tackle hills and longer distances with ease. Critics worry about safety risks and potential conflicts on crowded bike paths, but supporters claim that widespread e-bike use could reduce car traffic and pollution in major cities.

4. Which of the following best summarizes the main idea?

   A. E-bikes should replace cars entirely in major cities.
   B. E-bikes offer an easier, eco-friendly commute but raise questions about safety and path sharing.
   C. E-bikes are identical to traditional bicycles but have stronger brakes.
   D. Electric bicycles are not suitable for any urban environment.

Passage E

A growing number of universities are adopting "open educational resources"—freely available digital textbooks and course materials—to help students save money. While some faculty members worry these materials may lack depth or be harder to customize, many institutions report positive feedback from students who appreciate the reduced cost. Moreover, educational technology companies are creating high-quality open resources to compete with traditional publishers, suggesting that quality concerns may diminish over time.

5. What is the main idea of the passage?

   A. University students prefer paying for course materials because they trust traditional publishers.
   B. Many institutions are replacing traditional textbooks with open resources, though quality concerns remain.
   C. Some faculty refuse to use any digital materials in their classes.
   D. Publishers have stopped producing textbooks due to competition from open resources.

B. Detail Questions

These short passages require close attention to **specific information**. Answer the questions by **locating and interpreting** the relevant detail in the text.

Passage A

As part of her research, Dr. Sanchez tracked the migration patterns of monarch butterflies across three regions. She recorded the average travel distance, the types of plants monarchs frequented, and how climatic factors like temperature and rainfall influenced their journey. Her data revealed that cooler temperatures delayed the arrival time by about one week in certain northern areas.

Question 1. According to the passage, which factor delayed the butterflies' arrival in northern regions?

A. Reduced rainfall in the southern regions
B. A decline in the plants monarchs prefer
C. Cooler temperatures
D. Lack of proper sunlight

Passage B

In the summer of 1920, my great-grandfather opened a small café on Main Street. Business was slow at first, but with the support of close friends and family, he expanded the menu to include pastries and soups. By 1930, the café had become a popular gathering spot for locals, known especially for its homemade bread and cozy atmosphere.

Question 2. Which detail from the passage supports the café's eventual success?

A. It was located on Main Street.
B. The café also served pastries and soups.
C. The café opened in the summer of 1920.
D. It became a popular local gathering spot by 1930.

Passage C

A small coastal village depends on oyster harvesting for much of its income. Recently, however, many local harvesters have noticed a sharp decline in oyster populations along the shoreline. Scientists attribute this drop partly to warmer ocean temperatures and changes in salinity, which can disrupt oyster spawning. Meanwhile, the village council is considering limits on daily harvests to help replenish stocks.

Question 3. Which specific detail from the passage explains why oyster populations have dropped?

A. Local harvesters have noticed a decline in catch.
B. Scientists blame changes in temperature and salinity.
C. The village council is placing daily limits on harvests.
D. Oyster harvesting is an important source of income.

Passage D

Last spring, an archaeological team excavated a site near an ancient riverbed, uncovering multiple pottery fragments and stone tools. Most of these artifacts date back roughly two thousand years and appear to have been used for daily tasks like food preparation. The team's lead archaeologist believes that the settlement may have been a small farming community, relying heavily on the river's water supply for irrigation.

Question 4. Which detail indicates the **age** of the artifacts found at the site?

A. They were discovered near a riverbed.
B. Most artifacts were used for daily tasks like food preparation.
C. They date back roughly two thousand years.
D. The settlement might have been a small farming community.

Passage E

During the school's annual art exhibit, several students displayed sculptures made from recycled materials. One student created a metallic bird figure using bottle caps for feathers and a soda can for the body. Another showcased a garden scene constructed entirely from shredded newspapers. The panel of judges commended these innovative pieces for their environmental message and creative design.

Question 5. Which detail from the passage highlights how students incorporated recycled materials into their artwork?

A. The panel of judges praised the environmental message.
B. Shredded newspapers were used to create a garden scene.
C. The annual art exhibit is held at the school each year.
D. Each sculpture was made with strong adhesives.

C. Inference Questions

These brief excerpts test your ability to draw **logical conclusions** that the text implies, but does not explicitly state.

Passage A

Olivia stood at the art gallery's entrance, hesitating. She hadn't painted in years, yet her name was now listed among other exhibitors. Each brushstroke on the canvas represented a personal struggle she'd finally overcome. The gallery's director, smiling warmly, handed her a program. Olivia exhaled, stepping forward—ready to share her story.

Question 1. Which of the following can most reasonably be inferred about Olivia?

A. She only took up painting as a way to earn money.
B. She overcame a significant personal hurdle before exhibiting her work.
C. She does not care whether people appreciate her art.
D. She had exhibited her paintings at the gallery in previous years.

Passage B

The children were told they could play outside only after the new paint on the deck dried. While they waited, they quietly drew pictures on the living room floor, occasionally glancing out the window at the sunny yard. A couple of hours later, the youngest child set down his crayons and eagerly grabbed his shoes.

Question 2. What can be inferred about the children's attitude toward playing outside?

A. They were not allowed to go outside at all.
B. They were indifferent to playing outside.
C. They were excitedly awaiting permission to go outdoors.
D. They disliked being outdoors but wanted to help paint.

Passage C

Miguel checked the clock on his phone for the third time in ten minutes. He paced near the ticket counter, scanning the arrivals board overhead. A delayed flight from Chicago blinked in orange letters—exactly the one he was waiting on. At the first sign of passengers emerging from the gate, Miguel rushed forward, relief flooding his face.

Question 3. Based on the passage, what can the reader most likely infer about Miguel's situation?

A. He is angry at the airline for losing his luggage.
B. He is anxious about meeting someone arriving on the delayed flight.
C. He plans to depart on the next flight to Chicago.
D. He works for the airport and must announce incoming flights.

Passage D

Clarissa placed her last set of math flashcards in neat rows across the kitchen table. After weeks of preparation, she could recite each formula by heart. Her mother, noticing the effort, gave her a thumbs-up and said, "I don't think you need these cards anymore, kiddo." Clarissa sighed, then pulled out a sheet of fresh practice problems—just to be sure.

Question 4. Which inference can best be drawn from the passage?

A. Clarissa plans to abandon math completely after passing her next exam.
B. She's under pressure from her mother to learn new subjects.

C. She feels uncertain and wants to double-check her mastery of the material.
D. She used these flashcards for subjects other than math.

Passage E

The local bookstore advertised an evening book launch by a well-known mystery writer. When the author finally arrived—thirty minutes late—she apologized profusely, explaining that traffic had been heavier than anticipated. Despite her tardiness, the crowd greeted her with applause and quickly formed a line, clutching copies of her latest novel, eager to have them signed.

Question 5. Which of the following is the most reasonable inference about the audience?

A. They were angry that the event started behind schedule.
B. They were still enthusiastic about meeting the author even after her late arrival.
C. They had already read the entire book while waiting.
D. They had come only for the free refreshments.

D. Vocabulary In Context

Interpret the meaning of **bolded or underlined words** based on how they're used within the short passages.

Passage A

The old building's **ornate** façade drew travelers from across the region. Intricate carvings of mythological beasts and cascading floral patterns adorned every inch of the entrance, revealing the architect's extraordinary attention to detail.

Question 1. In this passage, "ornate" most nearly means:

A. plain and unattractive
B. elaborately decorated
C. outdated
D. structurally unstable

Passage B

Her initial attempts at baking were **rudimentary**, at best. She followed recipes precisely, but her cakes emerged dense and flavorless. Despite the failures, she persisted, gradually learning to measure ingredients by feel and developing a more refined palate for spices.

Question 2. The word "rudimentary" in this passage suggests that her baking attempts were:

A. advanced and sophisticated
B. basic and unrefined
C. overly sweet
D. meticulously planned

Passage C

For only a moment, the bright meteor's trail illuminated the night sky. It was so **fleeting** that many stargazers missed it entirely, catching only a brief glow out of the corner of their eyes.

Question 3. In context, the word "fleeting" most closely means:

A. burning brightly
B. lasting for an extended period
C. very short-lived
D. overwhelmingly intense

Passage D

The coffee's **robust** flavor surprised even the most experienced baristas. Though the beans had been roasted to a dark hue, the brew maintained a smooth richness without any hint of bitterness.

Question 4. Based on the passage, "robust" is best interpreted as:

A. weak and watery
B. strong and full-bodied
C. bitter and unpleasant
D. artificially flavored

Passage E

Before submitting her final paper, Ella reviewed every footnote with **meticulous** care. She double-checked citations, verified page numbers, and even corrected minor punctuation errors in her bibliography.

Question 5. The word "meticulous" here suggests that Ella's approach was:

A. casual and quick
B. overly lenient
C. extremely thorough
D. confusing and disorganized

Practice Tips

1. **Time Yourself**: Allocate a few minutes per passage to mimic testing conditions.
2. **Justify Your Answer**: For each question, identify the specific phrase or sentence that supports your choice.
3. **Track Common Pitfalls**: Notice if you repeatedly miss "main idea" questions or "inference" questions, so you can focus on improving those skills.

Next Steps

Once you've tackled these **targeted question sets**, move on to **8.2 Mixed Passage Exercises** to practice applying these skills in a single, more cohesive reading experience—mirroring the diversity of passages you'll face on test day. Afterward, you can consult **8.4 Explanations & Common Pitfalls** for a thorough review of each answer and any common misunderstandings.

8.2 MIXED PASSAGE EXERCISES (VARIED DIFFICULTY)

In this section, you'll encounter **three short passages** representing different subject areas—**Literary**, **Social Science**, and **Natural Science**—along with **varied question types** (main idea, detail, inference, and vocabulary in context). These exercises simulate the **range of complexity** you can expect on the ACT Reading section. By practicing under timed conditions and tackling a diverse set of passages, you'll refine your ability to adapt reading strategies on the fly.

Instructions for Use

1. **Set a Timer**: Allocate a specific amount of time (e.g., **10–12 minutes** total) to read each passage and answer the questions.
2. **Apply Active Reading**: Skim the passage first, make brief annotations (if helpful), and note key words or transitions.
3. **Answer Systematically**: Review each question carefully, refer back to relevant lines in the passage, and eliminate wrong answers based on clear evidence.
4. **Review Thoroughly**: After completing each passage, check your responses with the detailed explanations (found in **Section 8.4**). Understand any mistakes to prevent repeating them on test day.

Passage 1: Literary (Fiction)

Passage 1

Amelia wandered through the old orchard at dusk, her footsteps rustling fallen leaves that gave off a faint, sweet scent of apples. She remembered her grandfather's stories of early mornings spent gathering fruit for market—a tradition that died with him years ago. Now, the orchard's tangled branches and overripe apples were the only witnesses to her quiet visit.

Each tree bore the signs of neglect: twisted limbs, moss-covered bark, and fruit that lay half-eaten on the ground. Still, Amelia felt an odd sense of belonging here, as though the orchard's lingering warmth extended from her grandfather's memory, guiding her back to simpler times.

Questions (3)

1. Which statement best expresses the main idea of the passage?
A. Amelia's family orchard has been thriving ever since her grandfather passed away.
B. The orchard's current condition reflects Amelia's longing for a simpler, bygone era.
C. Amelia dislikes the orchard because it reminds her of hard work.
D. The orchard is being revitalized by new planting methods.

2. The imagery of "fallen leaves" and "overripe apples" primarily serves to:
A. symbolize Amelia's eagerness to rebuild the orchard.
B. highlight the orchard's prosperity and growth.
C. convey a mood of neglect and nostalgia.
D. suggest that nature is reclaiming her grandfather's land.

3. It can be most reasonably inferred that:
A. Amelia wants to restore the orchard to its former glory.
B. The orchard has been purchased by a neighboring farmer.
C. Amelia's grandfather disliked the orchard.
D. The orchard's fruit was renowned for its unique flavor.

Passage 2: Social Science

Passage 2

The rise of telecommuting—working remotely rather than in a traditional office—has transformed modern employment. Companies initially adopted telecommuting to save on office expenses, but more recent studies highlight additional benefits, including improved employee satisfaction and reduced commuting-related pollution. However, critics argue that remote work can foster isolation, potentially weakening team cohesion and stalling innovation. Some experts suggest a hybrid model, combining office and remote days, as a balance between cost efficiency and workforce well-being.

Questions (3)

4. Which sentence from the passage best summarizes the primary focus?
A. "The rise of telecommuting…has transformed modern employment."
B. "Critics argue that remote work can foster isolation…"
C. "Some experts suggest a hybrid model, combining office and remote days…"
D. "Companies…adopted telecommuting to save on office expenses."

5. The passage implies that one potential downside of telecommuting is:
A. a notable decrease in overall work productivity.
B. the possibility of employees feeling disconnected from colleagues.

C. a lack of available technology to enable remote work.
D. excessive spending on communication tools.

6. The author's overall tone toward telecommuting can best be described as:
A. dismissive, portraying remote work as a temporary fad.
B. critical, emphasizing the negative aspects of isolation.
C. balanced, presenting both advantages and drawbacks.
D. enthusiastic, endorsing telecommuting for all companies.

Passage 3: Natural Science

Passage 3

Coral reefs, often dubbed the "rainforests of the sea," support immense biodiversity by providing shelter and nourishment to countless marine species. However, these ecosystems face grave threats from warming ocean temperatures and acidification. Both conditions stress coral polyps, driving them to expel the symbiotic algae necessary for their survival in a process called bleaching. Repeated or prolonged bleaching events can lead to mass coral die-offs, disrupting food chains and diminishing fish populations that depend on reefs for habitat.

Questions (3)

7. Based on the passage, which statement best captures the effect of warming seas on coral?
A. It promotes a sudden increase in algae growth, benefiting coral reefs.
B. It causes coral reefs to expand into cooler regions of the ocean.
C. It leads to coral bleaching, harming the symbiotic relationship corals rely on.
D. It has had no notable impact on coral reef ecosystems so far.

8. The phrase "rainforests of the sea" is used to:
A. emphasize the dangerous predatory environment found in coral reefs.
B. compare the biological diversity of coral reefs to that of tropical rainforests.
C. highlight the humidity and rainfall common in marine habitats.
D. suggest that coral reefs are more important than actual rainforests.

9. Which of the following can be inferred regarding coral bleaching?
A. It permanently prevents corals from ever regaining their algae.
B. It is a phenomenon that only affects tropical reefs.
C. It can be triggered by both temperature increase and ocean acidification.
D. It leads directly to an increase in the fish population near affected reefs.

Practice Tips for Mixed Passages

1. **Vary Your Timing**: Some passages might feel easier or more familiar; try to move quicker through those to save time for more complex texts.
2. **Identify Passage Type**: Recognizing whether a passage is literary, social science, or natural science can guide how you approach skimming and annotation.
3. **Cross-Check**: After selecting an answer, briefly re-read the relevant line or paragraph to confirm your choice is grounded in textual evidence.
4. **Track Mistakes**: If you miss detail questions more frequently than main idea questions, for instance, focus your future practice on scanning for specific evidence.

8.3 TIMED MINI-TESTS & REVIEW

Putting all your reading skills to the test under **timed conditions** is crucial for preparing effectively for the ACT. These **mini-tests** feature **short passages** followed by **multiple questions**. Each mini-test is designed to be completed in **10–12 minutes**, reflecting the pace you must maintain during the actual exam (roughly **8–9 minutes** per passage on the ACT Reading section).

Tip: Practice your **annotation**, **skimming**, and **timing** strategies. If you find yourself consistently running out of time, try abbreviating your notes or reading slightly faster. Then, revisit challenging questions if time remains.

Mini-Test 1 (Approx. 10–12 Minutes)

Passage A: Humanities

Passage A

The early Renaissance was not merely an explosion of artistic talent—it was also a shift in the way people viewed humanity's place in the world. Scholars revisited ancient Greek and Roman texts, discovering human-centered philosophies that championed free will and individual achievement. This intellectual movement, later referred to as Humanism, opened new avenues for education, science, and art. Yet it also drew criticism from those who perceived an overemphasis on secular knowledge at the expense of spiritual devotion. The tension between religious tradition and emerging humanist ideas would shape European thought for centuries.

Questions (5)

1. **Which statement best captures the primary focus of the passage?**
   A. The Renaissance period saw a decline in religious devotion.
   B. Humanist ideas fundamentally changed European cultural and intellectual life.
   C. Renaissance scholars entirely rejected the teachings of Greek and Roman thinkers.
   D. Religious leaders remained indifferent to the rise of human-centered philosophies.
2. **The passage suggests that one of the key influences on early Renaissance thought was:**
   A. the rejection of ancient Greek and Roman philosophies.
   B. renewed interest in classical texts emphasizing the individual.
   C. a movement toward purely secular living.
   D. an abandonment of art in favor of education.
3. **The phrase "opened new avenues" in context most nearly means:**
   A. transformed physical pathways for trade and travel.
   B. restricted artistic freedom due to religious tension.
   C. created fresh opportunities for exploration in multiple disciplines.
   D. limited the scope of intellectual study to secular matters only.
4. **Based on the passage, which inference is most supported regarding the critics of Humanism?**
   A. They advocated for the full acceptance of Greek and Roman philosophies.
   B. They believed Humanism gave too little importance to spiritual considerations.
   C. They recognized the need for a balanced blend of classical knowledge and religion.
   D. They were primarily concerned with scientific progress overshadowing artistic pursuits.
5. **According to the passage, Humanist thinking influenced all of the following EXCEPT:**
   A. art
   B. education
   C. scientific inquiry
   D. agricultural methods

(Pause—if you've used about 5–6 minutes, move on to Passage B.)

Passage B: Natural Science

Passage B

Bioluminescence, the ability of living organisms to produce light, fascinates scientists and casual observers alike. Certain marine species of plankton glow faintly when disturbed, creating a nighttime spectacle known as the "phosphorescent sea." This phenomenon not only amazes beachgoers but also serves a biological purpose: bioluminescent flashes can startle predators or help attract potential mates. Researchers hope that studying the chemical processes behind bioluminescence can lead to new technologies, such as bio-inspired lighting or medical imaging techniques. However, much remains unknown about the specific genetic and environmental factors that trigger these light-producing reactions in various organisms.

Questions (5)

6. **What is the main focus of the passage?**
   A. The decline of bioluminescence in certain marine species
   B. Ways scientists use bioluminescent organisms to create decorative lighting
   C. The potential uses and scientific importance of bioluminescence
   D. The contrast between freshwater and marine bioluminescent species
7. **In line with the passage, the phosphorescent glow observed at night is caused by:**
   A. specialized plankton that emit light when agitated.
   B. fish that feed on glowing bacteria.
   C. beachgoers shining lights into the water.
   D. infrared light absorbed by ocean waves.
8. **Which statement best reflects the passage's view on the study of bioluminescence?**
   A. It is a completely understood biological phenomenon.
   B. It is significant because it may lead to innovative applications in technology and medicine.
   C. It only serves an aesthetic purpose for tourists and beachgoers.
   D. It is less complex than most other marine biological processes.
9. **Which of the following could be reasonably inferred from the passage?**
   A. Bioluminescent reactions are always triggered by the same environmental factor.
   B. Research on bioluminescence has progressed rapidly, leaving no unanswered questions.
   C. Different species may rely on bioluminescence for varied survival functions.
   D. Bioluminescence likely evolved in terrestrial mammals before appearing in marine creatures.
10. **The phrase "potential mates" (in reference to bioluminescence) suggests that:**
   A. some marine species use light displays as a way to signal readiness to reproduce.
   B. only predators can detect the light emitted by plankton.
   C. the production of light deters all possible reproduction efforts.
   D. most bioluminescent creatures are solitary and avoid mating.

Review for Mini-Test 1

Time Check

- If you have time left (target ~10–12 minutes total), quickly scan back over any tricky questions.
- If you're out of time, move on. You'll find explanations in **Section 8.4**.

Mini-Test 2 (Approx. 10–12 Minutes)

Passage C: Social Science

Passage C

In recent decades, crowdfunding has altered how individuals and small businesses raise capital. Rather than relying solely on banks or traditional investors, entrepreneurs can pitch their ideas directly to the public via online platforms. Supporters often contribute modest amounts, but collectively, these small pledges accumulate, transforming passionate projects into reality. Critics argue that this approach sometimes lacks professional oversight, leading to potential fraud or overpromised, under-delivered products. Nonetheless, proponents highlight that crowdfunding democratizes finance, enabling innovative ventures that might otherwise remain unfunded.

Questions (5)

1. **Which statement best reflects the central argument of the passage?**
   A. Crowdfunding always guarantees success for small businesses.
   B. Crowdfunding has become the primary method of raising capital worldwide.
   C. Crowdfunding offers both opportunities for innovation and potential drawbacks regarding oversight.
   D. Banks have largely replaced crowdfunding as a main source of venture funding.
2. **The phrase "transforming passionate projects into reality" suggests that crowdfunding can:**
   A. render conventional investment strategies obsolete.
   B. unite investors who focus strictly on profit margins.
   C. bring creative or niche ideas to fruition by pooling multiple small contributions.
   D. prevent fraud in all entrepreneurial endeavors.
3. **Which detail is provided as a critique of crowdfunding?**
   A. Limited public interest in new inventions
   B. A minimal chance of being scammed
   C. Over-promised results with insufficient scrutiny
   D. High bank interest rates for crowdfunded projects
4. **The author's attitude toward crowdfunding is best described as:**
   A. purely negative due to the risks involved.
   B. cautiously optimistic, acknowledging both advantages and potential flaws.
   C. indifferent, suggesting that crowdfunding doesn't affect traditional investing.
   D. skeptical of any benefits crowdfunding claims to have offered innovators.
5. **It can be inferred that "professional oversight" in the context of the passage means:**
   A. an official court system evaluating each business idea.
   B. banks and venture capitalists performing due diligence before investing.
   C. oversight by government agencies punishing unsuccessful entrepreneurs.
   D. peer review from other crowdfunding users.

(After ~5–6 minutes, move to Passage D.)

Passage D: Literary (Fiction)

Passage D

Marcus reread the letter that had arrived in the morning's post. His childhood friend, Anthony, announced plans to visit the old neighborhood after an absence of nearly ten years. Marcus felt both excitement and unease—so many things had changed, and he wasn't sure how Anthony would fit into the new rhythm of the place. Strolling by the abandoned playground and the remodeled community center, Marcus realized that time had reshaped not just the neighborhood's physical landmarks but also the memories they carried.

Questions (5)

6. **Which sentence best describes the main focus of this passage?**
   A. Marcus has received an invitation to a community meeting.
   B. Marcus expects Anthony to buy property in the neighborhood.
   C. Marcus anticipates a reunion with a friend and reflects on the changes in their hometown.
   D. Marcus wants to move away before Anthony arrives.
7. **Why does Marcus experience a sense of unease?**
   A. He dislikes Anthony and regrets hearing from him.
   B. He fears Anthony will dislike the remodeled community center.
   C. He is uncertain how Anthony will react to the changes in the neighborhood.
   D. He no longer recognizes any of his former friends.

8. **Which of the following details from the passage indicates that the neighborhood has evolved significantly?**
   A. The presence of an abandoned playground
   B. Marcus reading a letter in the morning
   C. Anthony being absent for ten years
   D. Marcus walking instead of driving
9. **The phrase "time had reshaped … the memories" suggests that:**
   A. The neighborhood's external changes have no impact on Marcus's inner feelings.
   B. As the neighborhood changed physically, Marcus's recollections also took on a different meaning.
   C. Marcus wishes to erase all memories of his childhood.
   D. Anthony's visit motivated the changes that Marcus sees.
10. **Which inference is supported by the passage?**
   A. Anthony left the neighborhood due to a personal dispute with Marcus.
   B. Marcus believes the neighborhood's new additions have improved everything.
   C. The evolution of the neighborhood triggers both nostalgia and uncertainty for Marcus.
   D. Marcus plans to surprise Anthony with a neighborhood tour.

Review for Mini-Test 2

- Use **any remaining time** (aiming for ~10–12 minutes total) to revisit confusing questions.
- Note which passages or question types slowed you down, so you can address these in future practice.
- Compare your answers to **Section 8.4: Explanations & Common Pitfalls** to clarify misunderstandings.

Post-Test Review Tips

1. **Identify Patterns**: Which question types (main idea, detail, inference, vocab) did you miss most often? Why?
2. **Check Annotation & Timing**: Did you skip annotation altogether? Did you linger too long on a tricky question?
3. **Refine Your Strategy**: Adjust your reading pace, consider scanning questions first (if it helps), or focus on more concise annotations.

By completing these **timed mini-tests**, you'll simulate the pressure of ACT Reading and refine techniques for handling various passage types. Once you've reviewed your performance, proceed to **8.4 Explanations & Common Pitfalls** for detailed solutions and guidance on avoiding typical reading comprehension errors.

8.4 DETAILED ANSWER EXPLANATIONS

Answer Key: Reading Practice Drills

A. Main Idea Questions

Passage A (Question 1)

Analysis: The text highlights the **tension** between offering recreational space and preserving wildlife habitats. The key point is that **finding a balance is both crucial and difficult**.
Correct Answer: **B**

Passage B (Question 2)

Analysis: The paragraph shows the **evolution of aviation navigation** from simple visual methods to advanced satellite systems.
Correct Answer: **C**

Passage C (Question 3)

Analysis: It describes how **sustainable farming** can reduce yields initially but provides **long-term benefits** (soil health, reduced pollution) and is bolstered by consumer interest.
Correct Answer: **C**

Passage D (Question 4)

Analysis: Electric bicycles (e-bikes) offer an **easier, eco-friendly** commute but raise **safety/path-sharing concerns**.
Correct Answer: **B**

Passage E (Question 5)

Analysis: Universities increasingly use **open educational resources** to lower student costs, although some **quality concerns** remain.
Correct Answer: **B**

Answer Key Summary

1. **B**
2. **C**
3. **C**
4. **B**
5. **B**

B. Detailed Questions

Question 1 (Passage A)

Prompt: Which factor delayed the butterflies' arrival in northern regions?

- **Key line**: "Her data revealed that **cooler temperatures** delayed the arrival time by about one week…"
- **Answer**: **C. Cooler temperatures**

Question 2 (Passage B)

Prompt: Which detail supports the café's eventual success?

- **Key line**: "By 1930, the café had **become a popular gathering spot** for locals…"
- **Answer**: **D. It became a popular local gathering spot by 1930.**

Question 3 (Passage C)

Prompt: Which specific detail explains why oyster populations have dropped?

- **Key line**: **"Scientists attribute this drop partly to warmer ocean temperatures and changes in salinity…"**
- **Answer**: **B. Scientists blame changes in temperature and salinity.**

Question 4 (Passage D)

Prompt: Which detail indicates the age of the artifacts?

- **Key line**: "Most of these artifacts **date back roughly two thousand years**…"
- **Answer**: **C. They date back roughly two thousand years.**

Question 5 (Passage E)

Prompt: Which detail highlights how students used recycled materials?

- **Key line**: “Another showcased a garden scene constructed entirely from **shredded newspapers**.”
- **Answer**: **B. Shredded newspapers were used to create a garden scene.**

Answer Key Summary

1. C
2. D
3. B
4. C
5. B

C. Inference Questions

Question 1 (Passage A)

Prompt: Which inference about Olivia is most reasonable?

- **Clue**: She hesitates, having “finally overcome” a personal struggle, yet her paintings are displayed.
- **Conclusion**: She overcame a significant hurdle before exhibiting.
- **Correct Answer**: **B**

Question 2 (Passage B)

Prompt: What can be inferred about the children’s attitude?

- **Clue**: They glance longingly outside and the youngest eagerly grabs his shoes when it’s time.
- **Conclusion**: They’re excitedly waiting to play outdoors.
- **Correct Answer**: **C**

Question 3 (Passage C)

Prompt: Miguel’s situation regarding the delayed flight.

- **Clue**: He frequently checks the arrivals board and looks relieved when passengers emerge.
- **Conclusion**: He’s anxious about someone arriving on that flight.
- **Correct Answer**: **B**

Question 4 (Passage D)

Prompt: Clarissa’s mindset about math flashcards.

- **Clue**: She knows each formula “by heart,” yet she continues practicing.
- **Conclusion**: She’s still unsure and wants to confirm her mastery.
- **Correct Answer**: **C**

Question 5 (Passage E)

Prompt: The audience’s reaction to the late author.

- **Clue**: They applaud and line up eagerly for autographs despite the delay.
- **Conclusion**: They remain enthusiastic to meet her.
- **Correct Answer**: **B**

Answer Key Summary

1. B
2. C
3. B
4. C
5. B

D. Vocabulary In Context

Question 1 (Passage A)

Word: "ornate"

*The old building's **ornate** façade drew travelers from across the region. Intricate carvings...revealing the architect's extraordinary attention to detail.*

- **Context Clues**: "Intricate carvings" and "attention to detail" indicate the façade is richly, elaborately decorated.
- **Correct Answer**: **B. elaborately decorated**

Question 2 (Passage B)

Word: "rudimentary"

*Her initial attempts at baking were **rudimentary**, at best. She followed recipes precisely... cakes emerged dense and flavorless.*

- **Context Clues**: Basic, lacking sophistication—her baking skills aren't advanced.
- **Correct Answer**: **B. basic and unrefined**

Question 3 (Passage C)

Word: "fleeting"

*It was so **fleeting** that many stargazers missed it entirely... only a brief glow.*

- **Context Clues**: "Brief glow," "for only a moment." The meteor's trail lasts a very short time.
- **Correct Answer**: **C. very short-lived**

Question 4 (Passage D)

Word: "robust"

*The coffee's **robust** flavor surprised even the most experienced baristas... maintained a smooth richness without any hint of bitterness.*

- **Context Clues**: "strong," "full-bodied," yet not bitter—suggests depth of flavor.
- **Correct Answer**: **B. strong and full-bodied**

Question 5 (Passage E)

Word: "meticulous"

*Before submitting her final paper, Ella reviewed every footnote with **meticulous** care... double-checked citations, verified page numbers... corrected minor punctuation errors.*

- **Context Clues**: She's extremely thorough, going over details carefully.
- **Correct Answer**: **C. extremely thorough**

Answer Key Summary

1. B
2. B
3. C
4. B
5. C

Answer Key: Mixed Passage Exercises (Varied Difficulty)

Passage 1 (Literary / Fiction)

Question 1

Prompt: Main idea of Amelia's visit to the orchard.

- **Analysis**: The orchard is neglected, evoking a sense of nostalgia tied to Amelia's grandfather's legacy. The text emphasizes her longing for simpler times rather than growth or revitalization.
- **Correct Answer**: **B.** The orchard's condition reflects Amelia's longing for a simpler, bygone era.

Question 2

Prompt: Purpose of the imagery "fallen leaves" and "overripe apples."

- **Analysis**: Both "fallen leaves" and "overripe apples" symbolize *neglect* and *nostalgia*, contributing to a mood rather than highlighting prosperity or replanting.
- **Correct Answer**: **C.** Convey a mood of neglect and nostalgia.

Question 3

Prompt: An inference about Amelia's intentions or feelings.

- **Analysis**: The passage never explicitly says she wants to restore the orchard, but she "felt an odd sense of belonging" connected to her grandfather's memory. The only plausible inference from the choices is that she's drawn to the idea of **reclaiming** or **restoring** what once was.
- **Correct Answer**: **A.** Amelia wants to restore the orchard to its former glory.

Passage 2 (Social Science)

Question 4

Prompt: Which sentence best summarizes the primary focus of telecommuting?

- **Analysis**: The passage starts with "The rise of telecommuting… has transformed modern employment," describing both pros and cons. That initial statement encapsulates the overall thrust.
- **Correct Answer**: **A.** "The rise of telecommuting… has transformed modern employment."

Question 5

Prompt: Potential downside of telecommuting.

- **Analysis**: The text highlights "isolation" and potential weakening of team cohesion as a drawback—**feeling disconnected**.
- **Correct Answer**: **B.** The possibility of employees feeling disconnected from colleagues.

Question 6

Prompt: The author's overall tone regarding telecommuting.

- **Analysis**: They acknowledge benefits (lower costs, improved satisfaction) and downsides (possible isolation), then mention a hybrid approach. It's balanced, not dismissive or overly enthusiastic.
- **Correct Answer**: **C.** Balanced, presenting both advantages and drawbacks.

Passage 3 (Natural Science)

Question 7

Prompt: Effect of warming seas on coral.

- **Analysis**: Warmer temperatures (and acidification) lead to bleaching, harming corals by driving out the algae they need.
- **Correct Answer**: **C.** It leads to coral bleaching, harming the symbiotic relationship.

Question 8

Prompt: "Rainforests of the sea" phrase usage.

- **Analysis**: The passage compares the **biodiversity** of coral reefs to that of tropical rainforests.
- **Correct Answer**: **B.** Compare reef biodiversity to tropical rainforests.

Question 9

Prompt: Inference regarding coral bleaching.

- **Analysis**: The text clearly states bleaching can occur with warming **and** acidification, potentially causing coral die-offs.
- **Correct Answer**: **C.** It can be triggered by both temperature increase and ocean acidification.

Answer Key Summary

1. B	6. C
2. C	7. C
3. A	8. B
4. A	9. C
5. B	

Answer Key: Timed Mini-Tests

Mini-Test 1

Passage A: Humanities (Questions 1–5)

1. **(Main Idea)**
   - **Prompt**: "Which statement best captures the primary focus of the passage?"
   - **Analysis**: The passage discusses Humanism's major impact, contrasting it with religious tradition.
   - **Correct Answer**: **B.** Humanist ideas fundamentally changed European cultural and intellectual life.
2. **(Detail / Influence)**
   - **Prompt**: The passage suggests the key influence on early Renaissance thought.
   - **Analysis**: Mentions "scholars revisited ancient Greek and Roman texts" that "championed free will," shaping the era.
   - **Correct Answer**: **B.** Renewed interest in classical texts emphasizing the individual.
3. **(Vocabulary in Context / "opened new avenues")**
   - **Prompt**: "opened new avenues" most nearly means…
   - **Analysis**: The passage says it led to fresh educational, scientific, and artistic developments—**not** literal roads.
   - **Correct Answer**: **C.** Created fresh opportunities for exploration in multiple disciplines.
4. **(Inference)**
   - **Prompt**: Inference about critics of Humanism.
   - **Analysis**: Critics felt it emphasized secular knowledge "at the expense of spiritual devotion."
   - **Correct Answer**: **B.** They believed Humanism gave too little importance to spiritual considerations.
5. **(Detail: EXCEPT)**
   - **Prompt**: Humanist thinking influenced which fields?
   - **Analysis**: Passage explicitly names art, education, science. No mention of agriculture.
   - **Correct Answer**: **D.** Agricultural methods

Passage B: Natural Science (Questions 6–10)

6. **(Main Idea)**
   - **Prompt**: The main focus of the bioluminescence passage.

- **Analysis**: It describes the phenomenon, its uses for organisms, and its potential scientific/tech importance.
- **Correct Answer**: **C.** The potential uses and scientific importance of bioluminescence

7. **(Detail)**
    - **Prompt**: What causes the nighttime phosphorescent glow?
    - **Analysis**: "Certain marine species of plankton glow faintly when disturbed."
    - **Correct Answer**: **A.** Specialized plankton that emit light when agitated
8. **(View / Significance)**
    - **Prompt**: The passage's view on studying bioluminescence.
    - **Analysis**: Researchers hope it leads to "bio-inspired lighting or medical imaging techniques."
    - **Correct Answer**: **B.** It may lead to innovative applications in technology and medicine
9. **(Inference)**
    - **Prompt**: Reasonable inference from the text.
    - **Analysis**: The passage notes that different species use bioluminescence for "startling predators" or "attracting mates," so it can serve varied survival roles.
    - **Correct Answer**: **C.** Different species rely on bioluminescence for varied survival functions
10. **(Vocabulary / "potential mates")**

- **Prompt**: Implied meaning of using light displays for mates.
- **Analysis**: The text says it "helps attract potential mates," i.e., for reproduction signals.
- **Correct Answer**: **A.** Some marine species use light displays to signal readiness to reproduce

Mini-Test 2

Passage C: Social Science (Questions 1–5)

1. **(Main Idea)**
    - **Prompt**: Central argument about crowdfunding.
    - **Analysis**: The passage states it offers big opportunities (innovation) but also has drawbacks (lack of oversight).
    - **Correct Answer**: **C.** Crowdfunding offers both opportunities for innovation and potential drawbacks.
2. **(Vocabulary / Phrase Interpretation)**
    - **Prompt**: "transforming passionate projects into reality" implies…
    - **Analysis**: Pooling small amounts of money from many supporters can bring creative ideas to life.
    - **Correct Answer**: **C.** Bring creative or niche ideas to fruition by pooling multiple small contributions
3. **(Detail / Critique)**
    - **Prompt**: Which detail is a critique of crowdfunding?
    - **Analysis**: The text specifically mentions "lack of professional oversight" and "overpromised, under-delivered products."
    - **Correct Answer**: **C.** Over-promised results with insufficient scrutiny
4. **(Author's Tone)**
    - **Prompt**: The author's attitude about crowdfunding.
    - **Analysis**: They discuss positives (democratizes finance) and negatives (fraud risk).
    - **Correct Answer**: **B.** Cautiously optimistic, acknowledging both advantages and potential flaws
5. **(Inference / "professional oversight")**
    - **Prompt**: What does "professional oversight" mean in context?
    - **Analysis**: Typically, banks or venture capitalists review business ideas before funding—**not** a court system or peer review.
    - **Correct Answer**: **B.** Banks and venture capitalists performing due diligence before investing

Passage D: Literary (Questions 6–10)

6. **(Main Idea)**
    - **Prompt**: Best description of the focus (Marcus's perspective).
    - **Analysis**: He gets a letter from Anthony and reflects on the changed neighborhood.

- **Correct Answer**: **C.** Marcus anticipates a reunion with a friend and reflects on changes in their hometown

7. **(Detail / Emotional Reaction)**
    - **Prompt**: Why Marcus feels unease.
    - **Analysis**: He wonders how Anthony will "fit" now that so much has changed.
    - **Correct Answer**: **C.** He's uncertain how Anthony will react to the neighborhood's changes
8. **(Specific Detail)**
    - **Prompt**: Which detail shows the neighborhood's significant evolution?
    - **Analysis**: The "abandoned playground and remodeled community center" directly point to physical transformations.
    - **Correct Answer**: **A.** The presence of an abandoned playground (and presumably the remodeled center)
9. **(Phrase Interpretation)**
    - **Prompt**: "time had reshaped … the memories" means…
    - **Analysis**: As physical landmarks changed, Marcus's old recollections also took on different meanings.
    - **Correct Answer**: **B.** As the place changed physically, the meaning of Marcus's memories changed too
10. **(Inference)**
    - **Prompt**: Which conclusion is supported about Marcus's feelings?
    - **Analysis**: The passage conveys both nostalgia for the past and uncertainty about the future.
    - **Correct Answer**: **C.** The neighborhood's evolution triggers both nostalgia and uncertainty for Marcus

Answer Keys Summaries

Mini-Test 1

Passage A (Q1–5):

1. B
2. B
3. C
4. B
5. D

Passage B (Q6–10):
6) C
7) A
8) B
9) C
10) A

Mini-Test 2

Passage C (Q1–5):

1. C
2. C
3. C
4. B
5. B

Passage D (Q6–10):
6) C
7) C
8) A
9) B
10) C

SECTION D: SCIENCE

CHAPTER 9

SCIENCE REASONING & DATA ANALYSIS

9.1 UNDERSTANDING EXPERIMENTS (VARIABLES, CONTROLS, HYPOTHESES)

A core component of the ACT Science section involves understanding how scientific experiments are designed, how variables are manipulated or measured, and how results are interpreted. Recognizing the roles of **independent** and **dependent variables**, the significance of **control groups**, and the formulation of a **testable hypothesis** can help you interpret research summaries and answer questions efficiently.

1. Defining Variables

Variables are the elements of an experiment that can change (or be changed) and influence the outcome of scientific research. Here are the key types you'll encounter:

1. **Independent Variable (IV)**
    - Sometimes called the **manipulated variable**.
    - The factor that the researcher **deliberately changes** to see how it affects other variables.
    - Example: If you're testing the effect of different fertilizers on plant growth, the **type of fertilizer** is your independent variable.
2. **Dependent Variable (DV)**
    - Sometimes called the **responding variable**.
    - The factor that is **measured or observed** to determine the effect of the independent variable.
    - Example: In the same fertilizer experiment, **plant height** or **biomass** might be the dependent variable.
3. **Controlled Variables (Constants)**
    - Factors kept **the same** throughout the experiment to ensure that changes in the dependent variable are truly caused by variations in the independent variable.
    - Example: Amount of water, sunlight exposure, and soil type might be kept constant for all test plants.

2. Controls and Control Groups

1. **Control Group**
    - A group in which the **independent variable is not applied** or is applied at a **standard/unchanged** level.
    - Functions as a **baseline** to compare against experimental groups.
    - Example: Plants receiving **no fertilizer** or a standard fertilizer might serve as the control group in the fertilizer experiment.
2. **Experimental Group(s)**
    - Group(s) in which the **independent variable is manipulated** in one or more ways.
    - Example: Plants receiving **different brands or types of fertilizer** are experimental groups.
3. **Why Controls Matter**
    - Controls help researchers ensure that **any observed changes** in the dependent variable are due to the **independent variable**, not random variation or outside factors.

3. Formulating and Testing Hypotheses

A hypothesis is an informed prediction or explanation that a researcher aims to test. It usually takes the form "If XX is done, then YY will result."

1. **Characteristics of a Good Hypothesis**

   - **Testable**: It can be confirmed or refuted through experimentation or observation.
   - **Specific**: Clearly states the relationship between the independent and dependent variables.
   - **Logical**: Based on existing theories or observations.
2. **Examples**
   - "If fertilizer A is used, then the plant growth rate will be higher than with fertilizer B."
   - "If temperature increases, then dissolved oxygen in water will decrease."
3. **Refining Hypotheses**
   - After initial observations, scientists might **reformulate** the hypothesis to be more precise.
   - Hypotheses can evolve as more data is collected or if initial assumptions prove inaccurate.

4. Common Experimental Designs

1. **Single-Factor Experiments**
   - Focus on **one** independent variable while keeping everything else constant.
   - Straightforward to analyze but may not capture real-world complexities.
2. **Multi-Factor (Factorial) Experiments**
   - Investigate **two or more** independent variables simultaneously.
   - More complex but can reveal how multiple factors interact (e.g., temperature and humidity effects on plant growth).
3. **Repeated Trials & Sample Size**
   - Repetition increases **reliability**: If the same results appear consistently, the findings are more credible.
   - Larger sample sizes help account for **individual variations** and reduce the influence of outliers.

5. ACT Science Implications

1. **Identifying Variables in Research Summaries**
   - Look for statements like "In Experiment 1, the researcher added 10 mL of acid to beakers at different temperatures."
     - The **independent variable** could be temperature.
     - The **dependent variable** might be reaction rate or pH change over time.
2. **Spotting Control Conditions**
   - Find references to "baseline," "placebo," or "room temperature" conditions—often the "control" scenario.
   - If you see multiple experimental setups, see if one is described as unchanged or standard.
3. **Understanding Null vs. Alternative Hypotheses** (Though not always explicitly named in ACT passages, the concept might be implied.)
   - **Null Hypothesis** (H0H_0): States there is **no relationship** or **no difference**.
   - **Alternative Hypothesis** (HaH_a): States **there is** a difference or a relationship.
4. **Common Pitfalls**
   - Mixing up the independent and dependent variables.
   - Assuming correlation implies causation. The ACT may present data that shows a relationship but doesn't necessarily prove a cause-effect link.
   - Overlooking the presence (or absence) of a control group, leading to incorrect conclusions about the experiment's design.

Key Takeaways

- **Independent variable**: The factor you change.
- **Dependent variable**: The factor you measure.
- **Control group**: Baseline comparison to confirm the effect of the independent variable.
- **Hypothesis**: A testable prediction guiding the experiment's purpose.

Grasping these fundamentals will equip you to parse experiments quickly, identify each component's role, and answer questions with confidence. In **Section 9.2: Interpreting Graphs, Tables, and Figures**, we'll build on these concepts by examining how data is presented visually and how to draw correct conclusions from charts and diagrams.

9.2 INTERPRETING GRAPHS, TABLES, AND FIGURES

Scientific data on the ACT often appears in **visual formats**—such as **graphs, tables, and figures**—requiring you to quickly interpret relationships and draw conclusions. Mastering this skill not only helps answer questions about experimental results, but also supports broader reasoning tasks (like evaluating a hypothesis or comparing multiple studies).

1. Common Data Presentation Formats

1. **Tables**
   - Present data in **rows and columns**, often comparing different conditions (e.g., time, temperature, groups).
   - You may see multiple variables listed side by side; be ready to **scan horizontally** (for comparisons across a single trial) and **vertically** (for trends down a column).
2. **Line Graphs**
   - Show how one variable **changes over time** or with respect to another variable (often the **independent variable** on the x-axis and the **dependent variable** on the y-axis).
   - Look for **trends**: increasing, decreasing, or fluctuating lines.
3. **Bar Graphs**
   - Compare **discrete categories** or groups (e.g., species A vs. species B).
   - Height (or length) of bars typically indicates the **magnitude** of the measured variable.
4. **Scatter Plots**
   - Depict **correlations** or relationships between two variables.
   - Data points may form patterns suggesting a positive, negative, or no correlation.
5. **Pie Charts** (Less Common on ACT)
   - Show **proportional** data, where each "slice" represents part of a whole.
6. **Diagrams or Schematics**
   - Illustrate **experimental setups**, labeling apparatus and control features.
   - May also display **biological processes** or **chemical reaction pathways**.

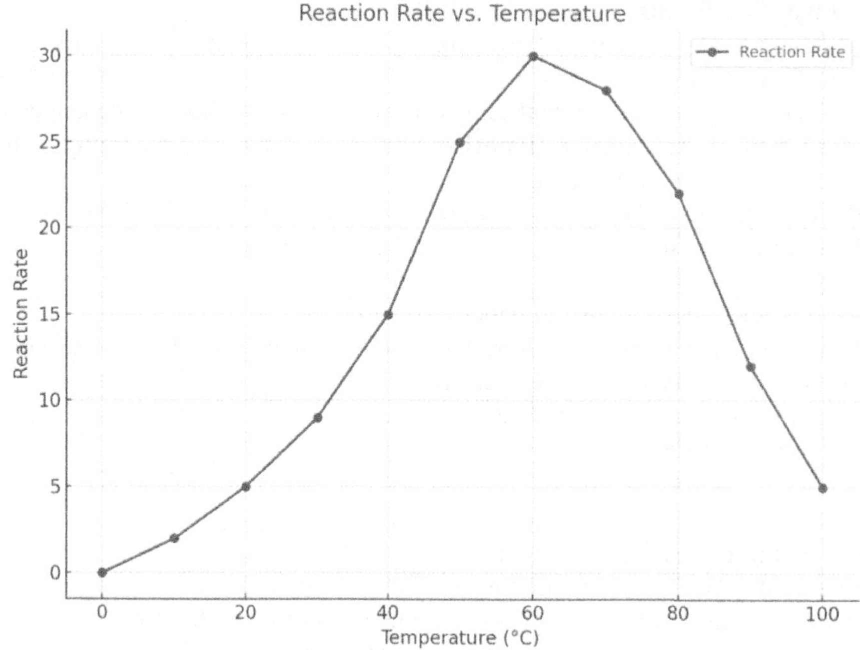

2. Strategies for Efficient Data Interpretation

2.1 Skim the Visual First

1. **Identify Axes and Labels**
   - Pinpoint which variable is on each axis.

    - Note any units (e.g., °C, mg/L, seconds).
2. **Check Legends and Keys**
    - Graphs might have multiple lines or bars, each color-coded or patterned.
    - A legend clarifies what each color/pattern represents (e.g., "Trial 1," "Trial 2").
3. **Look for Anomalies**
    - Outliers or breaks in data can be crucial clues about experimental error or unexpected findings.

Temperature (°C)	Reaction Rate	pH
10	0.5	7.0
20	1.2	6.8
30	3.5	6.5
40	7.8	6.2
50	15.0	6.0
60	12.4	5.8
70	5.6	5.5

2.2 Understand the Scales and Ranges

- **Linear vs. Logarithmic**
    - Some graphs use a **log scale** to accommodate very large or very small values.
    - Always note the numbering pattern on each axis: are they evenly spaced or does each increment represent a tenfold change?
- **Axis Limits**
    - The x-axis or y-axis might not start at zero. A truncated axis can exaggerate or minimize changes in the data.

2.3 Correlate with the Experimental Context

- If a line graph shows an increase in reaction rate as temperature rises, confirm how it aligns with the textual description of the experiment.
- Tables might indicate multiple experimental conditions (e.g., different pH levels); check whether the experiment manipulated each condition separately or simultaneously.

3. Typical Question Types Involving Visual Data

1. **Trend Identification**
    - "Based on Figure 2, how does the reaction rate change as temperature increases from 20°C to 40°C?"
    - **Approach**: Look for slope direction (increasing, decreasing) or changes in bar height.
2. **Interpolation & Extrapolation**
    - "Predict the reaction rate at 25°C given the trend shown."
    - **Approach**: Estimate between known data points (interpolation) or beyond them (extrapolation), but use caution if the passage warns about the validity of predictions outside tested ranges.
3. **Comparisons & Contrasts**
    - "Which trial had the highest final temperature?" or "Which species showed the greatest growth rate under Condition X?"
    - **Approach**: Scan bars or data points across multiple lines or columns.
4. **Identify Possible Errors or Outliers**
    - "Which data point, if any, appears inconsistent with the overall trend?"
    - **Approach**: Spot data that significantly deviates from the best-fit line or from other values in a table.
5. **Finding Missing or Implied Data**

- "If the trend continues, what would the pH be after 60 minutes?"
- **Approach**: Use a best-fit line or the rate of change from the dataset to approximate.

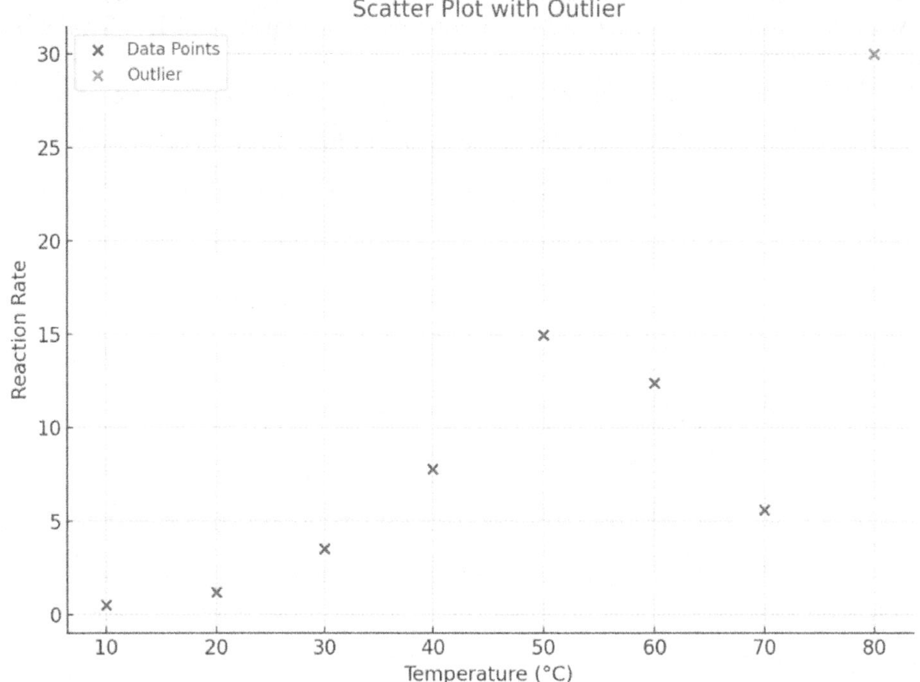

4. Common Pitfalls

1. **Mixing Up the Axes**
   - Always verify which variable is on the x-axis vs. the y-axis.
   - If you assume incorrectly, you'll draw the wrong conclusion.
2. **Ignoring Units**
   - Be mindful of whether data is in grams, kilograms, or milligrams. A single decimal place can drastically change an interpretation.
3. **Forgetting about Multiple Scales**
   - Some graphs combine two y-axes (one on the left, another on the right), each with distinct scales. Pay attention to the correct axis for each data set.
4. **Overlooking Footnotes or Annotations**
   - Tables or figures may include small notes indicating exceptions, measurement intervals, or definitions of abbreviations.

5. Integrating Data with Textual Descriptions

The ACT Science section often pairs data visuals with short paragraphs or bullet points describing the experiment. When answering questions:

- **Cross-reference**: Use both the figure and the passage text to confirm your understanding.
- **Resolve Contradictions**: If the text and graph seem to disagree, reread the text carefully—there might be a mention of a separate experiment or special condition.
- **Synthesize**: Some questions ask you to combine info from **multiple** figures or from different paragraphs within the same experiment summary.

Key Takeaways

- **Start with the Basics**: Identify axes, variables, scales, and legends immediately.
- **Check Consistency**: Align what's on the graph with the experimental design or hypothesis.
- **Extract the Trend or Relationship**: Summarize whether data shows a positive/negative correlation, a peak, a plateau, etc.
- **Stay Alert to Details**: Watch for outliers, multiple data sets, and tricky scaling.

9.3 CONFLICTING VIEWPOINTS & EVALUATING CLAIMS

Not all ACT Science passages revolve around straightforward experiments. Some present **multiple hypotheses** or **perspectives** on a scientific issue—often referred to as **Conflicting Viewpoints** passages. These scenarios require you to **compare**, **contrast**, and **evaluate** different claims. Understanding each viewpoint's **key evidence**, **assumptions**, and **conclusions** helps you answer questions about why authors disagree and which data might resolve their conflicts.

1. Identifying Contrasting Hypotheses or Perspectives

1. **Labels or Headings**
   - Passages often label each viewpoint as "**Scientist 1**," "**Scientist 2**," etc., or "**Theory A**," "**Theory B**," "**Theory C**."
   - Each viewpoint proposes a different explanation for the same phenomenon.
2. **Key Differences**
   - Notice words like "**however**," "**in contrast**," or "**unlike the others**" to find points of disagreement.
   - Look for each perspective's **main argument** and **supporting evidence**.
3. **Points of Agreement**
   - Sometimes multiple viewpoints share certain assumptions or data but **interpret them differently**. Recognizing areas of agreement vs. disagreement can help you navigate questions about which claim is strongest.

2. Evaluating the Strength of Each Claim

To judge or compare claims, consider:

1. **Evidence Base**
   - Does the viewpoint rely on **experimental data**, **observations**, or **theoretical models**?
   - More robust data or broader experimental support can strengthen a hypothesis.
2. **Logical Consistency**
   - Does the perspective contain **internal contradictions** or leaps of logic?
   - If a viewpoint fails to address clear counterexamples, it may be less convincing.
3. **Relevance & Scope**
   - Check if the claim's data truly relates to the phenomenon it's explaining.
   - A theory might be partially right but only addresses a specific subset of scenarios.
4. **Alternative Explanations**
   - Some viewpoints might acknowledge **other factors** (e.g., environmental conditions, different assumptions) that the competing viewpoint ignores.

3. Typical Conflicting Viewpoints Questions

1. **Comparison of Positions**
   - "How does Scientist 1's view on **x** differ from Scientist 2's?"
   - **Approach**: Scan for each scientist's stance on the key variable or process.
2. **Identifying Support/Evidence**
   - "Which statement would Scientist 2 most likely use to support his position?"
   - **Approach**: Align each claim with the data or logical reasoning found in that viewpoint's paragraph.
3. **Resolving the Conflict**
   - "Which new experimental finding would best help determine which viewpoint is correct?"
   - **Approach**: Pinpoint what each scientist's argument depends on—often the missing data or additional test that would confirm or disprove an assumption.
4. **Strength of Arguments**
   - "Based on the evidence provided, which scientist's argument is stronger?"

- **Approach**: Look for which viewpoint uses more direct evidence or addresses contradictions more thoroughly.

4. Strategies for Conflicting Viewpoints Passages

1. **Summarize Each Viewpoint**
   - Take quick notes (mentally or on scratch paper) about each viewpoint's **central claim**, **reasoning**, and **key evidence**.
   - Condense them into a short phrase if possible (e.g., "Scientist 1: Evolution primarily driven by climate changes; Scientist 2: By competition and natural selection.").
2. **Spot Overlaps vs. Disagreements**
   - They might agree on certain premises (e.g., "both believe species adapt over time") yet differ on causation or mechanism ("Scientist 1 says it's climate-based; Scientist 2 says competition is key").
3. **Examine Emotional/Subjective Language** (Less common but possible)
   - If a viewpoint uses strong language or speculation ("it seems likely," "it must be that…"), confirm whether it's backed by factual data or purely hypothetical.
4. **Avoid Bias**
   - Stay neutral. The test doesn't ask which side you personally agree with, but rather which is better supported by or consistent with the provided info.

5. Example: Multiple Theories, One Phenomenon

Consider a passage describing the extinction of a species:

- **Theory A (Scientist 1)**: Attributes extinction to a **sudden climate shift**, citing fossil evidence of temperature changes.
- **Theory B (Scientist 2)**: Claims an **asteroid impact** caused drastic habitat loss, referencing geological layers containing iridium.
- **Theory C (Scientist 3)**: Suggests **disease** decimated the species, noting an absence of older individuals in late fossils.

Questions might ask:

- How each scientist **interprets** certain fossil data, or
- Which additional finding (e.g., crater evidence, temperature records, disease markers) might **resolve** which theory fits best.

Key Takeaways

- **Identify Each Claim**: Know precisely what each viewpoint states.
- **Compare and Contrast**: Find how viewpoints agree or disagree on evidence, causes, or outcomes.
- **Look for Missing Data**: Often the ACT asks which experiment or piece of evidence could clarify the debate.
- **Evaluate Objectively**: Base your answers on the text's evidence, not personal beliefs about the subject.

9.4 ESSENTIAL SCIENCE VOCAB & QUICK REASONING TIPS

The ACT Science section doesn't require advanced coursework in biology, chemistry, or physics. Instead, it tests **reasoning skills** and **basic scientific literacy**. A crucial part of scientific literacy is familiarity with **key terminology**—words and phrases that frequently appear in experimental design, data representation, and theoretical discussions. Equally important are **fast, effective reasoning techniques** that help you navigate passages and questions under time pressure.

1. Core Scientific Terms and Concepts

These terms appear often in research summaries, conflicting viewpoints, and data analysis questions.

1. **Accuracy vs. Precision**

- **Accuracy**: How close a measurement is to the true or accepted value.
    - **Precision**: How consistent multiple measurements are with each other, regardless of how close they are to the true value.
2. **Correlation vs. Causation**
    - **Correlation**: Two variables appear to be related (as one changes, so does the other).
    - **Causation**: One variable **directly** causes the change in the other. Correlation does not necessarily imply causation.
3. **Constants / Controlled Variables**
    - Factors that remain the same throughout an experiment to ensure the independent variable is the only difference.
4. **Range, Median, Mean**
    - **Range**: The difference between the highest and lowest values in a set.
    - **Median**: The middle value when data is ordered from smallest to largest.
    - **Mean**: The average value (sum of all data points divided by the number of points).
5. **Replication / Reproducibility**
    - **Replication**: Repeating an experiment or observation to verify results.
    - **Reproducibility**: The ability for the same experiment, done by different researchers or at different times, to produce the same outcome.
6. **Control vs. Experimental Group**
    - **Control Group**: Baseline with no experimental manipulation or with a standard treatment.
    - **Experimental Group**: Group(s) exposed to the changed or tested condition.
7. **Qualitative vs. Quantitative Data**
    - **Qualitative**: Descriptive (colors, textures, behaviors).
    - **Quantitative**: Numerical (measurements, counts, rates).

Term	Definition
Accuracy	How close a measurement is to the true or accepted value.
Precision	How consistent multiple measurements are with each other.
Correlation	Two variables appear to be related (as one changes, so does the other).
Causation	One variable directly causes the change in the other.
Constants / Controlled Variables	Factors that remain the same throughout an experiment to ensure the independent variable is the only difference.
Range	The difference between the highest and lowest values in a set.
Median	The middle value when data is ordered from smallest to largest.
Mean	The average value (sum of all data points divided by the number of points).
Replication	Repeating an experiment or observation to verify results.
Reproducibility	The ability for the same experiment, done by different researchers or at different times, to produce the same outcome.
Control Group	Baseline group with no experimental manipulation or with a standard treatment.
Experimental Group	Group(s) exposed to the changed or tested condition.
Qualitative Data	Descriptive (e.g., colors, textures, behaviors).
Quantitative Data	Numerical (e.g., measurements, counts, rates).

2. Quick Reasoning Strategies for ACT Science

2.1 Skim, Then Detail

1. **Initial Scan**
   - Glance over the passage to identify the type (Data Representation, Research Summary, or Conflicting Viewpoints).
   - Note the main variables, the experiment's purpose, or the hypotheses in conflict.
2. **Deep Dive**
   - Move systematically through figures or experiments, clarifying how data is presented.
   - Pay special attention to units and axes in any graphs or tables.

2.2 Answer the Question Being Asked

- **Avoid Over-Interpretation**: If a question says "According to the data," your answer must come directly from tables/graphs, not from external scientific knowledge.
- **Look for Key Phrases**: Questions may specify "What best explains this increase…?" or "Which claim would Scientist 2 likely disagree with?" Focus on the relevant viewpoint or data set.

2.3 Process of Elimination (POE)

When unsure, eliminate answer choices that:

1. **Contradict** the passage's data or statements.
2. **Go Beyond** the scope (introduce info not suggested by the text).
3. **Ignore Key Details** (e.g., a choice might rely on an incorrect assumption about the independent variable).

3. Rapid-Fire Tips

1. **Highlight Trends**: Most ACT Science questions revolve around identifying or interpreting trends in data.
2. **Don't Panic over Complex Terminology**: Often you can decode meaning from context (e.g., "photosynthesis rate" might just be how quickly plants produce oxygen).
3. **Watch for Negatives and Inverses**: If a graph or a statement says "as X increases, Y decreases," keep that relationship in mind—some answer choices might flip it.
4. **Estimate Carefully**: Some questions require approximate values from a graph. Check the scale closely to avoid rounding errors.
5. **Conflicting Viewpoints**: Summarize each argument in simple bullet points to see exactly where they differ.

4. Putting It All Together

When you apply **essential vocabulary** and **quick reasoning techniques** effectively:

1. **You Recognize** the structure of the experiment or argument (independent vs. dependent variables, type of hypothesis).
2. **You Navigate** data visuals with ease, interpreting trends, correlations, and outliers.
3. **You Compare** viewpoints or contradictory findings logically, pinpointing how new evidence might favor one perspective over another.
4. **You Resist** the temptation to rely on external knowledge—sticking instead to what the passage and visuals provide.

Final Takeaways

- Familiarity with **basic scientific terms** and **experimental design** is essential for quick comprehension.
- Employ **reading and reasoning strategies** to handle a range of question types (data trend, hypothesis comparison, conflicting viewpoints, etc.).
- Stay systematic: identify the passage type, quickly parse relevant data, and align each question with the correct experiment or argument section.

With these **vocab essentials** and **reasoning tips** in mind, you're prepared to tackle even the trickiest ACT Science passages. Next, in **Chapter 10: Science Practice Drills**, you'll apply these principles via **data representation sets**, **research summaries**, **conflicting viewpoints mini-tests**, and **timed drills**—all designed to boost your confidence and accuracy on test day.

CHAPTER 10

SCIENCE PRACTICE DRILLS

10.1 DATA REPRESENTATION & GRAPH INTERPRETATION SETS

Interpreting visual data—whether in **line graphs**, **bar charts**, **tables**, or **scatter plots**—is at the core of the ACT Science section. In these practice sets, you'll hone your ability to read and interpret scientific data quickly and accurately. Apply the strategies from **Chapter 9** to answer the following questions, focusing on trends, variables, and any potential outliers.

Data Representation Set 1

Scenario: A group of researchers studied the growth rate of a bacterial culture at different temperatures (10°C, 20°C, 30°C, and 40°C). They measured the population count (in millions of cells per mL) every 8 hours over a 24-hour period.

Table A (Hypothetical Data)

Time (hours)	10°C (millions/mL)	20°C (millions/mL)	30°C (millions/mL)	40°C (millions/mL)
0	5	5	5	5
8	6	15	25	20
16	8	28	47	41
24	9	40	72	58

Questions (6)

1. **Which temperature showed the greatest overall increase in bacterial count from 0 to 24 hours?**
   A. 10°C
   B. 20°C
   C. 30°C
   D. 40°C

2. **At which temperature did the bacterial population reach approximately 25 million/mL first, based on the table?**
   A. 10°C at 16 hours
   B. 20°C at 8 hours
   C. 30°C at 8 hours
   D. 40°C at 24 hours

3. **Which of the following best describes the trend for the culture at 10°C over the 24-hour period?**
   A. The bacterial count nearly triples from 0 to 24 hours.
   B. The bacterial count remains roughly the same throughout.
   C. The bacterial count increases gradually but by less than at higher temperatures.
   D. The bacterial count peaks at 16 hours, then decreases.

4. **Suppose the researchers extended the experiment to 32 hours. Based on the overall trends, what is the most reasonable prediction for the culture at 30°C?**
   A. The population would likely decrease to near 5 million/mL.
   B. The population would likely continue to increase, surpassing 72 million/mL.
   C. The population would likely remain constant at 72 million/mL.
   D. No trend can be inferred from the data provided.

5. **If the researchers want to see how quickly the culture multiplies before reaching a plateau, which temperature's data should they examine most closely for signs of slowing growth?**
   A. 10°C, because it shows minimal changes in each time interval.
   B. 20°C, because it shows exponential growth followed by a decline.
   C. 30°C or 40°C, as these have higher growth rates and may eventually level off.
   D. All temperatures remain linear, so none will show a plateau.
6. **Which factor was most likely the dependent variable in this experiment?**
   A. The duration of the growth period (time in hours)
   B. The temperature of the environment (10°C, 20°C, 30°C, 40°C)
   C. The population count (millions of cells per mL)
   D. The type of bacterial strain used

(End of Set 1. Take about 8–10 minutes for these 6 questions.)

Data Representation Set 2

Scenario: In a different study, an environmental scientist recorded the dissolved oxygen (DO) levels in a river at two different sites (Site A near a wooded area and Site B near an industrial zone) over the course of a week.

Table B (Hypothetical Data)

Day	Site A DO (mg/L)	Site B DO (mg/L)
1	9.2	7.8
2	9.0	7.5
3	8.8	7.4
4	8.5	7.2
5	8.7	7.1
6	8.9	7.0
7	9.1	6.9

Questions (5)

1. **Which statement best summarizes the DO levels at Site A throughout the week?**
   A. They decrease steadily from 9.2 mg/L to 6.9 mg/L.
   B. They fluctuate slightly but remain in the 8.5–9.2 mg/L range.
   C. They show a sharp decline for the first 3 days before stabilizing at around 7.0 mg/L.
   D. They consistently rise from 7.8 mg/L to 9.2 mg/L.
2. **On which day is the difference between Site A and Site B's DO levels the smallest?**
   A. Day 1
   B. Day 3
   C. Day 5
   D. Day 7
3. **How do the DO levels at Site B compare to Site A across most of the week?**
   A. Site B remains higher than Site A by about 1 mg/L.
   B. Site B and Site A DO levels are approximately equal by Day 6.
   C. Site B remains consistently lower than Site A throughout the week.
   D. Site B surpasses Site A on Day 4 before dropping again.
4. **Which factor in the passage is most likely the independent variable if the scientist is investigating how location affects DO levels?**
   A. Dissolved oxygen (mg/L)

B. The day of the week
C. Site location (A vs. B)
D. The temperature of the river

5. **If the scientist wanted to examine whether temperature influenced DO levels, what additional data should be collected?**
A. pH level of the water at both sites
B. Daily temperature readings of the river at both sites
C. The species diversity of aquatic organisms in the river
D. The flow rate (speed) of the river water

(End of Set 2. Take about 6–8 minutes for these 5 questions.)

Practice Tips

- **Use Active Reading**: Quickly note key variables (time, temperature, DO levels, etc.) and what each column or axis represents.
- **Watch for Patterns**: Identify whether data is increasing, decreasing, or fluctuating.
- **Double-Check Units**: mg/L vs. millions/mL, hours vs. days, etc.—mixing them up can lead to errors.
- **Estimate Carefully**: Some questions might ask you to approximate values between measured points or to identify which data set has the highest rate of change.

After completing these **Data Representation & Graph Interpretation Sets**, proceed to **10.2 Research Summaries (Experimental Results)** to practice analyzing more detailed experimental setups and results. You'll find thorough solutions and explanations for all practice sets in **Section 10.4**.

10.2 RESEARCH SUMMARIES (EXPERIMENTAL RESULTS)

In **Research Summaries** passages, the ACT Science section presents **one or more experiments** or observational studies, often describing methods, variables, and outcomes. Your goal is to interpret the **experimental design**, **data trends**, and **conclusions**—and sometimes propose logical extensions or critiques of the work. Below are **two sets** of practice drills, each focusing on a particular experimental scenario. Use the strategies from **Chapter 9** to pinpoint independent/dependent variables, analyze results, and answer the accompanying questions.

Research Summaries Set 1

Background & Experiment Description

Experiment 1:

A group of ecologists wanted to see if the presence of different pollinator species (e.g., bees, butterflies, beetles) affected the seed production of a flowering plant called *Zanta floris*. They set up four test plots in a field:

1. **Plot 1**: Net covering excluded all pollinators (control condition, minimal pollination).
2. **Plot 2**: Net covering allowed only bees to enter.
3. **Plot 3**: Net covering allowed only butterflies to enter.
4. **Plot 4**: Open access to all pollinators (bees, butterflies, beetles).

At the end of 6 weeks, they measured **average seed count per plant** and recorded the **plant height** in each plot.

Result Highlights

- Plot 1 (No Pollinators): 5 seeds/plant (avg), 20 cm height
- Plot 2 (Bees Only): 30 seeds/plant (avg), 23 cm height
- Plot 3 (Butterflies Only): 25 seeds/plant (avg), 22 cm height
- Plot 4 (All Pollinators): 40 seeds/plant (avg), 24 cm height

Experiment 2:

To confirm the role of beetles specifically, the ecologists repeated the test with the same net coverings but added **Plot 5**, which allowed **only beetles**. They measured seed production again after 6 weeks.

Questions (6)

1. **In Experiment 1, which plot served as the control group?**
   A. Plot 1 (no pollinators)
   B. Plot 2 (bees only)
   C. Plot 3 (butterflies only)
   D. Plot 4 (all pollinators)
2. **Based on Experiment 1's data, which statement is best supported?**
   A. Butterflies are more effective pollinators than bees.
   B. Both bees and butterflies increase seed production compared to no pollinators.
   C. Allowing all pollinators reduces seed production significantly.
   D. Plant height is not affected by pollinator presence.
3. **Which variable is the primary dependent variable in both experiments?**
   A. The type of pollinator allowed
   B. The net covering used
   C. The average seed count per plant
   D. The plant species (*Zanta floris*)
4. **If Plot 5 (beetles only) yields an average of 15 seeds/plant, which conclusion could be drawn regarding beetles as pollinators?**
   A. Beetles produce more seeds than bees.
   B. Beetles alone are more effective than having no pollinators but less effective than having bees or butterflies.
   C. Beetles alone produce the highest seed counts.
   D. Beetles hinder pollination by reducing seed production.
5. **Which factor do the researchers most need to keep constant across all plots to ensure valid comparisons of seed production?**
   A. The length of each observation period (e.g., 6 weeks)
   B. The species of pollinators in each plot
   C. The number of plants in each plot and their initial health conditions
   D. The color of the net coverings
6. **If the ecologists want to see if soil quality affects plant height in addition to pollinator presence, what additional measurement would be most relevant?**
   A. The number of seeds that are viable post-harvest
   B. A soil nutrient analysis or pH reading in each plot
   C. The flowering time for *Zanta floris*
   D. The rainfall data for the entire region

(End of Research Summaries Set 1)

Research Summaries Set 2

Background & Experiment Description

A chemist investigates how temperature and pH influence the activity of **Enzyme X**, which catalyzes a specific reaction converting Substance A to Substance B.

Experiment 1 (Temperature Variation):

- The chemist prepares multiple test tubes, each containing the same concentration of Enzyme X and Substance A.
- She places each test tube at a different temperature (15°C, 25°C, 35°C, 45°C) for 10 minutes.

- At the end of 10 minutes, she measures the **amount of Substance B produced (in mg)** in each test tube.

Result Highlights

- 15°C: 2 mg B produced
- 25°C: 5 mg B produced
- 35°C: 9 mg B produced
- 45°C: 3 mg B produced

Experiment 2 (pH Variation):

- The chemist fixes the temperature at 35°C (optimal from Experiment 1) but varies the pH in different test tubes (pH 4, 6, 8, 10).
- Reaction time is again 10 minutes.
- Measures mg of Substance B produced.

(Hypothetical data for pH test)

- pH 4: 4 mg B
- pH 6: 6 mg B
- pH 8: 10 mg B
- pH 10: 5 mg B

Questions (6)

1. **In Experiment 1, which temperature yielded the highest enzyme activity?**
   A. 15°C
   B. 25°C
   C. 35°C
   D. 45°C
2. **Which statement is best supported by the temperature data?**
   A. Enzyme X is most active at 45°C.
   B. Enzyme X activity increases steadily as temperature rises, with no peak.
   C. There is an optimal temperature around 35°C where activity peaks before dropping off.
   D. The enzyme fails to produce any Substance B at high temperatures.
3. **From Experiment 2's data, which pH level produces the most Substance B at 35°C?**
   A. pH 4
   B. pH 6
   C. pH 8
   D. pH 10
4. **Given the results of both experiments, what conditions appear optimal for Enzyme X within the tested ranges?**
   A. 25°C and pH 8
   B. 35°C and pH 8
   C. 15°C and pH 4
   D. 45°C and pH 10
5. **Which factor was the chemist deliberately manipulating (independent variable) in Experiment 1?**
   A. The pH of the solution
   B. The temperature of each test tube
   C. The mg of Substance B produced
   D. The concentration of Enzyme X

6. **If the chemist wants to confirm these findings, what additional step could she take?**
   A. Measure how many times the enzyme can be reused.
   B. Repeat each temperature and pH test multiple times to ensure consistent results.
   C. Alter the substrate from Substance A to a different molecule.
   D. Lengthen the reaction time to 24 hours.

Practice Recommendations

1. **Skim the Summary**: Identify the research question, how the experiment is set up, and which variable(s) are being manipulated vs. measured.
2. **Check for Trends/Peaks**: Notice if there's an "optimal" condition (like 35°C) or if results show a clear rise and fall pattern.
3. **Analyze Both Experiments**: Some questions ask you to combine insights from multiple experiments—be prepared to do so quickly.
4. **Time Yourself**: Aim for about **8–10 minutes** per set, simulating ACT pacing.

After you finish both sets, refer to the **answer explanations** (which may appear in **Section 10.4** or at the end of this chapter) to clarify any mistakes or confusions.

10.3 CONFLICTING VIEWPOINTS MINI-TESTS

Conflicting Viewpoints passages challenge you to compare and contrast **multiple scientific perspectives** on a single phenomenon. Rather than analyzing a single experiment's design or data, you'll see **different hypotheses** or interpretations and must determine **where they agree, where they differ, and how new evidence might resolve their conflict**. Below are **two short practice passages** with questions that mirror this format.

Mini-Test 1

Passage A: Dinosaur Extinction Theories

Scientist 1

Believes that dinosaurs went extinct primarily due to **long-term volcanic activity** in what is now India (the Deccan Traps). This volcanic activity released massive amounts of ash and sulfur dioxide, blocking sunlight and triggering global cooling. According to this view, the resultant environmental changes—cooler temperatures, disrupted food chains, and acidic oceans—led to a gradual decline in dinosaur populations over tens of thousands of years.

Scientist 2

Asserts that dinosaurs died out following a **catastrophic asteroid impact** near the Yucatán Peninsula. Evidence includes a layer of iridium in geological strata worldwide, typically rare on Earth but common in meteorites, and the Chicxulub Crater's dating to around 66 million years ago. The impact would have caused widespread fires, shock waves, and dust clouds blocking sunlight, drastically affecting plant life and causing a sudden mass extinction event.

Questions (6)

1. **Which statement best summarizes the main point of contention between Scientist 1 and Scientist 2?**
   A. Whether dinosaurs survived into modern times
   B. Whether the extinction happened gradually or was triggered by a single catastrophic event
   C. Whether the extinction occurred in the ocean or on land
   D. Whether mammals or reptiles were more affected by climate change
2. **According to Scientist 1, what was the principal cause of global cooling?**
   A. The Chicxulub asteroid impact
   B. Dust clouds from a meteorite collision

C. Volcanic ash and sulfur dioxide from the Deccan Traps
D. A sudden shift in ocean currents

3. **Which piece of evidence supports Scientist 2's argument?**
A. Fossil records showing dinosaur populations slowly declining over thousands of years
B. Geological layers with high iridium concentrations, uncommon in Earth's crust
C. A significant drop in volcanic output data prior to 66 million years ago
D. Ancient ice cores indicating a long temperature decrease

4. **Scientist 1 would most likely respond to the iridium layer evidence by suggesting that:**
A. Iridium is not actually rare on Earth, so its presence is meaningless.
B. The asteroid impact never happened, and the crater is an unrelated feature.
C. The asteroid may have occurred, but the real long-term killer was volcanic-driven climate change.
D. Volcanic eruptions release far more iridium than an asteroid could.

5. **Which new finding would most help determine if the extinction was sudden or gradual?**
A. Proof that mammals also contained high levels of iridium in their bones
B. A precise timeline showing how quickly dinosaur fossils disappeared from the record
C. Evidence that ocean temperatures rose dramatically at the time of extinction
D. A measurement of how large the asteroid was relative to the crater size

6. **If a massive crater in India dating to 66 million years ago is discovered and found to be from meteorite impact, which scientist's position is strengthened?**
A. Scientist 1, because it supports the volcano theory
B. Scientist 2, because it implies multiple large impacts occurred globally
C. Both scientists equally, indicating volcanoes and asteroids combined
D. Neither scientist, as it contradicts both theories

(End of Mini-Test 1)

Mini-Test 2

Passage B: Salinity Changes in a Coastal Ecosystem

Scientist A

Maintains that **increased freshwater runoff** from nearby rivers is the primary driver of declining salinity levels in a coastal lagoon. This scientist points to records of heavier rainfall in the region over the past decade and the construction of upstream dams that redirect greater flow toward the lagoon. The resulting influx of fresh water dilutes the lagoon's salt content, affecting marine life adapted to higher salinity.

Scientist B

Argues that **ocean currents** shifting along the coast reduce the inflow of salty ocean water into the lagoon. According to this perspective, large-scale changes in prevailing wind patterns and ocean circulation have diverted the flow that once refreshed the lagoon with high-salinity seawater. Even with occasional spikes in river runoff, the lack of a consistent saltwater supply is the key factor in the lagoon's overall lower salinity trend.

Questions (5)

1. **What central disagreement exists between Scientist A and Scientist B?**
A. The extent to which rainfall patterns have changed over the decade
B. Whether ocean currents can increase salinity in an enclosed area
C. Whether lower salinity stems mainly from increased freshwater inflow or decreased marine inflow
D. The effect of pollution vs. climate change on coastal ecosystems

2. **Which piece of data would best support Scientist A's viewpoint?**
A. Measurements showing the lagoon's salinity dropping only during times of reduced tidal inflow
B. Records indicating river discharge into the lagoon doubled in the last decade

C. Evidence that ocean currents have strengthened along the coast
D. A study showing minimal changes in annual rainfall levels

3. **Scientist B's emphasis on "ocean circulation changes" suggests that:**
A. Freshwater inflow has virtually no impact on lagoon salinity.
B. The lagoon is entirely cut off from the ocean.
C. Even slight alterations in current direction or strength can reduce saltwater flow.
D. Rainfall has drastically decreased in recent years.

4. **Which finding would weaken Scientist B's claim?**
A. Satellite images confirming strong marine currents near the lagoon persist year-round
B. Yearly data revealing a fourfold increase in river outflow
C. Evidence that salinity remains stable during extreme low tide
D. Records of short-term pollution events in the lagoon

5. **Which statement is both scientists most likely to agree on?**
A. Salinity changes have no effect on marine organisms in the lagoon.
B. Fluctuations in rainfall are unrelated to lagoon salinity.
C. The lagoon's declining salinity adversely affects species that require saltier water.
D. Stronger ocean currents near the lagoon have significantly raised salinity levels.

(End of Mini-Test 2. Aim for 8–10 minutes per mini-test.)

Practice Tips

- **Summarize Each Scientist's Core Claim**: Conflicting Viewpoints often hinge on subtle differences in cause-and-effect or evidence emphasis.
- **Identify Overlaps**: If both scientists agree on certain data or outcomes, keep that in mind for questions about points of agreement.
- **Spot Potential Resolutions**: Look for new evidence or experiments that could confirm or contradict a specific viewpoint.
- **Time Yourself**: Keep practicing under **test-like conditions**, then compare your answers to the official explanations (located in **Section 10.4** or provided at the end of this chapter).

10.4 TIMED PRACTICE DRILLS WITH SOLUTIONS

Answers & Explanations: Data Representation Sets

Data Representation Set 1

Table A Recap

Time (hrs)	10°C	20°C	30°C	40°C
0	5	5	5	5
8	6	15	25	20
16	8	28	47	41
24	9	40	72	58

1. **Which temperature showed the greatest overall increase…?**
Answer: C. 30°C
    - At 30°C, the count rose from 5 to 72—a total increase of 67, exceeding the increases at other temperatures.

2. **At which temperature did the bacterial population reach ~25 million/mL first…?**
Answer: C. 30°C

- By the 8-hour mark, 30°C was already at 25 million/mL. Other temperatures reached or exceeded 25 million/mL later (if at all).

3. **Which best describes the trend for 10°C from 0 to 24 hours?**
   Answer: C. Increases gradually but by less than at higher temperatures
   - 10°C rose from 5 to 9 (a modest change), unlike the dramatic growth at 20–40°C.
4. **If extended to 32 hours, the most reasonable prediction for 30°C is...?**
   Answer: B. The population would likely continue to increase beyond 72 million/mL
   - The data show a consistently rising trend at 30°C, suggesting further growth.
5. **Which temperature's data is best for examining a pre-plateau growth rate?**
   Answer: C. 30°C or 40°C
   - At these temperatures, growth is faster and likely to plateau eventually; 10°C and 20°C are slower or less dramatic in changes.
6. **Which factor was the dependent variable in this experiment?**
   Answer: C. The population count (millions of cells per mL)
   - The researchers manipulated temperature (independent variable) and measured bacterial population changes (dependent variable).

Data Representation Set 2

Table B Recap

Day	Site A DO (mg/L)	Site B DO (mg/L)
1	9.2	7.8
2	9.0	7.5
3	8.8	7.4
4	8.5	7.2
5	8.7	7.1
6	8.9	7.0
7	9.1	6.9

1. **Which statement best summarizes DO levels at Site A?**
   Answer: B. They fluctuate slightly but remain in the 8.5–9.2 mg/L range
   - The values for Site A only vary between 8.5 and 9.2, never dropping below 8.5 or exceeding 9.2.
2. **On which day is the difference between Site A and Site B smallest?**
   Answer: D. Day 4
   - Compute differences for each day; Day 4 yields an 8.5 – 7.2 = 1.3 difference, which is less than on other days.
3. **How do Site B's DO levels compare overall?**
   Answer: C. Site B remains consistently lower than Site A throughout the week
   - Every data point for Site B is below Site A's corresponding value.
4. **If investigating how location affects DO, which is the independent variable?**
   Answer: C. Site location (A vs. B)

- The location changes; the measured DO is the dependent variable.

5. **What additional data is needed to see if temperature influences DO?**
   Answer: B. Daily temperature readings of the river at both sites
   - Temperature data would help correlate or compare DO changes to temperature changes.

Answers & Explanations: Research Summaries Sets

Use these detailed answers to check your work on **Research Summaries Set 1** and **Set 2**. Each explanation highlights the key reasoning steps so you can pinpoint any errors and adjust your approach accordingly.

Research Summaries Set 1

Recap of Experiments:

- **Experiment 1**:
  - Four plots:
    1. Plot 1 (No pollinators)
    2. Plot 2 (Bees only)
    3. Plot 3 (Butterflies only)
    4. Plot 4 (All pollinators)
  - Measured **seed count** and **plant height** after 6 weeks.
  - Results:
    - Plot 1: 5 seeds/plant, 20 cm height
    - Plot 2: 30 seeds/plant, 23 cm height
    - Plot 3: 25 seeds/plant, 22 cm height
    - Plot 4: 40 seeds/plant, 24 cm height
- **Experiment 2**:
  - Same setup, plus **Plot 5 (Beetles only)**.
  - Goal: Assess the contribution of beetles specifically.

Answers & Explanations

1. **Which plot served as the control group?**
   Answer: A. Plot 1 (no pollinators)
   - The control group is the baseline with **no** exposure to the independent variable (pollinators). Plot 1 has a net covering that excludes all pollinators, thus providing a "no pollination" comparison.
2. **Which statement is best supported by Experiment 1's data?**
   Answer: B. Both bees and butterflies increase seed production compared to no pollinators
   - Plot 1 (no pollinators) had only 5 seeds, whereas bees-only and butterflies-only plots yielded 30 and 25 seeds, respectively, indicating a clear boost from having these pollinators present.
3. **Primary dependent variable in both experiments?**
   Answer: C. The average seed count per plant
   - The researchers manipulate which pollinators can access the plants (independent variable), then measure seed count (dependent variable). Plant height is also measured, but seed production is more central to the hypothesis about pollinator efficiency.
4. **If Plot 5 (beetles only) yields ~15 seeds/plant, which conclusion follows?**
   Answer: B. Beetles alone are more effective than no pollinators but less effective than bees or butterflies
   - With 15 seeds, it's higher than Plot 1's 5 seeds, but less than bees (30) or butterflies (25). So beetles help, though not to the same extent as other pollinators.
5. **Which factor must be kept constant to ensure valid comparisons of seed production?**
   Answer: C. The number of plants and their initial health conditions

- Consistent plant density, planting conditions, and initial health allow a fair comparison of pollinator effects. Time length (6 weeks) is also the same, but ensuring the same plant conditions is critical to avoid skewing results.

6. **If the ecologists want to see if soil quality affects plant height, what extra measurement is relevant?**
   Answer: B. A soil nutrient analysis or pH reading in each plot
   - Soil quality measurements (like nutrient levels or pH) would reveal whether differences in plant height could stem from pollinator presence or from underlying soil differences.

Research Summaries Set 2

Recap of Experiments:

- **Experiment 1 (Temperature Variation)**
  - Test tubes with Enzyme X and Substance A at 15°C, 25°C, 35°C, 45°C.
  - Reaction time: 10 minutes.
  - Measured **Substance B** produced (mg).
  - Results:
    - 15°C: 2 mg
    - 25°C: 5 mg
    - 35°C: 9 mg
    - 45°C: 3 mg
- **Experiment 2 (pH Variation)**
  - Temperature fixed at 35°C (based on Exp 1's optimal result).
  - pH varied: 4, 6, 8, 10.
  - Measured mg of Substance B produced in 10 minutes.
  - Hypothetical results:
    - pH 4: 4 mg
    - pH 6: 6 mg
    - pH 8: 10 mg
    - pH 10: 5 mg

Answers & Explanations

1. **Temperature with highest enzyme activity in Exp 1?**
   Answer: C. 35°C
   - At 35°C, 9 mg of Substance B is produced, more than any other temperature tested.
2. **Which statement is best supported by the temperature data?**
   Answer: C. There is an optimal temperature around 35°C where activity peaks
   - Activity rises from 2 mg (15°C) to 9 mg (35°C), then drops to 3 mg (45°C). This suggests a peak in the middle temperature range.
3. **Which pH level produces the most Substance B at 35°C?**
   Answer: C. pH 8
   - At pH 8, the reaction yields 10 mg, the highest among pH values tested (4, 6, 8, 10).
4. **Optimal conditions within tested ranges?**
   Answer: B. 35°C and pH 8
   - Combining the best temperature (35°C) and the best pH (8) yields the maximum observed enzyme activity.
5. **Independent variable in Experiment 1?**
   Answer: B. The temperature of each test tube
   - The researcher changes (manipulates) temperature to see its effect on how much Substance B is produced. The measured outcome (Substance B) is the dependent variable.

6. **Additional step to confirm findings?**
   Answer: B. Repeat each temperature and pH test multiple times
    - Replication strengthens reliability. Changing the substrate or drastically altering time might introduce new variables, but repeating tests under the same conditions verifies consistency.

Answers & Explanations: Conflicting Viewpoints Mini-Tests

Use these answer keys and rationales to check your responses for **Mini-Test 1** and **Mini-Test 2**. Pay special attention to the reasoning behind each correct choice—this will help refine your approach to future Conflicting Viewpoints passages.

Mini-Test 1: Dinosaur Extinction Theories

Passage Recap

- **Scientist 1**: Gradual extinction driven by long-term **volcanic activity** (Deccan Traps), causing global cooling and environmental stress.
- **Scientist 2**: Sudden extinction from a **catastrophic asteroid impact** (Chicxulub Crater), with fires, dust clouds, and iridium layer as evidence.

Answers & Brief Explanations

1. **Main point of contention between Scientist 1 and Scientist 2?**
   Answer: B. Whether the extinction happened gradually or was triggered by a single catastrophic event
    - Scientist 1 proposes a long-term volcanic cause; Scientist 2 proposes a sudden asteroid strike.
2. **Principal cause of global cooling per Scientist 1?**
   Answer: C. Volcanic ash and sulfur dioxide from the Deccan Traps
    - Scientist 1 attributes cooling to volcanic emissions, not an asteroid dust cloud or ocean currents.
3. **Evidence supporting Scientist 2's argument?**
   Answer: B. Geological layers with high iridium concentrations, uncommon in Earth's crust
    - The global iridium layer is a classic signature of extraterrestrial impact, aligning with Scientist 2's asteroid hypothesis.
4. **Scientist 1's likely response to the iridium layer evidence?**
   Answer: C. The asteroid may have occurred, but the real long-term killer was volcanic-driven climate change
    - Scientist 1 wouldn't outright deny the impact but would argue that volcanic activity was the more sustained factor in dinosaur extinction.
5. **Which new finding would clarify if the extinction was sudden or gradual?**
   Answer: B. A precise timeline showing how quickly dinosaur fossils disappeared
    - If fossils vanish abruptly, that supports a sudden event. If they decline over thousands of years, that supports a gradual process.
6. **If a massive crater in India (66 million years old) is found from a meteorite, whose position strengthens?**
   Answer: B. Scientist 2, because it implies multiple large impacts occurred globally
    - Another major crater from the same period would bolster the asteroid-impact hypothesis (Scientist 2). It wouldn't reinforce the volcanic theory (Scientist 1).

Mini-Test 2: Salinity Changes In A Coastal Ecosystem

Passage Recap

- **Scientist A**: Salinity decline is mainly due to **increased freshwater runoff** from rivers (heavier rainfall, dam redirects).
- **Scientist B**: Salinity decline is mainly due to **reduced inflow of salty ocean water** because of shifts in ocean currents/wind patterns.

Answers & Brief Explanations

1. **Central disagreement between Scientist A and B?**
   Answer: C. Whether lower salinity stems mainly from increased freshwater inflow or decreased marine inflow
   - They differ on the primary cause: more fresh water vs. less salty water intrusion.
2. **Which data best supports Scientist A?**
   Answer: B. Records indicating river discharge into the lagoon doubled in the last decade
   - Scientist A focuses on increased freshwater, so significantly higher river flow aligns perfectly with that claim.
3. **Scientist B's emphasis on ocean circulation changes suggests that…**
   Answer: C. Even slight alterations in current direction/strength can reduce saltwater flow
   - Scientist B argues that shifting ocean currents hamper the usual infusion of saltwater, leading to overall lower salinity.
4. **Which finding would weaken Scientist B's claim?**
   Answer: B. Yearly data revealing a fourfold increase in river outflow
   - If freshwater runoff has increased dramatically, it becomes a more likely explanation for salinity decline, undermining the idea that reduced ocean inflow is the main cause.
5. **Statement both scientists likely agree on?**
   Answer: C. The lagoon's declining salinity adversely affects species needing higher salinity
   - Both presumably accept that lower salinity impacts marine organisms, even if they disagree on the cause. They wouldn't agree that salinity changes have no effect or that rainfall is irrelevant.

Review & Next Steps

- **Check Patterns in Mistakes**: Did you misunderstand the viewpoints' primary disagreements, or overlook clues pointing to a viewpoint's preferred data?
- **Reinforce Comparison Skills**: Always summarize each scientist's argument before you tackle the questions.
- **Practice Timing**: Conflicting Viewpoints passages often require close reading; use process-of-elimination and quick referencing to maintain speed.

CHAPTER 11

THE OPTIONAL WRITING TEST

11.1 UNDERSTANDING THE PROMPT & PERSPECTIVES

Though optional, the ACT Writing Test can strengthen your college application by showcasing your ability to craft a **cohesive, analytical essay**. The prompt presents a **contemporary issue** and provides **three distinct perspectives** on that issue, each with its own viewpoint or rationale. Your task is to **analyze** these perspectives, **develop** your own position, and **explain** how it relates to the others. Mastering this structure is the first step toward a clear, well-supported argument.

1. Examining the Prompt

Each prompt typically covers a **broad social or cultural theme**—for instance, the impact of technology on personal privacy or the role of public funding in education. To effectively respond:

1. **Read Carefully**
   - Identify key terms or phrases that reveal the central debate (e.g., "privacy vs. security," "innovation vs. tradition," "individual rights vs. public welfare").
   - Note any **focus** or **limitations** (e.g., "in the workplace," "in high schools," "for government programs").
2. **Paraphrase the Issue**
   - Reformulate the topic in your own words: "This prompt is asking if businesses should monitor employee internet use…"
   - Clarify **why** this issue might matter—what's at stake, and for whom?
3. **Spot Sub-Questions**
   - The prompt often hints at tensions or trade-offs: e.g., "Should convenience outweigh individual privacy?"
   - These sub-questions can guide your argument's framework.

2. The Three Perspectives

After the prompt sets the stage, you'll see **three perspectives**, each representing a **distinct** stance on the issue. For example, if the topic is about implementing a new public transportation system:

- **Perspective 1** might emphasize **economic efficiency** ("It saves money and reduces traffic").
- **Perspective 2** might focus on **environmental or social benefits**.
- **Perspective 3** might stress **personal freedom** or **funding concerns** ("It's unfair to raise taxes for a project everyone won't use").

Analyzing Each Perspective

1. **Restate**
   - Capture the essence of each perspective in your own words.
   - E.g., "Perspective 1 suggests the new system's cost savings outweigh potential downsides."
2. **Evaluate**
   - What **evidence** or assumptions underpin each view?
   - Does the perspective address certain aspects of the prompt while ignoring others?
3. **Compare & Contrast**
   - How do the perspectives **agree** or **clash**?
   - Are they focusing on **short-term** vs. **long-term** outcomes, **practical** vs. **ethical** considerations, or something else?

3. Forming Your Own Position

You're not required to invent a **fourth** perspective from scratch—though you can. Often, you might **align** with one of the provided perspectives but **tweak** or **expand** it to create your unique stance. Or you may synthesize aspects of multiple perspectives into a more nuanced view.

1. **Choose Your Basis**
   - Decide whether your thesis aligns most with **Perspective 1**, **2**, or **3**, or if you want to combine them.
   - Make sure you have enough **reasons** and potential examples to support this choice.
2. **Acknowledge Other Views**
   - Even if you embrace one perspective strongly, you should **address** the opposing or alternative ideas. This shows complexity in your thinking.
3. **Be Specific**
   - A broad statement ("We must do what's best for everyone!") lacks the detail ACT scorers look for.
   - Outline **why** and **how** your position responds to the central debate.

4. Time Management & Brainstorming

Given the **short timeframe** on the ACT Writing Test (40 minutes), you must quickly unpack the prompt and plan your response:

1. **Initial Read-Through (1–2 minutes)**
   - Understand the topic, perspectives, and what's being asked.
2. **Quick Brainstorm (3–5 minutes)**
   - Jot down bullet points for each perspective: potential pros, cons, and real-world or hypothetical examples.
   - Decide on your stance—which perspective(s) do you support or modify?
3. **Draft the Essay (around 30 minutes)**
   - Introduce the issue and your position.
   - Discuss each perspective, weaving in your own argument.
   - Offer examples or analogies to illustrate why your view is reasonable or superior.
4. **Review (2–3 minutes)**
   - Check for clarity, grammar slips, and a coherent flow.

Key Takeaways

- **Read the Prompt Thoroughly**: Identify key issues and the scope of the debate.
- **Understand Each Perspective**: Restate, evaluate, and compare them to see where strengths and weaknesses lie.
- **Craft Your Own Position**: You may side with one perspective, blend multiple, or present a distinct viewpoint—just ensure you address other perspectives.
- **Manage Time**: Efficiently plan your approach, then write and revise for best clarity.

11.2 STRUCTURING YOUR ARGUMENT (INTRODUCTION, BODY, CONCLUSION)

Once you've **interpreted the prompt** and **identified key perspectives**, the next step is to **construct a cohesive essay** that showcases your reasoning skills. The ACT Writing Test rewards clear organization and logical transitions; a strong structure helps you deliver your ideas persuasively and ensures the reader follows your argument from start to finish. Below is a **three-part framework**—introduction, body, conclusion—that will keep your essay focused and coherent.

1. Introduction: Engaging and Focused

Your introduction should do two main things: **grab the reader's attention** and **signal your thesis**. On the ACT, with limited time, aim for a **concise yet clear** opening.

1. **Contextualize the Issue**
   - Briefly restate the core debate or problem the prompt poses (e.g., the role of technology in schools, or balancing personal freedom with public safety).
   - Show **why** it matters—how does it affect individuals, communities, or society?
2. **Acknowledge the Perspectives**
   - Indicate that multiple viewpoints exist without diving into exhaustive detail.
   - Example: "Some argue for stricter policies to ensure security, while others emphasize personal autonomy above all else."
3. **State Your Position (Thesis Statement)**
   - Let the reader know where you stand—or if you plan to combine multiple perspectives into a nuanced stance.
   - A clear thesis might look like this: "While security measures are vital, maintaining personal freedoms ultimately fosters a healthier, more innovative society."

Introduction Example (Brief)

"Modern schools face a dilemma: Should they fully integrate personal digital devices into the classroom, or maintain strict restrictions on technology to minimize distraction? Some perspectives emphasize the need for innovative tech-based learning, while others worry about negative effects on attention and academic integrity. I believe that a balanced approach—allowing certain devices under structured guidelines—offers the best pathway to both engage students and preserve academic standards."

Notice how this introduction:

- Summarizes the conflict (tech in schools).
- Mentions multiple viewpoints (tech integration vs. restriction).
- States a clear stance (a **balanced** approach is best).

2. Body Paragraphs: Development and Support

The body of your essay is where you **examine perspectives** more thoroughly and **defend your viewpoint** with **examples** or **explanations**. Typically, you'll have **2–3 body paragraphs**. Here's a common approach:

1. **Paragraph 1**: Address or compare **Perspective 1**
   - Explain what the perspective is.
   - Discuss its strengths and weaknesses.
   - Relate it briefly to your stance (e.g., "Although Perspective 1 raises valid concerns, it overlooks …").
2. **Paragraph 2**: Address or compare **Perspective 2**
   - Same process: restate that viewpoint, analyze it, compare/contrast it with yours.
   - If your essay strongly aligns with one perspective, use this paragraph to highlight why it resonates with your position.
3. **Paragraph 3** (Optional/As Time Allows): Integrate or refute **Perspective 3**
   - You can also use this paragraph to propose **your** solution or perspective in greater detail if you've only briefly mentioned it.
   - If you have time, incorporate **counterarguments**—discuss why an opposing perspective is less convincing or how your viewpoint addresses potential pitfalls.

Writing Effective Body Paragraphs

- **Topic Sentence**: Each paragraph begins with a clear, guiding idea (e.g., "Perspective 1 emphasizes the value of hands-on skill development, but it underestimates the role of theoretical knowledge.").
- **Evidence and Examples**:

    - Real-world scenarios, hypothetical illustrations, or historical/societal references can bolster your reasoning.
    - Stay focused: Choose examples that tie directly to the prompt's issue.
- **Logical Transitions**:
    - Words like "Furthermore," "Nevertheless," "By contrast," help the reader follow your thought progression.
    - Linking back to the thesis ensures consistency.

3. Conclusion: Summarize and Extend

Your conclusion should **restate** your overall stance, succinctly **acknowledge** the significance of the issue, and leave the reader with a **sense of closure**. Even if pressed for time, aim for at least **2–3 sentences** that neatly wrap up your argument.

1. **Re-emphasize Your Position**
    - Don't introduce brand-new evidence. Instead, briefly reaffirm how the points made in the body paragraphs support your stance.
2. **Offer a Forward-Looking Statement**
    - Consider the broader implications or next steps: "Adopting balanced policies ensures that schools adapt to modern technology while preserving academic integrity."
3. **Avoid a Weak "In Conclusion"**
    - A generic concluding phrase can be fine, but try to be direct and purposeful. A statement like "Ultimately, by acknowledging each perspective's concerns and focusing on balanced solutions, society can …" shows more engagement.

Conclusion Example (Brief)

"By recognizing the merits and drawbacks of each perspective, we see that technology need not be all-or-nothing in education. A balanced approach—embracing tools that foster creativity while maintaining clear guidelines—can uphold both student engagement and academic rigor. Such a strategy prepares learners for a tech-driven future without sacrificing the focused environment essential to genuine learning."

Practical Tips for Strong Structuring

1. **Outline Quickly**: In your 40-minute window, spend a couple of minutes planning paragraph topics and examples.
2. **Use the Prompt's Language**: Echo key terms (but don't plagiarize). This ensures clarity and direct relevance to the question.
3. **Adapt as Needed**: If you only have time for two body paragraphs, ensure they're well-developed. Quality > quantity.
4. **Stay Focused**: Each paragraph should connect back to your thesis—avoid tangents or filler.

By following this structured approach—**introduction**, **body**, **conclusion**—you'll create a clear, compelling argument that addresses each perspective thoughtfully. Next, in **Section 11.3**, we'll deepen your essay by incorporating **effective examples** and **rebutting counterarguments** to further strengthen your case.

11.3 EFFECTIVE EXAMPLES & COUNTERARGUMENTS

A strong ACT Writing essay must illustrate your stance with **concrete, relevant examples** and demonstrate your **critical thinking** by engaging with counterarguments. Showing the reader that you can balance multiple viewpoints—and still defend a coherent position—raises the sophistication of your response and boosts your score. Below, we delve deeper into selecting robust examples and addressing opposing perspectives.

1. Selecting and Shaping Your Examples

When constructing examples, consider **what type** of illustration will best support your argument and fit within the limited time you have:

1. **Real-World Events or Case Studies**
    - **Why They Work**: They lend **credibility** to your argument because they're grounded in actual occurrences.
    - **Tips**:
        - Choose examples that **most readers can recognize** (e.g., referencing a well-known environmental initiative, a notable historical policy, or a commonly reported social trend).
        - Briefly summarize the event or outcome—focus on the key details directly relevant to the essay prompt.
2. **Historical or Cultural References**
    - **Why They Work**: They show an awareness of broader contexts and how similar issues were handled in the past.
    - **Tips**:
        - Keep them succinct. For instance: "During the Great Depression, government programs like the TVA exemplified how targeted investments can revitalize communities."
        - Highlight the **lessons learned** or parallels to the current issue.
3. **Statistical or Scientific Illustrations**
    - **Why They Work**: Numbers can be **persuasive** if they clearly back your point.
    - **Tips**:
        - If you don't have an exact figure, you can still use an **approximate** or **hypothetical** statistic as long as it's reasonable and consistent with the prompt (e.g., "A 2020 survey found that nearly 60% of college students…")
        - Ensure the statistic is relevant—random data without a link to the argument is ineffective.
4. **Personal Anecdotes or Hypotheticals**
    - **Why They Work**: They can be **engaging** and easy to generate under time pressure.
    - **Tips**:
        - Tie them directly to the **prompt**: "Growing up in a rural area, I experienced the challenges of limited internet access, illustrating how crucial connectivity is for student success."
        - Avoid overly detailed or random stories—focus on how the anecdote exemplifies a broader principle.
5. **Comparative or Contrasting Examples**
    - **Why They Work**: By showcasing two different instances—one successful, one failing— you highlight the **factors** that support or undermine your stance.
    - **Tips**:
        - Example: "While City A's recycling program thrived due to strong community engagement, City B's attempts stagnated without clear incentives, proving that public support is key."

2. Integrating Examples into Your Paragraphs

Examples are most powerful when they flow **naturally** and are **fully explained**. Here's a step-by-step method to integrate them effectively:

1. **Topic Sentence or Transition**
    - Prepare the reader: "One pertinent illustration of technology's impact on education is…"
    - This sets up why you're introducing the example.
2. **State the Example Clearly**
    - Give the **who, what, when**: "In 2019, Greenridge High School rolled out a tablet-based curriculum across all grade levels…"
3. **Discuss the Outcome/Significance**
    - Focus on **relevance**: "Within six months, students' average math scores rose by 15%, attributed partly to interactive learning apps."

   - Connect it **directly** to your argument: "This improvement underpins the idea that technology, used responsibly, can bolster academic performance rather than distract."
4. **Transition Back to the Main Argument**
   - Reinforce your stance: "Hence, while some fear devices lead to distraction, Greenridge's results suggest structured guidance can channel technology toward legitimate educational gains."

(Aim for a succinct but complete illustration, typically 3–5 sentences in a single paragraph.)

3. The Importance of Counterarguments

Demonstrating that you're aware of and can **address opposing views** sets your writing apart. It proves you're not ignoring valid concerns.

1. **What is a Counterargument?**
   - A perspective that **challenges** or **refutes** part (or all) of your main claim.
   - For instance, if you advocate for mandatory community service in high school, a counterargument might be that forcing students to volunteer undermines the spirit of volunteerism.
2. **Where to Place It**
   - Typically after you've established your own stance, so the reader first understands **your** position.
   - You can introduce it within the body paragraphs, dedicating a section to "While some might argue X…"
3. **How to Address It**
   - **Concession**: If you find some **merit** in the opposing view, briefly acknowledge that. This can soften the "us vs. them" feeling: "It's true that mandatory service might feel forced, yet it can still cultivate broader community awareness and empathy."
   - **Refutation**: Identify a flaw or limitation: "However, this argument fails to note that well-designed service programs offer students choice, preserving genuine engagement."
4. **Bridge Back to Your Thesis**
   - Always conclude with a **return** to your main argument: "Thus, while concerns about voluntarism are valid, these can be mitigated by flexible program design."

4. Potential Counterarguments to Look For

Depending on the **prompt's topic**, counterarguments can take many forms:

- **Financial Constraints**: If you propose a large-scale policy, critics might question cost or budget implications.
- **Freedom vs. Regulation**: If you support stricter regulations or safety measures, expect pushback on personal liberties.
- **Unintended Consequences**: A new policy or technology might have side effects you must address.
- **Cultural or Ethical Objections**: Some solutions may clash with societal values or moral perspectives.

When scanning the prompt's **provided perspectives**, identify the position(s) that conflict with yours. If you're creating a fresh angle, anticipate what one of the official perspectives would say against it.

5. Balancing Example and Counterargument Time

In a **40-minute** essay, time is tight. Here's how to balance effectively:

1. **Plan**:
   - Spend 2–4 minutes deciding which **main** example(s) you'll use and which **key** counterargument you'll address.
2. **One Solid Counterargument**:
   - Typically, you only need **one** developed counterargument paragraph—or a portion of a paragraph—to show nuance. More than that risks shortchanging your main points.
3. **Approximate Distribution**:
   - **Introduction**: 1 short paragraph

    - **Body**: 2–3 paragraphs (some or all referencing examples, 1 including counterargument)
    - **Conclusion**: 1 short paragraph

6. Pitfalls to Avoid

1. **Irrelevant or Forced Examples**
    - Don't pick an example simply because you recall it well if it barely connects to the prompt.
2. **Overly Long Anecdotes**
    - A drawn-out personal story can overshadow the central issue—be concise.
3. **"Straw Man" Counterarguments**
    - Don't misrepresent the opposing viewpoint in an oversimplified way. Your essay is stronger if you tackle a **reasonable** version of the opposing stance.
4. **Dropping the Counterargument**
    - After mentioning the opposing view, **resolve** it. Don't leave it hanging—show how it influences or fails to alter your conclusion.

Key Takeaways

- **Examples** breathe life into your thesis. Choose **specific, relevant** ones that clearly illustrate why your stance matters or makes sense.
- **Counterarguments** demonstrate critical thinking. Briefly present an opposing viewpoint, **concede** anything valid, and **refute** its core weaknesses.
- **Efficiency** is crucial. You have limited time, so plan your examples and your main counterargument in advance to ensure they align with and **strengthen** your argument.
- **Stay Grounded** in the prompt. Keep returning to the central issue and the perspectives you must address.

Armed with purposeful examples and a logical approach to counterarguments, you'll craft a thorough, persuasive ACT Writing essay. Next, in **Section 11.4**, we'll cover **common mistakes** to watch out for—ranging from grammar slips to unclear structure—and apply **quick revision methods** to maximize clarity under exam conditions.

11.4 COMMON MISTAKES & QUICK REVISION METHODS

Even the most insightful argument can lose effectiveness if it's hampered by **organizational flaws**, **grammatical errors**, or **unclear connections** between ideas. In the pressure of a 40-minute ACT Writing Test, some lapses are natural—but staying aware of frequent pitfalls and employing quick fixes can help you submit a polished essay. Here are **common mistakes** and methods for fast but effective revision.

1. Common Mistakes

1.1 Misinterpreting or Straying from the Prompt

- **Symptom**: Your essay drifts into irrelevant tangents, or you fixate on a sub-issue not central to the question.
- **Solution**: Re-read the prompt. Ensure each paragraph directly addresses the **given topic** and the **perspectives**.

1.2 Neglecting to Address All Perspectives

- **Symptom**: Your essay focuses on your viewpoint but ignores or barely mentions the provided perspectives.
- **Solution**: Even if you strongly agree with one perspective, devote at least a sentence or two per perspective to show you've considered each. This is essential for a higher score.

1.3 Weak or Confusing Thesis

- **Symptom**: Readers can't pinpoint your main stance or how you'll approach the perspectives.

- **Solution**: Craft a **clear, concise** thesis that states your position (or how you blend multiple perspectives). Place it near the end of the introduction.

1.4 Lack of Specific Examples

- **Symptom**: Your paragraphs rely on vague statements like "It will be good for society," without concrete illustration.
- **Solution**: Include at least one or two **specific** examples or mini-case studies. Even a succinct real-world reference can strengthen credibility.

1.5 Poor Organization and Transition

- **Symptom**: Paragraphs feel randomly arranged; readers struggle to see how each point builds on the last.
- **Solution**: Use **topic sentences** to introduce each paragraph's main focus. Insert transitional words or phrases ("However," "For instance," "In contrast," "Additionally") to signal shifts or continuations of thought.

1.6 Overloading with Grammar/Mechanical Errors

- **Symptom**: Frequent run-ons, spelling slips, or punctuation mistakes can distract from your ideas.
- **Solution**: Plan to **save a brief moment** at the end for a final scan. Focus on obvious errors that hamper clarity.

1.7 Ignoring Counterarguments Entirely

- **Symptom**: Your essay reads as one-sided. Readers might suspect you haven't considered alternative views.
- **Solution**: Briefly present an opposing idea and either concede a valid point or refute it. This elevates the sophistication of your argument.

1.8 Rushed or Incomplete Conclusion

- **Symptom**: The essay ends abruptly without restating the thesis or summarizing key points.
- **Solution**: Allocate **at least 2–3 sentences** for a conclusion that reiterates your stance and leaves a sense of closure.

2. Quick Revision Methods

Given the **tight timing** (40 minutes), revision must be **swift** but strategic. Aim for a **1–2 minute** review if possible.

2.1 Skim for Clarity

- **Process**: After writing, read each paragraph's first and last sentences. Check: Do these lines reflect what the paragraph is supposed to convey? Does the conclusion match your introduction's promise?

2.2 Check Thesis Consistency

- **Process**: Re-read your thesis, then ensure each body paragraph aligns with it. If any paragraph contradicts or strays, add a clarifying sentence or transition.

2.3 Confirm You Addressed All Perspectives

- **Process**: Quickly scan for explicit references to the prompt's three perspectives. If one is missing or underdeveloped, insert a short paragraph or sentence acknowledging it.

2.4 Target Grammar & Punctuation Hot Spots

- **Process**: Look for common pitfalls:
  - **Run-on Sentences**: Split or use proper conjunctions.
  - **Comma Use**: Ensure clarity in compound or complex sentences.
  - **Homophones**: Watch for "their/there/they're," "your/you're," etc.

2.5 Eliminate Redundancies & Fillers

- **Process**: Phrases like "in order to," "the fact that," or repeated words slow the reader. Simplify for directness.
- **Example**: Replace "due to the fact that technology is widely used" with "because technology is widely used."

2.6 Strengthen Transitions If Needed

- **Process**: Insert or adjust linking phrases so paragraphs flow logically.
- **Examples**: "Furthermore," "On the other hand," "Nevertheless," "Consequently."

2.7 Ensure a Polished Conclusion

- **Process**: If your conclusion is missing, write a **very short final paragraph** recapping your stance. A single polished statement can suffice over none at all.

3. Final Tips for Maximizing Impact

1. **Write Legibly** (for handwritten tests): Unclear handwriting can hinder grading, even if your logic is sound.
2. **Stay Confident**: If time is running low, prioritize clarity in your last statements. Don't panic—focus on finishing strong.
3. **Maintain a Formal Yet Approachable Tone**: Avoid slang, but also skip overly convoluted vocabulary if it doesn't serve clarity.

Conclusion

By anticipating common pitfalls—like failing to address all perspectives, losing focus on the prompt, or letting grammar errors slip through—you can apply **quick, targeted revisions** that significantly improve your essay's polish. Combining these revision tactics with a well-structured argument and concrete examples ensures a persuasive, high-scoring ACT Writing response.

You're now equipped with the core strategies to handle every aspect of the Writing Test: from understanding the prompt to structuring your argument, supporting it with examples, addressing counterarguments, and finally revising effectively.

CHAPTER 12

WRITING PRACTICE

12.1 SHORT PRACTICE PROMPTS & OUTLINES

Practice is key to building confidence and speed for the ACT's optional Writing Test. Below are **four short prompts** reflecting the style of ACT essay questions—each featuring **multiple perspectives** on a contemporary issue. After each prompt, you'll find a **brief outline** illustrating how you could structure a response.

Prompt 1: Technology in Public Spaces

Prompt

Society debates the merits of introducing advanced technology (e.g., facial recognition, digital tracking) in public spaces for security and convenience. Three perspectives emerge:

- **Perspective 1**: High-tech surveillance fosters public safety by preventing crime and aiding law enforcement.
- **Perspective 2**: Deploying such technology invades personal privacy and sets a dangerous precedent for government overreach.
- **Perspective 3**: A balanced system with transparent oversight and opt-in models could enhance public safety while respecting individual rights.

Outline Example

1. **Introduction** (Context + Thesis)
    - Mention how technology has rapidly evolved, creating tension between **safety** and **privacy**.
    - State your position (e.g., that a **regulated approach** aligns best with both security and civil liberties).
2. **Body Paragraph 1**: Address Perspective 1 (Pro-Surveillance)
    - **Strengths**: Evidence of crime prevention, faster law enforcement response.
    - **Weaknesses**: Potential for abuse, cost considerations.
    - **Tie to Thesis**: While beneficial, needs checks to avoid overreach.
3. **Body Paragraph 2**: Address Perspective 2 (Privacy Concerns)
    - Acknowledge legitimate fears: data misuse, chilling effect on public life.
    - Counterargument: With strict regulations, many privacy risks can be mitigated.
    - **Example**: Countries implementing robust data protection laws.
4. **Body Paragraph 3**: Discuss Perspective 3 (Balanced System) & Own Take
    - Argue why combining oversight committees, public transparency, and user consent can strike a workable compromise.
    - Possibly highlight real-world example (e.g., pilot programs with community feedback).
5. **Conclusion**
    - Reiterate the necessity of striking a balance: we can deploy advanced tech while safeguarding fundamental rights.

Prompt 2: College Admissions Policies

Prompt

Rising college tuition and competitive admissions prompt debates on the best approach to college entry. Three perspectives:

- **Perspective 1**: Prioritize **standardized test scores** for fairness and objectivity.
- **Perspective 2**: Emphasize **holistic reviews** (essays, community service, personal background) to reflect the student's true potential.

- **Perspective 3**: Implement **lotteries** or guaranteed admissions for a wider demographic reach, increasing socioeconomic diversity.

Outline Example

1. **Introduction**
    - Frame the issue: the tension between standardized criteria vs. broader definitions of merit.
    - Thesis: Argue for a **hybrid** admissions system that weights both academic performance and holistic factors.
2. **Body Paragraph 1**: Perspective 1 (Test Scores)
    - **Pros**: Clear benchmark, less subjective.
    - **Cons**: Ignores creativity, personal growth, resource disparities in test prep.
3. **Body Paragraph 2**: Perspective 2 (Holistic Review)
    - **Pros**: Captures character, leadership, unique talents; fosters diverse student bodies.
    - **Counterargument**: Subject to bias or inconsistent evaluation.
4. **Body Paragraph 3**: Perspective 3 (Lotteries / Guaranteed Spots) + Personal Stance
    - Discuss potential to improve representation but question feasibility (e.g., might overlook academic readiness).
    - Suggest a **balanced** approach: combine minimum academic thresholds with deeper personal reviews.
5. **Conclusion**
    - Summarize how a multi-faceted system respects both quantitative measures and individual experiences.

Prompt 3: Mandatory Community Service

Prompt

Some high schools now require students to complete community service hours to graduate. Three perspectives:

- **Perspective 1**: Mandatory service fosters civic responsibility and empathy in youth.
- **Perspective 2**: Forcing "volunteering" undermines genuine charity and places undue burden on students.
- **Perspective 3**: Schools should offer **incentives** (e.g., scholarship points) rather than outright mandates to encourage service without coercion.

Outline Example

1. **Introduction**
    - Highlight the increasing trend of service requirements.
    - Thesis: Argue that **guided service** with choice can create a beneficial experience that remains voluntary in spirit.
2. **Body Paragraph 1**: Perspective 1 (Benefits of Required Service)
    - Emphasize positive impacts: empathy, community engagement, practical skills.
    - Possible example: "X High School's success with structured service programs."
3. **Body Paragraph 2**: Perspective 2 (Opposition to Coercion)
    - Valid concern: authenticity of volunteerism compromised, potential stress on students.
    - Counter: Provide means for **flexibility** (choice of service area, alternative tasks) to preserve genuine interest.
4. **Body Paragraph 3**: Perspective 3 (Incentive-Based Approach) + Your Position
    - Incentives (credits, recognition) might motivate students, but risk overshadowing altruistic values.
    - Conclude with your stance: a balanced plan that merges mandatory hours with ample choice and reflection.
5. **Conclusion**
    - Reassert that well-designed programs can strengthen student development without sacrificing the genuine spirit of service.

Prompt 4: The Role Of Arts Funding

Prompt

As public budgets tighten, some argue for reducing or eliminating funding for arts programs, believing those resources should go to more critical services. Three perspectives:

- **Perspective 1**: Arts funding is vital for cultural identity and innovation; reducing it harms societal growth.
- **Perspective 2**: Essential services (healthcare, infrastructure, education basics) must come first; arts can be funded privately.
- **Perspective 3**: A **middle ground** could scale back arts budgets but keep key community programs alive through partnerships and targeted grants.

Outline Example

1. **Introduction**
   - Note how the arts often face budget cuts during economic downturns.
   - Thesis: Argue that **art programs** are integral to community well-being and can be funded responsibly.
2. **Body Paragraph 1**: Perspective 1 (Importance of Arts)
   - **Pros**: Cultural enrichment, tourism, creative thinking.
   - **Support with an Example**: A city that revitalized its economy via arts festivals or museums.
3. **Body Paragraph 2**: Perspective 2 (Prioritize Essentials)
   - Concede that vital services must be funded.
   - Refutation: Demonstrate how arts can be part of essential community development (e.g., therapy programs, education synergy).
4. **Body Paragraph 3**: Perspective 3 (Compromise) + Own View
   - Partnerships with local businesses, partial public funding, philanthropic contributions.
   - Affirm that a balanced approach avoids undermining creativity while still respecting budget constraints.
5. **Conclusion**
   - Reiterate that thoughtful allocation and cooperation can sustain arts programs without jeopardizing fundamental services.

Final Suggestions for Practice

1. **Draft Briefly**
   - For each prompt, spend **5 minutes** creating your own outline, focusing on the **thesis** and **paragraph flow**.
2. **Time Yourself**
   - If you want a full simulation, attempt to **write a complete essay** in **40 minutes**: 2–3 minutes reading the prompt, 4–5 minutes outlining, 30 minutes drafting, 2–3 minutes revising.
3. **Compare Approaches**
   - Try different angles or stances—practice writing for or against a prompt's perspective to stretch your argumentative range.

EXAMPLE OF ESSAY STRUCTURES

Sample Essay For Prompt 1: Technology In Public Spaces

Prompt Recap

Society debates the merits of introducing advanced technology (e.g., facial recognition, digital tracking) in public areas for security and convenience.

- **Perspective 1**: High-tech surveillance fosters safety by preventing crime.
- **Perspective 2**: This technology invades personal privacy and sets a risky precedent.

- **Perspective 3**: A balanced system with transparent oversight could enhance safety while respecting individual rights.

Sample Essay

Introduction

Public spaces worldwide are increasingly adopting advanced surveillance tools—ranging from facial recognition to license plate readers. While these systems promise heightened security, they also raise concerns about privacy and potential misuse of personal data. Although some contend that comprehensive monitoring deters crime (Perspective 1), others argue it endangers civil liberties (Perspective 2). In my view, a **regulated, transparent approach** (Perspective 3) can indeed bolster public safety without sacrificing fundamental freedoms.

Body Paragraph 1

Proponents of widespread surveillance emphasize concrete benefits. For instance, major cities utilizing real-time facial recognition claim lower crime rates, as law enforcement can identify suspects faster. This aligns with Perspective 1, suggesting such measures protect citizens by swiftly catching criminals. However, challenges remain—these technologies are expensive and occasionally inaccurate, leading to false matches and potential bias. Thus, while their security potential is genuine, unchecked deployment risks error and overreach.

Body Paragraph 2

On the other side, critics warn of privacy erosion (Perspective 2). In a world where cameras track every movement, individuals may feel constantly watched, chilling free expression. Moreover, data breaches or government misuse can escalate from possibility to reality if adequate safeguards are absent. Recent controversies over unauthorized facial recognition databases underscore the vulnerability of personal data. Though these concerns are legitimate, they do not necessarily mean all surveillance should be abandoned. Instead, it implies that we need robust oversight.

Body Paragraph 3

A middle ground (Perspective 3) recognizes the need for public safety while instituting accountability and transparency. Cities could establish independent review boards, stringent data-retention limits, and well-defined rules on when and how such technology is used. For example, pilot programs that require clear signage indicating camera use or allow individuals to request deletion of personal data can protect citizen rights. By fusing the benefits of advanced surveillance with strong checks, we maintain order without sliding into an Orwellian reality.

Conclusion

Ultimately, technology in public spaces can enhance security but must be applied judiciously. Embracing a balanced, well-regulated approach reduces crime and abuse simultaneously. With transparent oversight, we retain the advantages of modern surveillance while safeguarding civil liberties—the hallmark of a society that values both safety and freedom.

Sample Essay For Prompt 2: College Admissions Policies

Prompt Recap

Debates arise over how to admit students fairly amid rising tuition and competition.

- **Perspective 1**: Prioritize standardized test scores for objectivity.
- **Perspective 2**: Emphasize holistic reviews (essays, background) to capture true potential.
- **Perspective 3**: Implement lotteries or guaranteed admissions for broader access.

Sample Essay

Introduction
As the pool of college applicants expands, determining fair admissions policies becomes more pressing. Some favor standardized testing for a clear benchmark (Perspective 1), while others stress character and life experiences (Perspective 2). Alternatively, a lottery approach (Perspective 3) attempts to grant wider access regardless of academic metrics. In my view, a **hybrid system** that uses both objective scores and holistic reviews strikes the best balance between merit and equity.

Body Paragraph 1

Standardized tests offer a straightforward, if imperfect, measure. Proponents of Perspective 1 note that such exams minimize subjective bias and reward diligent academic preparation. Indeed, historically, tests have helped identify talented students who might otherwise be overlooked. Yet, critics point out that not all students have equal test-prep resources, leading to disparities. Solely relying on scores can overlook leadership, creativity, or resilience factors that a test can't measure.

Body Paragraph 2

Holistic evaluations (Perspective 2) aim to capture these intangible qualities—essays, community service, extracurricular achievements, and personal hardships. This approach champions a more rounded view of each applicant, acknowledging that students are more than just their test results. However, holistic methods can vary in consistency. One admissions officer's interpretation of a personal story may differ drastically from another's, introducing subjectivity. Still, many elite universities successfully blend these measures, which implies the method can work with robust guidelines.

Body Paragraph 3

While a lottery system (Perspective 3) does promote broader socioeconomic representation, it risks admitting students unprepared for rigorous programs. It also diminishes recognition of academic dedication. A more viable path is to set baseline academic benchmarks—ensuring readiness—while also giving significant weight to personal qualities. This hybrid ensures that those who excel academically aren't penalized, while students from diverse backgrounds get a fair shot to highlight unique experiences.

Conclusion
Ultimately, no single admissions metric can flawlessly gauge student potential. By integrating test scores with holistic criteria, colleges can maintain fairness, reflect the range of student achievements, and uphold academic standards. Such a balanced policy respects academic merit while enriching campuses with diverse talents and perspectives.

Sample Essay For Prompt 3: Mandatory Community Service

Prompt Recap

High schools debate requiring community service hours to graduate.

- **Perspective 1**: Mandatory service fosters civic responsibility.
- **Perspective 2**: Forced volunteering undermines genuine charity.
- **Perspective 3**: Offering incentives (rather than mandates) encourages service without coercion.

Sample Essay

Introduction
Amid calls for greater civic engagement, many high schools have introduced mandatory community service hours. Some educators believe these requirements teach compassion (Perspective 1), while critics worry enforced volunteering is contradictory (Perspective 2). Others recommend incentivized service (Perspective 3) to preserve

voluntarism. I propose that **structured but flexible service**—with student input—can harness the benefits of community engagement while maintaining a sense of genuine contribution.

Body Paragraph 1

Requiring volunteer hours can indeed cultivate empathy and teamwork in teenagers. Perspective 1 highlights that practical experience—like serving at food banks or tutoring peers—broadens students' awareness of social needs. For instance, a local high school program that mandates 20 hours of service found students reported higher satisfaction with their sense of purpose. However, critics worry compulsion undercuts sincerity. This concern is valid but can be mitigated if schools allow students to choose causes that resonate with their interests.

Body Paragraph 2

From Perspective 2's viewpoint, mandatory service risks superficial involvement—students may simply chase hours without internalizing lessons. Yet genuine altruism can still develop if reflection and choice are part of the curriculum. Schools can encourage journaling or group discussions, helping participants connect the service to broader social issues. Thus, even if an initial push is "required," it can evolve into a more heartfelt commitment.

Body Paragraph 3

As for Perspective 3, offering incentives such as scholarships or credit points is attractive but may inadvertently shift focus to extrinsic rewards. To me, a balanced approach merges the mandatory element with freedom: students must complete community hours but have broad categories to pick from, plus reflection tasks. This way, the sense of volunteering remains largely self-directed, preserving authenticity.

Conclusion

In the end, making community service a well-designed component of graduation fosters social awareness and personal growth. While forced volunteering alone isn't ideal, flexible structures and reflective practices can ensure students' experiences are both fulfilling and genuinely valuable to the community.

Sample Essay For Prompt 4: The Role Of Arts Funding

Prompt Recap

As public budgets shrink, some advocate cutting arts funding to prioritize essential services.

- **Perspective 1**: Arts funding is vital for cultural growth.
- **Perspective 2**: Basic services must come first; let private donors support the arts.
- **Perspective 3**: Reduce arts budgets but retain critical programs via partnerships and targeted grants.

Sample Essay

Introduction

With municipal budgets under strain, arts programs are frequently on the chopping block. Proponents of arts funding (Perspective 1) emphasize the cultural and economic benefits of a vibrant arts scene, while others (Perspective 2) insist resources should go to core public services such as healthcare or infrastructure. Another perspective (Perspective 3) seeks a middle ground, trimming arts budgets but preserving core initiatives. I believe arts funding, though scalable, is crucial to societal well-being and should not be dismissed outright.

Body Paragraph 1

Perspective 1 underscores the intangible yet significant value of the arts: fostering cultural identity, spurring local tourism, and stimulating innovation. For example, cities like Glasgow or Bilbao reinvented themselves around museums and festivals, boosting visitor numbers and revitalizing neighborhoods. While cost-saving critics may question devoting funds to "non-essentials," these cultural hubs often pay back in job creation and civic pride.

Body Paragraph 2

Meanwhile, Perspective 2 rightly contends that life-saving services like emergency responses or infrastructure upkeep must rank high. If governments face severe deficits, it may appear more prudent to cut museum expansions than a hospital. Yet the arts do not necessarily conflict with these priorities. In fact, some art programs directly benefit health—like public art in hospitals or community outreach that fosters therapeutic expression. Painting arts as purely extraneous overlooks their interdisciplinary value.

Body Paragraph 3

Thus, Perspective 3's notion of compromise is sensible. Rather than slashing arts completely, targeted reductions coupled with public-private partnerships allow essential programs to continue. Private sponsors can adopt cultural institutions, bridging shortfalls. This synergy ensures that fundamental social services remain robust while still nurturing creative expression. Though the arts may not always be "first-tier" necessities, they remain a crucial pillar for a thriving society.

Conclusion

Ultimately, the arts invigorate communities in ways that purely functional services cannot. Balancing budgets should not equate to erasing cultural lifelines. By refining funding strategies—allocating smaller but sustainable grants and inviting private support—municipalities can uphold the arts' invaluable role in shaping civic identity and fostering collective well-being.

Next Steps

- **Practice Under Timed Conditions**: Attempt writing a complete essay for at least one prompt, aiming for ~40 minutes total.
- **Review**: Compare your work to these samples—did you **address all perspectives**? **State a clear thesis**? Provide **examples** or a **counterargument**?
- **Refine**: Each essay can be improved by stronger transitions, more concrete illustrations, or crisper conclusions. Apply the revision tips from **Chapter 11** to elevate clarity and coherence.

12.2 SAMPLE ESSAYS (HIGH-, MID-, AND LOW-SCORING EXAMPLES)

Below are **three essays** responding to the **same prompt**—each sample aims to illustrate a **different scoring tier** (high, mid-range, and low) in an ACT Writing-style response. As you read, notice how the essays handle:

- **Clarity of Argument** (thesis and focus)
- **Use of Examples** and development of ideas
- **Engagement with Multiple Perspectives** (addressing or acknowledging each)
- **Organization** (intro, body, conclusion) and **Language Control**

Prompt: Social Media's Influence on Public Opinion

Social media platforms have gained enormous power in shaping public opinion. Some argue that these platforms broaden access to information and democratize voices (**Perspective 1**). Others believe social media fosters misinformation and erodes meaningful discourse (**Perspective 2**). Yet another perspective sees social media as a neutral tool—potentially useful or harmful depending on how it's regulated or used (**Perspective 3**). In your essay, analyze the relationship between social media and the formation of public opinion, evaluate each perspective, and develop your own stance.

A. High-Scoring Example

Introduction

In the last decade, social media has evolved from casual friend updates to a central force shaping global conversations. Today, platforms like Twitter, Facebook, and TikTok can amplify marginalized voices (Perspective 1), yet they can also spread rumors and hostility at lightning speed (Perspective 2). A third view notes that social media is neither inherently good nor bad—its impact depends on how society and policymakers choose to govern it (Perspective 3). While social media inherently offers unique opportunities for inclusive dialogue, **robust moderation and transparent rules** are crucial to curb misinformation and maintain constructive discourse.

Body Paragraph 1: Perspective 1

Proponents of the first perspective emphasize the democratizing effect: social media grants individuals from diverse backgrounds the ability to reach large audiences without traditional gatekeepers. For instance, grassroots activists frequently rally global support using hashtags and live streams, shedding light on issues that mainstream media outlets might overlook. This effect is indeed transformative, as it enables grassroots movements to flourish—consider how the "Arab Spring" protests gained momentum via social media, rallying international attention. However, the absence of filters or fact-checking means that while many voices can be heard, not all are reliable, blending constructive activism with potential false narratives.

Body Paragraph 2: Perspective 2

Critics worry that this same openness fuels misinformation. Perspective 2 warns that viral rumors or polarizing headlines can overshadow truth, creating echo chambers where users only see content reinforcing their preconceptions. Recent studies on conspiracy theories demonstrate how quickly unverified claims can circulate. The emotional, rapid-fire nature of social media can reward sensationalism over facts. Despite this valid concern, banning social media or dismissing its benefits altogether might be extreme. It seems more effective to implement responsible governance—like fact-checks or community-driven reporting systems—rather than discredit the platforms entirely.

Body Paragraph 3: Perspective 3 & My Position

A third stance correctly points out that social media itself is merely a "tool," shaped by its design and regulations. My view closely aligns here: *if* platforms and policymakers invest in transparent guidelines—clearly labeling misleading content, discouraging harassment, and promoting authoritative sources—social media can remain a powerful means for global dialogue while minimizing misinformation. For example, certain platforms have begun partnering with reputable fact-checking organizations, reducing the spread of spurious headlines. When properly regulated, these networks serve as communal spaces for diverse opinions, bridging geographical divides without succumbing to disinformation.

Conclusion

Ultimately, social media reflects the intentions and policies of those who run it and use it. By integrating the best elements of open communication (Perspective 1) with stricter ethical standards to combat misinformation (addressing Perspective 2), we uphold the notion that social platforms are tools that can be shaped for positive impact (Perspective 3). With vigilant governance and user responsibility, social media can continue fostering inclusive engagement without devolving into chaos or echo chambers.

B. Mid-Scoring Example

Introduction

Social media has rapidly changed how people share news and opinions. Some believe it's a great way for everyone to have a voice (Perspective 1). Others think it leads to fake news and negative arguments (Perspective 2). A third viewpoint says social media itself isn't to blame—regulations and user behavior determine if it's good or bad (Perspective 3). I think social media can benefit society if we find the right balance of freedom and responsibility.

Body Paragraph 1

First, social media does let ordinary people speak up, which is important for democracy. For instance, during certain political elections, candidates with fewer resources can still get noticed online. However, there are also accounts that spread rumors. People share stories without verifying facts. So while it gives a voice to many, it also pushes misinformation sometimes.

Body Paragraph 2

We also see how it can be a place for harmful content. Some pages spread hate speech or false conspiracies. This matches Perspective 2 about misinformation. But even so, shutting down social media wouldn't solve the problem. It's more about guidelines and possible controls. So I relate more to Perspective 3: the platform's impact depends on how it's used. With better moderation or fact-checking, social media might still remain open for healthy discussions.

Conclusion
In conclusion, social media can both help and harm public opinion. It's not simply positive or negative—human behavior and regulations matter a lot. If we manage it wisely, people can continue enjoying free expression (Perspective 1) while minimizing the downsides (Perspective 2). Ultimately, we should treat social media like any powerful tool, making sure it's used responsibly so society benefits overall.

C. Low-Scoring Example

Introduction
Social media is everywhere. Some say it gives power to people, some say it spreads lies, and some say it's just a tool. I think social media is good but also can be bad.

Body Paragraph

First, if you want to talk to your friends or share your ideas, you can do that with social media. That's what Perspective 1 talks about, freedom and stuff. On the other hand, some people spread rumors or false things. So that's Perspective 2. But if we do something about it, maybe it's fine—like Perspective 3 says. Also, it's not easy to fix everything because we have so many posts every day. People need to be careful.

Conclusion
In the end, social media is big. We can't ignore it. I guess if we watch out for fake news, it's okay. Maybe just have rules to stop misinformation. That's all.

Analysis of Each Example

1. **High-Scoring Essay**
   - **Depth of Analysis**: Thoroughly discusses each perspective with examples (Arab Spring, fact-checking initiatives).
   - **Organization**: Clear intro-body-conclusion structure, logical transitions, direct engagement with each perspective.
   - **Development**: Solid real-world illustrations, strong concluding statement.
2. **Mid-Scoring Essay**
   - **Clarity**: Addresses all perspectives and has a decent stance, though less detailed.
   - **Organization**: Decent but paragraphs are shorter, with fewer specific examples or references.
   - **Analysis**: Recognizes basic arguments but lacks the depth or stronger examples of the high-scoring essay.
3. **Low-Scoring Essay**
   - **Depth**: Minimal. Mentions perspectives superficially without substantial development.
   - **Organization & Detail**: Merged "body" paragraph is short, ideas are not expanded.
   - **Language**: Basic phrasing, limited transitions, lacks real examples or deeper reasoning.

Using These Essays for Practice

- **Compare & Contrast**: Note how the **high-scoring** version addresses each perspective comprehensively and uses well-chosen examples.

- **Identify Improvements**: If you find your essay resembles the mid-range or low-scoring format, add more specific **support**, clearer **structure**, and references to each perspective.
- **Time Yourself**: Recreate these essays under a 40-minute constraint to gauge pacing.

By analyzing these models, you can refine your own writing to approach the thoroughness and clarity of a **high-scoring** ACT Writing response.

12.3 SELF-EVALUATION CHECKLIST & PEER REVIEW SUGGESTIONS

After drafting practice essays, **reflecting on your own work** and seeking **constructive feedback** can significantly enhance your writing. Below is a **self-evaluation checklist** to guide you in reviewing your essay for clarity, organization, and depth. We also provide **peer review tips**, so you can exchange feedback with classmates or friends in a focused, productive way.

1. Self-Evaluation Checklist

Use this checklist after you've written a full practice essay under timed conditions. Spend a few minutes (ideally 5–10) reviewing your draft against these criteria:

1. **Prompt Alignment**
   - Did I fully **address the topic** given in the prompt (or inadvertently stray into unrelated details)?
   - Did I **acknowledge** and **integrate** the three provided perspectives in some way?
2. **Thesis Statement & Position**
   - Is my **main claim** or thesis apparent in the introduction (and perhaps revisited in the conclusion)?
   - Do I make it clear how my stance relates to the perspectives—whether I adopt one outright, modify it, or propose a blended view?
3. **Organization & Paragraph Flow**
   - Does each paragraph begin with a **topic sentence** that indicates its focus?
   - Are **transitions** between paragraphs (and within them) smooth and logical? (e.g., "However," "On the other hand," "In addition," etc.)
4. **Example Quality & Relevance**
   - Did I use **at least one or two concrete examples** to illustrate my points (e.g., real-world case, historical reference, or well-constructed hypothetical)?
   - Are these examples **explained** sufficiently—not just dropped in?
5. **Counterargument Treatment**
   - Is there a brief acknowledgment of an **opposing viewpoint**, followed by a **refutation** or **concession**?
   - Do I show why my stance remains strong despite that opposing argument?
6. **Clarity & Style**
   - Do my sentences read **smoothly**, or are there areas with repetitive language or unclear phrasing?
   - Are there **grammar, spelling, or punctuation** errors that might confuse readers?
7. **Conclusion Effectiveness**
   - Do I wrap up by **reiterating** my main stance without merely repeating the introduction?
   - Is there a **forward-looking** statement or final insight about the broader significance of the topic?
8. **Length & Time Management**
   - Did I produce a coherent essay within the **40-minute** limit?
   - If too short, did I cut crucial analysis? If too long, did I risk unpolished writing or run out of revision time?

2. Peer Review Suggestions

When offering or receiving peer feedback, **focus on constructive critique** rather than just identifying mistakes. Here's how to make peer review sessions more effective:

1. **Agree on Specific Goals**
   - Ask your peer: "What do you want feedback on the most—organization, argument clarity, examples, or grammar?"
   - This ensures the reviewer pays attention to those areas, providing targeted advice.
2. **Start with Strengths**
   - Even if an essay has weaknesses, highlight **what's working**: strong introduction, compelling example, a smooth transition, etc.
   - Positive comments encourage the writer to build on what they're doing well.
3. **Use "I" Statements & Open-Ended Questions**
   - Instead of "This paragraph is bad," say "I found it hard to follow your point here—could you clarify how it ties to your thesis?"
   - This tone fosters a more supportive environment and invites the writer to reflect.
4. **Offer Specific Advice**
   - Vague feedback like "needs more detail" is less helpful than "You mention data from a survey—consider explaining the year or result to illustrate your point more concretely."
   - If grammar is an issue, point to a specific sentence structure or punctuation rule.
5. **Look at Overall Structure**
   - Check if paragraphs follow a **logical sequence** and if transitions connect ideas.
   - Suggest rearranging paragraphs if the argument would flow better.
6. **Watch the Time Constraint**
   - In a group or class setting, keep peer reviews **timely and purposeful**. Spending too long dissecting minor flaws could overshadow bigger structural feedback.
7. **Conclude with a Positive Outlook**
   - Encourage the writer to revise key points but also reaffirm that their essay can be strong with focused improvements.

3. Putting It All into Practice

1. **Use the Checklist Yourself**: After each practice essay, mark where you feel confident and where you see gaps.
2. **Exchange Essays with a Peer**: Spend ~5 minutes reading each other's work, then ~5 minutes offering direct verbal or written notes.
3. **Revise with Purpose**: Implement the clearest, most impactful suggestions in your next draft.

By methodically **evaluating your own essays** and sharing them for **peer review**, you'll continue refining your ACT Writing skills. This cycle of writing, self-checking, and revising—plus outside feedback—builds a solid foundation for a **clear, well-structured, and insightful** essay on test day.

PART III

FULL-LENGTH PRACTICE TESTS

CHAPTER 13

FULL LENGTH PRACTICE TEST 1

ACT English Exam Section

PASSAGE I (Questions 1–15)

A Conversation with My Grandfather

My grandfather, a former school principal (1) have seen more cultural changes than anyone I know. He (2) grew up in an era when radios were a novelty, and television had not yet dominated living rooms. (3)His stories always captivate me, because I learn how quickly technology and social norms can shift.

Despite his advanced age, (4) my grandfather remains energetic. He volunteers at a local historical society, (5) collects old vinyl records, and mentors students in math. (6)I especially admire how he uses his experiences to show young people that knowledge is a lifelong pursuit.

"(7)I may be old," he jokes, "but I'm still learning something new everyday." (8)He often invites me to join him at the library, where we dig into newspapers from decades ago to investigate how times have changed. (9)We also watch documentaries about scientific breakthroughs from the last half-century (10) to appreciate the leaps humanity has made.

Grandfather's advice is simple (11) but crucial. He believes in reading widely, listening carefully, and (12) never to stop questioning the world around us. (13)He insists that each generation must build upon the lessons of the previous one while forging its own path.

Although he's seen an entire lifetime of transformation, (14) my grandfather's genuine curiosity about the future never fades. (15)He continues to live by his motto: stay curious, stay active, and share what you learn with others.

PASSAGE I Questions (1–15)

1.

A. NO CHANGE
B. has saw
C. has seen
D. had saw

2.

F. NO CHANGE
G. having grown
H. grew
J. growing

3.

A. NO CHANGE
B. His stories, always captivating, remind me

C. His captivating stories are reminding me

D. His stories always captivating remind me

4.

F. NO CHANGE

G. being so old

H. at his age

J. (Delete the underlined portion)

5.

A. NO CHANGE

B. collects old vinyl records; and mentors

C. collects old vinyl records and mentors

D. collects old, vinyl records and mentors

6.

F. NO CHANGE

G. I especially admire him because he uses

H. I especially admire him using

J. Especially admiring him, I watch how he uses

7.

A. NO CHANGE

B. "I may be old," he jokes. "But I'm still

C. "I may be old," he jokes, "but I'm still

D. "I may be old." He jokes, "but I'm still

8.

F. NO CHANGE

G. He occasionally invites me to join him at the library, where we dig into newspapers,

H. He often invites me to join him, we go to the library,

J. Inviting me to the library, he often goes,

9.

A. NO CHANGE

B. We also watch documentaries, about scientific breakthroughs from the last half-century

C. We watch documentaries also, about scientific breakthroughs from the last half-century

D. We also watch documentaries about scientific breakthroughs, from the last half-century

10.

F. NO CHANGE

G. for appreciating all the leaps

H. to appreciate leaps

J. to appreciate all of the great leaps

11.

A. NO CHANGE

B. simple, but crucial—

C. simple; but crucial
D. simple but; crucial

12.

F. NO CHANGE
G. never stop
H. never stopping
J. to never stop

13.

A. NO CHANGE
B. He insists, each generation must build upon the lessons of the previous one while forging
C. He insists that each generation must build, upon the lessons of the previous one while forging
D. He insists that each generation builds upon the lessons of the previous one while forging

14.

F. NO CHANGE
G. transformation
H. transformations
J. transformation:

15.

A. NO CHANGE
B. He continues living by his motto, "Stay curious, stay active, and share what you learn with others."
C. He continues to live by his motto: Stay curious, stay active, and share.
D. He continues to live by his motto: "Stay curious, stay active, and share what you learn with others."

PASSAGE II (Questions 16–30)

The Community Garden Project

A local organization recently started a community garden in our neighborhood. (16)It's purpose is to provide residents with plots of land to grow fresh produce. The garden also (17)aims to bring people together and foster a sense of unity.

I was immediately intrigued by the concept, I decided to volunteer on the first day it opened. (19)Families, retirees, and students gathered to build raised beds, lay mulch, and sow seeds of hope. (20)We spent hours working side by side and sharing gardening tips.

The most inspiring moment occurred when Ms. Andrews, (21)one of the oldest residents in our community, passed down her grandmother's heirloom tomato seeds. She explained (22)that these seeds had been in her family for generations, a legacy of both heritage and flavor.

A few weeks later, the sprouts emerged. (23)Seeing vibrant green leaves pop out of the soil, I felt a surge of pride. This project wasn't just about fresh vegetables; (24)it was a living example of what cooperation could accomplish.

In an effort to expand, the organizers plan to (25)install a small greenhouse for year-round planting, set up a compost system, (26)and are offering gardening workshops. (27)They want to ensure anyone, from novice to expert, can learn how to grow healthy food.

The community garden stands as a testament to (28)our shared desire for healthier living and a more connected neighborhood. As we water each plant and watch it (29)develop, we cultivate friendships that will also flourish. (30)It is a constant reminder that positive change can start with just a few seeds and a united effort.

PASSAGE II Questions (16–30)

16.

F. NO CHANGE
G. Its
H. It's'
J. Its'

17.

A. NO CHANGE
B. also is aiming
C. also aimed
D. also will aim

18.

F. NO CHANGE
G. I was immediately intrigued by the concept; I decided
H. Intrigued by the concept. I decided
J. Intrigued by the concept, I decided

19.

A. NO CHANGE
B. Families—retirees, and students
C. Families, retirees and students
D. Families, retirees, and students,

20.

F. NO CHANGE
G. side-by-side, and sharing
H. side by side sharing
J. side by side, while we shared

21.

A. NO CHANGE
B. one of the oldest residents in our community—
C. one of the oldest residents in our community;
D. one of the oldest residents in our community

22.

F. NO CHANGE
G. that these seeds had been in her family for generations: a legacy
H. that these seeds had been in her family for generations—a legacy
J. that these seeds had been in her family for generations a legacy

23.

A. NO CHANGE
B. Seeing vibrant green leaves pop out of the soil, a surge of pride overcame me.
C. I saw the vibrant green leaves pop out of the soil, I felt a surge of pride.
D. As the vibrant green leaves popped out of the soil, a surge of pride was what I felt.

24.

F. NO CHANGE
G. it was a living example of cooperation's accomplishments
H. it was an example, living, of what cooperation could accomplish
J. it was a living example of what cooperation can accomplish

25.

A. NO CHANGE
B. install a small greenhouse for year-round planting; set up a compost system
C. install a small greenhouse for year-round planting, set up a compost system
D. installing a small greenhouse for year-round planting, setting up a compost system

26.

F. NO CHANGE
G. and offering gardening workshops
H. and will be offering gardening workshops
J. and offer gardening workshops

27.

A. NO CHANGE
B. They want to ensure that anyone—novice to expert—can learn how
C. They want to ensure that anyone from novice, to expert, can learn how
D. They want to ensure that anyone, from novice to expert can learn how

28.

F. NO CHANGE
G. our shared, desire for healthier living, and
H. our shared desire for healthier living, and
J. our shared desire for healthier living and

29.

A. NO CHANGE
B. grow
C. leap
D. flourish

30.

F. NO CHANGE
G. It is a consistent reminder
H. It is a constant reminder; that positive change
J. It is a constant reminder that positive change

PASSAGE III (Questions 31–45)

Finding the Perfect Study Spot

(31)As exams approach, students often seek out quiet corners on campus to concentrate. While libraries remain a popular choice, (32)some individuals prefer the bustling ambiance of coffee shops. (33)Determining the right environment, however, depends on personal study habits.

When I need absolute silence, I head to the (34)far corner, in the library's second floor. The hush there is almost sacred, with only the faint rustling of pages (35)interrupting. This atmosphere helps me (36)focus; still, I sometimes crave a livelier background.

(37)Therefore, a local coffee shop becomes my next option. The background chatter and gentle clinking of cups create (38)a lively symphony that keeps me motivated. (39)For short study sessions, I find that the mild noise level actually boosts my concentration.

Some students claim that the variety of sounds in a coffee shop can be (40)distractions. Others say the (41)presence of people coming in and out helps them avoid feeling isolated and bored. (42)So, each person must strike a balance between silence and stimulation, analyzing what fosters productivity.

A friend of mine (43)calls the library "my sanctuary," rarely stepping foot in a café with her textbooks. Another friend insists she cannot concentrate at all without a bit of (44)noise. Ultimately, (45)where you study is less important than how effectively you manage your time and attention.

PASSAGE III Questions (31–45)

31.

A. NO CHANGE
B. As exams approach; students often seek out quiet corners on campus to concentrate.
C. As exams approach students, often seek out quiet corners on campus to concentrate.
D. As exams approach, students often seek out quiet corners, on campus to concentrate.

32.

F. NO CHANGE
G. certain individuals prefer
H. some, individuals, prefer
J. some individuals they prefer

33.

A. NO CHANGE
B. Determining the right environment, though,
C. Determining the right environment, on the other hand,
D. Nevertheless, determining the right environment

34.

F. NO CHANGE
G. far corner in the library's second floor.
H. far corner on the library's second floor.
J. far corner. On the library's second floor.

35.

A. NO CHANGE
B. to interrupt.
C. that might interrupt.
D. interrupting it.

36.

F. NO CHANGE
G. focus, still, I sometimes crave
H. focus. Still, I sometimes crave
J. focus still I sometimes crave

37.

A. NO CHANGE
B. Consequently, a local coffee shop
C. For instance, a local coffee shop
D. On the other hand, a local coffee shop

38.

F. NO CHANGE
G. a lively, symphony, that keeps me
H. a lively symphony that keep me
J. a lively symphony that kept me

39.

A. NO CHANGE
B. For short study sessions, I find, that the mild noise level actually boosts
C. During short study sessions: I find that the mild noise level actually boosts
D. For short study sessions I find that, the mild noise level actually boosts

40.

F. NO CHANGE
G. distraction
H. distract
J. distracting

41.

A. NO CHANGE
B. presence, of people,
C. presence, of people coming in and out,
D. presence of people, coming in and out

42.

F. NO CHANGE
G. So each person must strike a balance between silence and stimulation: analyzing what fosters productivity.
H. So each person must strike a balance between silence, and stimulation, analyzing what fosters productivity.
J. So each person must strike a balance between silence and stimulation, analyzing what fosters productivity.

43.

A. NO CHANGE
B. refers to the library as "my sanctuary," and rarely steps
C. calls the library "my sanctuary;" rarely stepping
D. calls the library "my sanctuary," rarely steps

44.

F. NO CHANGE
G. noise. Ultimately,
H. noise ultimately
J. noise, ultimately

45.

A. NO CHANGE
B. your study location is less important than how effectively time and attention are managed.
C. where you study is less important, than how effectively you manage your time and attention.
D. it is less important, where you study, than how effectively you manage your time and attention.

PASSAGE IV (Questions 46–60)

The World of Amateur Astronomy

If you have ever gazed at the night sky with fascination, (46)you might find amateur astronomy an exciting hobby. (47)Many amateurs start by observing the moon and planets with binoculars or a simple telescope.

Yet, the real fun begins when you start (48)recognizing star patterns, known as constellations, and learning how they move with the seasons. (49)For instance, Orion is a prominent constellation in winter skies, while Scorpius (50)reigns in summertime.

To deepen your interest, you might join a local astronomy club. (51)These groups typically host star parties, gatherings in which enthusiasts share equipment and stories. (52)Through these events you can get advice, test out different telescopes, and discover new celestial targets.

(53)Moreover, some amateurs try astrophotography. Using cameras attached to telescopes, they capture stunning images of galaxies, nebulae, and star clusters. (54)Patience, along with specialized gear, is crucial because these objects are extremely faint.

Amateur astronomers also help with scientific research. (55)They monitor variable stars, track asteroids, and occasionally detect new comets. (56)Modern technology, such as digital sensors and advanced software, have made such discoveries more accessible than ever.

(57)Ultimately, the joy of amateur astronomy arises from the sense of wonder that the cosmos inspires. Whether you're capturing images of distant galaxies or simply gazing at (58)the luminous band of the Milky Way overhead. (59)There is always something breathtaking to see. (60)All it takes is a clear night, a bit of curiosity, and a willingness to explore.

PASSAGE IV Questions (46–60)

46.

F. NO CHANGE
G. you might find, that amateur astronomy is
H. you might find that amateur astronomy is
J. you might find amateur astronomy, is

47.

A. NO CHANGE
B. Many amateurs starts
C. Many amateurs will have started
D. Many amateurs has started

48.

F. NO CHANGE
G. recognizing star patterns. Known as constellations,
H. recognizing star patterns known as constellations
J. recognizing star patterns, known as constellations

49.

A. NO CHANGE
B. For example, Orion is a prominent constellation, in winter skies, while Scorpius
C. For instance, Orion is a prominent constellation in winter skies while Scorpius
D. For instance: Orion is a prominent constellation in winter skies, while Scorpius

50.

F. NO CHANGE
G. reign
H. reigned
J. is reigning

51.

A. NO CHANGE
B. This group typically hosts
C. This group typically host
D. These group's typically host

52.

F. NO CHANGE
G. Through these events, you can get advice, test out different telescopes,
H. Through these events you can get advice; test out different telescopes
J. Through these events: you can get advice, test out different telescopes

53.

A. NO CHANGE
B. In addition
C. However,
D. For instance,

54.

F. NO CHANGE
G. Patience and specialized gear, are crucial,
H. Patience along with specialized gear; is crucial
J. Patience—along with specialized gear—is crucial

55.

A. NO CHANGE
B. They monitored variable stars, tracked asteroids
C. They monitors variable stars, track asteroids
D. They are monitoring variable stars, track asteroids

56.

F. NO CHANGE
G. have made, such discoveries
H. has made such discoveries
J. has made, such discoveries

57.

A. NO CHANGE
B. Ultimately, the joy of amateur astronomy arises from a sense of wonder
C. Ultimately, the joys of amateur astronomy arise from the sense of wonder
D. Ultimately, the joys of amateur astronomy arises from the sense of wonder

58.

F. NO CHANGE
G. the luminous band of the Milky Way overhead,
H. the luminous band of the Milky Way overhead, you'll find
J. the luminous band of the Milky Way overhead

59.

A. NO CHANGE
B. Always, there is something breathtaking to see.
C. There is, always, something breathtaking to see.
D. There is always, something breathtaking, to see.

60.

F. NO CHANGE
G. All it takes is, a clear night, a bit of curiosity, and a willingness to explore.
H. All it takes: is a clear night, a bit of curiosity, and a willingness to explore.
J. All it takes is a clear night, a bit of curiosity, and a willingness, to explore.

PASSAGE V (Questions 61–75)

Urban Beekeeping

In many major cities, interest in urban beekeeping has soared. (61)Concerned about declining honeybee populations, residents have taken to rooftops and small gardens to house hives. (62)These beekeepers not only harvest honey but also help pollinate local plants.

Before starting a hive, prospective beekeepers should learn their local regulations. (63)Many cities requires permits, and some buildings have specific rules about rooftop installations. (64)Next, aspiring keepers must study honeybee behavior to ensure they can maintain healthy colonies.

Hives typically flourish where flowers are abundant. (65)However, even dense urban areas often offer enough blooms, (66)from public parks to balcony gardens. Surprisingly, many city beekeepers report high honey yields thanks to (67)diverse plantings in ornamental landscapes.

Caring for bees is both an art and a science. (68)Regular hive inspections, tracking the queen's health, (69)and prevent pests like varroa mites are crucial tasks. (70)Most keepers also harvest honey carefully, leaving enough for the bees to survive winter.

Despite the rewards, urban beekeeping can present challenges. (71)Neighbors may worry about stings, (72)requiring keepers to practice good hive management and maintain positive communication. (73)In addition, beekeepers must watch for pesticide use in surrounding areas, as chemicals can harm pollinators.

Ultimately, urban beekeeping (74)fosters environmental awareness. It reminds city dwellers (75)that pollinators play a vital role in sustaining biodiversity, even among skyscrapers and busy streets.

PASSAGE V Questions (61–75)

61.

A. NO CHANGE
B. Because they are concerned about declining honeybee populations,
C. Declining honeybee populations concern many residents,
D. Concerned about declining honeybee populations.

62.

F. NO CHANGE
G. They not only harvest honey but also pollinate
H. These beekeepers not only harvest honey, but they also pollinate
J. These beekeepers not only harvest honey, but they also are pollinating

63.

A. NO CHANGE
B. Many cities require
C. Many cities requiring
D. Many cities have required

64.

F. NO CHANGE
G. Next, aspiring keepers must study honeybee behavior, to ensure
H. Next, aspiring keepers, must study honeybee behavior to ensure
J. Next aspiring keepers must study honeybee behavior, to ensure

65.

A. NO CHANGE
B. However, even dense, urban areas
C. However even dense urban areas
D. However, even dense urban areas,

66.

F. NO CHANGE
G. from public parks, to balcony gardens.
H. from public parks to balcony gardens
J. from public parks, to balcony gardens,

67.

A. NO CHANGE
B. diverse plants in ornamental landscapes.
C. diverse, plantings in ornamental, landscapes.
D. diverse plantings in ornamental landscapes.

68.

F. NO CHANGE
G. Inspections of hives on a regular basis, tracking the queen's health,
H. Inspecting hives regularly, tracking the queen's health,
J. Regular hive inspections, track the queen's health,

69.

A. NO CHANGE
B. and preventing pests like varroa mites
C. and to prevent pests like varroa mites
D. as well as prevention of pests like varroa mites

70.

F. NO CHANGE
G. keepers also harvest honey carefully leaving
H. keepers also carefully harvest honey leaving
J. keepers also harvest honey, carefully, leaving

71.

A. NO CHANGE
B. Neighbors, may worry about stings,
C. Neighbors may worry about stings;
D. Neighbors may worry about stings

72.

F. NO CHANGE
G. which requires
H. it requires
J. requiring that keepers

73.

A. NO CHANGE
B. Meanwhile, beekeepers must watch for pesticide
C. However, beekeepers must also watch for pesticide
D. Also, beekeepers must watch for pesticide

74.

F. NO CHANGE
G. fosters environmental awareness, it
H. fosters environmental awareness, which
J. fosters environmental awareness; it

75.

A. NO CHANGE
B. that pollinators playing a vital role in sustaining biodiversity
C. that pollinators play a vital role sustaining biodiversity
D. that pollinators do play a vital role in sustaining biodiversity

ACT Math Exam Section

60 Questions — 60 Minutes

1.

If $8k - 12 = 36$, what is the value of k?

A. 6
B. 8
C. 9
D. 12
E. 15

2.

Which of the following is equivalent to $\frac{4}{5} \times \frac{5}{6}$?

A. $\frac{4}{6}$
B. $\frac{4}{5}$
C. $\frac{2}{3}$
D. $\frac{5}{4}$
E. $\frac{4}{6} + \frac{5}{6}$

3.

A small business sells notebooks at $2.50 each. If the company sells 400 notebooks, what is the total revenue from these notebook sales?

A. 250$
B. 500$
C. 750$
D. 900$
E. 1000$

4.

If $\frac{3}{4} = 0.75$, which of the following is $\frac{1}{8}$ expressed as a decimal?

A. 0.02
B. 0.125
C. 0.25
D. 0.5
E. 1.25

5.

What is the greatest integer less than π?

A. 1

B. 2

C. 3

D. 4

E. 5

6.

Evaluate: $2 + 3 \times 4 - 6$.

A. 6

B. 8

C. 12

D. 14

E. 18

7.

What is the value of $\sqrt{144}$?

A. 10

B. 12

C. 16

D. 18

E. 24

8.

Simplify: $(y^2)(y^3)$.

A. y^5

B. y^6

C. y^8

D. y^9

E. $y^{2.5}$

9.

Which of the following is the largest integer less than $\frac{25}{4}$?

A. 4

B. 5

C. 6

D. 7

E. 8

10.

If $2n + 3 = 15$, then $4n - 6 =$

A. 18

B. 20

C. 22

D. 24
E. 26

11.

Simplify the expression $5(x-2)-2(x+1)$.

A. $3x-9$
B. $3x-12$
C. $7x-10$
D. $5x-14$
E. $x-1$

12.

In the coordinate plane, a line passes through $(0,0)$ and $(2,4)$. What is the slope of this line?
A. 2
B. 3
C. 4
D. $\frac{1}{2}$
E. -2

13.

What is the value of $3x$ if $x=\frac{1}{3}$?
A. $\frac{1}{9}$
B. $\frac{2}{3}$
C. 1
D. $1\frac{1}{2}$
E. 3

14.

If $4^m=4^3$, what is m?
A. -3
B. 0
C. 1
D. 2
E. 3

15.

Which integer satisfies $-2<x<1$?
A. -3
B. -2
C. -1
D. 0
E. 2

16.

If $7x - 4 = 31$, then $x =$

A. 3

B. 5

C. 6

D. 7

E. $\frac{35}{7}$

17.

What is the sum of the first 4 positive odd integers?

A. 10

B. 12

C. 16

D. 20

E. 24

18.

If $x < 0$ and $| x |= 5$, what is x?

A. -5

B. 5

C. 0

D. 4

E. -6

19.

Which of the following is a solution to $3y + 2 = y + 8$?

A. $y = 3$

B. $y = -3$

C. $y = 2$

D. $y = -2$

E. $y = 1$

20.

A line in the xy-plane has the equation $y = 2x + 3$. If $x = 4$, what is y?

A. 2

B. 8

C. 9

D. 11

E. 12

21.

Which inequality is **true** for $2 \leq x < 5$?

A. $x < 2$

B. $x = 5$

C. $3 \leq x < 5$

D. $x \geq 5$

E. $2 \leq x < 5$

22.

Solve for x: $\frac{x}{3} = 6$.

A. $\frac{1}{2}$
B. 2
C. 6
D. 9
E. 18

23.

What is the **greatest common divisor (GCD)** of 36 and 48?
A. 4
B. 6
C. 12
D. 16
E. 24

24.

A car traveled 300 miles in 5 hours. What was its average speed in miles per hour (mph)?
A. 50
B. 55
C. 60
D. 65
E. 75

25.

Which of the following expressions is equivalent to $3(2a + 1) + 2a$?
A. $6a + 3 + 2a$
B. $6a + 3$
C. $8a + 3$
D. $8a + 1$
E. $8a + 5$

26.

If $2 < a < 3$, then $a + 5$ is between which two integers?
A. 7 and 8
B. 8 and 9
C. 6 and 7
D. 5 and 6
E. 2 and 3

27.

Which of the following is a **prime** number?
A. 21
B. 25
C. 27
D. 31
E. 39

28.

Simplify: $\frac{8x+4}{4}$.

A. $2x + 1$

B. $8x$

C. $8x + 4$

D. $2x + 4$

E. $x + 1$

29.

If $(x + 3)^2 = x^2 + 6x + 9$, which of the following is another correct expansion for $(x + 4)^2$?

A. $x^2 + 8x + 16$

B. $x^2 + 4x$

C. $x^2 + 16x + 8$

D. $x^2 + 8x + 8$

E. $x^2 + 4$

30.

What is the solution set for $n^2 = 36$?

A. $\{0\}$

B. $\{-6,6\}$

C. $\{-36,36\}$

D. $\{6\}$

E. {-9, 9}

31.

What is the slope of the line in the xy-plane given by $2y = 6x + 4$?

A. -3

B. $\frac{6}{2} = 3$

C. 6

D. 4

E. 2

32.

Which ordered pair (x, y) satisfies $y = -2x + 4$?

A. $(0,4)$

B. $(2,0)$

C. $(3, -2)$

D. $(4, -8)$

E. $(1, -6)$

33.

If the area of a rectangle is 48 square units and its length is 8 units, what is its width?

A. 3

B. 4

C. 6

D. 8
E. 12

34.

Simplify: $(x+2)(x-2)$.
A. $x^2 - 4$
B. $x^2 - 4$
C. $x^2 + 4$
D. $x^2 - 2$
E. $x^2 + 2$

35.

A triangle has angles measuring $30°, 60°$, and $90°$. What is the ratio of the side opposite the $30°$ angle to the side opposite the $90°$ angle?
A. $1: 2$
B. $1: \sqrt{2}$
C. $\sqrt{3}: 2$
D. $2: 3$
E. $\frac{1}{2}: 1$

36.

Which of the following is the equation of a line with slope -1 and y-intercept 5?
A. $y = -x + 5$
B. $y = x - 5$
C. $y = -x - 5$
D. $y = x + 5$
E. $y = -5x + 1$

37.

If $\sin(\theta) = \frac{\text{opposite}}{\text{hypotenuse}}$, what is $\cos(\theta)$?
A. $\frac{\text{adjacent}}{\text{hypotenuse}}$
B. $\frac{\text{opposite}}{\text{adjacent}}$
C. $\frac{\text{adjacent}}{\text{opposite}}$
D. $\sin(\theta) - 1$
E. $\frac{\text{hypotenuse}}{\text{adjacent}}$

38.

What is the distance between the points $(1,3)$ and $(5,3)$ in the coordinate plane?
A. 2
B. 4
C. 6
D. 5
E. 8

39.

Factor the expression $x^2 - 9x$.

A. $x(x - 9)$

B. $(x - 3)(x - 6)$

C. $x(x + 9)$

D. $(x - 3)(x - 3)$

E. Cannot be factored

40.

Solve for x: $\frac{2}{x} = 4$.

A. $\frac{1}{2}$

B. 2

C. $\frac{1}{4}$

D. $-\frac{1}{2}$

E. 4

41.

Which of the following is closest to $\sqrt{50}$?

A. 5.0

B. 6.2

C. 7.1

D. 7.7

E. 8.0

42.

If $(a, b) = (4,3)$, then $a + b =$

A. 1

B. 4

C. 6

D. 7

E. 12

43.

A bag contains 5 blue marbles, 4 red marbles, and 1 green marble. If one marble is chosen at random, what is the probability it is **not** red?

A. $\frac{6}{10}$

B. $\frac{4}{10}$

C. $\frac{3}{5}$

D. $\frac{1}{2}$

E. $\frac{5}{10}$

44.

What is the midpoint of the line segment with endpoints $(-2,2)$ and $(4,6)$?

A. $(1,4)$
B. $(6,8)$
C. $(2,4)$
D. $(1,2)$
E. $(3,4)$

45.

Simplify: $\sqrt{81a^2}$. Assume $a \geq 0$.

A. $9a$
B. $81a^2$
C. $9a^2$
D. $3a$
E. $9\sqrt{a^2}$

46.

What is the next term in the geometric sequence 2,6,18,54, ...?

A. 72
B. 108
C. 162
D. 216
E. 324

47.

Which expression is equivalent to $(x^3)^2$?

A. x^1
B. x^5
C. x^6
D. $2x^3$
E. x^9

48.

If the perimeter of a square is 24, what is its area?

A. 24
B. 36
C. 49
D. 144
E. 576

49.

What is the solution for $(x + 1)(x + 2) = 0$?

A. $x = -1$ or $x = -2$
B. $x = 0$ or $x = 1$
C. $x = 1$ or $x = 2$
D. $x = -2$ or $x = 2$
E. $x = 0$ or $x = 2$

50.

What is the distance between the points $(0,0)$ and $(3,4)$?

A. 3

B. 4

C. 5

D. 7

E. 12

51.

Let $f(x) = x^2 - 4$. What is $f(3)$?

A. 0

B. 1

C. 2

D. 5

E. 9

52.

Which fraction is **equivalent** to 0.6%?

A. $\frac{6}{100}$

B. $\frac{3}{500}$

C. $\frac{6}{10}$

D. $\frac{6}{1{,}000{,}000}$

E. $\frac{6}{1{,}000{,}000} \times 10$ *(nonsensical—ignore, but we'll keep to keep 5 choices)*

53.

For what value of x is the expression $\frac{1}{x}$ undefined?

A. $x = 0$

B. $x = 1$

C. $x = -1$

D. $x = 10$

E. $x = \frac{1}{2}$

54.

The measure of an interior angle of a regular pentagon is how many degrees?

(Recall: The sum of interior angles of a pentagon is $540°$*; each angle in a* ***regular*** *pentagon is* $\frac{540°}{5} = 108°$*.)*

A. $72°$

B. $90°$

C. $108°$

D. $120°$

E. $135°$

55.

If $\tan(\alpha) = \frac{\text{opposite}}{\text{adjacent}}$, and α is in a right triangle, then by the Pythagorean identity, $\sin^2(\alpha) + \cos^2(\alpha) =$

A. $\tan^2(\alpha)$

B. 0

C. $\sec^2(\alpha)$

D. 1

E. $\csc^2(\alpha)$

56.

If $\sin(\beta) = \frac{3}{5}$ in a right triangle, which of the following is $\cos(\beta)$ **if** β **is acute**?

(Use $\sin^2(\beta) + \cos^2(\beta) = 1$.*)*

A. $\frac{4}{5}$

B. $\frac{3}{4}$

C. $\frac{3}{5}$

D. $\frac{9}{25}$

E. $\frac{5}{3}$

57.

What is the sum of the first n positive integers (i.e., $1 + 2 + 3 + \cdots + n$)?

A. $\frac{n(n+1)}{2}$

B. $\frac{n(n-1)}{2}$

C. $n^2 + 1$

D. $\frac{(n+1)(n+2)}{2}$

E. $n(n + 1)$

58.

A right circular cylinder has a radius r and a height h. Which formula gives its **volume**?

A. $\pi r^2 h$

B. $2\pi rh$

C. $\frac{1}{3}\pi r^2 h$

D. $\pi r(h^2)$

E. πr^3

59.

If (4,5) lies on the circle $x^2 + y^2 = R^2$, what is R^2?

A. 1

B. 9

C. 16

D. 25

E. 41

60.

For real numbers a and b, the expression $(a+b)^2$ expands to

A. $a^2 + 2ab + b^2$

B. $a^2 - 2ab + b^2$

C. $a^2 + ab + b^2$

D. $a^2 + b^2$

E. $2a^2 + 2b^2$

ACT Reading Exam Section

PASSAGE I (Questions 1–10)

Literary Narrative

Evelyn stepped off the bus at Sunrise Station with a mixture of relief and trepidation. She had not seen the sleepy town of Lyndale in six years, and the dusty roads and peeling paint on the storefronts looked much as she remembered. When she was fifteen, she had left Lyndale with her parents, believing they would never return. Now, at twenty-one, she was back on her own terms. Clutching a worn leather suitcase, Evelyn inhaled the warm air, recalling the tang of pine from her grandmother's backyard and the taste of fresh peach pie she and her best friend used to share on the diner's porch every summer afternoon.

Her return had a purpose: she wanted to see if home truly could remain unchanged despite the passage of time. Yet she already sensed that whatever she might find—be it the same old quiet sidewalks or brand-new developments—she herself was the one who had changed the most. She was no longer the timid teenager who had feared she might never leave. Instead, she had chosen to come back, stronger and determined to make peace with all she'd left behind: her grandmother's unspoken advice, her father's bitter departure, her friend's sudden silence. Lyndale had shaped who she was, and now, she was about to find out if it still held the power to guide her future.

Questions 1–10 refer to Passage I.

1. The main focus of the passage is:
   - **A.** Evelyn's decision to move to a new city with her parents.
   - **B.** Evelyn's reflections on her past in Lyndale and her reason for returning.
   - **C.** The rundown buildings and shops along the dusty roads of Lyndale.
   - **D.** A friendship that ended when Evelyn was fifteen.
2. It can most reasonably be inferred that Evelyn's mood when stepping off the bus is:
   - **F.** purely elated.
   - **G.** a blend of uncertainty and anticipation.
   - **H.** disappointed by how little the town has changed.
   - **J.** indifferent to the town's appearance.
3. The passage most strongly suggests that Evelyn:
   - **A.** expects her grandmother to greet her at the bus station.
   - **B.** has come back to Lyndale unwillingly.
   - **C.** has fond memories of certain experiences in Lyndale.
   - **D.** resents her parents for leaving Lyndale.
4. Based on the passage, which of the following best describes Evelyn's perspective on "home"?
   - **F.** It is a place that inevitably deteriorates over time.
   - **G.** It is a place whose physical details matter more than personal growth.
   - **H.** It is a concept tied both to memory and personal evolution.
   - **J.** It is where her father forced her to return.
5. As used in the first paragraph, the word *trepidation* most nearly means:
   - **A.** eagerness.
   - **B.** confusion.

- C. amusement.
- D. apprehension.

6. The statement "Yet she already sensed … she herself was the one who had changed the most" primarily emphasizes that:
   - **F.** Evelyn's life experiences outside of Lyndale have transformed her.
   - **G.** Lyndale had become drastically different in her absence.
   - **H.** Evelyn fears she hasn't truly matured since her teenage years.
   - **J.** Her parents forced her to return as a changed person.
7. It can most logically be inferred that Evelyn's relationship with her grandmother is:
   - **A.** strained by arguments.
   - **B.** one that included unspoken but meaningful guidance.
   - **C.** based solely on frequent written letters.
   - **D.** the reason Evelyn vowed never to leave Lyndale.
8. The passage implies that when Evelyn left Lyndale at age fifteen, she:
   - **F.** already planned to return at exactly twenty-one.
   - **G.** had little hope of coming back someday.
   - **H.** was determined to open a business upon returning.
   - **J.** moved to a more rural area with her family.
9. Which of the following best describes the overall tone of the passage?
   - **A.** Reflective and cautiously optimistic.
   - **B.** Sarcastic and dismissive of the past.
   - **C.** Overwhelmingly regretful and ashamed.
   - **D.** Amused by the people and places in Lyndale.
10. The primary purpose of the second paragraph (lines 8–14) is to:
    - **F.** criticize Lyndale for its lack of economic opportunity.
    - **G.** highlight Evelyn's changed outlook and the reasons behind her visit.
    - **H.** list all the people she once knew in Lyndale.
    - **J.** reveal that she never wanted to leave Lyndale in the first place.

PASSAGE II (Questions 11–20)

Social Science

The idea of "public green space" in urban areas traces back centuries, with city planners long recognizing the importance of parks, gardens, and communal recreation areas. In the nineteenth century, many Western cities underwent rapid industrial expansion. Public green spaces served as a respite from crowded living conditions, offering fresh air and a place for leisure. In modern times, research has demonstrated that proximity to green space correlates positively with improved mental health, reduced stress, and lower rates of cardiovascular disease.

However, city planners today must grapple with competing demands: housing shortages, commercial development, and the high cost of urban land. While new parks improve neighborhood well-being and boost property values, they can also accelerate gentrification, sometimes pushing out longtime residents. As a result, some planners advocate multi-use or "shared" green spaces, which combine affordable housing or commercial areas with open-air courtyards, rooftop gardens, and small playgrounds.

Balancing the need for greenery with economic realities requires creative solutions. Cities that prioritize equitable access to green space frequently deploy zoning rules mandating a minimum percentage of open land in developments. Others encourage the use of vacant lots for community gardens, offering tax incentives to owners who convert unused space into small urban farms. These strategies highlight how green space has evolved from a merely aesthetic asset to a vital component of public health and social equity.

Questions 11–20 refer to Passage II.

11. According to the passage, public green spaces originally served which of the following purposes in 19th-century Western cities?

- **A.** Showcases for expensive landscaping
- **B.** Areas to test new construction materials
- **C.** Community retreats from overcrowded conditions
- **D.** Areas designated only for the wealthy

12. The passage indicates that recent research on green space has found a correlation between:
    - **F.** new park construction and declining property values.
    - **G.** exposure to nature and improved health outcomes.
    - **H.** fewer city regulations and increased stress levels.
    - **J.** overcrowding in urban centers and better mental health.
13. The author describes a drawback of creating new parks in urban areas, noting that:
    - **A.** green spaces automatically lead to high unemployment.
    - **B.** residents generally prefer large commercial developments.
    - **C.** building parks can unintentionally push housing prices up.
    - **D.** neighbors dislike sharing open-air courtyards.
14. As used in line 9, the word *grapple* most nearly means:
    - **F.** wrestle.
    - **G.** ignore.
    - **H.** defeat.
    - **J.** simplify.
15. The passage cites "multi-use or 'shared' green spaces" primarily as an example of:
    - **A.** a temporary solution requiring no funding.
    - **B.** a compromise that allows both development and green areas.
    - **C.** a design that historically failed in most urban environments.
    - **D.** an obsolete concept never tested in modern cities.
16. Which statement from the passage best supports the idea that green space is considered critical for public health?
    - **F.** "Public green spaces served as a respite from crowded living conditions…" (lines 3–4)
    - **G.** "While new parks improve neighborhood well-being…they can also accelerate gentrification…" (lines 7–8)
    - **H.** "Cities that prioritize equitable access…deploy zoning rules mandating a minimum percentage of open land…" (lines 14–16)
    - **J.** "…green space has evolved from a merely aesthetic asset to a vital component of public health and social equity." (lines 18–19)
17. According to the passage, one method cities use to increase green space is to:
    - **A.** only build parks on the most expensive real estate.
    - **B.** prohibit new commercial buildings.
    - **C.** convert empty plots of land into community gardens.
    - **D.** remove existing playgrounds.
18. The passage suggests that gentrification might be a concern when:
    - **F.** older parks are renovated instead of replaced.
    - **G.** property values remain stable in high-income districts.
    - **H.** new green amenities lead to rising costs, displacing residents.
    - **J.** communal gardens reduce maintenance fees for homeowners.
19. The main idea of the final paragraph (lines 12–19) is that:
    - **A.** having green space in a city is unimportant unless it features advanced recreational equipment.
    - **B.** many cities are using new strategies and regulations to ensure fair access to green space.
    - **C.** city planners are giving up on public parks.
    - **D.** social equity decreases when neighborhoods gain new gardens.
20. The passage most strongly implies that in the future, green space in cities will:
    - **F.** be replaced entirely by private commercial development.
    - **G.** become a secondary concern compared to zoning changes.
    - **H.** remain a critical and debated issue in urban planning.
    - **J.** cease to affect property values or community health.

PASSAGE III (Questions 21–30)

Humanities

Anna Reyes, an award-winning journalist, was once better known for her gritty investigative articles about political corruption than for her recent pivot to writing a biography of a nineteenth-century poet. Many fans were initially puzzled by her shift in subject matter. According to Reyes, however, the change was a natural progression. "I've always loved uncovering hidden truths," she explains. "In my investigative pieces, that meant shining light on secret financial deals or bribery. In this biography, I'm shining light on a forgotten figure's life."

The poet in question is Eliza Sutton, born in 1837 in rural England. Despite publishing only two volumes of verse, Sutton influenced many later poets, including some recognized by the British literary establishment. Reyes's project began after she chanced upon one of Sutton's out-of-print books in a secondhand shop. Fascinated by the poet's delicate yet powerful language, Reyes spent months chasing down personal letters, diaries, and contemporary reviews, eventually piecing together a portrait of a woman who struggled for visibility in a male-dominated literary scene.

Reyes's biography not only examines Sutton's writing but also explores the broader cultural context of her work. By delving into Victorian-era publishing, social expectations, and gender norms, Reyes strives to show readers why Sutton's modest output mattered to so many. "She wrote with uncommon precision about women's emotional landscapes," says Reyes. "And she did so during a time when women were rarely encouraged to publish—let alone publish bold, introspective poetry."

Questions 21–30 refer to Passage III.

21. The primary purpose of the passage is to:
    - **A.** provide an overview of a journalist's transition to literary biography.
    - **B.** highlight political scandals uncovered by a journalist.
    - **C.** argue that nineteenth-century poets were largely ignored.
    - **D.** prove that Eliza Sutton's poetry is better than modern verse.
22. According to the passage, Reyes's fans were:
    - **F.** upset that she never returned to investigative work.
    - **G.** puzzled by her move away from political reporting.
    - **H.** excited that she wrote a novel based on Sutton's life.
    - **J.** unaware that she had ever written about corruption.
23. Reyes compares her investigative pieces to her biography work by pointing out that both:
    - **A.** were unprofitable but fulfilling.
    - **B.** faced strict censorship.
    - **C.** involved uncovering hidden information.
    - **D.** focused primarily on historical figures.
24. The passage suggests that Eliza Sutton's writing career was limited partly because:
    - **F.** her poetry was overshadowed by other famous female writers.
    - **G.** she only published her books late in her life.
    - **H.** she was uninterested in writing beyond her diaries.
    - **J.** social norms in her era discouraged women writers.
25. As used in line 6, the word *chanced* most nearly means:
    - **A.** intentionally searched.
    - **B.** happened upon by luck.
    - **C.** persuaded a friend.
    - **D.** traveled a long distance.
26. The passage indicates that Eliza Sutton's influence included:
    - **F.** guiding new literary movements in the British establishment.
    - **G.** affecting later poets who gained recognition.
    - **H.** prompting a nationwide ban on certain verses.

- **J.** enabling her to earn a significant fortune during her lifetime.

27. Reyes's research process for the biography:
    - **A.** involved traveling to multiple countries for primary sources.
    - **B.** depended solely on oral testimonies from Sutton's relatives.
    - **C.** required examining original letters, diaries, and reviews.
    - **D.** was completed in just a few weeks.
28. The passage indicates Reyes is interested in Victorian-era publishing because:
    - **F.** it helps her understand the challenges female writers faced.
    - **G.** she wants to mimic older marketing strategies for her own book.
    - **H.** she hopes to prove women wrote better than men in that period.
    - **J.** it offers proof that Sutton never attempted to publish.
29. Which of the following statements best summarizes Reyes's perspective on Sutton's poetry?
    - **A.** It was overly sentimental and lacked depth.
    - **B.** It was advanced for its time because it was bold and introspective.
    - **C.** It was identical in style to many other Victorian writers.
    - **D.** It was too controversial to be printed in mainstream publications.
30. According to Reyes, one reason Sutton's verses were unique for her time is that they:
    - **F.** relied mainly on popular literary tropes.
    - **G.** expanded into novels and plays about women's rights.
    - **H.** offered keen insights into women's emotional experiences.
    - **J.** were published anonymously in several magazines.

PASSAGE IV (Questions 31–40)

Natural Science

Bats, the only mammals capable of sustained flight, exhibit remarkable adaptations that allow them to navigate and feed in the dark. Most species rely on echolocation, emitting high-frequency sounds that bounce off objects in their path. When bats receive the echoes, they can determine the size, shape, and distance of potential obstacles or prey. This sensory system is incredibly precise; certain bats can even detect individual insect wingbeats.

Contrary to popular belief, bats are not blind. Many species have well-developed vision that, combined with echolocation, helps them hunt effectively. However, their reliance on high-frequency calls presents challenges in noisy or cluttered environments. Scientists studying bat colonies in urban areas have observed that traffic noise and dense building structures can interfere with echolocation signals, leading bats to adjust flight routes or switch foraging times.

Despite these challenges, bats play a vital role in many ecosystems. They help control insect populations, pollinate fruit trees, and disperse seeds. Growing awareness of their ecological importance has prompted conservation efforts, especially as some species face threats from habitat loss and diseases such as white-nose syndrome. By understanding the complexities of bat echolocation and the environments that support it, researchers hope to protect these unique and beneficial creatures.

Questions 31–40 refer to Passage IV.

31. The primary function of bat echolocation is to allow bats to:
    - **A.** produce mating calls at lower frequencies.
    - **B.** maintain body temperature during flight.
    - **C.** detect and interpret echoes to navigate and hunt.
    - **D.** hibernate for longer periods in winter.
32. As described in the passage, one misconception about bats is that they:
    - **F.** are the only winged mammals.
    - **G.** exist in nearly every part of the world.
    - **H.** have poor eyesight.
    - **J.** never adjust their foraging times.

33. According to the passage, echolocation can be adversely affected in urban areas by:
    - **A.** the presence of other bats competing for food.
    - **B.** intense light sources that disrupt flight.
    - **C.** excessive noise and building structures.
    - **D.** the natural predatory instincts of birds.
34. As used in line 3, the phrase *bounce off* most nearly means:
    - **F.** stick to.
    - **G.** fail to impact.
    - **H.** reflect from.
    - **J.** amplify in volume.
35. The passage implies that bats are able to detect individual insect wingbeats primarily because:
    - **A.** their hearing is attuned to the low-pitched calls that insects produce.
    - **B.** they use echolocation signals precise enough to capture very fine details.
    - **C.** their vision allows them to see high-frequency waves.
    - **D.** the insects they hunt move extremely slowly.
36. The passage credits bats with all of the following ecological roles **except**:
    - **F.** seed dispersal.
    - **G.** pest control.
    - **H.** pollinating certain plants.
    - **J.** increasing greenhouse gas emissions.
37. Which of the following statements best describes the passage's central point?
    - **A.** Bats are declining rapidly, and only urban areas can protect them.
    - **B.** Bats rely on echolocation for flight and feeding, and they play crucial ecological roles.
    - **C.** Bats are the most important pollinators of all fruit-bearing plants.
    - **D.** Humans should avoid studying bats because of dangerous diseases they carry.
38. In discussing white-nose syndrome, the passage suggests that:
    - **F.** this disease is especially common in tropical environments.
    - **G.** it poses a significant threat to certain bat populations.
    - **H.** it helps bats fight off insects and other pests.
    - **J.** it has no known impact on bat colonies.
39. The passage indicates that when bats experience interference with their echolocation calls, they might:
    - **A.** form larger roosting colonies to limit distractions.
    - **B.** remain completely inactive and refuse to feed.
    - **C.** switch to diurnal (daytime) living permanently.
    - **D.** modify their flight paths or change when they forage.
40. Which of the following best reflects the author's perspective on bat conservation?
    - **F.** Bats pose more harm than benefits to ecosystems.
    - **G.** Maintaining bat populations is useful only for rural areas.
    - **H.** Understanding bats' needs helps protect them and benefits the environment.
    - **J.** Conservation efforts are unnecessary because bats adapt to any condition.

ACT Science Exam Section

PASSAGE I

(6 questions)

Data Representation

Background: A researcher measured **net photosynthetic rate (NPR)** of a certain plant at different **temperatures** and **light intensities**. NPR is measured in $\mu mol\ CO_2\ m^{-2}\ s^{-1}$. Table 1 summarizes the results.

Table 1: Net Photosynthetic Rate (NPR) at Different Temperatures and Light Intensities

Temp (°C)	Light Intensity (μmol photons $m^{-2}\ s^{-1}$)	NPR ($\mu mol\ CO_2\ m^{-2}\ s^{-1}$)

15	200	2.1
15	400	4.3
15	600	5.8
25	200	3.9
25	400	7.5
25	600	9.2
35	200	3.2
35	400	6.1
35	600	8.7

Use this table to answer Questions 1–6.

1.

According to Table 1, at $25°C$ and a light intensity of 400 $\mu mol\ photons\ m^{-2}\ s^{-1}$, NPR is:
A. 3.9
B. 6.1
C. 7.5
D. 9.2

2.

Based on the data, which of the following statements is **best supported** regarding temperature and NPR at the **highest** light intensity measured (600)?
F. NPR remains the same for all three temperatures.
G. NPR is highest at $15°C$.
H. NPR is highest at $25°C$.
J. NPR is highest at $35°C$.

3.

Suppose the researcher tested a light intensity of 200 $\mu mol\ photons\ m^{-2}\ s^{-1}$ at $20°C$. If the trend between $15°C$ and $25°C$ holds, the NPR at $20°C$ would most likely be:
A. slightly higher than 2.1 but lower than 3.9.
B. higher than 5.8.
C. lower than 2.1.
D. very close to 9.2.

4.

According to the table, at **400** light intensity, the **largest increase** in NPR (compared to the next lower temperature's NPR at the same light) occurs when going from:
F. $15°C$ to $25°C$.
G. $25°C$ to $35°C$.
H. $15°C$ to $35°C$.
J. There is no increase from lower to higher temperature at 400 light intensity.

(Note: Compare 4.3 at 15°C to 7.5 at 25°C, and 7.5 at 25°C to 6.1 at 35°C. Choose carefully.)

5.

A student claims that **higher temperature always** results in higher NPR **at any given light level**. Do the data support this claim?
A. Yes, because NPR at 35°C is higher than at both 15°C and 25°C for all light intensities.
B. No, because NPR at 35°C (400 light) is lower than NPR at 25°C (400 light).
C. Yes, because NPR at 25°C is consistently the lowest.
D. No, because NPR is always highest at 15°C.

6.

Which of the following **best describes** how NPR changes with light intensity (holding temperature constant)?
F. NPR decreases as light intensity increases.
G. NPR increases as light intensity increases.
H. NPR remains the same for all light intensities.
J. NPR first decreases, then increases.

PASSAGE II

(6 questions)

Data Representation

Background: A chemist measured the **solubility** of three different salts (Salt A, Salt B, and Salt C) in water at various temperatures. **Solubility** is defined as the maximum grams of salt that can dissolve in 100 g of water at a given temperature.

Figure 1: Solubility of Salt A, Salt B, and Salt C over Temperatures from $0°C$ to $100°C$. (Values below are approximate.)

Temp (°C)	Salt A (g/100g H_2O)	Salt B (g/100g H_2O)	Salt C (g/100g H_2O)
0	25	12	40
20	35	20	46
40	45	28	50
60	58	36	56
80	70	45	62
100	85	55	68

Use the data to answer Questions 7–12.

7.

At $20°C$, which salt is **most** soluble?
A. Salt A
B. Salt B
C. Salt C
D. They all have equal solubility

8.

Which salt shows the **largest** overall increase in solubility from $0°C$ to $100°C$?
F. Salt A

G. Salt B
H. Salt C
J. All increase by the same amount

9.

If a solution has **55 g** of Salt A dissolved in **100 g** of water at $60°C$, based on Figure 1, the solution is:
A. unsaturated (can still dissolve more Salt A).
B. saturated (at the max for Salt A).
C. supersaturated (beyond the solubility limit).
D. frozen.

10.

Between $40°C$ and $80°C$, Salt B's solubility increases from 28 g to 45 g. Therefore, the **average rate of increase** in that range is about:
F. $(45 - 28)/(80 - 40) = 17/40 = 0.43$ g/°C
G. $(45 - 28)/(40 - 80) = -0.43$ g/°C
H. $(28 - 45)/(80 - 40) = -17/40$
J. 17 g/°C

11.

If a scientist needs a salt that dissolves **at least 50 g per 100 g water at** $40°C$, which salt(s) meets this requirement?
A. Only Salt A
B. Only Salt B
C. Only Salt C
D. Both Salt A and Salt C

12.

A student claims that Salt C's solubility is always greater than Salt B's solubility **at every temperature** in Figure 1. Do the data support this?
F. Yes, because Salt C is higher than Salt B from $0°C$ to $100°C$.
G. No, because Salt B has higher solubility than Salt C at $80°C$.
H. No, because Salt C only exceeds Salt B at $0°C$.
J. Yes, because Salt C equals Salt B at every temperature.

PASSAGE III

(7 questions)

Research Summaries

Background: A team of biologists studied the **growth rates** of a fungus under different **pH** conditions. They set up three experiments (Experiments 1, 2, and 3), each measuring fungal colony diameter (in mm) over 7 days under different pH levels (4.0, 5.0, 6.0).

- **Experiment 1**: Fungal culture plates at pH 4.0
- **Experiment 2**: Fungal culture plates at pH 5.0
- **Experiment 3**: Fungal culture plates at pH 6.0

Figure 2: Average Colony Diameter for Each Experiment Over 7 Days

Day	Exp 1 (pH 4.0)	Exp 2 (pH 5.0)	Exp 3 (pH 6.0)
1	2 mm	4 mm	5 mm
2	5 mm	8 mm	10 mm
3	10 mm	15 mm	18 mm
4	14 mm	20 mm	25 mm
5	16 mm	26 mm	32 mm
6	18 mm	30 mm	38 mm
7	20 mm	33 mm	45 mm

Use this information for Questions 13–19.

13.

Which experiment had the **greatest** average colony diameter on Day 4?

A. Exp 1 (pH 4.0)
B. Exp 2 (pH 5.0)
C. Exp 3 (pH 6.0)
D. All are the same

14.

Based on Figure 2, which statement **best** describes the relationship between pH and fungus growth rate?

F. Lower pH always leads to higher growth.
G. Higher pH (within the range tested) appears to promote faster growth.
H. pH has no effect on fungal growth.
J. pH 4.0 is optimal for fungus growth.

15.

On Day 2, the difference in colony diameter between Exp 2 and Exp 3 is:

A. 10 − 8 = 2 mm
B. 8 − 5 = 3 mm
C. 10 + 8 = 18 mm
D. 10 − 4 = 6 mm

16.

A student hypothesizes that **beyond pH 6.0**, the fungus might grow even faster. Which of the following findings from the data would support this hypothesis?

F. Growth rate in Exp 3 (pH 6.0) is consistently higher than in Exp 2 (pH 5.0).
G. Growth rate in Exp 1 (pH 4.0) was higher than in Exp 3 (pH 6.0).
H. Exp 1 (pH 4.0) and Exp 2 (pH 5.0) had nearly the same day-to-day increases.
J. All experiments show identical growth patterns.

17.

On which day did Exp 2 (pH 5.0) **first** exceed a colony diameter of 25 mm?

A. Day 3
B. Day 4

C. Day 5
D. Day 6

(Check the table: Day 4 = 20 mm, Day 5 = 26 mm...)

18.

If the researchers measured Exp 3 (pH 6.0) on Day 8 and found the colony diameter to be 48 mm, which conclusion is most consistent with the trend from Days 1–7?
F. The fungus likely stopped growing after Day 7.
G. The fungus likely continued growing by about 3 mm after Day 7.
H. The fungus likely shrank in size after Day 7.
J. The fungus likely grew by at least 10 mm after Day 7.

19.

If the researchers repeated the study at **pH 7.0** and found the fungus grew **much slower** than at pH 6.0, which of the following hypotheses about the fungus's growth range might be supported?
A. The optimal pH for this fungus is between 4.0 and 6.0.
B. The fungus does not grow in acidic conditions.
C. The fungus can only grow at exactly pH 6.0.
D. The fungus can thrive in any alkaline environment.

PASSAGE IV

(7 questions)

Research Summaries

Background: Two scientists, Dr. Li and Dr. Gupta, studied the **effects of different carbon dioxide (CO_2) concentrations** on algae growth in flasks over 10 days.

- **Dr. Li's Method (Study 1)**: Prepared flasks with algae in a growth medium. Each flask was bubbled with air containing 400 ppm (parts per million) of CO_2. Counted algae cells daily.
- **Dr. Gupta's Method (Study 2)**: Prepared flasks with the same algae species. Each flask was bubbled with air containing 700 ppm CO_2. Counted algae cells daily.

Figure 3: Algae Cell Count (in thousands of cells/mL) Over 10 Days

- **Study 1 (400 ppm CO_2)**:
  Day 1: 5
  Day 2: 8
  Day 3: 14
  Day 4: 20
  Day 5: 27
  Day 6: 35
  Day 7: 40
  Day 8: 45
  Day 9: 48
  Day 10: 50

- **Study 2 (700 ppm CO_2)**:
  Day 1: 5
  Day 2: 10
  Day 3: 18
  Day 4: 26
  Day 5: 36
  Day 6: 46
  Day 7: 54
  Day 8: 60
  Day 9: 64
  Day 10: 68

Use the information to answer Questions 20–26.

20.

On Day 5, which study shows more algae cells?
F. Study 1
G. Study 2
H. Both are the same
J. Not enough data

21.

Between Day 2 and Day 3 in **Study 2**, algae cell count increases from 10 to 18. Which of the following best describes that change?
A. 2 thousand cells/mL
B. 8 thousand cells/mL
C. 18 thousand cells/mL
D. 28 thousand cells/mL

22.

If a scientist hypothesizes that **higher CO_2 concentrations** speed up algae growth, which result in Figure 3 would **support** that hypothesis?
F. Study 2 consistently shows higher cell counts than Study 1 by each day.
G. Study 1 has a higher final cell count than Study 2.
H. Both studies show identical rates of increase.
J. Both studies have the same final cell count on Day 10.

23.

Which of the following is a **controlled variable** common to both studies based on the descriptions?
A. Concentration of CO_2
B. The species of algae used
C. The cell count after 10 days
D. The number of flasks in total

24.

In Study 2, from Day 7 to Day 10, the cell count increases from 54 to 68. What is the **total increase** for that period?
F. 14 thousand cells/mL
G. 24 thousand cells/mL
H. 68 thousand cells/mL
J. 122 thousand cells/mL

25.

If a new Study 3 used 1,000 ppm of CO_2, and the algae grew **even faster** than in Study 2, which of the following conclusions would that most likely support?
A. Algae are unaffected by CO_2 levels.
B. CO_2 concentration may be a limiting factor for algae growth.
C. Algae cannot survive above 400 ppm CO_2.
D. The presence of CO_2 kills the algae.

26.

After Day 10, Dr. Gupta observed that algae growth in Study 2 **began to plateau** around 70 thousand cells/mL. Which of the following is a **reasonable explanation** for this plateau?
F. The algae reached a limit imposed by nutrient availability or flask space.
G. The CO_2 concentration instantly dropped to 0 ppm.
H. The algae died off immediately after Day 10.
J. There was no real plateau; it was a data recording error.

PASSAGE V

(7 questions)

Research Summaries

Background: A geologist investigates how different rock types erode under **acidic rainfall** conditions. Three sets of rock samples—limestone, sandstone, and granite—were placed in chambers that simulate acidic rain (pH 3.5). The mass of each sample was measured initially and then after 6 weeks.

Table 2: Rock Mass Loss (in grams) after 6 Weeks of Acidic Rain Exposure

Rock Type	Initial Mass (g)	Final Mass (g)	Mass Loss (g)
Limestone	200	190	10
Sandstone	200	197	3
Granite	200	199.5	0.5

Use this information to answer Questions 27–33.

27.

Which rock type shows the **highest** mass loss under the given conditions?
A. Limestone
B. Sandstone
C. Granite
D. All lose the same mass

28.

Based on Table 2, which statement best **compares** limestone to granite regarding susceptibility to acid rain?
F. Granite erodes more quickly than limestone.
G. Limestone erodes more than granite under the same conditions.
H. Both have no significant erosion.
J. Both lose over 10 grams of mass.

29.

A student claims that **increasing the pH** (making the solution less acidic) would result in **less** erosion for all rock types. Do the data alone confirm or deny this?
A. The data confirm it because all pH values above 3.5 must erode less.
B. The data deny it because the mass losses are independent of pH.
C. The data cannot confirm or deny because they only show results at pH 3.5.
D. The data deny it because limestone gained mass.

30.

A second experiment used pH 2.5 instead of 3.5 for sandstone. The mass loss was **6 g** (instead of 3 g) after 6 weeks. Which conclusion is most consistent with these results?
F. Lower pH (more acidic) causes greater erosion.
G. Lower pH (more acidic) causes less erosion.
H. pH has no effect on erosion.
J. The sample gained mass at lower pH.

31.

If a 250 g granite sample underwent the same experiment at pH 3.5, assuming the **same erosion rate** as Table 2, what **final mass** would be expected after 6 weeks?
A. 249.0 g
B. 249.5 g
C. 240.0 g
D. 199.5 g

(Hint: Original 200 g sample lost 0.5 g. That's 0.25% mass loss. Apply that to 250 g.)

32.

A farmer uses crushed limestone to neutralize acidic soil. Based on the data, which property of limestone might be **relevant** for this purpose?
F. Limestone hardly reacts with acid, so it will have little effect on soil pH.
G. Limestone reacts noticeably with acid, suggesting it can buffer acidity.
H. Limestone has no mass change in acidic conditions.
J. Limestone is the least reactive of all rocks tested.

33.

Which of the following is **most directly** measured in this experiment?
A. Change in color of each rock
B. Change in pH of the acid solution
C. Time it takes for the rock to dissolve completely
D. Loss of mass of each rock sample

PASSAGE VI

(7 questions)

Conflicting Viewpoints

Background: Two scientists disagree on whether **asteroid mining** could be a viable solution to resource scarcity on Earth.

Scientist 1: Asteroid mining could provide valuable metals (like platinum, nickel, iron) in large quantities. Since asteroid compositions can be rich in metals, transporting them back to Earth would eventually reduce mining on Earth. Although initial costs are high, new technologies could offset them by enabling repeated missions. The environmental impact on Earth would decrease because we'd minimize destructive terrestrial mining.

Scientist 2: While asteroid mining might yield metals, the energy cost of launching rockets, extracting materials, and shipping them back is far too large. The process's carbon footprint might negate any supposed environmental benefits. Also, unpredictable factors (e.g., cosmic radiation, micro-meteoroids) could damage equipment. Developing advanced robotics to mine asteroids is complex and expensive, with no guarantee of cost-effectiveness. Humans should focus instead on improving Earth-based recycling and less resource-intensive manufacturing.

Use this information to answer Questions 34–40.

34.

Which of the following best describes the **point of disagreement** between the two scientists?
A. Whether asteroid metals are valuable
B. Whether asteroid mining is feasible and environmentally beneficial
C. Whether advanced robotics can function in space
D. Whether we should continue mining on Earth for common metals

35.

Which statement would **Scientist 1** most likely agree with?
F. "Asteroid mining will be cheap from the very first mission."
G. "Reducing Earth-based mining activities could be an environmental benefit."
H. "No metals exist in asteroids."
J. "Space missions are always affordable and safe."

36.

Which statement would **Scientist 2** most likely use to **counter** Scientist 1's argument regarding reduced environmental impact?
A. "Asteroids are too far away to be reached by any spacecraft."
B. "The robotic technology needed is quite simple."
C. "Launching and returning with heavy payloads could produce significant emissions."
D. "Recycling on Earth is environmentally hazardous."

37.

According to **Scientist 1**, the **main advantage** of asteroid mining for Earth is:
F. preventing the formation of cosmic radiation.
G. gathering water from comets to supply Earth.
H. obtaining metals in space to reduce damage to Earth's environment.
J. proving that manned space missions are safer than robotic missions.

38.

Which of the following best **summarizes** Scientist 2's stance on energy and cost?
A. The long-term benefits easily outweigh the upfront costs.
B. Energy usage and cost are likely so high that the project may never be practical.
C. Nuclear power can solve the rocket energy issue.
D. The cost is negligible, but the energy usage is extreme.

39.

If new rocket technology drastically **reduced the cost** of launching and returning payloads, which scientist's viewpoint would be **strengthened** the most?
F. Scientist 1
G. Scientist 2
H. Both equally
J. Neither viewpoint

40.

Which of the following is the **best** alternative solution **Scientist 2** proposes to address resource scarcity?

A. Expand manned space travel to all nearby asteroids

B. Increase Earth-based recycling efforts

C. Purchase metals directly from other countries

D. Develop advanced robots to reduce cosmic radiation

ACT Writing Exam Section (Optional)

PROMPT

Background Information

Over the last decade, **telemedicine**—the practice of providing healthcare remotely via video or phone consultations—has significantly expanded. Proponents say it improves access for people in rural or underserved communities, allowing them to receive advice and treatment without traveling long distances. Opponents caution that telemedicine may reduce the quality of care or depersonalize the doctor-patient relationship. Others see telemedicine as a helpful supplement to in-person care but not a replacement.

Essay Task

Read and consider the following three perspectives on the growing role of telemedicine in healthcare. Then, develop your own perspective on the issue. You may agree with one of the perspectives, or you may present a different point of view. Support your ideas with logical reasoning and detailed examples.

Perspective One

Telemedicine provides critical services for those who otherwise struggle to access healthcare. By allowing consultations and follow-up visits online, it reduces travel burdens, time off work, and costs for both providers and patients. This convenient option significantly improves public health outcomes.

Perspective Two

Telemedicine undermines the quality of care by eliminating in-person diagnosis. Some ailments require physical exams and cannot be accurately assessed via webcam. Telemedicine is prone to misdiagnoses and impersonal interactions, potentially endangering patients.

Perspective Three

Telemedicine works best as a supplemental tool alongside traditional care. It should be limited to services like basic follow-ups, mental health consultations, or preliminary screenings. For complex conditions, patients still benefit most from in-person evaluation.

DIRECTIONS

Write a unified, coherent essay in which you evaluate multiple perspectives on telemedicine's expanding role in healthcare. In your essay, be sure to:

- Analyze and evaluate at least one of the three provided perspectives.
- State and develop your own perspective on the issue.
- Explain the relationship between your perspective and those given.
- Organize your essay clearly, providing logical reasoning and detailed support.

Your essay should demonstrate:

- A clear thesis and logical organization.
- Development and support for ideas.
- Careful use of language and mechanics.

You will have **40 minutes** to write the essay.

CHAPTER 14

FULL LENGTH PRACTICE TEST 2

ACT English Exam Section

PASSAGE I (Questions 1–15)

A New View of "Home"

Nina [1]was born in a small village of rolling hills, sheep farms, and winding dirt roads. From her earliest memory, she admired [2]the bright meadow's each spring. Running barefoot across dewy grass, she would imagine painting every pastel color that surrounded her.

But Nina's family relocated to a bustling city when she was ten. [3]In those first months, the towering buildings, busy streets, and constant noise felt unbelievably disorienting. Yet in time, Nina learned to see beauty in the skyscrapers that reflected pink and orange hues at sunrise, and [4]the vibrancy of local art found it's way into her heart. She realized that "home" could be [5]somewhere in the comfort of farmland or the excitement of an urban metropolis.

Throughout her teenage years, Nina traveled [6]back, and forth to visit relatives in the countryside, witnessing the village's evolving identity. Old barns were renovated, while new businesses [7]has sprouted up near the main road. Meanwhile, the city itself revealed hidden pockets of serenity, such as [8]lush community gardens, quiet reading nooks at libraries, and small neighborhood bakeries.

Today, Nina no longer divides her time between "rural" or "urban" experiences. She [9]observes the details of both worlds with an appreciative eye. Each environment fosters creativity, reflection, and a distinct sense of belonging. In truth, Nina recognizes that [10]home was never about geography but about the places in which she felt authentically herself.

She hopes her story might remind others that [11]a sense of place, in fact, can be shaped by personal growth rather than by geographic limitations. [12]As she once put it: "No matter how many roads you cross, you can always carry the best memories along." She firmly believes we can learn to embrace new settings without losing [13]the roots that shaped our earliest dreams.

For Nina, it no longer matters if she's in the heart of a buzzing city, or on a quiet path near sheep-dotted hills. [14]Her greatest freedom is knowing that home is not a single point on the map. [15]Its a living tapestry woven from each experience she treasures.

PASSAGE I Questions (1–15)

1.

A. NO CHANGE
B. was born, in a small village,
C. was born in a small village:
D. was born, in a small village

2.

F. NO CHANGE
G. the bright meadows every spring
H. the bright meadow's each Spring
J. the bright meadows each spring

3.

A. NO CHANGE
B. In those first months the towering buildings, busy streets, and constant noise, felt unbelievably disorienting.
C. In those first months, the towering buildings and busy streets, and constant noise, felt unbelievably disorienting.
D. In those first months, the towering buildings, busy streets and constant noise, felt unbelievably disorienting.

4.

F. NO CHANGE
G. the vibrancy of local art found its
H. the vibrancy, of local art found it's
J. the vibrancy, of local art found its

5.

A. NO CHANGE
B. both somewhere
C. anywhere
D. anywhere she wanted

6.

F. NO CHANGE
G. back and forth
H. back, and forth,
J. back-and-forth

7.

A. NO CHANGE
B. had sprouted
C. has sprout
D. have sprouted

8.

F. NO CHANGE
G. lush, community gardens, quiet
H. lush community gardens quiet
J. lush community gardens: quiet

9.

A. NO CHANGE
B. is observing
C. observe
D. would observe

10.

F. NO CHANGE
G. home was never about geography, but
H. home, was never about geography but
J. home never was about geography, but

11.

A. NO CHANGE
B. a sense of place in fact, can be shaped
C. a sense of place, in fact can be shaped
D. a sense of place, in fact, can be shaped

12.

F. NO CHANGE
G. As she once put it: "no matter how many roads you cross,
H. As she once put it, "No matter how many roads you cross,
J. As she once put it, "no matter how many roads you cross,

13.

A. NO CHANGE
B. the roots, that shaped
C. the roots; that shaped
D. the roots that shape

14.

F. NO CHANGE
G. Her greatest freedom is: knowing
H. Her greatest freedom, is knowing
J. Her greatest freedom is, knowing

15.

A. NO CHANGE
B. It's
C. It is
D. Its'

PASSAGE II (Questions 16–30)

At the Archaeological Site

Dr. Kincaid spent years analyzing ancient artifacts from a remote settlement along the coast. [16]Woven baskets, carved figurines, and pottery shards were meticulously cataloged. Her goal was to piece together the cultural practices and daily routines of a lost civilization.

Because of shifting sands, the site [17]was partly concealed for centuries, archaeologists [18]only recently discovered evidence of entire living quarters beneath the dunes. Dr. Kincaid's team uncovered a complex network of stone foundations. [19]She believed that these dwellings indicated a sophisticated social structure; one that included designated communal areas and private spaces.

Yet not everyone agreed with her conclusion. Some argued that the settlement [20]serves mostly as a seasonal fishing camp, lacking permanent inhabitants. Dr. Kincaid, however, pointed to the variety of artifacts—[21]including intricate jewelry items and tool sets—as proof of a long-term community presence.

Over the next few months, Dr. Kincaid planned to analyze organic remnants [22]like seashell fragments, fish bones, and grain seeds. By examining these materials, her team could better understand the local diet and, possibly, how trade routes developed. [23]In spite of the fact that some colleagues remain skeptical, she believed that further excavation would reveal new patterns.

For Dr. Kincaid, archaeology was never [24]just about unearthing objects: it was about reconstructing the voices of those who came before. [25]She often states "Each artifact holds a narrative; we just need the patience to read it carefully." In her eyes, the hidden settlement along the coast was [26]like a puzzle that begs to be solved. If her theory holds true, [27]the understanding of ancient coastal societies will expand significantly.

Still, doubts linger regarding her interpretation. She remains [28]undaunted. She meticulously documents every discovery with the hope that, one day, the site's secrets will become as clear as the footprints left behind in the shifting sands.

PASSAGE II Questions (16–30)

16.

F. NO CHANGE
G. Woven baskets carved figurines, and pottery shards
H. Woven baskets, carved figurines and pottery shards
J. Woven baskets, carved figurines, and, pottery shards

17.

A. NO CHANGE
B. was partly concealed for centuries, so archaeologists
C. was partly concealed for centuries. Archaeologists
D. was partly concealed for centuries archaeologists

18.

F. NO CHANGE
G. only recently discovering
H. only recently discovered, evidence
J. only recently discovered evidence

19.

A. NO CHANGE
B. She believed that these dwellings indicated a sophisticated social structure. One that included designated communal areas and private spaces.
C. She believed that these dwellings indicated a sophisticated social structure, one that included designated communal areas, and private spaces.
D. She believed that these dwellings indicated a sophisticated social structure, one that included designated communal areas and private spaces.

20.

F. NO CHANGE
G. served mostly
H. had served mostly
J. would serve mostly

21.

A. NO CHANGE
B. including, intricate jewelry items, and tool sets
C. including intricate jewelry items and tool sets
D. including intricate jewelry items, and tool sets.

22.

F. NO CHANGE
G. such as
H. such like
J. in which

23.

A. NO CHANGE
B. In spite of some colleagues remain skeptical, she believed
C. Despite some colleagues remain skeptical, she believed
D. Although some colleagues remain skeptical, she believed

24.

F. NO CHANGE
G. never, just about unearthing objects: it was
H. never just, about unearthing objects it was
J. never just about unearthing objects it was

25.

A. NO CHANGE
B. She often states, "Each artifact holds a narrative; we just need the patience to read it carefully."
C. She often states: "each artifact holds a narrative; we just need the patience to read it carefully."
D. She often states, "each artifact holds a narrative; We just need the patience to read it carefully."

26.

F. NO CHANGE
G. like a puzzle that begged to be solved
H. as a puzzle that begs to be solved
J. like a puzzle, it begs to be solved

27.

A. NO CHANGE
B. understanding ancient coastal societies will expand significantly
C. it would expand the understanding of ancient coastal societies significantly
D. it would expand significantly, the understanding of ancient coastal societies

28.

F. NO CHANGE
G. undaunted, she meticulously
H. undaunted: she meticulously
J. undaunted; She meticulously

29.

Which choice best concludes the paragraph in [6], considering Dr. Kincaid's optimism and ongoing research?
A. She grew frustrated that the dunes obscured any chance of further discovery.
B. She envisions the settlement forever out of reach.
C. She anticipates many more questions will arise as they dig deeper.
D. She decides to leave archaeology and become a historian instead.

30.

Which choice most effectively combines the underlined sentences in [6] for clarity and flow?
Dr. Kincaid remains undaunted. She meticulously documents every discovery with hope.
F. Dr. Kincaid remains undaunted, and she meticulously documents every discovery with hope.
G. Remaining undaunted, Dr. Kincaid meticulously documents every discovery, hoping for clarity one day.
H. Dr. Kincaid remains undaunted, she meticulously documents every discovery, hopefully, for clarity.
J. Undaunted, remains Dr. Kincaid, who, with hope, documents every discovery.

PASSAGE III (Questions 31–45)

A Chorus of Voices

Amelia joined the community choir on a whim. [31]She had never read music nor received formal vocal training. However, the director's welcoming smile convinced her to try. On her first day, she stood among strangers who opened their sheet music with practiced ease.

As they [32]begin to warm up, Amelia mimicked the exercises, carefully listening to the notes. She could feel her anxiety subside each time the voices around her formed harmonious chords. [33]She realized that singing was more about blending and less about perfection. Whenever her pitch wavered, a friendly neighbor helped her find the correct melody line.

The choir rehearsed weekly in a local school auditorium. [34]Sometimes, the overhead lights flickered, but the group pressed on. Over time, Amelia discovered that each rehearsal was an opportunity to learn from small mistakes. [35]Though her confidence grew, she recognized there was always more to master.

During the final rehearsal before a holiday concert, [36]Amelia had a moment of doubt. She questioned whether she truly belonged. Yet, the director's encouraging words reminded her why she joined in the first place. [37]Song, after all, was meant to be shared.

[38]At the performance, family, friends, and neighbors filled the seats, the choir's voices soared through the auditorium, weaving a tapestry of sound that brought tears to many eyes. Amelia discovered that singing, though demanding of skill and practice, was fundamentally a collective experience of unity.

Now, Amelia plans to continue with the choir. [39]She cherishes the camaraderie, the creative expression, and the personal growth singing fosters in each member. Even if a single note occasionally goes flat, Amelia knows the entire group stands together, lifting each other up. [40]In that sense, her voice merges with countless others, culminating in something far greater [41]then any single sound.

PASSAGE III Questions (31–45)

31.

A. NO CHANGE
B. She had never read music, nor had she received formal vocal training.
C. She never read music; nor received formal vocal training.
D. She had never read music, nor receiving formal vocal training.

32.

F. NO CHANGE
G. began
H. begins
J. would begin

33.

A. NO CHANGE
B. She realized that singing was about more blending and less about perfection.
C. She realized that singing was about more blending, and not about perfection.
D. She realized that singing was more about blending, and about less perfection.

34.

F. NO CHANGE
G. Sometimes the overhead lights flickered but, the group pressed on.
H. Sometimes, the overhead lights flickered but the group pressed on.
J. Sometimes the overhead lights flickered, but the group pressed on.

35.

A. NO CHANGE
B. As her confidence grew, she recognized that there would always be more to master.
C. Her confidence grew, recognized there was always more to master.
D. With her confidence grown, there was always more to master recognized.

36.

F. NO CHANGE
G. Amelia had, a moment of doubt.
H. Amelia: had a moment of doubt.
J. Amelia would have a moment: of doubt.

37.

A. NO CHANGE
B. Song, after all was meant to be shared.
C. Song after all, was meant to be shared.
D. Song, after all, was meant, to be shared.

38.

F. NO CHANGE
G. At the performance, as family, friends, and neighbors filled the seats, the choir's voices soared
H. At the performance: family, friends, and neighbors filled the seats; the choir's voices soared
J. At the performance—family, friends, and neighbors filled the seats—the choir's voices soared

39.

A. NO CHANGE
B. She cherishes camaraderie, creative expression, and personal growth that singing fosters
C. She cherishes the camaraderie, the creative expression and the personal growth, that singing fosters
D. She cherishes the camaraderie: the creative expression: and the personal growth singing fosters

40.

F. NO CHANGE
G. In that sense her voice merges with countless others culminating
H. In that sense, her voice merges with countless others; culminating
J. In that sense, her voice merges with countless others, culminating

41.

A. NO CHANGE
B. than any single sound
C. then, any single sound
D. than any single sound.

42.

Which choice provides the **best transition** from the end of paragraph [2] to the beginning of paragraph [3]?

- **A.** "Amelia wondered if the audience would appreciate her efforts."
- **B.** "The group sometimes shared snacks after rehearsal, which she enjoyed."
- **C.** "Their weekly rehearsals offered Amelia a routine and a steady environment for growth."
- **D.** "She disliked the auditorium's dim lighting, which caused eye strain."

43.

In the context of the passage, which phrase in paragraph [5] most clearly conveys the effect of the choir's singing on the audience?

- **F.** "weaving a tapestry of sound that brought tears to many eyes."
- **G.** "filling the seats with family and friends."
- **H.** "the performance was short but entertaining."
- **J.** "the group sang in unison without reading sheet music."

44.

Which of the following alternatives to the underlined portion in paragraph [4], "She questioned whether she truly belonged," would **best** maintain the meaning and tone?

- **A.** She lost her place in the sheet music.
- **B.** She momentarily doubted she fit in with the others.
- **C.** She worried the director might remove her from the ensemble.
- **D.** She concluded that singing was definitely not for her.

45.

Which statement **best** sums up Amelia's overall realization by the end of the passage?

- **F.** She regrets joining the choir and plans to quit.
- **G.** She resents the high expectations of the director.
- **H.** She recognizes that communal singing is more important than individual perfection.
- **J.** She believes practicing alone at home is the only way to improve vocal skills.

PASSAGE IV (Questions 46–60)

Supporting a Local Orchard

Hector's family owns a small orchard that produces peaches, apples, and plums. [46]Every autumn they invite neighbors to come and harvest fruit on weekends. The orchard's tradition started decades ago, as Hector's grandparents believed in sharing the bounty with the entire community.

However, modern challenges emerged. [47]A surge in pests threatened to reduce yields, and unpredictable weather patterns made harvest timing more difficult. Instead of using heavy pesticides, Hector proposed natural solutions, such as introducing beneficial insects and rotating which tree rows were harvested each week to allow regrowth. [48]Although the orchard encountered obstacles, it thrived by focusing on sustainable methods.

Word spread about the orchard's new approach. Soon, local chefs and bakers began visiting, praising Hector's family for prioritizing flavor and environmental responsibility over mass production. [49]One baker commented,

"Freshness is the key, your peaches taste better than anything shipped from far away." Hearing such feedback reaffirmed [50]Hector's convictions and made him proud.

[51]The orchard organizes workshops where they teach visitors to craft homemade jams, pies, and dried fruit snacks. At first, only a handful of people attended, but the classes quickly became popular. Families started scheduling group outings to learn about sustainable farming. [52]Hector realized the orchard could be more than just a place to buy fruit, it could be a hub for education and connection.

Of course, not every experiment succeeded. [53]One year, Hector tried growing pears in a shady corner, which produced only a handful of usable fruit. [54]Nevertheless, each setback was a lesson—an opportunity to refine techniques and adapt. Over time, the orchard thrived not by chasing perfection, but by embracing collaboration, creativity, and respect for the land.

Today, the orchard stands as a testament to family tradition and environmental stewardship. [55]Neighbors still gather, the trees still blossom, and the fruit still sweetens every autumn day. Hector's family remains committed to passing on these values, ensuring that future generations [56]will enjoy in the orchard's legacy.

PASSAGE IV Questions (46–60)

46.

A. NO CHANGE
B. Every autumn, they invite neighbors to come, and harvest fruit on weekends.
C. Every autumn; they invite neighbors, to come and harvest fruit on weekends.
D. Every autumn they invite neighbors, to come and harvest fruit, on weekends.

47.

F. NO CHANGE
G. A surge in pests, threatened to reduce yields, and unpredictable
H. A surge in pests threatened to reduce yields—and unpredictable
J. A surge in pests threatened to reduce yields, and unpredictable

48.

A. NO CHANGE
B. The orchard encountered obstacles, thriving by focusing on sustainable methods though.
C. Though the orchard encountered obstacles, it thrived by focusing on sustainable methods.
D. The orchard encountered obstacles, but thriving by focusing on sustainable methods.

49.

F. NO CHANGE
G. A baker commented, "Freshness is the key; your peaches taste better than anything shipped from far away."
H. A baker commented "Freshness is the key. Your peaches taste better than anything shipped from far away."
J. A baker commented. "Freshness is the key, your peaches taste better than anything shipped from far away."

50.

A. NO CHANGE
B. Hector's convictions making him proud.
C. Hector's conviction's and made him proud.
D. Hector's convictions, which made him proud.

51.

F. NO CHANGE
G. The orchard organizes workshops, they teach visitors to craft homemade jams, pies, and dried fruit snacks.
H. The orchard organizes workshops, teaching visitors to craft homemade jams, pies, and dried fruit snacks.
J. The orchard organizes workshops; teaching visitors, to craft homemade jams, pies, and dried fruit snacks.

52.

A. NO CHANGE
B. Hector realized the orchard could be more than just a place to buy fruit—it could be a hub for education and connection.
C. Hector realized the orchard could be more than just a place to buy fruit; it could be a hub for education and connection,
D. Hector realized the orchard could be more: than just a place to buy fruit, it could be a hub for education, and connection.

53.

F. NO CHANGE
G. One year Hector tried growing pears, in a shady corner, which produced only a handful
H. One year, Hector tried growing pears in a shady corner which produced only a handful
J. One year: Hector tried growing pears in a shady corner: which produced only a handful

54.

A. NO CHANGE
B. Notwithstanding, each setback was a lesson—an opportunity
C. Regardless, every setback was a lesson; an opportunity
D. Regardless every setback was a lesson—an opportunity

55.

F. NO CHANGE
G. Neighbors still gather; the trees still blossom, and the fruit, still sweetens every autumn day.
H. Neighbors still gather. The trees still blossom and the fruit still sweetens every autumn day.
J. Neighbors still gather, the trees still blossom and the fruit still sweetens, every autumn day.

56.

A. NO CHANGE
B. will partake in the orchard's legacy.
C. will enjoy the orchard's legacy.
D. will partake in orchard's legacy.

57.

Which choice best introduces the idea of small-scale sustainability in paragraph [2]?

- **F.** "Unlike many large farms, Hector's orchard relies on creative pest control methods."
- **G.** "Hector was frustrated that he could not spray more pesticides."
- **H.** "The orchard was first established by his grandparents."
- **J.** "Weather changes made planting schedules unpredictable."

58.

The writer wants to convey that the orchard's educational programs expanded quickly. Which choice best accomplishes this?

- **A.** “At first, only a handful of people attended, but the classes quickly became more elaborate.”
- **B.** “At first, only a handful of people attended, but soon attendance soared as word spread.”
- **C.** “At first, they had too many sign-ups, so they had to stop offering classes.”
- **D.** “At first, kids came by themselves, and later, adults also showed up in small numbers.”

59.

In the context of the passage, the phrase “passing on these values” (paragraph [6]) primarily refers to:

- **F.** continuing the orchard’s unique fruit distribution system.
- **G.** preserving the orchard’s social traditions of jam-making.
- **H.** teaching sustainability, community, and family heritage.
- **J.** planting more trees for purely economic reasons.

60.

Which concluding sentence would **best** strengthen paragraph [6] by emphasizing the orchard’s broader significance?

- **A.** “Most fruits grown on large-scale farms are distributed throughout the country.”
- **B.** “In essence, the orchard remains a place where nature, heritage, and community spirit thrive.”
- **C.** “Experts say plums are the hardest fruit to grow in certain climates.”
- **D.** “Of course, not every visitor knows how to pick peaches from tall branches.”

PASSAGE V (Questions 61–75)

Revisiting Classical Music

Jonas grew up listening to pop music on the radio. [61]He rarely gave classical compositions a chance. One day, however, he attended a live orchestra performance by chance. Surprised at how deeply he was moved, Jonas decided to explore the genre further.

Initially, he felt overwhelmed by the number of composers, symphonies, and concertos. [62]He approached his friend, a music major, who recommended Jonas start with accessible pieces from the Romantic period. Jonas found himself captivated by the sweeping melodies, dramatic contrasts, and [63]unique emotional tension. Over time, he ventured into Baroque and contemporary works, deepening his appreciation for the genre’s variety.

Jonas realized that classical music was not [64]exclusively for a small group of “elite” audiences. Instead, it offered a universal language capable of stirring powerful emotions in [65]everyone who gave it a honest listen. He began attending free community concerts, joining online music forums, and sharing favorite recordings with friends.

Of course, some remained skeptical of the music’s relevance. Jonas responded by highlighting how certain modern films, commercials, and even pop songs [66]incorporate orchestral elements that evoke timeless feelings. [67]Rather than dismiss older compositions as outdated, Jonas argued that reimagining them is the key to connecting with new generations.

Before long, Jonas started a small club at his college. [68]They called it “Classical Crossroads.” Students from all majors [69]came to watch performance clips, discuss composer backstories, or simply relax while listening to a string quartet. The club grew rapidly, reflecting a renewed curiosity in discovering what Jonas described [70]as an ocean of musical treasures.

By sharing classical music in accessible ways, Jonas hoped [71]to bridging the gap between centuries-old compositions and modern listeners. For him, it wasn’t about living in the past but about [72]celebrating the enduring beauty that resonates across any era. Through each new piece, Jonas found a deeper connection not only to the music, but also [73]two himself and those who joined him in this musical journey.

Today, Jonas acknowledges that [74]the significance that classical music has on culture is often underestimated. Still, he believes that anyone who invests even a little time exploring it [75]will discover entire worlds hidden within each orchestral score.

PASSAGE V Questions (61–75)

61.

A. NO CHANGE
B. He rarely gave classical compositions, a chance.
C. Rarely giving classical compositions, a chance
D. He rarely gave classical compositions a chance,

62.

F. NO CHANGE
G. Approaching a friend who was a music major, who recommended Jonas start with
H. He approached his friend: a music major who recommended Jonas start with
J. He approached his friend, a music major, recommending Jonas to start with

63.

A. NO CHANGE
B. unique, emotional tension
C. uniquely, emotional tension
D. unique emotional tension

64.

F. NO CHANGE
G. exclusive for a small group of "elite"
H. exclusive to a small group of "elite"
J. exclusively to a small group of "elite"

65.

A. NO CHANGE
B. everyone who gave it an honest listen
C. everyone that gave it a honest listen
D. everyone who gave it honest listens

66.

F. NO CHANGE
G. incorporate
H. had incorporate
J. are incorporating

67.

A. NO CHANGE
B. Instead of dismiss older compositions as outdated, Jonas argued that
C. Rather than dismiss older compositions as outdated, Jonas argues that
D. Instead, dismiss older compositions as outdated, Jonas argued that

68.

F. NO CHANGE
G. He named it "Classical Crossroads."
H. They named the club as "Classical Crossroads."
J. The small club was named "Classical Crossroads."

69.

A. NO CHANGE
B. came to watch performance clips; they discussed composer backstories or simply relaxed
C. came to watch performance clips, discuss composer backstories, or simply relax
D. came to watch performance clips and discussing composer backstories or relaxing

70.

F. NO CHANGE
G. as an ocean, of musical treasures
H. like an ocean, of musical treasures
J. as an ocean of musical treasures,

71.

A. NO CHANGE
B. bridging
C. to bridge
D. that bridging

72.

F. NO CHANGE
G. celebrating, the enduring beauty that resonates
H. celebrating the enduring beauty who resonates
J. celebrating in enduring beauty that resonates

73.

A. NO CHANGE
B. too himself, and those
C. to himself, and those
D. to himself and those

74.

F. NO CHANGE
G. the significance classical music has on culture
H. that the significance of classical music
J. that classical music's significance

75.

A. NO CHANGE
B. would discover entire worlds hidden
C. will have discovered entire worlds hidden
D. will discover entire worlds that are hidden

ACT Math Exam Section

1.

If $x + 4 = 10$, then $x =$

A. 4

B. 6

C. 7

D. 10

E. 14

2.

What is the value of $5 \times 3 - 4$?

A. 11

B. 12

C. 13

D. 15

E. 19

3.

A bag contains 6 red marbles and 9 blue marbles. What fraction of the marbles in the bag are blue?

A. $\frac{3}{9}$

B. $\frac{6}{15}$

C. $\frac{9}{15}$

D. $\frac{2}{3}$

E. $\frac{3}{5}$

4.

What is 0.7×0.05?

A. 0.35

B. 0.035

C. 0.0035

D. 0.014

E. 0.00035

5.

If $n < 0$ and $| n |= 8$, which of the following is n?

A. -8

B. 8

C. 0

D. -1

E. $\frac{1}{8}$

6.

Which of the following **inequalities** is **true** for any real x?

A. $x + 1 < x$

B. $2x > 2x + 1$

C. $x - x = 1$
D. $2x = 2 + x$
E. $x - x = 0$

7.

What is the **sum** of the first 4 positive even integers?
A. 6
B. 12
C. 16
D. 20
E. 24

(Hint: The first 4 positive even integers are 2, 4, 6, 8.)

8.

If $x = 5$, what is $\frac{2x}{10}$?
A. 0.5
B. 1
C. 1.5
D. 2
E. 10

9.

The expression $(a^2)(a^3)$ simplifies to:
A. a^5
B. a^6
C. a^8
D. $a^{2.5}$
E. $a^{5/2}$

10.

Solve for p:

$$4p + 3 = 15.$$

A. 1
B. 2
C. 3
D. 4
E. 5

11.

A line in the coordinate plane passes through the points $(0,2)$ and $(2,6)$. What is the slope of this line?
A. 2
B. 3
C. 4
D. $\frac{1}{2}$
E. -2

12.

Which of the following is **closest** to $\sqrt{90}$?

A. 8.1

B. 9.2

C. 9.5

D. 10.1

E. 11.2

13.

Which value of x satisfies $10 - x = 4$?

A. 6

B. -6

C. 4

D. -14

E. 14

14.

If $(x + 2)^2 = x^2 + 4x + 4$, then $(x + 5)^2 =$

A. $x^2 + 5$

B. $x^2 + 25$

C. $x^2 + 10x + 25$

D. $x^2 + 25x + 5$

E. $x^2 + 5x + 10$

15.

What is the largest integer less than $\frac{27}{4}$?

A. 4

B. 5

C. 6

D. 7

E. 8

16.

Simplify: $\frac{2}{3} \times \frac{6}{5}$.

A. $\frac{4}{5}$

B. $\frac{6}{10}$

C. $\frac{12}{5}$

D. $\frac{12}{15}$

E. $\frac{6}{5}$

17.

What is the total cost of 6 notebooks priced at $2.75each?

A. $11.00

B. $13.50

C. \$15.00
D. \$16.50
E. \$18.00

18.

If $b < 0$ and $| b |= 2$, then $3b =$
A. -6
B. -3
C. 1
D. 6
E. $\frac{-1}{2}$

19.

What is the value of $3\left(\frac{4}{2} + 2\right)$?
A. 9
B. 10
C. 12
D. 15
E. 18

20.

A hotel charges \$80 per night plus a one-time tax of \$20. If a guest stayed for x nights, which expression represents the total cost?

A. $80 + 20x$
B. $20 + 80x$
C. $(20 + 80)x$
D. $100x$
E. $80x - 20$

21.

Which of the following is the **greatest common divisor (GCD)** of 24 and 36?
A. 4
B. 6
C. 8
D. 12
E. 24

22.

A line has the equation $y = -x + 8$. If $x = 3$, what is y?
A. -3
B. 5
C. 8
D. 11
E. 14

23.

The sum of the first n positive integers is given by $\frac{n(n+1)}{2}$. If $n = 5$, what is that sum?

A. 10
B. 12
C. 15
D. 20
E. 25

24.

A rectangle's length is 8 inches, and its width is 3 inches. What is the **perimeter** of this rectangle?
A. 11 inches
B. 22 inches
C. 24 inches
D. 48 inches
E. 64 inches

25.

If $3n + 2 = 17$, then $6n + 4 =$
A. 17
B. 20
C. 30
D. 34
E. 40

26.

In the coordinate plane, which point (x, y) lies on the line $y = 2x - 1$?
A. (0,1)
B. (2,3)
C. (1,1)
D. (3,5)
E. (2,2)

27.

Which of the following is a **prime** number?
A. 21
B. 28
C. 31
D. 36
E. 40

28.

If a and b are integers and $a < b$, which of the following sets of inequalities is possible?
A. $a = 4$ and $b = 3$
B. $a = 5$ and $b = 5$
C. $a = 2$ and $b = 7$
D. $a = -1$ and $b = -2$
E. $a = 0$ and $b = 0$

29.

A car travels 240 miles in 4 hours. What is its **average speed** in miles per hour (mph)?

A. 40

B. 50

C. 60

D. 70

E. 80

30.

Simplify: $\frac{10x+5}{5}$.

A. $2x + 1$

B. $10x$

C. $10x + 5$

D. $2x + \frac{5}{5}$

E. $x + 1$

31.

What is the **distance** between the points $(1,2)$ and $(5,2)$ in the coordinate plane?

A. 2

B. 3

C. 4

D. 5

E. 6

32.

Which of the following expressions is equivalent to $(x^2)^3$?

A. x^5

B. x^6

C. x^8

D. x^9

E. $x^{2/3}$

33.

If $(x + 4)(x + 1) = 0$, which of the following is a possible value for x?

A. -4

B. -3

C. 4

D. 3

E. 0

34.

A right triangle has legs of lengths 3 and 4. What is the length of the **hypotenuse**?

A. 3

B. 4

C. 5

D. 6
E. 7

35.

If $2m = 6$, then $4m - 3 =$
A. 3
B. 6
C. 9
D. 12
E. 21

36.

What is the **area** of a rectangle with length 10 inches and width 4 inches?
A. 14 sq. inches
B. 20 sq. inches
C. 28 sq. inches
D. 40 sq. inches
E. 50 sq. inches

37.

What is the slope of the line $2y = 4x - 2$?
A. $\frac{2}{1}$
B. $\frac{4}{2} = 2$
C. 4
D. $\frac{1}{2}$
E. -2

38.

A hexagon has **6 sides**. What is the sum of the interior angles of a **hexagon**?
(The sum of interior angles of an n-sided polygon is $(n - 2) \times 180°$.*)*
A. $360°$
B. $540°$
C. $720°$
D. $900°$
E. $1,080°$

39.

If $\frac{2}{x} = 1$, what is x?
A. $\frac{1}{2}$
B. -2
C. 1
D. 2
E. 0

40.

Which inequality is **true** for any real number k?

A. $k^2 \geq 0$

B. $k^2 \leq 0$

C. $-k^2 \geq 1$

D. $k^2 - 1 = 0$

E. $k^2 < 0$

41.

The expression $(x-3)(x+3)$ simplifies to:

A. $x^2 + 9$

B. $x^2 - 9$

C. $x^2 + 3x - 3x + 9$

D. $x^2 - 3$

E. $x^2 + 3$

42.

Which of the following is the **greatest common divisor** of $15x$ and $9x$?

(Assume x is a positive integer.)

A. $3x$

B. $6x$

C. $9x$

D. $15x$

E. $\frac{15}{9}x$

43.

If a circle has radius r, which formula gives its **circumference**?

A. πr^2

B. $\frac{1}{2}\pi r$

C. $2\pi r$

D. πd^2

E. πd

44.

The length of a rectangle is twice its width. If the width is 4, what is the **perimeter** of the rectangle?

A. 8

B. 12

C. 16

D. 24

E. 32

45.

Solve for y: $\frac{y}{5} = 7$.

A. $\frac{5}{7}$

B. 12

C. $\frac{7}{5}$
D. 35
E. 2

46.

Which ordered pair (p, q) **satisfies** the equation $q = 3p - 4$?
A. $(1, -1)$
B. $(2,2)$
C. $(0, -4)$
D. $(1,2)$
E. $(4,0)$

47.

What is the **area** of a right triangle with legs of 6 cm and 10 cm?
A. 16 cm^2
B. 30 cm^2
C. 60 cm^2
D. 64 cm^2
E. 120 cm^2

48.

Factor completely: $x^2 - 16x$.
A. $(x - 4)(x - 4)$
B. $x(x - 16)$
C. $(x - 8)(x - 2)$
D. $x(x - 16x)$
E. $(x - 8)(x + 2)$

(Check the factoring carefully!)

49.

A line has slope -2 and a y-intercept of 3. Which is its equation?
A. $y = -2x + 3$
B. $y = 2x + 3$
C. $y = -\frac{1}{2}x + 3$
D. $2y = -x + 3$
E. $y = -2(x - 3)$

50.

If $\sin(\theta) = \frac{\text{opposite}}{\text{hypotenuse}}$, then $\tan(\theta)$ is:

A. $\frac{\text{adjacent}}{\text{hypotenuse}}$
B. $\frac{\text{opposite}}{\text{adjacent}}$
C. $\frac{\text{opposite}}{\text{hypotenuse}} + 1$

D. $\frac{\text{hypotenuse}}{\text{opposite}}$

E. $\frac{\text{adjacent}}{\text{opposite}}$

51.

Which of these angles is an **obtuse angle**?

A. $25°$

B. $45°$

C. $89°$

D. $90°$

E. $120°$

52.

Which of the following points lies on the circle $x^2 + y^2 = 25$?

A. $(0,6)$

B. $(5,5)$

C. $(3,4)$

D. $(10,0)$

E. $(4,4)$

53.

What is the solution set for $z^2 = 49$?

A. {7}

B. {-7}

C. {-7, 7}

D. {49}

E. {-49, 49}

54.

A box has dimensions $l = 5, w = 4, h = 3$. The **volume** of this rectangular prism is:

A. $5 + 4 + 3$

B. $5 \times 4 \times 3$

C. $2(5 + 4 + 3)$

D. $5 \times 4 \times 3 \times 2$

E. 5×4

55.

If $x = \frac{2}{3}$, then $6x + 1 =$

A. 5

B. 6

C. 7

D. 2

E. 3

56.

What is the simplified form of $\frac{6x+9}{3}$?

A. $2x + 3$

B. $6x + 9$

C. $\frac{6x}{3} + 9$

D. $2x + \frac{9}{3}$

E. $2x + 3 + 3$

57.

If $\sin(\alpha) = \frac{3}{5}$ in a right triangle, and α is acute, what is $\cos(\alpha)$?

A. $\frac{2}{5}$

B. $\frac{3}{4}$

C. $\frac{4}{5}$

D. $\sqrt{\frac{3}{5}}$

E. $\frac{5}{3}$

(Use $\sin^2(\alpha) + \cos^2(\alpha) = 1$*.)*

58.

Solve for n: $5n - 2 = 18$.

A. 4

B. 5

C. 20

D. $\frac{18+5}{2}$

E. $\frac{1}{4}$

59.

Which is **true** for any acute angle θ?

A. $\sin(\theta) + \cos(\theta) > 1$

B. $\sin(\theta) + \cos(\theta) = 0$

C. $\sin^2(\theta) = \cos^2(\theta)$

D. $\sin(\theta) = 0$

E. $\sin(\theta) > 1$

60.

Which expression represents the **volume of a cylinder** with radius r and height h?

A. $\frac{1}{2}\pi rh$

B. $\pi r^2 h$

C. $2\pi rh$

D. $\frac{4}{3}\pi r^3$

E. πr^3

ACT Reading Exam Section

PASSAGE I (Questions 1–10)

Literary Narrative

Elena perched on the rickety fence bordering her grandfather's orchard, watching the sun slip behind distant hills. It was her first summer back in years. As a child, she'd raced through these rows of peach trees, sticky juice running down her chin, unconcerned about the future. Now, at eighteen, Elena was on the cusp of deciding where to attend college—if she attended at all.

Her grandfather appeared beside her, quiet as ever. He offered a gentle nod toward the orchard. "Looks like this year's peaches will be good," he said. She noticed deeper lines across his face, shaped by a lifetime of farm work and laughter shared at family gatherings. The orchard, he reminded her, was more than a place for fruit; it was a testament to enduring traditions.

Elena's parents, however, wanted her to enroll in a prestigious university hundreds of miles away, believing that a rural orchard had nothing left to teach her. The tension weighed heavily on Elena. She'd grown up hearing that success lay in sprawling cities and corporate towers. Yet something about her grandfather's steady presence made her question if she should rush toward an unknown future.

Early the next morning, she helped him gather the first peaches of the season. As she moved among the branches, Elena found her senses overwhelmed by the orchard's lush fragrance and the hum of bees dancing around the blossoms. Each tree bore marks from storms and harvests gone by, standing tall despite harsh winters. She felt unexpectedly at peace, as though the orchard's resilience seeped into her own soul.

That afternoon, her grandfather asked her to record the harvest numbers. In doing so, Elena recognized the skill behind each row's yield: the careful pruning, watering schedules, and forecasting that came from decades of careful observation. She realized the orchard might be a living classroom, offering lessons in patience, diligence, and hope. Though she still planned to pursue her education, the orchard reminded her that learning could happen anywhere.

PASSAGE I Questions (1–10)

1. The passage primarily focuses on Elena's:
   A. decision to abandon all plans for higher education.
   B. frustration with her grandfather's orchard and its routine tasks.
   C. reflections on her future while revisiting a place filled with memories.
   D. certainty that her parents' advice about college is wrong.
2. It can most reasonably be inferred that Elena's parents:
   F. grew up working in the orchard alongside her grandfather.
   G. see little value in the orchard's traditions for Elena's future success.
   H. want Elena to take over the orchard immediately.
   J. believe the orchard will help her gain scholarships.
3. As used in the first paragraph, Elena's memories of "sticky juice running down her chin" serve mainly to:
   A. illustrate her long dislike of peaches.
   B. highlight that she was never carefree as a child.
   C. depict carefree childhood moments in contrast to her current worries.
   D. suggest the orchard was unsanitary.
4. Elena's grandfather's attitude toward the orchard can best be described as:
   F. indifferent and dismissive.
   G. resentful and discontented.
   H. fearful and anxious.
   J. appreciative and proud.
5. The line "The orchard, he reminded her, was more than a place for fruit; it was a testament to enduring traditions" suggests that:
   A. the orchard has failed to produce a meaningful harvest in years.

B. the orchard holds cultural or familial significance beyond its economic value.
C. Elena's grandfather secretly dislikes the orchard's traditions.
D. Elena's parents created the orchard for family bonding.

6. Which of the following best describes Elena's emotional state while she gathers peaches the next morning?
F. Irritated by the orchard's swarming bees
G. Overwhelmed by how strenuous orchard work is
H. Calm and renewed by the orchard's atmosphere
J. Eager to leave as soon as possible

7. The orchard's trees bearing marks from storms and harvests primarily symbolizes:
A. the orchard's continuous struggle with pests.
B. the orchard's inability to survive adverse conditions.
C. the orchard's resilience and long history.
D. the orchard's decoration for tourists.

8. By helping record the harvest numbers, Elena learns that:
F. orchard work requires no real skill or precision.
G. orchard tasks are too boring for someone with ambition.
H. orchard success relies on observation and careful planning.
J. orchard yields never change year to year.

9. From the passage, Elena's perspective on learning is best described as:
A. resentful of any education outside the orchard.
B. dismissive of formal schooling.
C. recognizing that valuable lessons come from both academic and practical experiences.
D. convinced that the orchard is the only place she can learn meaningful skills.

10. Overall, the passage most strongly implies that Elena:
F. will likely drop out of high school to work full-time in the orchard.
G. sees the orchard and college as completely incompatible.
H. no longer feels any doubt about leaving for college.
J. is discovering the orchard's deeper importance as she faces her next steps.

PASSAGE II (Questions 11–20)

Social Science

In many communities, **urban farming** initiatives have become a grassroots response to food deserts—areas lacking access to fresh produce. Local residents reclaim unused plots of land, plant vegetables and fruit trees, and manage small-scale farms right in the city. Over time, these projects have evolved to address broader issues like community building, youth education, and sustainable living.

Historically, urban farming gained attention during wartime shortages when citizens planted "victory gardens" to supplement the national food supply. However, modern efforts often arise from health and equity concerns rather than an immediate food crisis. For example, neighborhoods with few grocery stores might struggle with nutrition-related health problems, and urban farms help provide fresh, affordable foods.

Critics question the feasibility of producing enough food within city limits to make a real impact. Urban agriculture proponents acknowledge that city farms can't replace large-scale rural production. Nevertheless, they contend that even modest local harvests can create a sense of empowerment among residents. People learn about soil quality, composting, and even business skills when they sell surplus at local farmers' markets.

Moreover, these green spaces serve as communal hubs, bringing neighbors together for planting sessions, shared meals, and workshops. Some urban farms partner with schools for educational programs, teaching children about plant biology, nutrition, and environmental stewardship. In this way, urban farming initiatives extend beyond just growing vegetables—they aim to cultivate community resilience.

PASSAGE II Questions (11–20)

11. According to the passage, one major reason modern urban farming initiatives have emerged is:
    A. to fill vacant city lots with decorative art sculptures.
    B. to address food insecurity and access to fresh produce in certain neighborhoods.
    C. to replace large-scale rural farming entirely.
    D. to discourage local markets from selling produce.

12. The passage suggests that during wartime, citizens planted "victory gardens" primarily to:
    F. protest against government restrictions.
    G. learn more about organic farming methods.
    H. reinforce the scarcity caused by global trade issues.
    J. supplement the national food supply in times of shortage.

13. A critic who doubts the effectiveness of urban farms might argue that:
    A. urban residents already have unlimited grocery options.
    B. city-based farming cannot produce enough food for all residents.
    C. rural areas must rely on urban farms for increased production.
    D. city dwellers have never shown interest in growing food.

14. Supporters of urban farms acknowledge they're not meant to replace large-scale agriculture but insist that:
    F. any locally grown produce is more nutritious than rural produce.
    G. urban farms can strengthen community ties and empower residents.
    H. rural farms should move into city centers.
    J. only the wealthiest citizens benefit from small gardens.

15. Which of the following best describes a **broader impact** of urban farming mentioned in the passage?
    A. Using farmland only for ornamental flowers
    B. Decreasing literacy rates among local children
    C. Offering a space where neighbors can learn and collaborate
    D. Causing real estate prices to drop

16. The passage most strongly implies that urban farms:
    F. typically reject partnerships with schools to keep land private.
    G. only produce exotic fruits and flowers.
    H. can serve as educational sites for children and adults alike.
    J. function exclusively during wartime shortages.

17. Based on the passage, which of the following best characterizes the role of local farmers' markets in urban farming?
    A. They have no connection to city farms.
    B. They allow city farmers to sell surplus and develop business skills.
    C. They are strictly regulated by the federal government.
    D. They discourage the sale of produce from small plots.

18. The passage's use of the term "empowerment" (paragraph 3) most nearly means:
    F. humiliating others.
    G. giving people a sense of control and confidence.
    H. transferring total authority from local to state agencies.
    J. forcing communities to adopt uniform farming methods.

19. Which statement from the passage best supports the idea that urban farming efforts improve social cohesion?
    A. "Local residents reclaim unused plots of land…" (paragraph 1)
    B. "…address broader issues like community building…" (paragraph 1)

C. "Critics question the feasibility…" (paragraph 3)
D. "Urban agriculture proponents acknowledge that city farms can't replace large-scale rural production." (paragraph 3)

20. Which of the following is the author's overall view of modern urban farming?
    F. It's a short-lived fad with little practical value.
    G. It's an emerging alternative with both limitations and significant community benefits.
    H. It's a required practice mandated by city governments worldwide.
    J. It's primarily an economic strategy to raise real-estate prices.

PASSAGE III (Questions 21–30)

Humanities

Throughout her life, composer and pianist Mira Lewis sought ways to blend traditional classical structures with the sounds of her childhood: folk tunes, lullabies, and rhythmic dances she heard at local festivals. Born into a family of farmers, Lewis found creative inspiration in everyday experiences—cicadas humming at dawn, the gentle sway of wind through wheat fields, and the laughter of neighbors sharing stories after harvest.

Lewis's earliest piano lessons focused on standard pieces by European composers, which she admired but felt lacked the warmth of her familiar melodies. Determined to carve her own path, she began incorporating folk motifs into her compositions, threading them through the classical forms she had painstakingly studied. The resulting music caught the attention of local concert halls.

At first, some critics dismissed her work as "simple," implying that her rural influences diminished its sophistication. Undeterred, Lewis continued to refine her style, blending the emotive cadences of folk songs with the structured complexity of classical arrangements. Over time, audiences grew to appreciate how her music captured a sense of place while upholding rigorous compositional standards.

When an international orchestra performed one of her symphonies, Lewis's unique sound reached a global audience. Listeners remarked on the captivating interplay between lush orchestral harmonies and earthy, foot-tapping rhythms. In interviews, she explained that her goal was not to replace classical traditions but to expand them, showing that one could embrace both formal discipline and the raw spirit of folk roots.

Today, Mira Lewis is hailed as a pioneer who bridged divides between "high" art and community traditions. She still lives near the wheat fields of her youth, and on warm summer nights, she leaves her windows open to let nature's chorus infuse her next piece.

PASSAGE III Questions (21–30)

21. The passage mainly focuses on Mira Lewis's:
    A. rejection of all classical forms in favor of purely folk music.
    B. journey to combine classical music with the folk influences from her upbringing.
    C. frustration with orchestras that refused to play her work.
    D. decision to move away from her rural home and settle in a large city.

22. Lewis's initial piano instruction involved:
    F. primarily European classical repertoire.
    G. only folk tunes from her local festival.
    H. exclusively jazz lessons.
    J. no written compositions.

23. According to the passage, critics who first heard Lewis's work described it as "simple" because they:
    A. disapproved of her classical background.
    B. felt her music was overly complex and confusing.
    C. believed rural or folk elements lacked sophistication.
    D. thought her compositions were plagiarized from older symphonies.

24. The statement "her goal was not to replace classical traditions but to expand them" implies that Lewis:
F. saw no merit in classical forms.
G. wanted to destroy mainstream classical music.
H. respected classical conventions while introducing folk elements.
J. aimed to make classical music simpler for students.

25. Which of the following best describes the initial reception of Lewis's music by critics and audiences?
A. Instant and overwhelming praise
B. Complete rejection by all listeners
C. Skepticism from some critics, eventually warming acceptance by audiences
D. Total disinterest from local concert halls

26. As used in the last paragraph, the phrase "bridged divides" most closely refers to Lewis's ability to:
F. create conflicts between two distinct musical styles.
G. keep her personal life and professional life separate.
H. unify contrasting musical traditions in a harmonious way.
J. prevent orchestras from performing standard compositions.

27. The author presents Lewis's experiences with nature (in paragraph 1) mainly to:
A. highlight the random sounds she disliked.
B. reveal how these influences shaped her musical style.
C. criticize her for ignoring classical composers.
D. show that living near farms prevented her from composing.

28. Listeners' reactions to Lewis's symphony performed by an international orchestra can best be described as:
F. unimpressed because the music sounded too traditional.
G. dismissive of any folk-inspired components.
H. intrigued by the blend of classical harmonies and energetic folk rhythms.
J. disappointed by her disregard for formal discipline.

29. By choosing to remain near the wheat fields of her youth, Lewis demonstrates:
A. a continued commitment to the rural inspirations that inform her work.
B. a rejection of all performance opportunities in cities.
C. an inability to travel abroad.
D. a fear of meeting critics who disliked her music.

30. The passage as a whole suggests that Lewis's musical approach is characterized by:
F. an effort to erase classical standards and rely on folk tunes alone.
G. a respectful merging of formal complexity and rustic inspiration.
H. a focus on modern electronic experimentation.
J. a refusal to adapt her works for large orchestras.

PASSAGE IV (Questions 31–40)

Natural Science

The **Greenland ice sheet** is one of the largest ice masses on Earth. Spanning over 1.7 million square kilometers, it holds enough frozen water to raise global sea levels significantly if it were to melt entirely. Scientists closely monitor changes in its thickness, extent, and melting rate to understand possible impacts on coastal regions worldwide.

One factor affecting the Greenland ice sheet is **surface temperature**. Warmer summer months can lead to increased melting on the ice surface. Meltwater then forms lakes and streams on top of the ice, sometimes draining through crevasses to the base. This water can act as a lubricant between the ice and bedrock, accelerating the flow of glaciers toward the ocean.

Another factor is **snowfall**, which can replenish lost ice. In certain high-altitude areas, increased precipitation compensates for melting. However, if overall melting surpasses snowfall, the ice sheet experiences a net loss of mass. Regional differences in precipitation patterns contribute to the complexity of measuring total ice change across Greenland's vast terrain.

Satellite measurements have revealed that some parts of the ice sheet are losing mass more quickly than others. Warmer ocean currents can speed the calving of icebergs at glacier fronts, contributing to sea-level rise. Such variations emphasize the need for detailed studies that combine ground-based observations, satellite data, and climate models.

Predicting how quickly the ice sheet will diminish remains challenging. Scientific projections indicate that continued global warming will lead to an acceleration of melting, although the exact timeline is uncertain. Nevertheless, researchers agree that understanding Greenland's ice dynamics is critical for preparing vulnerable coastal communities and guiding international policies on climate change mitigation.

PASSAGE IV Questions (31–40)

31. The passage mainly focuses on:
   A. the history of snowfall in Greenland prior to modern times.
   B. the role of ocean currents in landlocked deserts.
   C. factors influencing changes in the Greenland ice sheet and implications for sea-level rise.
   D. how Greenland's ice is unaffected by global temperature shifts.

32. According to the passage, one consequence of meltwater draining through crevasses is that it:
   F. contributes to year-round drought conditions on the surface.
   G. acts as a lubricant between ice and bedrock, accelerating glacier flow.
   H. prevents calving of icebergs at the glacier front.
   J. permanently stops precipitation in the region.

33. The passage indicates that the net mass of the ice sheet depends on the balance between:
   A. iceberg calving and ocean temperature.
   B. satellite measurements and ground-based observations.
   C. precipitation and melting losses.
   D. volcanic activity and polar bears.

34. Warmer ocean currents can speed the:
   F. formation of ice crystals in the upper atmosphere.
   G. freezing of glaciers.
   H. generation of thicker bedrock layers.
   J. calving of icebergs at glacier edges.

35. Which of the following best describes the role of high-altitude snowfall on the ice sheet?
   A. It has no effect on ice mass changes.
   B. It can offset some melting in certain regions, contributing to ice replenishment.
   C. It melts immediately and never accumulates.
   D. It remains constant regardless of climate fluctuations.

36. As used in paragraph 3, the word *replenish* most nearly means:
   F. study in depth.
   G. decrease gradually.
   H. fill up again.
   J. freeze permanently.

37. The passage suggests that measuring ice changes in Greenland is complex partly because:
   A. satellites cannot penetrate cloud cover.
   B. precipitation varies significantly across different regions.
   C. the bedrock under the ice is too flat to detect melting.
   D. no scientists are allowed to visit Greenland's interior.

38. The author states that predicting how quickly the ice sheet will diminish is difficult because:
F. we lack any global climate models.
G. scientists do not agree on the basic principles of ice formation.
H. multiple factors, including ocean currents and regional precipitation, affect melting rates.
J. satellites cannot detect changes smaller than 10 meters.

39. The passage implies that continued global warming will most likely:
A. reduce ocean levels worldwide.
B. slow down the flow of glaciers.
C. cause more dust storms across Greenland.
D. accelerate the melting of the Greenland ice sheet.

40. The author's overall perspective on the Greenland ice sheet can best be described as:
F. emphasizing the urgent need to understand its changes for coastal impact mitigation.
G. dismissing it as too minor to influence global sea levels.
H. focusing on geological history with little regard for current climate trends.
J. insisting that no further research is needed because the trends are fully known.

ACT Science Exam Section

PASSAGE I

(Data Representation; 5 Questions)

A biologist measured the **growth rate** of a microalga under three different **light intensities**. The microalga was grown in separate flasks, each receiving either Low, Medium, or High light intensity. The biologist recorded the **cell density** (in thousands of cells/mL) every other day for 8 days.

Table 1: Microalga Cell Density (thousands of cells/mL) at Different Light Intensities

Day	Low Intensity	Medium Intensity	High Intensity
0	2	2	2
2	3	6	8
4	5	10	15
6	7	16	24
8	9	21	35

Use this table to answer Questions 1–5.

1.

On **Day 4**, which flask shows the **highest** cell density?
A. Low Intensity
B. Medium Intensity
C. High Intensity
D. They are all equal

2.

Based on the data, which of the following statements best describes the effect of **increasing light intensity** on cell growth by **Day 8**?
F. Growth is lower at high light intensity than at low light intensity.
G. There is no difference between medium and high intensities.

H. Higher light intensity generally leads to higher cell density.
J. All flasks reach the same cell density at the end.

3.

On **Day 2**, the cell density in the **Low Intensity** flask is 3 (thousands of cells/mL). According to the table, approximately how many times greater is the **High Intensity** flask's cell density at **Day 2** than the Low Intensity?

A. $\frac{6}{3} = 2$ times
B. $\frac{8}{3} \approx 2.7$ times
C. $\frac{3}{2} = 1.5$ times
D. $\frac{3}{8} = 0.375$ times

4.

If the biologist extended the experiment to **Day 10**, which flask would most likely show the greatest cell density, based on the trend?

F. Low Intensity
G. Medium Intensity
H. High Intensity
J. They would all be the same

5.

A student claims the microalga stops growing after **Day 6** under Low Intensity. Do the data support this claim?

A. Yes, because the cell density at Low Intensity is highest on Day 6.
B. No, because the Low Intensity density continues to increase from Day 6 to Day 8.
C. Yes, because the Low Intensity population declined from Day 6 to Day 8.
D. No, because the Low Intensity shows a decrease in cell density by Day 4.

PASSAGE II

(Data Representation; 6 Questions)

A chemist measured the **pH** of three different solutions (Solution A, B, and C) and how each solution's pH changed when **10 mL** of a dilute acid was gradually added. The pH was recorded after each 2 mL increment of acid.

Table 2: pH Changes in 3 Solutions Upon Acid Addition

Acid Volume Added (mL)	Sol A pH	Sol B pH	Sol C pH
0	7.5	8.0	5.0
2	6.8	7.2	4.5
4	6.4	6.8	4.2
6	6.1	6.3	4.0
8	5.8	5.9	3.8
10	5.4	5.6	3.6

Use this table for Questions 6–11.

6.

At **0 mL** acid added, which solution is **most alkaline** (highest pH)?
A. Sol A
B. Sol B
C. Sol C
D. They are all at the same pH

7.

According to the data at **4 mL** of acid added, which solution has the **lowest** pH?
F. Sol A
G. Sol B
H. Sol C
J. All are equal

8.

Compared to **Sol A**, how does **Sol B**'s pH change from **2 mL** acid to **6 mL** acid?
A. Sol B remains above Sol A's pH throughout that range.
B. Sol B's pH is consistently lower than Sol A in that range.
C. Both solutions have identical pH values in that range.
D. Sol B starts lower than Sol A at 2 mL but ends higher by 6 mL.

9.

If the chemist continued adding acid in 2 mL increments beyond 10 mL, which solution would likely reach a pH **below 3** first, based on the trend?
F. Sol A
G. Sol B
H. Sol C
J. They would all reach pH 3 at the same time

10.

What is the **overall** change in pH for **Sol C** from 0 mL to 10 mL acid?
A. 5.0 → 3.6; a decrease of 1.4
B. 3.6 → 5.0; an increase of 1.4
C. 5.0 → 3.6; a decrease of 1.2
D. 5.0 → 4.0; a decrease of 1.0

(Note: Double-check the math for the difference: $5.0 - 3.6 = 1.4$.*)*

11.

A student claims that **Sol B** is the **most resistant** to acidification, meaning its pH drops the least. Do the data support this?
F. Yes, because Sol B shows the smallest drop overall from 0 to 10 mL.
G. No, because Sol A remains more alkaline than Sol B at every measurement.
H. Yes, because Sol C's pH ends lower than Sol B's does.
J. No, because Sol B experiences a drop of 2.4, while Sol A experiences a drop of 2.1.

PASSAGE III

(Research Summaries; 7 Questions)

A researcher investigated how **salinity** (salt concentration) affects the growth of a certain plant. Three experiments were conducted, each with a different salinity level in the soil. The plant's **average height** (in cm) was measured over 4 weeks.

- **Experiment 1**: 0.5% salt in soil
- **Experiment 2**: 1.0% salt in soil
- **Experiment 3**: 2.0% salt in soil

Table 3: Average Plant Height (cm) Over 4 Weeks

Week	Exp 1 (0.5%)	Exp 2 (1.0%)	Exp 3 (2.0%)
1	4.0	3.5	2.5
2	6.0	5.0	3.8
3	9.5	7.0	4.2
4	12.0	8.5	5.0

Use this info for Questions 12–18.

12.

Which experiment shows the **greatest plant height** by **Week 4**?
A. Exp 1
B. Exp 2
C. Exp 3
D. All are the same

13.

Based on the data, how does **increasing salinity** from 0.5% to 2.0% affect plant growth?
F. It appears to have no effect on final height.
G. Plant height increases as salinity increases.
H. Higher salinity is associated with lower plant height.
J. Plants in Exp 3 show the same height as Exp 1 by Week 4.

14.

A student hypothesizes that the plant can grow effectively at **2.5% salinity**. According to the **trend** from 0.5%, 1.0%, and 2.0% salinity, which outcome is most likely if salinity increased to 2.5%?
A. Plants will exceed 12 cm by Week 4.
B. Plants would likely show even **less** growth than at 2.0%.
C. Plants would match the height of the 1.0% salinity group.
D. Data do not allow any speculation about 2.5%.

15.

In Week 3, which experiment has the **lowest** average height?
F. Exp 1
G. Exp 2
H. Exp 3
J. They all have equal heights

16.

A teacher suggests that **Exp 2** might still be too salty for optimal growth. Which piece of data best supports that suggestion?
A. Exp 1's plants are consistently taller than Exp 2's across all weeks.
B. Exp 2 has the tallest plants at Week 4.
C. Exp 2's final height is 12.0 cm.
D. Exp 3 surpasses Exp 2 at Week 2.

17.

If the researcher continued **Exp 3** to **Week 5**, and the trend continues, the average plant height in Exp 3 would likely be:
F. greater than 12 cm.
G. around 6 cm or slightly more.
H. less than the Week 4 measurement.
J. exactly 10 cm.

18.

Which of the following conclusions is best supported by the data from all three experiments?
A. Plants thrive in extremely salty soils and always exceed 10 cm by Week 4.
B. Moderate salinity (1.0%) yields the highest growth.
C. Lower salinity (0.5%) supports greater growth compared to higher salinity (2.0%).
D. Changing salinity does not affect plant growth in any significant way.

PASSAGE IV

(Research Summaries; 7 Questions)

Two scientists studied the **movement** of a freshwater snail species in a pond. They wanted to see how water temperature affects snail movement speed. Each scientist performed a separate experiment.

Scientist 1 (Experiment A):

- Placed 10 snails in a tank at **15°C** water temperature.
- Timed how long it took each snail to travel 10 cm along the tank's bottom.
- Computed the **average speed** (cm/min) from the 10 snails.

Scientist 2 (Experiment B):

- Placed 10 snails of the same species in a tank at **25°C** water temperature.
- Timed how long it took each snail to travel 10 cm.
- Computed the average speed (cm/min).

The results:

- Experiment A (15°C) average: **2.0 cm/min**
- Experiment B (25°C) average: **3.5 cm/min**

Use this information for Questions 19–25.

19.

According to the results, which temperature produced **faster** snail movement on average?
A. 15°C
B. 25°C

C. Both were the same
D. No difference is implied

20.

A student claims that **warmer** water speeds up snail movement. Which data point would **support** that claim?
F. The average snail speed in Experiment B is higher than in Experiment A.
G. All 10 snails in Experiment A were faster than those in Experiment B.
H. Snail speeds are unpredictable at any temperature.
J. Experiment A had fewer snails total.

21.

If **Scientist 1** repeated the experiment at **5°C** with the same snail species, what speed might be predicted, based on the results?
A. A speed slower than **2.0 cm/min**.
B. A speed faster than **3.5 cm/min**.
C. Exactly **2.0 cm/min** again.
D. Higher than any measured speed so far.

22.

Which of the following is a **constant** variable in both experiments, as described?
F. The water temperature used.
G. The species of snail being studied.
H. The length each snail was timed traveling.
J. Both G and H

23.

Scientist 1's data show an average snail speed of **2.0 cm/min** at **15°C**. This average is derived from:
A. The fastest snail in the group.
B. The slowest snail in the group.
C. A single trial with one snail.
D. The times of all 10 snails in the group.

24.

A teacher suggests that **oxygen levels** in the water might also influence snail speed. Which statement would best **strengthen** the validity of the two scientists' comparison, given this new suggestion?
F. Both scientists used water with the same oxygen concentration, controlling that factor.
G. Scientist 1 used higher oxygen levels than Scientist 2.
H. Scientist 2 used multiple snail species with varying oxygen needs.
J. The teacher's suggestion is not relevant to snail movement.

25.

Which of the following is a **reasonable conclusion** based on both experiments' results?
A. Warmer water (25°C) tends to produce faster snail movement than cooler water (15°C).
B. Snails cannot survive in 15°C water.
C. Snails always move at the same speed, regardless of temperature.
D. The snail species prefer 5°C to 25°C water for faster movement.

PASSAGE V

(Research Summaries; 7 Questions)

Researchers studied how the **pollen count** of a flowering plant species changes over time in a controlled greenhouse. They monitored three variables: **temperature**, **humidity**, and **time of day**. The greenhouse's temperature was 25°C, and humidity was 60%. They recorded pollen release at four different times each day: 6 AM, 12 PM, 6 PM, and 12 AM.

Table 4: Average Pollen Count (particles/m³) Over a 2-Day Period

Time	Day 1	Day 2
6 AM	150	160
12 PM	400	410
6 PM	600	620
12 AM	250	255

Use this table for Questions 26–32.

26.

At which time is pollen count the **highest** on both Day 1 and Day 2?
F. 6 AM
G. 12 PM
H. 6 PM
J. 12 AM

27.

How does the pollen count at **6 PM** on Day 2 compare to the count at **6 PM** on Day 1?
A. Day 2's 6 PM is lower than Day 1's 6 PM.
B. Day 2's 6 PM is higher than Day 1's 6 PM.
C. They are the same.
D. The table does not provide that information.

28.

A student claims the **lowest** pollen count occurs at **6 AM**. Do the data support this claim?
F. Yes, because 6 AM has the lowest count for both days.
G. No, because 12 AM is consistently lower for both days.
H. Yes, because 6 PM is always the highest.
J. No, because 12 AM is higher than 6 AM.

29.

If the humidity were **increased** significantly, the researchers predict pollen release might **decrease** slightly. However, in this experiment, humidity remained at 60%. Why is it difficult to draw conclusions about humidity's effect on pollen count from this data alone?
A. Humidity was not varied; it stayed constant throughout the observations.
B. Temperatures changed drastically in the greenhouse.
C. The times of day were not recorded consistently.
D. Humidity is irrelevant to plant pollen release.

30.

During which time slot do the pollen counts appear to rise most sharply between 6 AM and 6 PM on Day 1?
F. 6 AM to 12 PM
G. 12 PM to 6 PM
H. 6 AM to 6 PM directly
J. 12 AM to 6 AM

31.

A researcher suggests repeating the measurements for an additional 2 days. Which outcome would **increase confidence** that the time-based pattern is real?
A. The next 2 days show random, unpredictable pollen release times.
B. The next 2 days replicate a similar pattern of higher pollen counts around 6 PM.
C. The next 2 days have the highest pollen count at 6 AM.
D. The next 2 days have no measurable pollen at all.

32.

If the greenhouse temperature is lowered to **20°C** (with humidity still at 60%) for future studies, which of the following is a **reasonable** approach to see the temperature effect?
F. Repeat the same time-of-day measurements over 2 days at 20°C, then compare to current data.
G. Add 2 more plants to the greenhouse with the same 25°C temperature.
H. Stop measuring time of day and only track daily rainfall.
J. Replace all plants with different species that don't produce pollen.

PASSAGE VI

(Conflicting Viewpoints; 8 Questions)

Two researchers, **Scientist A** and **Scientist B**, disagree about how **invasive plant species** impact local ecosystems.

- **Scientist A**: Invasive plant species often **outcompete** native flora, reducing biodiversity. Because they frequently lack natural predators or diseases in the new environment, their populations grow unchecked. This disrupts local food webs, as certain insects or animals depend on native plants for survival. Over time, entire ecosystems can be altered or degraded.
- **Scientist B**: While some invasive plants do harm local habitats, many introduced species become **neutral or even beneficial**. They can provide additional food sources for wildlife or help stabilize soil in eroded areas. Furthermore, some introduced plants can fill ecological niches once vacant or restore vegetation in places where natives have declined due to climate or human impact.

Use this scenario for Questions 33–40.

33.

Which of the following best describes the point of disagreement between the two scientists?
A. Whether invasive plants exist at all
B. Whether non-native species should be eradicated entirely
C. Whether introduced plants always harm local ecosystems
D. Whether climate change affects native flora

34.

Scientist A would most likely say which of the following about invasive species?
F. They provide essential nutrients to the soil without any negative side effects.

G. They can displace native plants, leading to reduced biodiversity.
H. They replace climate-stressed natives with no negative outcomes.
J. They hardly spread, so they pose minimal threat.

35.

Scientist B mentions that some introduced species can "fill ecological niches once vacant." This statement implies that:
A. Invasive plants always kill off local flora.
B. Certain habitats might benefit from having a non-native plant occupy a missing role.
C. Natives occupy every possible niche, leaving no room for new species.
D. Non-native plants only thrive in deserts.

36.

Scientist A's reasoning that invasive plants "lack natural predators or diseases in a new environment" mainly suggests:
F. They cannot survive in foreign habitats.
G. Their population is often unchecked and can rapidly expand.
H. They require more herbicides for control.
J. They only spread in mountainous areas.

37.

Which hypothetical example would best support **Scientist A**'s position?
A. A new plant species introduced to a wetland area prevents erosion and increases fish populations.
B. A non-native tree that coexists peacefully with indigenous shrubs.
C. A foreign vine that covers vast areas, blocking sunlight and killing off native plants.
D. A newly introduced flower that quickly dies in the local climate.

38.

Which statement would **Scientist B** most likely use to **counter** Scientist A's emphasis on reduced biodiversity?
F. "Some ecosystems already contain too many native plants."
G. "Introduced species occasionally help pollinators by providing extra food sources."
H. "Eradicating invasive species is easy and inexpensive."
J. "No plants can possibly adapt to a foreign environment."

39.

If a government agency proposed removing every non-native plant from a region, Scientist B would probably respond by arguing that:
A. all non-native plants definitely pose a threat and must be removed.
B. some non-native plants are beneficial, so a case-by-case approach might be better.
C. only new non-native species matter; older ones should be kept.
D. removing them solves no problems because new non-natives will arrive soon anyway.

40.

Based on the viewpoints, which statement reflects a **possible area of agreement** between the two scientists?
F. Some introduced plants can have negative impacts on native species.
G. All introduced species are beneficial in every ecosystem.
H. No invasive plants survive more than one generation.
J. Eliminating all non-native plants is the only solution.

ACT Writing Exam Section (Optional)

PROMPT

Background

As urban populations grow, some cities are considering banning personal cars from their downtown areas. Proponents say this measure would reduce pollution, ease traffic congestion, and promote safer, more walkable streets. Critics argue that such a ban inconveniences residents, hurts local businesses reliant on customer car access, and may not significantly improve air quality. Others believe the solution lies in improving public transit systems or employing other strategies that balance individual freedom with communal needs.

Essay Task

Read and consider the following three perspectives on banning personal cars from downtown districts. Then, develop your own perspective on the issue. You may agree with one of the perspectives, or you may present a different point of view. Support your ideas with logical reasoning and detailed examples.

Perspective One

Car-free zones would revolutionize city life. Fewer cars on the streets mean safer roads, fresher air, and an environment where pedestrians and cyclists can flourish. Banning personal vehicles is the only effective path to a truly healthy and vibrant downtown.

Perspective Two

Completely banning private cars from city centers is drastic and unrealistic. It undermines local business interests, restricts accessibility for those who cannot use public transit, and disproportionately impacts those who rely on personal cars for work or medical reasons.

Perspective Three

Instead of an outright ban, a combination of improved mass transit options and targeted regulations (like congestion pricing or time-based restrictions) can relieve traffic and reduce pollution. A flexible approach respects both individual choices and community welfare.

DIRECTIONS

Write a unified, coherent essay in which you evaluate multiple perspectives on banning personal cars from downtown areas. In your essay, be sure to:

- Analyze and evaluate at least one of the three provided perspectives.
- Present and develop your own perspective on the issue.
- Explain the relationship between your perspective and those given.
- Organize your essay clearly, providing logical reasoning and detailed support.

Your essay should demonstrate:

- A clear thesis and logical organization.
- Development and support for ideas.
- Careful use of language and mechanics.

You will have **40 minutes** to write your essay.

CHAPTER 15

EXAM SOLUTIONS

SOLUTIONS FULL LENGTH PRACTICE TEST 1

ENGLISH SECTION

PASSAGE I (Questions 1–15)

1. C	6. F	11. A
2. F	7. A	12. H
3. A	8. F	13. A
4. F	9. A	14. H
5. A	10. F	15. D

PASSAGE II (Questions 16–30)

16. G	21. A	26. J
17. A	22. H	27. A
18. J	23. A	28. F
19. A	24. F	29. A
20. F	25. A	30. F

PASSAGE III (Questions 31–45)

31. A	36. F	41. A
32. F	37. D	42. J
33. A	38. F	43. A
34. H	39. A	44. F
35. A	40. J	45. A

PASSAGE IV (Questions 46–60)

46. F	51. A	56. H
47. A	52. G	57. A
48. F	53. A	58. G
49. A	54. F	59. A
50. F	55. A	60. F

PASSAGE V (Questions 61–75)

61. A	66. F	71. A
62. F	67. A	72. F
63. B	68. F	73. A
64. F	69. B	74. F
65. A	70. F	75. A

MATH SECTION

1–10

1. A	6. B
2. C	7. B
3. E	8. A
4. B	9. C
5. C	10. A

11–20

11. B	16. B
12. A	17. C
13. C	18. A
14. E	19. A
15. C	20. D

21–30

21. E	26. A
22. E	27. D
23. C	28. A
24. C	29. A
25. C	30. B

31–40

31. B	36. A
32. A	37. A
33. C	38. B
34. A	39. A
35. A	40. A

41–50

41. C	46. C
42. D	47. C
43. C	48. B
44. A	49. A
45. A	50. C

51–60

51. D	56. A
52. B	57. A
53. A	58. A
54. C	59. E
55. D	60. A

READING SECTION:

PASSAGE I (Questions 1–10)

1. B	6. F
2. G	7. B
3. C	8. G
4. H	9. A
5. D	10. G

PASSAGE II (Questions 11–20)

11. C	16. J
12. G	17. C
13. C	18. H
14. F	19. B
15. B	20. H

PASSAGE III (Questions 21–30)

21. A	26. G
22. G	27. C
23. C	28. F
24. J	29. B
25. B	30. H

PASSAGE IV (Questions 31–40)

31. C
32. H
33. C
34. H
35. B

36. J
37. B
38. G
39. D
40. H

SCIENCE SECTION:

PASSAGE I (Questions 1–6)

1. C
2. H
3. A

4. F
5. B
6. G

PASSAGE II (Questions 7–12)

7. C
8. F
9. A

10. F
11. C
12. F

PASSAGE III (Questions 13 19)

13. C
14. G
15. A
16. F

17. C
18. G
19. A

PASSAGE IV (Questions 20–26)

20. G
21. B
22. F
23. B

24. F
25. B
26. F

PASSAGE V (Questions 27–33)

27. A
28. G
29. C
30. F

31. B
32. G
33. D

PASSAGE VI (Questions 34–40)

34. B
35. G
36. C
37. H

38. B
39. F
40. B

WRITING SECTION:

SAMPLE “SOLUTION” ESSAY

ESSAY EXAMPLE

As digital technology integrates ever more deeply into everyday life, telemedicine has emerged as an efficient way for patients to receive healthcare services without the constraints of geography or travel time. Some believe that telemedicine can effectively replace traditional care, while others criticize its potential to lower the standard of doctor-patient interaction. Still others argue telemedicine should be treated as a partial measure rather than a full replacement. In my view, **telemedicine can bring considerable benefits—particularly for routine services or preliminary consultations—when paired with traditional, in-person treatment for more complex conditions.**

Perspective One highlights telemedicine’s ability to **improve access** for patients who might otherwise struggle with location or limited mobility. This benefit is crucial. For example, in remote communities without adequate clinics or hospitals, online consultations help individuals manage chronic illnesses more effectively. In such cases, telemedicine ensures patients can routinely connect with specialists many miles away. Given the growing shortage of healthcare providers in certain regions, telemedicine’s capacity to **bridge this gap** cannot be overstated.

However, Perspective Two warns of the **limitations and risks** of remote healthcare. Indeed, conditions such as broken bones, serious infections, or heart irregularities typically require in-person procedures or diagnostic equipment (such as X-rays or EKGs). A video call might not reveal subtle signs that an in-person examination would catch, increasing the risk of misdiagnosis. This critique is valid: telemedicine cannot replicate certain hands-on evaluations, which means it must not serve as a universal substitute for physical examinations.

Perspective Three strikes a **compromise**, recognizing telemedicine’s value while advocating it primarily for follow-ups and preliminary assessments. I agree with this middle ground. For example, patients with long-term conditions like diabetes can benefit from virtual checkups about medication dosage, meal planning, or lab results. In contrast, a newly identified lump or an acute injury should probably be evaluated face-to-face for accuracy and safety.

Ultimately, telemedicine should be understood as a **complement** to traditional healthcare, rather than an outright replacement. It excels at **routine tasks** and addresses important **accessibility challenges**, but still relies on physical clinics for full diagnostic capabilities. By balancing these strengths and limitations, the healthcare system can expand services to more people while maintaining the thoroughness of in-person examinations. In this way, telemedicine stands to **enrich** healthcare overall, if used judiciously and in combination with standard care.

SOLUTIONS FULL LENGTH PRACTICE TEST 2

ENGLISH SECTION

PASSAGE I (Questions 1–15)

1. A	**6. G**	**11. D**
2. J	**7. D**	**12. H**
3. A	**8. F**	**13. A**
4. G	**9. A**	**14. F**
5. C	**10. F**	**15. B**

PASSAGE II (Questions 16–30)

16. F	**21. C**	**26. F**
17. C	**22. G**	**27. A**
18. J	**23. D**	**28. G**
19. D	**24. F**	**29. C**
20. G	**25. B**	**30. G**

PASSAGE III (Questions 31–45)

31. B	**36. F**	**41. B**
32. G	**37. A**	**42. C**
33. A	**38. J**	**43. F**
34. J	**39. A**	**44. B**
35. B	**40. J**	**45. H**

PASSAGE IV (Questions 46–60)

46. B	**51. F**	**56. C**
47. F	**52. B**	**57. F**
48. C	**53. F**	**58. B**
49. G	**54. A**	**59. H**
50. A	**55. H**	**60. B**

PASSAGE V (Questions 61–75)

61. A	**64. F**	**67. A**
62. F	**65. B**	**68. F**
63. A	**66. G**	**69. C**

70. F	72. F	74. J
71. C	73. D	75. A

MATH SECTION

Below are the final answers for each question, organized in grouped intervals as requested.

1–10

1. B	6. E
2. A	7. D
3. E	8. B
4. B	9. A
5. A	10. C

11–20

11. A	16. A
12. C	17. D
13. A	18. A
14. C	19. C
15. C	20. B

21–30

21. D	26. B
22. B	27. C
23. C	28. C
24. B	29. C
25. D	30. A

31–40

31. C	36. D
32. B	37. B
33. A	38. C
34. C	39. D
35. C	40. A

41–50

41. B	42. A

43. C
44. D
45. D
46. A

47. B
48. B
49. A
50. B

51–60

51. E
52. C
53. C
54. B
55. A

56. A
57. C
58. A
59. A
60. B

READING SECTION:

PASSAGE I (Questions 1–10)

1. C
2. G
3. C
4. J
5. B

6. H
7. C
8. H
9. C
10. J

PASSAGE II (Questions 11–20)

11. B
12. J
13. B
14. G
15. C

16. H
17. B
18. G
19. B
20. G

PASSAGE III (Questions 21–30)

21. B
22. F
23. C
24. H
25. C

26. H
27. B
28. H
29. A
30. G

PASSAGE IV (Questions 31–40)

31. C
32. G
33. C
34. J
35. B

36. H
37. B
38. H
39. D
40. F

SCIENCE SECTION:

PASSAGE I (Questions 1–5)

1. C
2. H
3. B

4. H
5. B

PASSAGE II (Questions 6–11)

6. B
7. H
8. A

9. H
10. A
11. J

PASSAGE III (Questions 12–18)

12. A
13. H
14. B
15. H

16. A
17. G
18. C

PASSAGE IV (Questions 19–25)

19. B
20. F
21. A
22. J

23. D
24. F
25. A

PASSAGE V (Questions 26–32)

26. H
27. B

28. F
29. A

30. F
31. B

32. F

PASSAGE VI (Questions 33–40)

33. C
34. G
35. B
36. G
37. C
38. G
39. B
40. F

WRITING SECTION:

SAMPLE "SOLUTION" ESSAY

ESSAY EXAMPLE

Urban centers often face gridlocked streets, higher pollution levels, and noisy traffic—problems that intensify as populations grow. One proposed solution is to ban personal vehicles from downtown areas. While removing cars entirely might seem like a direct route to cleaner and safer streets, it can also lead to unintended consequences. In my view, we should **not completely ban** personal cars from city centers; instead, we must adopt a **flexible approach** that combines robust public transportation with selective regulations to reduce congestion and pollution without severely limiting residents' access and mobility.

Perspective One claims that banning personal vehicles in city centers is the only way to achieve a healthier environment. Indeed, reducing vehicular traffic can significantly lower carbon emissions, create safer walking corridors, and encourage alternative travel modes like bicycles. Proponents point to successful car-free experiments in certain European cities, noting that downtown areas become more pleasant and economically vibrant once the streets open up to pedestrians. This perspective highlights the potential environmental gains: fewer car fumes, cleaner air, and revitalized public spaces.

However, **Perspective Two** warns that a total ban on private cars is an overly rigid policy. It could inconvenience residents who rely on vehicles for commuting or medical appointments, particularly in regions lacking extensive public transit. Additionally, businesses in downtown areas might suffer if customers cannot easily park. While such negative outcomes are plausible, it is also true that many people adapt to new systems, such as using ride-shares or improved mass transit. The question becomes whether these alternatives can sufficiently address everyone's needs, especially people with physical limitations or hectic schedules.

Perspective Three offers a middle ground: combine improved public transportation with measures like congestion fees or limited-entry hours for private cars. Such policies let people drive downtown when necessary—paying a fee or working around certain hours—while discouraging casual driving that leads to gridlock. This approach aligns with my own perspective. Transforming public transit systems, such as adding more buses, subways, or trams, relieves dependence on private cars. Meanwhile, time-based restrictions (e.g., limiting car access during peak pollution times) balance environmental goals and personal freedom. This plan could achieve many of the benefits advocated by Perspective One—like reducing pollution—without fully alienating car owners, as Perspective Two fears.

Cities already experimenting with congestion charges, such as London or Singapore, have seen fewer cars on the road and reduced traffic. Such targeted policies encourage people to consider alternate modes of transportation. If a downtown area is also designed to be walkable and bicycle-friendly, the result can be a vibrant, people-centered space without placing an outright ban on personal vehicles. Additionally, revenue from congestion fees could be reinvested into public transit, further improving access and equity.

In conclusion, while banning personal cars outright might yield quick benefits for air quality and walkability, it overlooks legitimate concerns about accessibility, economic impact, and individual freedom. By **strengthening public transportation**, implementing **selective regulations** that discourage but not entirely forbid cars, and **allocating resources** to enhance infrastructure, city centers can become cleaner and less congested. This balanced solution ensures that people retain a measure of choice while the community at large gains a healthier, more sustainable urban environment.

Made in the USA
Coppell, TX
12 May 2025